全国部分高校化工类及相关专业
大学英语专业阅读教材编委会

主任委员
  朱炳辰 华东理工大学

副主任委员
  吴祥芝 北京化工大学
  钟　理 华南理工大学
  欧阳庆 四川大学
  贺高红 大连理工大学

委员
  赵学明 天津大学
  张宏建 浙江大学
  王延儒 南京化工大学
  徐以撒 江苏石油化工学院
  魏新利 郑州工业大学
  王　雷 抚顺石油学院
  胡惟孝 浙江工业大学
  吕廷海 北京石油化工学院
  陈建义 石油大学（东营）
  胡　鸣 华东理工大学

秘书
  何仁龙 华东理工大学教务处

教育部高等学校制药工程专业教学指导分委员会推荐教材

制药工程专业英语

大学英语专业阅读教材编委会组织编写

吴达俊　庄思永　主编

嵇汝运　主审

化学工业出版社

·北京·

图书在版编目(CIP)数据

制药工程专业英语/吴达俊　庄思永主编．—北京：化学工业出版社，2000.8（2024.7重印）
教育部高等学校制药工程专业教学指导分委员会推荐教材
ISBN 978-7-5025-2804-1

Ⅰ．制⋯　Ⅱ．①吴⋯②庄⋯　Ⅲ．制药工程-英语-高等学校-教材
Ⅳ．H31

中国版本图书馆 CIP 数据核字（2000）第 37696 号

责任编辑：何　丽　徐世峰　徐雅妮　　　　　　　装帧设计：田彦文
责任校对：蒋　宇

出版发行：化学工业出版社（北京市东城区青年湖南街 13 号　邮政编码 100011）
印　　装：大厂聚鑫印刷有限责任公司
787mm×1092mm　1/16　印张 18　字数 446 千字　2024 年 7 月北京第 1 版第 25 次印刷

购书咨询：010-64518888　　　　　　　　　　　售后服务：010-64518899
网　　址：http://www.cip.com.cn
凡购买本书，如有缺损质量问题，本社销售中心负责调换。

定　价：45.00 元　　　　　　　　　　　　　　　　　　　　　　版权所有　违者必究

前　　言

　　组织编审出版系列的专业英语教材，是许多院校多年来共同的愿望。在高等教育面向21世纪的改革中，学生基本素质和实际工作能力的培养受到了空前的重视。对非英语专业的学生而言，英语水平和能力的培养不仅是构成其文化素质的重要部分，在很大程度上也是其综合能力的补充和延伸。在此背景下，教育部几次组织会议研究加强外语教学的问题，制订有关规范，使外语教学更加受到重视。教材是教学的基本因素之一，与基础英语相比，专业英语教学的教材问题此时显得更为突出。

　　国家主管部门的重视和广大院校的呼吁引起了化学工业出版社的关注。他们及时地与原化工部教育主管部门和全国化工类专业教学指导委员会请示协商后，组织全国十余所院校成立了大学英语专业阅读教材编委会。经过必要的调查研究后，根据学校需求，编委会优先从各院校教学（交流）讲义中确定选题，同时组织力量进行编审工作。本套教材涉及的专业主要包括化学工程与工艺、石油化工、机械工程、信息工程、生产过程自动化、应用化学和精细化工、生化工程、环境工程、制药工程、材料科学与工程和化工商贸等。

　　根据"全国部分高校化工类及相关专业大学英语专业阅读教材编审委员会"的要求和安排编写的《制药工程专业英语》教材可供制药工程及相关专业的本科学生使用，也可作为同等程度（通过大学英语四级）的专业技术人员自学教材。

　　本书分为5个部分（PART），每个部分中有5个单元（UNIT）。每个单元由一篇课文和一篇阅读材料构成。阅读材料提供与课文相关的背景知识，以进一步拓宽课文内容，为学生自学（开拓视野和训练阅读技能）提供合适的材料。课文还配有相应的练习题。各篇课文之间、课文与相应的阅读材料之间既有一定的联系，又可独立成章，教学时可根据不同学时数灵活选用。课文与阅读材料共计50篇，均选自原版英文教科书、科技报告、专著、大型参考书和专业期刊，大部分为80年代末和90年代以来的出版物。

　　PART 1 为药物化学的内容，包括药物的生产，药物的结构特点和药理活性的关系，化学治疗学和药物的研究开发等；

　　PART 2 为生物制药的内容，包括植物化学，胰岛素化学，新抗生素的寻找，β-内酰胺类抗生素，肝素的制备和纯化以及脱氧核糖核酸等；

　　PART 3 为工业药剂的内容，包括片剂，灭菌制剂，缓释制剂，药物制剂的动力学原理和稳定性试验等；

　　PART 4 为制药工程的内容，包括反应器，发酵，蒸馏，超临界液体萃取，结晶，干燥以及空气和水的净化等；

　　PART 5 为制药工程前沿的内容，包括手性药物，干扰素，海洋药物，催化抗体，合成有机化学中的酶，药物设计原理和计算机辅助药物设计等。

　　附录内容有：The General Principles for Nomenclature of Chinese Approved Drug Names（包括原料药和制剂的命名），INN 采用的词干及其中文译名，英汉对照新药名选编和总词汇表。

本书在编写过程中得到了化学工业出版社、全国部分高校化工类及相关专业大学英语专业阅读教材编委会、华东理工大学教务处和浙江工业大学教务处的大力支持；中国科学院上海药物研究所嵇汝运院士审阅了全书，并提出了许多宝贵意见；本书稿于1999年10月在北京化工大学召开的审稿会议上进行了讨论，与会专家对本书提出了许多宝贵的修改意见；对此一并表示衷心的感谢。

本书由华东理工大学和浙江工业大学合编。华东理工大学朱为宏、吴达俊编写第一部分，卓超编写第三部分，庄思永、何斌编写第四部分，吴达俊、庄思永编写附录及总词汇表，浙江工业大学项斌编写第二部分，赵军编写第五部分，华东理工大学硕士研究生潘海港、梁冰等参加了本书的文稿整理和文字处理工作。

本教材从结构到练习设计都是一种尝试。由于时间仓促和编者的水平有限，不妥之处希望使用本书的师生、读者提出宝贵意见。

编　者

2000年元旦

Content

PART 1 MEDICINAL CHEMISTRY 1
 Unit 1 Production of Drugs 1
   Reading Material 1 Past Approaches to Discovering New Drugs as Medicines 7
 Unit 2 Structural Features and Pharmacologic Activity (I) 15
   Reading Material 2 Structural Features and Pharmacologic Activity (II) 23
 Unit 3 Chemotherapy: An Introduction (I) 29
   Reading Material 3 Chemotherapy: an Introduction (II) 35
 Unit 4 Novel Analgesics 42
   Reading Material 4 Mild Analgesics-Antipyretics 49
 Unit 5 Drug Development (I) 54
   Reading Material 5 Drug Development (II) 61

PART 2 BIOCHEMICAL PHARMACEUTICALS 67
 Unit 6 Isolation of Caffeine from Tea 67
   Reading Material 6 Medicinal of Plant Origin: Historical Aspects 71
 Unit 7 Developing Drugs from Traditional Medicinal Plants 76
   Reading Material 7 Naturally Occurring Flavans Unsubstituted in the Heterocyclic Ring 82
 Unit 8 The Chemistry of Insulin 86
   Reading Material 8 Steroid Saponins 91
 Unit 9 Multidrug-Resistant Bacterial Infections: Driving the Search for New Antibiotics 96
   Reading Material 9 Beta-Lactams Past and Present 101
 Unit 10 Preparation and Purification of Heparin 107
   Reading Material 10 Deoxyribonucleic Acid 113

PART 3 INDUSTRIAL PHARMACY 117
 Unit 11 Tablets (The Pharmaceutical Tablets Dosage Form) 117
   Reading Material 11 Evaluation 120
 Unit 12 Manufacture of Tablets 124
   Reading Material 12 Solids Mixing and Drying 127
 Unit 13 Sterile Products 131
   Reading Material 13 Processing 135
 Unit 14 Sustained Release Dosage Forms 139
   Reading Material 14 Tableted Slow Release Granulations 143
 Unit 15 Kinetic Principles and Stability Testing 146

Reading Material 15 Degradative Pathways ··· 150
PART 4 PHARMACEUTICAL ENGINEERING ··· 152
Unit 16 Reactor Technology ··· 152
Reading Material 16 Fermentation ··· 159
Unit 17 Distillation ··· 164
Reading Material 17 Supercritical Fluid Extraction ··· 170
Unit 18 Crystalization ··· 176
Reading Material 18 Drying ··· 181
Unit 19 Water and Air in the Chemical Process Industries ··· 187
Reading Material 19 Chemical Process Industries and Environmental Pollution Abatement ··· 192
Unit 20 Practical Process Engineering ··· 198
Reading Material 20 Valves ··· 203
PART 5 FRONTIERS OF PHARMACEUTICAL ENGINEERING ··· 210
Unit 21 Chiral Technology and Single-isomers ··· 210
Reading Material 21 When Drug Molecules Look in the Mirror ··· 213
Unit 22 Interferon ··· 217
Reading Material 22 Molecular Recognition: Chemical and Biochemical Problems ··· 220
Unit 23 The Marine Drug Potential ··· 223
Reading Material 23 Drugs from the Sea ··· 226
Unit 24 Catalytic Antibodies Generation of Novel Biocatalysts ··· 230
Reading Material 24 Enzymes in Synthetic Organic Chemistry ··· 233
Unit 25 Principles of Drug Design ··· 236
Reading Material 25 On Computer-Aided Drug Design ··· 239
APPENDIXES ··· 241
Appendix 1 The General Principles for Nomenclature of Chinese Approved Drug Names* ··· 241
Appendix 2 INN 采用的词干及其中文译名* ··· 244
Appendix 3 英汉对照新药名选编* ··· 247
总词汇表 ··· 256

PART 1 MEDICINAL CHEMISTRY

Unit 1 Production of Drugs

Depending on their production or origin pharmaceutical agents can be split into three groups:

  I. Totally synthetic materials (synthetics),
  II. Natural products, and
  III. Products from partial syntheses (semi-synthetic products).

The emphasis of the present book is on the most important compounds of groups I and III -thus Drug *synthesis*. This does not mean, however, that natural products or other agents are less important. They can serve as valuable lead structures, and they are frequently needed as starting materials or as intermediates for important synthetic products.

Table 1 gives an overview of the different methods for obtaining pharmaceutical agents.

Table 1 Possibilities for the preparation of drugs

Methods	Examples
1. Total synthesis	—over 75% of all pharmaceutical agents (synthetics)
2. Isolation from natural sources (natural products):	
2.1 Plants	—alkaloids; enzymes[1]; heart glycosides; polysaccharides; tocopherol; steroid precursors (diosgenin, sitosterin); citral (intermediate product for vitamins A, E, and K)
2.2 Animal organs	— enzymes; peptide hormones; cholic acid from gall; insulin[2] from the pancreas; sera and vaccines
2.3 Other sources	— cholesterol from wool oils; L-amino acids from keratin and gelatine hydrolysates
3. Fermentation	— antibiotics; L-amino acids; dextran; targeted modifications on steroids, e.g. 11-hydroxylation; also insulin, interferon, antibodies, peptide hormones, enzymes, vaccines
4. Partial synthetic modification of natural products (semisynthetic agents):	
	— alkaloid compounds; semisynthetic β-lactam antibiotics; steroids; human insulin

Several therapeutically significant natural products which were originally obtained from natural sources are today more effectively -i.e. more economically -prepared by total synthesis. Such examples include **L-amino acids**, **Chloramphenicol**, **Caffeine**, **Dopamine**, **Epinephrine**, **Levodopa**, **peptide hormones**, **Prostaglandins**, **D-Penicillamine**, **Vincamine**, and practically all vitamins.

Over the last few years fermentation - i.e. microbiological processes - has become extremely important. Through modern technology and results from genetic selection leading to the creation of high performance mutants of microorganisms, fermentation has already become the method of choice for a wide range of substances. Both Eukaryonts (yeasts and moulds) and Prokaryonts (single bacterial cells, and actinomycetes) are used as microorganisms. The following product types can be obtained:

1. cell material (single cell protein),
2. enzymes,
3. primary degradation products (primary metabolites),
4. secondary degradation products (secondary metabolites).

Disregarding the production of dextran from the mucous membranes of certain microorganisms, e.g. *Leuconostoc mesenteroides*, classes 2 and 3 are the relevant ones for the preparation of drugs. Dextran itself, with a molecular weight of 50,000~100,000, is used as a blood plasma substitute. Among the primary metabolites the L-amino acids from mutants of *Corynebacterium glutamicum* and *Brevibacterium flavum* are especially interesting. From these organisms some 350,000 tones of monosodium L-glutamate (food additive) and some 70,000 tones of L-lysine (supplement for vegetable proteins) are produced. Further important primary metabolites are the purina nucleotides, organic acids, lactic acid, citric acid, and vitamins, for example vitamin B_{12} from *Propionibacterium shermanii*.

Among the secondary metabolites the antibiotics must be mentioned first. The following five groups represent a yearly worldwide value of US-$ 17 billion:

penicillins[®] (*Penicillium chrysogenum*),
cephalosporins (*Cephalosporium acremonium*),
tetracyclines (*Streptomyces aureofaciens*),
erythromycins (*Streptomyces erythreus*),
aminoglycosides (e.g. streptomycin from *Streptomyces griseus*).

About 5000 antibiotics have already been isolated from microorganisms, but of these only somewhat fewer than 100 are in therapeutic use. It must be remembered, however, that many derivatives have been modified by partial synthesis for therapeutic use; some 50,000 agents have been semisynthetically obtained from β-lactams alone in the last decade. Fermentations are carried out in stainless steel fermentors with volumes up to 400 m³. To avoid contamination of the microorganisms with phages etc. the whole process has to be performed under sterile conditions. Since the more important fermentations occur exclusively under aerobic conditions a good supply of oxygen or air (sterile) is needed. Carbon dioxide sources include carbohydrates, e.g. molasses, saccharides, and glucose. Additionally the microorganisms must be supplied in the growth medium with nitrogen-containing compounds such as ammonium sulfate, ammonia, or urea, as well as with inorganic phosphates. Furthermore, constant optimal pH and temperature are required. In the case of penicillin G, the fermentation is finished after 200 hours, and the cell mass is separated by filtration. The desired active agents are isolated from the filtrate by absorption or extraction processes. The cell mass, if not the desired product, can be further used as an animal feedstuff owing to its high protein content.

By modern recombinant techniques microorganisms have been obtained which also allow production of peptides which were not encoded in the original genes. Modified E. *coli* bacteria make it thus possible to produce A- and B- chains of **human insulin** or **proinsulin** analogs. The disulfide bridges are formed selectively after isolation, and the final purification is effected by chromatographic procedures. In this way **human insulin** is obtained totally independently from any pancreatic material taken from animals.

Other important peptides, hormones, and enzymes, such as **human growth hormone (HGH)**, **neuroactive peptides**, **somatostatin**, **interferons**, **tissue plasminogen activator (TPA)**, **lymphokines**, calcium regulators like **calmodulin**, **protein vaccines**, as well as **monoclonal antibodies** used as diagnostics, are synthesized in this way.

The enzymes or enzymatic systems which are present in a single microorganism can be used for directed stereospecific and regiospecific chemical reactions. This principle is especially useful in steroid chemistry. Here we may refer only to the microbiological 11-α-hydro xylation of **progesterone** to 11-α-hydroxyprogesterone, a key product used in the synthesis of **cortisone**. Isolated enzymes are important today not only because of the technical importance of the enzymatic saccharification of starch, and the isomerization of glucose to fructose, They are also significant in the countless test procedures used in diagnosing illness, and in enzymatic analysis which is used in the monitoring of therapy.

A number of enzymes are themselves used as active ingredients. Thus preparations containing proteases (e. g. chymotrypsin, pepsin, and trypsin), amylases and lipases, mostly in combination with synthetic antacids, promote digestion. Streptokinase and urokinase are important in thrombolytics, and asparaginase is used as a cytostatic agent in the treatment of leukemia.

Finally mention must be made of the important use of enzymes as 'biocatalysts' in chemical reactions where their stereospecificity and selectivity can be used. Known examples are the enzymatic cleavage of racemates of N-acetyl-D, L-amino acids to give L-amino acids, the production of 6-aminopenicillanic acid from benzylpenicillin by means of penicillinamidase and the aspartase-catalysed stereospecific addition of ammonia to fumaric acid in order to produce L-aspartic acid.

In these applications the enzymes can be used in immobilized forms——somehow bound to carriers - and so used as heterogeneous catalysts. This is advantageous because they can then easily be separated from the reaction medium and recycled for further use.

Another important process depending on the specific action of proteases is applied for the production of semisynthetic human insulin. This starts with pig insulin in which the alanine in the 30-position of the B-chain is replaced by a threonine tert-butyl ester by the selective action of trypsin. The insulin ester is separated, hydrolyzed to human insulin and finally purified by chromatographic procedures.

Sources for enzymes include not only microorganisms but also vegetable and animal materials.

In Table 1 it was already shown that over 75% of all pharmaceutical agents are obtained by total synthesis. Therefore knowledge of the synthetic routes is useful. Understanding also makes it possible to recognize contamination of the agents by intermediates and by-products. For the reason of effective quality control the registration authorities in many countries demand as essentials for registration a thorough documentation on the production process. Knowledge of drug syntheses provides the R&D chemist with valuable stimulation as well.

There are neither preferred structural classes for all pharmaceutically active compounds nor preferred reaction types. This implies that practically the whole field of organic and in part also organometallic chemistry is covered. Nevertheless, a larger number of starting materials and intermediates are more frequently used, and so it is useful to know the possibilities for their preparation from primary chemicals. For this reason it is appropriate somewhere in this book to illustrate a tree of especially important intermediates. These latter intermediates are the key compounds used in synthetic processes leading to an enormous number of agents. For the most part chemicals are involved which are produced in large amounts. In a similar way this is also true for the intermediates based on the industrial aromatic compounds toluene, phenol and chlorobenzene. Further key compounds may be shown in a table which can be useful in tracing cross-relationships in syntheses.

In addition to the actual starting materials and intermediates solvents are required both as a reaction medium and for purification via recrystallization. Frequently used solvents are methanol, ethanol, isopropanol, butanol, acetone, ethyl acetate, benzene, toluene and xylene. To a lesser extent diethyl ether, tetrahydrofuran, glycol ethers, dimethylformamide (DMF) and dimethyl sulphoxide (DMSO) are used in special reactions.

Reagents used in larger amounts are not only acids (hydrochloric acid, sulfuric acid, nitric acid, acetic acid) but also inorganic and organic bases (sodium hydroxide, potassium hydroxide, potassium carbonate, sodium bicarbonate, ammonia, triethylamine, pyridine). Further auxiliary chemicals include active charcoal and catalysts. All of these supplementary chemicals (like the intermediates) can be a source of impurities in the final product.

In 1969 the WHO published a treatise on 'Safeguarding Quality in Drugs'. Appendix 2 is concerned with the 'Proper Practice for Reparation and Safeguarding Quality in Drugs' (WHO Technical Report No. 418,1969, Appendix 2; No. 567, 1975, Appendix 1A). This has in the meantime become known as 'Good Manufacturing Practices' or GMP rules, and these should now be obeyed in drug production. They form the basis for mutual recognition of quality certificates relating to the production of pharmaceuticals and for inspections of the production facilities.

For a long time the US drug authority, the Food and Drug Administration (FDA)[4], has issued regulations for the preparation of drugs analogous to the WHO rules, and it applies these strictly. Exports of drugs to the USA, like those of finished products, require regular inspection of the production facilities by the FDA.

It may merely be noted here that such careful control applies not only to the products, but also to the raw materials (control of starting materials), and also to the intermediates. Clearly the technical and hygienic equipment of the production and the storage areas have to fulfill set conditions.

Since only a few compounds, such as acetylsalicylic acid, paracetamol and vitamins, are prepared in large amounts, most of the actual production takes place in multi-purpose (multi-product) facilities. Special care has to be taken to avoid cross-contamination by other products what can be effected by good cleansing of used apparatus. A careful description and definition of all stored intermediates and products is needed.

Selected from H. J. Roth and A. Kleemann, *Pharmaceutical Chemistry*, Vol. 1, *Drug Synthesis*, Ellis Horwood Limited, England, 1988.

Words and Expressions

pharmaceutical [ˌfɑːməˈsjuːtikəl] *a.* 制药的，药学的；*n.* 药品，药剂
alkaloid [ˈælkələid] *n.* 生物碱
enzyme [ˈenzaim] *n.* 酶
polysaccharide [ˌpɔliˈsækəraid] *n.* 多糖，多聚糖
precursor [priˈkəːsə] *n.* 前体
steroid [ˈstərɔid] *n.* 甾类
peptide [ˈpeptaid] *n.* 肽，缩氨酸
hormone [ˈhɔːməun] *n.* 激素，荷尔蒙
gall [gɔːl] *n.* 胆汁
insulin [ˈinsjulin] *n.* 胰岛素
pancreas [ˈpæŋkriəs] *n.* 胰腺
serum [ˈsiərəm] *n.* 血浆
vaccine [ˈvæksiːn] *n.* 疫苗，牛痘疫苗
cholesterol [kəˈlestərəul] *n.* 胆固醇
gelatine [ˌdʒeləˈtin] *n.* 骨胶，明胶（亦作：gelatin）
antibiotic [ˌæntibaiˈɔtik] *a.* 抗生的，抗菌的；*n.* 抗生素
interferon [ˌintəˈfiərɔn] *n.* 干扰素
antibody [ˈæntiˌbɔdi] *n.* 抗体
fermentation [ˌfəːmenˈteiʃən] *n.* 发酵
therapeutical [ˌθerəˈpjuːtikəl] *a.* 治疗（学）的
Caffeine [ˈkæfiːn] *n.* 咖啡因，咖啡碱
dopamine [ˈdəupəˌmiːn] *n.* 多巴胺（一种神经递质）
yeast [jiːst] *n.* 酵母
mucous [ˈmjuːkəs] *a.* 粘液的，分泌粘液的
plasma [ˈplæzmə] *n.* 血浆，淋巴液，等离子体
Penicillin [ˌpeniˈsilin] *n.* 青霉素

Streptomycin [ˌstreptə'maisin] n. 链霉素
derivative [di'rivətiv] n. 衍生物
sterile ['sterail] a. 不能生育的，无细菌的
aerobic [eiə'rəubik] a. 需氧的，有氧的
feedstuff ['fi:dstʌf] n. 饲料
lymph [limf] n. 淋巴，淋巴液
starch [stɑ:tʃ] n. 淀粉
regiospecific reaction 区域专一性反应
stereospecific reaction 立体专一性反应
glucose ['glu:kəus] n. 葡萄糖
streptokinase ['streptəu'kaineis] n. 链球葡萄激酶
immobilize [i'məubilaiz] vt. 固定化
heterogeneous ['hetərəu'dʒi:niəs] a. 不均匀的，多相的
trypsin ['tripsin] n. 胰蛋白酶
contamination [kənˌtæmi'neiʃən] n. 玷污，污染，污染物
hygienic [hai'dʒi:nik] a. 卫生学的，卫生的
intermediate [ˌintə'mi:diət] n. 中间体
extraction [ik'strækʃən] n. 萃取，提取
recrystallization [ri:ˌkristəlai'zeiʃən] n. 重结晶
xylene ['zaili:n] n. 二甲苯
toluene ['tɔljui:n] n. 甲苯
ether ['i:θə] n. 醚
benzene ['benzi:n] n. 苯

Notes

① Enzyme——酶，一类由生物体产生的具有高效和专一催化功能的蛋白质。在生物体内，酶是参与催化几乎所有的物质转化过程，与生命活动有密切关系；在体外，也可作为催化剂进行工业生产。在工业生产中，酶主要从微生物发酵获得。

② Insulin——胰岛素，胰岛 β-细胞分泌的蛋白质激素，由两条肽链共 51 个氨基酸组成。胰岛素主要是促进碳水化合物的代谢，增加肝糖元和肌糖元的贮存，降低血糖，并能抑制脂肪的分解，减少酮体生成。胰岛素分泌不足会引起糖尿病。

③ Penicillin——青霉素，一种抗革兰氏阳性细菌的 β-内酰胺类抗生素，是 6-氨基青霉烷酸（简称 6-APA）的酰化衍生物。由青霉素产生菌培养所得的天然青霉素有多种成分。

④ FDA——美国联邦食品及药物管理局（The Federal Food and Drng Administration）。

Exercises

1. Answer the following questions:
   (1) How many groups can pharmaceutical agents be split into depending on their production or origin?
   (2) Can you illustrate any significant examples of pharmaceutical agents obtained by

total synthesis?

(3) What is the difference between the synthetic drugs and traditional Chinese herbal medicine?

2. Put the following into English:

生物碱　　　中间体　　　起始原料　　　重结晶　　　胆固醇
吡啶　　　　甲苯　　　　萃取　　　　　胰岛素　　　醛

3. Put the following into Chinese:

polysaccharide　　peptide　　　hormone　　vaccine　　heterogeneous catalyst
contamination　　 plasma　　　 steroid　　 penicillin　metabolite

4. Fill in the blanks with the following verb words:

derive　　term　　distinguish　　present　　compose

Nucleic acids are polyanionic molecules of high molecular weight. These polymers are _____ of a sequence of subunits or nucleotides so that the whole is usually _____ a polynucleotide. The nucleic acids are of two main varieties, ribonucleic (RNA) and deoxyribonucleic (DNA). DNA is found primarily in the chromatin of the cell nucleus, whereas 90% of RNA is _____ in the cell cytoplasm and 10% in the nucleolus. The two classes of nucleic acids are _____ primary on the basis of the five-carbon atom sugar or pentose present. Two general kinds of bases are found in all nucleic acids. One type is a derivative of the parent compound purine. Principle examples are guanine and adenine. The second class of bases found in all nucleic acids is _____ from the parent compound pyrimidine.

Reading Material 1

Past Approaches to Discovering New Drugs as Medicines

1 Introduction

New medicines are mainly developed by the modern pharmaceutical industry where also most of the new drugs have been discovered. To put the present situation into context it is helpful to recall some of the main approaches to drug discovery which have been taken in the relatively recent past. Broadly speaking, there are four main sources for new drug leads. These are:
- Natural products
- Existing drugs
- Screens
- Physiological transmitters

2 Drugs Derived from Natural Products

Natural products provide the oldest source for new medicines. Natural selection during evolution, and competition between the species, has produced powerful biologically active natural products which can serve as chemical leads. For example, moulds and bacteria produce substances that prevent other organisms from growing in their vicinity, e. g. Penicillin. The discovery of penicillin gave rise to the concept of seeking naturally occurring antibiotics and to its further development by microbiologists who argued that bacteria that cause infections in humans do not survive for long in soil because they are destroyed by other soil-inhabiting microbes. Extensive soil screening research programs have led to many antibiotics which have provided some very potent life-saving drugs, e. g. Streptomycin, Chloramphenicol, Chlortetracycline, and Erythromycin.

Microbial fermentation products may also provide leads to other types of drug when combined with a suitable screen. A classic example is that of the novel cholecystokinin (CCK)antagonist, obtained from *Aspergillus alliaceus* fermentation broths which served as the starting point for scientists at Merck Sharp and Dohme to develop very specific and potent nonpeptide antagonists at CCK-A and CCK-B receptors respectively. Screening against the binding of $[^{125}I]$CCK-33 to a membrane preparation from rat pancreas furnished a substance. Asperlicin, which had $IC_{50}=1.4$ μm; its structure was determined and served as a lead (Fig. 1). Structure-activity exploration led to a very potent synthetic inhibitor (MK-329, devazepide), having $IC_{50}=0.008$nm, i.e. over 10000 fold increase in potency; a nonpeptide antagonist of a peptide. Fermentation broths contain hundreds, if not thousands, of chemicals and are a potentially rich source of novel enzyme inhibitors and receptor blockers.

Venoms and toxins are used by animals as protection or to paralyse their prey; some are extremely potent, requiring only minute doses, e. g. tetrodotoxin (from puffer fish) which blocks sodium channels, charybdotoxin (from scorpion venom) which blocks Ca-activated potassium channels, α-bungarotoxin (from snake venom) which combines with acetycholine receptors, and batroxobin (from the venom of a pit viper) which is a thrombin-like enzyme. They have served as starting points for investigation of ion channels, hormone receptors, or enzymes. Recent subjects for study include frogs, spiders and sponges. Indeed, marine life offers a vast untapped resource for future investigation.

Another fruitful means for identifying pharmacologically active natural products has been the folk law remedies, which are mainly plant products. Alkaloids such as Atropine and Hyoscine (from plants of the Solanaceae family known to the ancient Greeks), Morphine (from the opium poppy known in ancient Egypt), and Reserpine (from *Rauwolfia serpentina*, the snakeroot popular in India as a herbal remedy), and non-nitrogenous natural products such as salicylates, e. g. salicin from the willow tree (genus *Salix*, botanical sources known to Hippocrates), and the glycosides, e. g. Digitoxin and Digoxin in digitalis from the foxglove (in folk use in England for centuries).

Natural products continue to provide a fruitful source of drug leads. A recent example is the anticancer drug, taxol, isolated from the pacific yew tree. Testing the natural products has become much more efficient now that the procedure can be coupled with robotic screens based on modern pharmacological or biochemical procedures, e. g. for enzyme inhibitors or

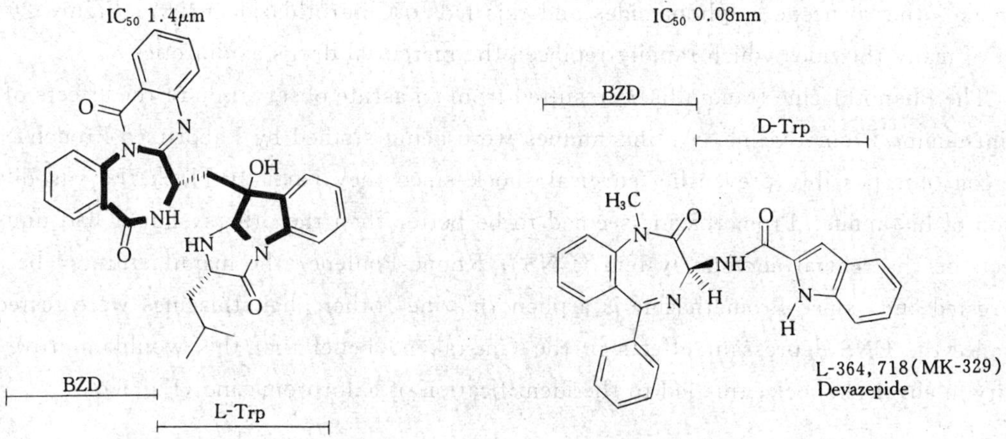

Fig. 1 Asperlicin, a natural product lead from Aspergillus alliaceus, was the starting point for designing potent nonpeptide inhibitors at CCK-A receptors. Two substructures were noticed, a benzodiazepine (BZD) and a tryptophan-derived group (L-Trp) in receptor binding assays.

3 Existing Drugs as a Source for New Drug Discovery

The most fruitful basis for the discovery of a new drug is still to start with an old drug. This has been the most common and reliable route to new products. Existing drugs may need to be improved, *e.g.* to get a better dosage form, to improve drug absorption or duration, to increase potency to reduce the daily dose, or to avoid certain side effects. For example antihistamines discovered in the 1940s, used for treating hay fever, often make people feel sleepy. This has led to development of the new antihistamines introduced in the 1980s (*e.g.* Terfenadine, Astemizole, Mequitazine) which have a much lower tendency to cause sedation.

Fig. 2 Sulphanilamide, an antibacterial drug, was the lead to chlorothiazide and the start of the new divretics

Sometimes it is possible to exploit a side effect. A discovery usually starts with astute observation during pharmacological studies in animals or from clinical investigation in patients. Sulphonamide diuretics were discovered in the 1950s following an observation involving Sulphanilamide (Fig. 2), *i.e* p-aminobenzenesulphonamide (the first antibacterial sulphonamide, see later). Sulphanilamide was found to cause alkaline diuresis in patients who had been given massive doses and this was later shown to be due to inhibition of the enzyme, carbonic anhydrase. The lead was eventually used by chemists at Sharp and Dohme to make other benzene sulphonamides and this led to Chlorothiazide (1957; Figure 2) the first of many thiazides which rapidly replaced the mercurial drugs as diuretics.

The Phenothiazine tranquillisers resulted from an astute observation of the effects of the antihistamine Promethazine. Antihistamines were being studied by Laborit, a French Navy surgeon, for possibly preventing surgical shock since they partially block the vasodilator action of histamine. Promethazine seemed to be better than the others, but it had unusual effects on the central nervous system (CNS). Rhone-Poulenc (the manufacturers) became interested and, since Promethazine is a phenothiazine, other phenothiazines were tested to enhance the CNS depressant effects in the (mistaken) belief that this would improve the utility in surgical shock; this led to the identification of chlorpromazine (Fig. 3).

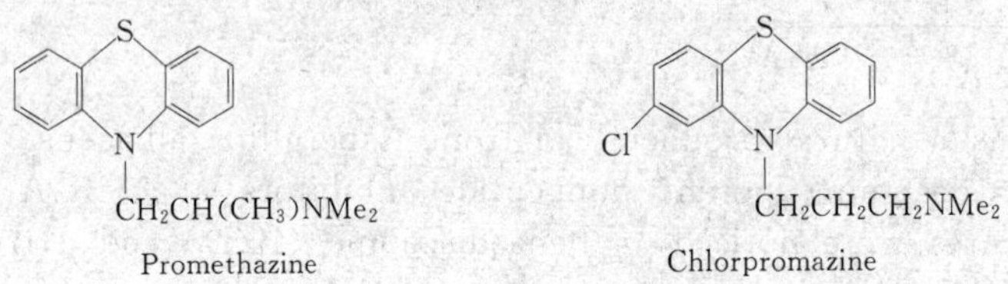

Fig. 3   The antihistamine Promethazine, which provided a lead to Chlorpromazine giving rise to the revolution in psychiatric medicine

When tested on patients undergoing surgery they seemed relaxed and unconcerned. The drug was therefore tried on a manic patient (1952) and the dramatic results led to Chlorpromazine being used for the treatment of schizophrenia, which transformed psychiatric medicine.

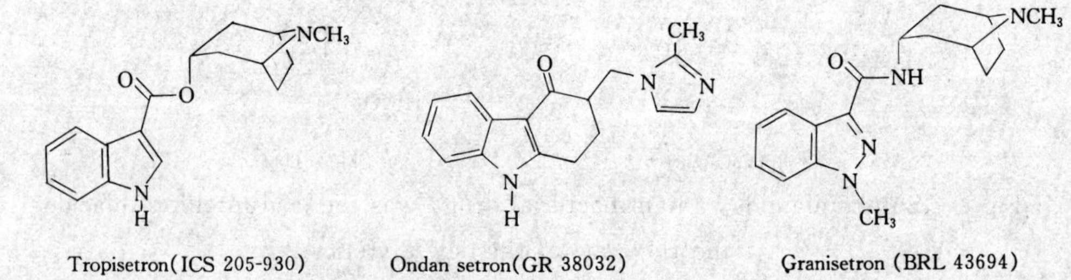

Fig. 4   Metoclopramide, a Dopamine antagonist, was later shown to act at 5-hydroxy-tryptamine 5-HT$_3$ receptors and provide the lead for the development of potent anti-emetic drugs Tropisertron and Granisetron

A much more recent example is Metoclopramide (Fig. 4), an antagonist of dopamine receptors, which was found to be useful in patients as an anti-emetic. More potent dopamine antagonists were not so effective, so that it was realised that the compounds were acting by another mechanism. It was shown that Metoclopramide and Cocaine analogues were also antagonists of a subtype of 5-hydroxytryptamine (5-HT) receptors, then known as 5-HT (M). Further structure-activity studies led to a 3,5-dichlorobenzoate, MDL 72222, which was 10 times more potent than Metoclopramide. Subsequently, chemists at Sandoz replaced the benzene ring by indole to give ICS 205-930 (Tropisetron) which has a $pA_2 = 10.6$. Later, the receptor was defined as $5-HT_3$ and work at Beecham and Glaxo led to the development of the new potent anti-emetics Granisetron and Ondansetron.

Many new products arise which may only represent minor improvements. These are the so-called 'Me-Too' products. It is hard to predict the success of a 'Me-Too' product but some have become the product of choice, replacing the original lead product or at least having a wider usage, e.g. the drug Cimetidine, from Smith Kline and French, revolutionised the treatment of peptic ulcers and for a while was the best selling prescription drug in the world; it was followed five years later by ranitidine from Glaxo which is more potent and less effect on liver enzymes; within a few years Ranitidine outsold Cimetidine to become the number one product.

Historically, 'Me-Too' drugs have provided the main route whereby a particular type of drug action has been optimised in terms both of selectivity (to avoid side effects) and application (for a particular patient population). Eventually, to realise the full potential of a new 'Me-Too' drug and to reveal its advantages, it is necessary to market it in order to gain access to a sufficiently wide patient population. Unfortunately, this can lead to the proliferation of products and it can take many years for clinicians to determine the most suitable drug treatment.

4 Using Disease Models as Screens for New Drug Leads

The screening approach with natural products for new antibiotics, receptor blockers, and enzyme inhibitors has also been used with synthetic chemicals. The idea has been to test large numbers of compounds on a relatively simple system to reveal the required activity. This has been a third main source of new drugs. The background for this approach lies in the dyestuffs industry. Paul Ehrlich discovered that synthetic dyes were absorbed differentially into tissues and that they could kill parasites and bacteria without affecting mammalian cells. From this work came Salvarsan in 1910, an arsenic compound for treating syphilis. Several large chemical companies followed up this discovery by establishing their own research programs seeking drugs against venereal diseases and initiated their own systematic examination of hundreds of synthetic chemicals.

In 1931 Gerhard Domagk, working for I. G. Farbenindustrie, turned to screening sulphonamide derivatives of azo dyes and discovered Prontosil Rubrum (red), published in1935, the first truly effective chemotherapeutic agent for any generalised bacterial infection. This activity was shown to be due to Sulphanilamide (Fig. 2) and this led to the development of the sulphonamide class of antibacterials.

The success of these discoveries in chemotherapy dominated the research approach in the pharmaceutical industry for many years and screens were also established for non-infectious disease, *e.g.* for anti-convulsants (useful in epilepsy), analgesics (in the hope of being non addictive), anti-hypertensives, anti-inflammatories, anti-ulcer agents, *etc*. There is, however, a fundamental distinction between the anti-infective screens, and the screens that seek a treatment for a 'metabolically-based' disease. In the anti-infective screens (antibacterial, antifungal, antihelmintic, antiprotozoal, antiviral) a drug is sought which is lethal to the pathogen, but leaves the host unharmed. It is a search for selective toxicity between species.

By contrast, in the metabolically-based diseases, *e.g.* allergy, asthma, cancer, duodenal ulcers, epilepsy, the cause is often unknown, and we seek selectivity within the same being. In these latter situations, an animal model was used as a screening test, in which a clinical condition was induced in a laboratory animal such as a rabbit or rat, and compounds were tested to see whether they would alleviate it. Such models often simulate the disease by presenting similar symptoms, but may be misleading if the underlying causes are quite different; the procedure then throws up false leads, *e.g.* compounds that protect the laboratory animal, but when tested clinically are found not to be active in man. Nevertheless, notable successes have been achieved, *e.g.* non-steroidal ant-inflammatory drugs were discovered by screening in animals in which various forms of inflammation had been artificially induced.

The potassium channel opening class of drug, exemplified by cromakalim, was discovered by testing compounds in the spontaneously hypertensive rat. The compounds were found to reduce blood pressure through vasodilation (relaxing the smooth muscle of blood vessels) and later the mechanism was shown to involve the efflux of potassium ions.

5 Physiological Mechanisms: the Modern 'Rational Approach' to Drug Design

With the advent of greater understanding of a physiological mechanism and with the use of modern technological developments it has become possible to take a more mechanistic approach to research and start from a rationally argued hypothesis to design drugs. Progress depends largely upon the current state of understanding of physiology in relation to diseases. This is the modern 'rational approach' to drug design which is becoming increasingly important with the development of information in cell biochemistry and cell biology, especially where this is understood at the molecular level. Indeed, there has been such a revolution in our ability to define new biological targets in a highly specific manner that the problem has now become one of the selection, *i.e.* which target next? The combination of radioligand binding, receptor cloning and laboratory robotics now makes it possible to screen thousands of compounds per week for blocking action at a specific site. Modern drug discovery requires very close collaboration between chemists and biologists and a truly 'rational approach' requires several essential ingredients for success:

- evidence of a physiological basis for understanding a disease, so that one may hypothesise that a drug with a particular action should be therapeutically beneficial
- an explicit chemical starting point

- bioassay systems which measure the desired drug activity in the laboratory
- a test which measures the activity of the drug in humans that can be related t a potential therapeutic treatment

Selected from F. D. King, *Medicinal Chemistry Principles and Practice*, the Royal Society of Chemistry, Thomas Graham House, G. B., 1994.

Words and Expressions

mould [məuld] n. 霉菌
Chlortetracycline [ˌklɔːtetrəˈsaiklain] n. 金霉素，氯四环素
Chloramphenicol [ˌklɔːræmˈfenikɔl] n. 氯霉素
Erythromycin [iˌriθrəuˈmaisin] n. 红霉素
antagonist [ænˈtægənist] n. 拮抗物（药），对抗剂
membrane [ˈmembrein] n. 细胞膜
paralyse [ˈpærəlaiz] vt. 使麻痹，使瘫痪，使无助
potent [ˈpəutənt] a. 有力的，有效的
venom [ˈvenəm] n. （蛇的）毒液，恶意
toxin [ˈtɔksin] n. 毒素
acetylcholine [ˌænsitilˈkəuliːn] n. 乙酰胆碱（副交感神经递质）
thrombin [ˈθrɔmbin] n. 凝血酶
Atropine [ˈætrəpin] n. 阿托品
Hyoscine [ˈhaiəsin] n. 莨菪碱，天仙子碱
Morphine [ˈmɔːfiːn] n. 吗啡
Opium [ˈəupiəm] n. 鸦片
salicylate [sæˈlisileit] n. 水杨酸盐，水杨酸酯
botanical [ˈbɔtənikəl] a. 植物学的
sedation [seˈdeiʃən] n. 镇静
alkaline [ˈælklain] a. 碱的，强碱的
anhydrase [ænˈhaidreis] n. 脱水酶
Phenothiazine [ˌfiːnəuˈθaiəziːn] n. 吩噻嗪
tranquilliser [ˈtræŋkwilaizə] n. （精神）安定药
Chlorpromazine [klɔːˈprəuməziːn] n. 氯丙嗪，冬眠灵
Cocaine [kəuˈkein] n. 可卡因
proliferation [ˌprəlifəˈreiʃən] n. 增殖
parasite [ˈpærəsait] n. 寄生虫
azo [ˈæzəu] n. 偶氮
anti-convualsant [ˈæntikənˈvʌlsənt] a.; n. 抗痉厥的（药）
inflammatory [inˈflæmətəri] a. 发炎的
metabolical [metəˈbɔlikl] a. 代谢作用的，变化的
pathogen [ˈpæθədʒin] n. 病原体，病原菌

lethal ['li:θəl] a. 致命的，致死的
alleviate [ə'li:vieit] vt. 减轻，缓和
exemplify [ig'zemplifai] vt. 例证，示范
vasodilation [ˌveizəudai'leiʃən] n. 血管扩张

Unit 2 Structural Features and Pharmacologic Activity (I)

A drug is subjected to many complex processes from the time it is administered to the time the biologic response is effected. Processes such as passage of the drug through biologic membranes and penetration to sites of action are major phenomena to be considered in a drug's action and depend to a large extent on the physical properties of the molecule. The stereochemistry[1] of a molecule, that is, the relative spatial arrangement of the atoms, or three-dimensional structure of the molecule, also plays a major role in the pharmacologic properties, because many of these processes are stereospecific.

Although stereochemistry does play a major role in a drug's biologic action, factors such as the lipid: water distribution function, the pK value, or perhaps the rate of hydrolysis or metabolism may differ between isomeric pairs and account for the observed differences in pharmacologic activity. Care, therefore, must be taken when considering structure-activity relationships to determine if major differences in physical properties exist before one makes firm correlations with the steric arrangement of the molecules. In many reported examples of steric relationships, these factors are ignored.

When stereochemistry alone is responsible for differences in the degree of pharmacologic activity between isomers, conclusions may be made regarding the steric requirements of the drug receptor site. On the other hand, if isomers differ in effectiveness and in other parameters, such as partition coefficient or pK values, the ability of one isomer to preferentially reach the active site or to be more readily metabolized is a real possibility. In these cases, therefore, steric factors are indirectly responsible for the observed differences in action.

The influence of steric factors on pharmacologic activity is considered under three major headings: (1) Optical and Geometric Isomerism and Pharmacologic Activity; (2) Conformational Isomerism and Pharmacologic Activity; (3) Isosterism and Pharmacologic Activity.

Optical and Geometric Isomerism and Pharmacologic Activity

The fact that enantiomorphic pairs, that is, optical isomers, may exhibit different biologic activities is by no means a recent discovery. Enantiomorphs were separated and their different activities observed as early as 1858 by Louis Pasteur[2]. He separated the isomers of tartaric acid by manually picking out the different crystals under magnification, and observed that one of the isomers of ammonium tartrate inhibits the growth of the mold *Penicillium glaucum*, while the other isomer has no effect on the growth of the mold.

Early in the 20th century, information relating biologic activity with optical isomerism[3] slowly began to appear with the work of investigators such as Cushny and Easson and

Stedman, who provided important initial studies. Today the studies are extensive and of primary importance in drug design. Optical isomers may be defined simply as compounds that differ only in their ability to rotate the plane of polarized light. The (+), or dextrorotatory(d), isomer rotates light to the right (clockwise) and the (−), or levorotatory (l), isomer rotates light to the left (counterclockwise). Enantiomorphs (also called optical antipodes or enantiomers) may be defined as optical isomers in which the atoms or groups about an asymmetric center are arranged in such a manner that the two molecules differ only as does the right hand from the left. In other words, they are nonsuperimposable mirror images. Enantiomorphs rotate the plane of polarized light in equal amounts but in opposite directions. Since there is no difference in physical properties between enantiomorphs, their difference in biologic activity must be due to their spatial arrangement, or stereochemistry.

The earliest nomenclature of asymmetric centers is the (D) and (L) designations. These terms were chosen arbitrarily to coincide with the (+) and (−) isomers of glyceraldehyde. The (D) configuration was assigned to the (+) isomer of glyceraldehyde, and other isomer that rotated light in the same direction were also designated (D). From this initial concept, it can be said that (D) and (L) represent configuration, whereas (+) and (−) denote the rotation of the plane of polarized light by the compound. With x-ray crystallography, it has been proved that many of the absolute configurations are in fact not related to the rotation, as previously thought, and it is possible, therefore, to have a D (−) or an L (+) isomer. The terms D and L are used only when referring to the absolute configuration and should not be confused with d and l, which denote rotation.

The more recent approach to nomenclature of asymmetric centers, widely reported in today's scientific literature, is the Cahn, Ingold and Prelog system. This system is much more convenient in most cases because it allows one to include the actual arrangements of the groups at a center in the standard nomenclature for a particular compound. An oversimplified explanation of this system is as follows: (1) the atoms or groups surrounding an asymmetric center are given priorities according to atomic number and various sequence considerations (for the purposes of this discussion, the atoms with highest atomic number will be given highest priority); (2) the molecule is rotated so that the group with lowest priority is away from the viewer; and (3) following descending priorities, one forms either clockwise or counterclockwise motion about the center. If the motion is clockwise, the compound is termed (R); if the motion is counterclockwise, the notation is (S).

Fig. 1, shows a pair of enantiomorphs with groups a, b, c, and d, the order of atomic number being a>b>c>d. The molecule is sighted to the side opposite the smallest group, in this case d. In Fig. 1, therefore, compound 1 has the R configuration, and compound 2 has the S configuration.

In Fig. 2, the optical isomers of tartaric acid are drawn and their (+) and (−) rotations are given along with the (R) and (S) nomenclature. Compounds 3 and 4 are enantiomorphs or nonsuperimposable mirror images, and compound 5 is a diastereoisomer of compounds 3 and 4, i.e., an isomer (with two or more asymmetric centers) that is not a mirror image of

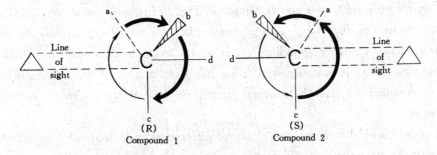

Fig. 1 Pair of enantiomorphs in which groups a, b, c, and d are in order of decreasing atomic numbers, i.e., a>b>c>d

any of the others. Diastereoisomers may exhibit significant differences in physical properties, such as solubility, partition coefficient, and melting point. Differences in biologic activity between diastereoisomers may, therefore, be due to differences in physical properties. Compound 5 show no optical activity, because it possesses a plane of symmetry (dotted line), and the (+) and (−) rotation around the two asymmetric centers is equal and opposite with a resultant cancellation of optical rotatory properties.

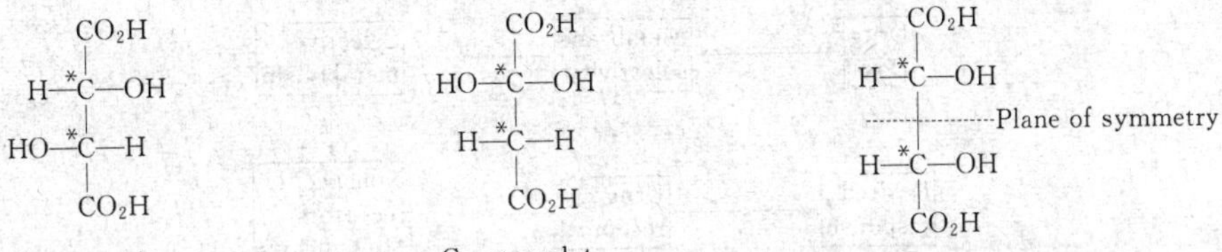

$$
\begin{array}{ccc}
\text{CO}_2\text{H} & \text{CO}_2\text{H} & \text{CO}_2\text{H} \\
\text{H}-\overset{*}{\text{C}}-\text{OH} & \text{HO}-\overset{*}{\text{C}}-\text{OH} & \text{H}-\overset{*}{\text{C}}-\text{OH} \\
\text{HO}-\overset{*}{\text{C}}-\text{H} & \text{H}-\overset{*}{\text{C}}-\text{H} & \text{H}-\overset{*}{\text{C}}-\text{OH} \\
\text{CO}_2\text{H} & \text{CO}_2\text{H} & \text{CO}_2\text{H} \\
\text{Compound 3} & \text{Compound 4} & \text{Compound 5} \\
(+)\text{Tartaric acid} & (-)\text{Tartaic acid} & \text{Mesotataric acid} \\
(R,R) & (S,S) & (R,S)
\end{array}
$$

Fig. 2 Optical isomers of tartaric acid. * indicates center of asymmetry.

Influence of Optical Isomerism on Pharmacologic Activity

The differences in biologic activity between optical isomers depend on their ability to react selectively at an asymmetric center in the biologic system. The reason for differences in

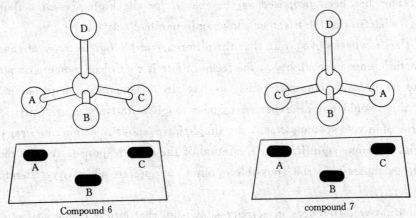

Fig. 3 Optical isomers. Only in compound 6 do the functional groups A, B, C align with the corresponding sites of binding on the asymmetric surface

activity at asymmetric centers is shown simply in Fig. 3. In the diagram, A, B, C and D on the molecule represent functional groups that either bind or have a place of fit on the asymmetric surface. The corresponding letters on the asymmetric surface are the individual sites of binding, or fit. It is easily seen from this diagram that of the two enantiomorphs, only one (compound 6) has the correct orientation for all three groups to fit at their respective sites.

In the case of optical isomers, the observed differences in biologic activity may be due to a difference in the distribution of the isomers or to a difference in the properties of the drug-receptor combination if less than the optimal number of binding groups is suitably located for binding. Differences in distribution occur as optical isomers are selected by some other asymmetric center in the biologic system before the isomer reaches the specific receptor. This may be due to optically active processes such as selective penetration of membranes, selective metabolism, or selective absorption at sites of loss. Fig. 4 shows the selective phases that optical isomers may be subjected to prior to the biologic response. An optically active drug may not be subjected to all of them, but these processes may contribute to superiority of biologic effect of one isomer.

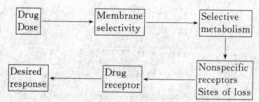

Fig. 4 Selective phases to which optical isomers may be subjected prior to biologic response

The difference in reactivity of enantiomorphs at the receptor site has been elegantly demonstrated in the receptor site and drug interaction hypothesis proposed by Beckett. Fig. 5 shows the interaction of the optical isomers of Epinephrine at the proposed receptor site. Only the (−) isomer has the OH group in the correct orientation to allow perfect binding by all groups. This has been proposed as the reason for the high pressor activity of (−) Epinephrine, whereas the (+) isomer shows only minimal activity.

One of the drawbacks of stating that the difference in biologic activity of enantiomorphs is due to the difference in reactivity at the receptor site is that often isomers do not reach the receptor site in the same concentrations, as has already been demonstrated in discussing Fig. 4, and thus would not be expected to possess quantitatively equal activities. This is especially true of in vivo systems, i.e., the simple intravenous injection of a drug, where the factors in Fig. 4 become significant in elicitation of the drug response. A brief discussion of documented examples of the possible points of stereo-selectivity therefore seems appropriate.

The quantitative differences in activity shown by the optical isomers of muscarine are thought to be good examples of selectivity at the receptor site. Since muscarine type molecules are not susceptible to enzyme hydrolysis by enzymes such as cholinesterase, their

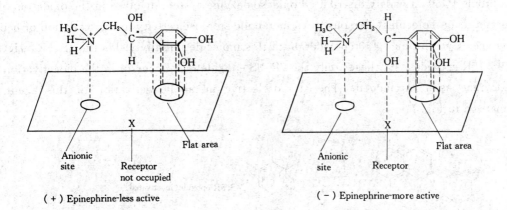

Fig. 5 Interaction of optical isomers of Epinephrine at the proposed receptor site,
* Indicates center of asymmetry

muscarinic potencies on isolated tissue preparations may be interpreted as being a direct measure of the interaction at the receptor site. The (+) muscarine isomer (5S, 4R, 2S), which is shown in Fig. 6, is 200 to 800 times more active than the (−) isomer with respect to its ability to contract various types of muscle tissue, such as guinea pig ileum.

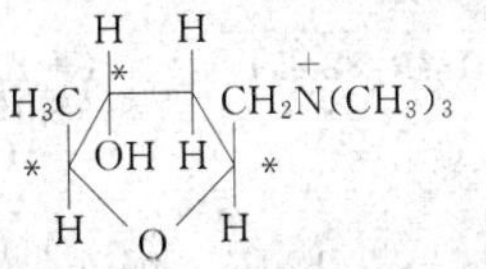

$$\underset{(+)\,\text{muscarine}}{\begin{array}{c}\\[-2pt]\end{array}}$$

Fig. 6 The (+) muscarine isomer, * Indicates center of asymmetry

It has long been recognized that stereochemical configuration can play a role in the metabolism of optically active drug molecules. The metabolizing enzymes (optical active) in binding with a racemic drug (substrate) will clearly produce diastereoisomeric complexes possessing differing physical and chemical properties, thus providing the possibility for metabolic reactions to occur at differing rates, i.e., stereoselective drug metabolism. A metabolized drug resulting from this stereoselective process may have decreased or increased activity, depending on whether the drug or the metabolite elicits the response. An example of how stereoselective metabolism may affect the potency of a drug is the action of the optical isomers of Hexobarbital[4]. Two major oxidative metabolic pathways exist for Hexobarbital: 1) allylic oxidation yielding the 3-hydroxy and 3-ketohexobarbitals, and 2) epoxidation which leads to the formation of 1,5-dimethylbarbituric acid. The L-Hexobarbital has a longer latency of action and longer half-life and achieves higher blood levels than does the D-Hexobarbital when injected into male rats. It has been proposed that this difference in activity is a result of the D enantiomer being more rapidly metabolized than the L species.

Selective metabolism may act through several stereoselective metabolic enzyme systems, e.g., amino acid oxidases, decarboxylases, hydrolytic enzymes, dehydrases, and dehydrogenases, all of which in specific cases are stereoselective. As an example,

Cytochrome P450, a widely distributed oxidase enzyme system involved in the oxidation of a variety of drug molecules, demonstrates metabolic stereoselectivity in the oxidation of benzo (a)pyrene. Cytochrome P450 epoxidation of this molecule initially yields the 4S,5R, 7R,8S and 9S,10R epoxides. Of these, only the 7R,8S epoxide is a precursor in the bioactivation of benzopyrene as a carcinogen. The stereoselective metabolic activation of this agent is summarized in Fig. 7.

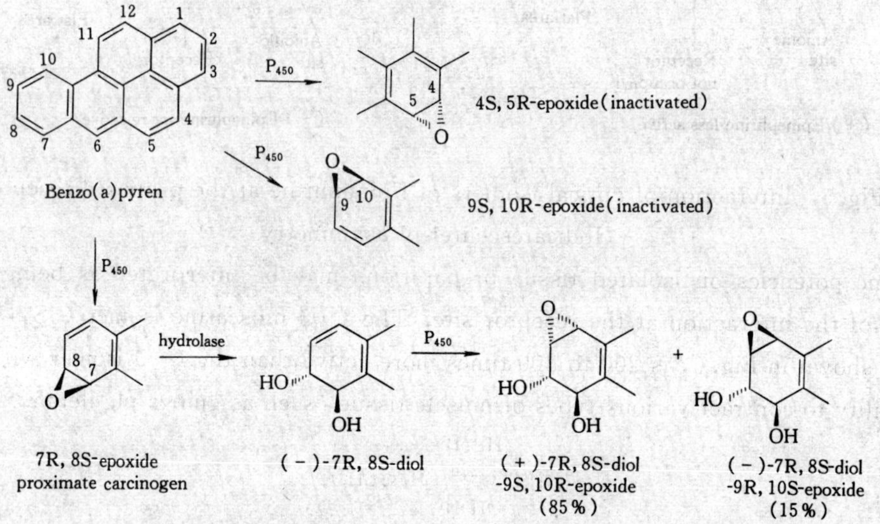

Fig. 7 Stereoselective metabolic activation of benzo (a) pyrene

Erythrocyte acetylcholinesterase, a hydrolytic enzyme that hydrolyzes lactoylcholine to its constituent lactic acid and choline, also demonstrates steric selectivity. The L (+) lactoylcholine undergoes hydrolysis by the enzyme much more readily than does the D (−) isomer. A hypothetical interaction between the enzyme and lactoylcholine has been proposed, and Fig. 8 shows how the spatial arrangement about the asymmetric center is important in lining up the other sites on the enzyme. The alternative arrangement about the asymmetric carbon atom would obviously not allow binding of either the OH grouping or the CH_3 grouping.

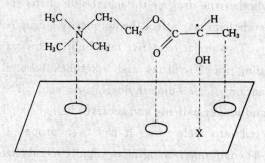

Fig. 8 Hypothetical interaction between L (+) lactoylchloine and erythrocyte acetylcholinesterase. * Indicates center of asymmetry

A rarely observed but interesting stereoselective metabolic phenomenon is inversion of configuration during metabolism. In man, R (−) ibuprofen (lesser active isomer) is excreted predominantly as the S (+) enantiomer (or its hydroxyl or carboxy derivative) as a result of an isomerase enzyme thought to be present in the gut wall (Table 1).

Table 1 Inversion of configuration of Ibuprofen in humans

Enantiomer	Administered Ibuprofen S/R isomer ratio	Excreted S/R ratio
II	95 : 5	95 : 5
III	6 : 94	80 : 20
I	50 : 50	70 : 30

$$\text{H}-\underset{\underset{CH_3}{|}}{\overset{\overset{CH_3}{|}}{C}}-CH_2-\underset{}{\bigcirc}-\underset{\underset{H}{|}}{\overset{\overset{CH_3}{|}}{C}}-CO_2H$$

Ibuprofen
I : racemate
II : (S) (+)
III : (R) (−)

Selectivity of passage of a drug through a membrane may occur as a result of asymmetric centers associated with the membrane, and thus may play a major role in determining the relative potencies of pairs of isomers. The asymmetric centers on the optically active drug molecule may bind selectively to the centers on the membrane, contributing to differences in penetration. If a drug must cross a membrane to reach a receptor, selectivity at the membrane is important in biologic response. Adsorption of only the (+) isomer of α-naphthylglycolic acid (a dye) by wool is a simple example of this type of surface adsorption. If a racemic mixture - equal amounts of both (+) and (−) isomers - of the dye is placed in a solution with wool, the wool preferentially adsorbs the (+) dye, leaving a significantly higher percentage of the (−) dye in the solution when the wool is removed.

Transportation of molecules across a membrane by transporting enzymes known as permeases may also be a selective process. The ability of only the L isomers of the amino acids valine, leucine, and isoleucine to penetrate the cell walls of bacteria such as *Escherichia coli* demonstrates this type of stereospecific transportation. In general, however, stereoselectivity in drug transport is not observed. Similarly, plasma and tissue binding of drugs generally shows little stereoselectivity, with the notable exceptions of Oxazepam, probably other benzodiazepines, and tryptophan.

Selected from W. O. Foye, *'Principles of Medicinal Chemistry'*, 3rd ed.,
Lea & Febigen, U. S. A., 1989.

Words and Expressions

stereochemistry [ˌstiəriə'kemistri] *n.* 立体化学
pharmacologic [fɑːmə'kɔlədʒik] *a.* 药理学的
distribution function 分布函数
hydrolysis [hai'drɔlisis] *n.* 水解（作用）
metabolism [me'tæbəlizəm] *n.* 新陈代谢

isomeric [ˌaisəu'merik] a. 同分异构的
parameter [pə'ræmitə] n. 参数
optical isomerism 旋光异构（现象）
conformation [kɔnfɔː'meiʃən] n. 构象
conformational isomerism 构象异构现象
isosterism [ˌaisəu'sterizm] n. 等排性，电子等排同物理性
enantiomorphic [enˌæntiə'mɔːfik] a. 对映异构的
enantiomer [en'æntiəmə] n. 对映异构体
diastereoisomer [ˌdaiə'steriəu'aisəumə] n. 非对映异构体
polarize ['pəuləraiz] vt. 使偏振，使极化
dextrorotatory [ˌdekstrəu'rəutətəri] a. 右旋的
levorotatory [ˌliːvəu'rəutətəri] a. 左旋的
asymmetric [ˌæsi'metrik] a. 不对称的，不均匀的
spatial ['speiʃəl] a. 空间的
nomenclature [ˌnəu'menklətʃə] n. 命名法，命名原则
glyceraldehyde [glisə'rældəhaid] n. 甘油醛
partion coefficient 分配系数
crystallography [ˌkristə'lɔgrəfi] n. 结晶学，结晶论
sequence ['siːqwəns] n. 次序，排序，序列
priority [prai'ɔriti] n. 优先权
solubility ['sɔljuː'biliti] n. 溶解度，溶解性
epinephrine [ˌepi'nefrin] n. 肾上腺素
orientation [ˌɔːrien'teiʃən] n. 定位，方位
intravenous [ˌintrə'viːnəs] a. 静脉内的
intravenous injection 静脉注射
hexobarbital [ˌheksəu'bɑːbitæl] n. 海索比妥，环己烯巴比妥
barbituric acid [ˌbɑːbi'tjuərik] n. 巴比妥酸
susceptible [sə'septəbl] a. 敏感的，易感染的，可被接受的
racemic [rə'simiːk] a. 外消旋的
oxidation [ˌɔksi'deiʃən] n. 氧化（作用）
latency ['leitənsi] n. 潜在（因素）；隐藏
oxidase ['ɔksideis] n. 氧化酶
epoxide [ep'ɔksaid] n. 环氧化合物
carcinogen [kɑː'sinədʒən] n. 致癌物质，诱癌因素
predominant [pri'dɔminənt] a. 占优势的，主要的
penetration [ˌpeni'treiʃən] n. 渗透，穿透力

Notes

① Stereochemistry——立体化学，是从三维空间来研究分子结构及其性能的化学，可分为立体异构、构象异构及光学异构等。

② Louis Pasteur（1822～1895）法国化学家，微生物科学的创始人。他证明了微生物能引起发酵和疾病，首创了疫苗并第一个用疫苗防治狂犬病、炭疽病和鸡霍乱，挽救了法国和其他国家的啤酒业、葡萄酒业及丝绸业，在立体化学领域中做出重要的先驱工作，研究出巴氏杀菌法。

③ Optical isomerism——旋光异构现象，是研究手性不同的旋光异构体。

④ Barbital：巴比妥，化学名称为 5,5-二乙基巴比妥酸，白色晶体，其钠盐曾广泛用做镇静药和催眠药。

Exercises

1. Answer the following questions:
   (1) What is quantitative structure-activity relationship (QSAR) of pharmacologic agents?
   (2) How many steric factors influence on the pharmacologic activity?
   (3) Why do enantiomophric pairs (optical isomers) exhibit different biological activities?

2. Put the following into English:
   静脉注射   旋光异构现象   溶解度   左旋   构象
   生物膜   巴比妥酸   偏振光   立体选择性 对映体

3. Put the following into Chinese:
   precursor   hydrolysis   diastereoisomer   geometric isomerism   steric effect
   partion coefficient   chirality   asymmetric carbon   epoxide   stereospecificity

4. Fill in the blanks with proper words:

The ____ of a novel drug molecule is a long, expensive, and tortuous process with no guarantee of success. Clearly, out of the almost infinite number of possible compounds, only a ____ number can ever be ____ for testing within a given time and the skill of medicinal chemist is in deciding which of those compounds to make first. Of course, there is then the ____ problem of how to synthesize them! In order to ____ that decision, the mass of biological data produced for compounds already tested needs to be analyzed in such a way that features which are important for the biological activity/activities can be identified and then ____ future molecules. The ____ of quantitative structure-activity relationship (QSAR) is to find predicative ____ between quantitative descriptions of physical properties of compounds and the response of the biological system under consideration. Hopefully the resulting QSAR will lead to an ____ of the molecular features/properties most important in derterming activity, and guide the ____ of biological activity within the compound series.

Reading Material 2

Structural Features and Pharmacologic Activity (II)

The enantiomers of a drug molecule may also show differences in activity because of stereoselective reactions at nonspecific receptors, or sites of loss. This means that one isomer reacts with a nonspecific receptor that is sterically similar to the specific receptor for the required response. Reaction of the isomer at this second receptor may cause no response and thus an overall loss of drug activity, or it may show a response different from the intended one.

It is possible, therefore, that the potentially more potent isomer may effect the lower response because it has reacted at the nonspecific site. In these cases, the activity may be enhanced by tying up the nonspecific receptor by reaction with another molecule that has an asymmetric center similar to that of the drug. As an illustration, a certain dosage of quinine fails to produce a complete response against chick malaria. When the same dosage is administered in combination with derivatives of quinine having the same optical asymmetry as quinine, the antimalarial response is enhanced. Optically dissimilar derivatives in combination with quinine do not enhance the response. Displacement of the quinine from the nonspecific receptor by sterically related molecules allow the quinine to react at the specific site and effect good antimalarial activity.

The most important and most likely area for stereoselectivity is the specific receptor site. As seen from the previously mentioned studies, however, one must be careful in drawing such conclusions. In a review article by Patil and co-workers, the various sites for selectivity are presented for the adrenergic drugs. At adrenergic synapses, stereoselectivity has been observed for: (1) all biosynthetic pathways; (2) transport in the adrenergic neuron; (3) binding and retention of the adrenergic drug in the granule; (4) action of the enzyme monoamine oxidase on the drug; and (5) the α-adrenergic and β-adrenergic receptors. The total action of these drugs therefore involves complex series of stereoselective events.

Regardless of where the selectivity takes place, the general conclusion is that many pairs of optically isomeric drugs exhibit quantitatively different responses.

The classic example is ephedrine. Of the optical isomer of ephedrine and its diastereoisomer pseudoephedrine, only the D (−) ephedrine significantly blocks the β-adrenergic receptor thereby lowering blood pressure. This high degree of specificity is seen from the structures of the four molecules in Fig. 9. The Cahn, Ingold, and Prelog designation for each asymmetric carbon is given in parenthese to the right of each asymmetric atom. For these molecules, the configuration around both asymmetric centers is particularly important, and as can be seen from Fig. 9, the β center must be (R) and the α center (S) for maximal activity.

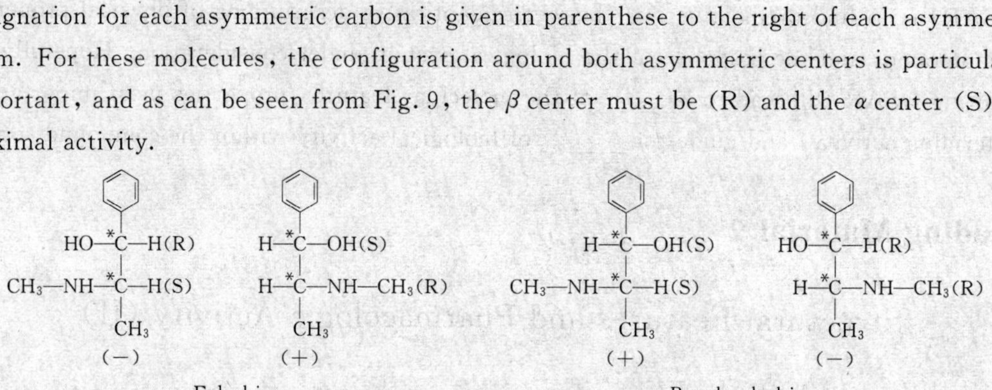

Fig. 9 The structures of the four molecules

While in many of the phenylethylamines isomeric potency differences of 100-fold are common, in the isomeric imidazolines synthesized to date adrenergic potency differences of only 5-to 10-fold have been observed. This indicates that the adrenergic receptors have stringent steric requirements for the former group as compared to the imidazolines.

Another drug in which the optical isomers have been isolated and the biologic activities studied is 1-(4-nitrophenyl)-2-isopropylaminoethanol (INPEA). This drug was tested in rats for its ability to antagonize several β-adrenergic receptor responses, namely: (1) the positive chronotropic response to epinephrine; (2) the calorigenic action produced by epinephrine; and (3) the arterial depression response to isoproterenol. In each case the L (+) INPEA had little or no effect, while the D(−) INPEA (Fig. 10) had a high degree of activity at the same dose levels.

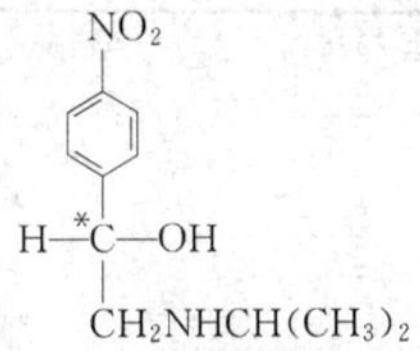

$$NO_2$$

H—*C—OH
|
$CH_2NHCH(CH_3)_2$
D(−)INPEA

Fig. 10 D(−) INPEA, * Indicates center of asymmetry

Optical stereoselectivity is shown in both dopaminergic and antidopaminergic agents, even though dopamine itself lacks asymmetry. It should be recognized, however, that dopamine is a flexible molecule and can thus assume a conformation to enable a "fit" with dopamine receptor. It is generally thought that of the possible dopamine conformations, the trans β-dopamine is preferred by the dopamine receptor. This preferred conformation, in addition, has α and β rotamers. Rigid rotameric analogs have been studied to determine the more desirable rotamer, with varying conclusions. Optically active dopamine agonists possess specific orientations, i.e., optical stereoselectivity, to elicit activity. For example, it has been shown that 6aS(+) apomorphine is devoid of dopaminergic activity, while the 6aR(−) isomer possesses significant activity. In the dopamine antagonists, the neuroleptic (+) butaclamol is able to block the agonist effects of apomorphine while (−) butaclamol is an inactive antagonist in this screening protocol.

An article by Portoghese and Williams clearly demonstrates the complexities involved in correlating the biologic activity with the optical isomeric configurations of drugs. When isomethadol was tested for analgesic activity, it was discovered that of the four possible isomers (Fig. 11), only one, the 3S, 5S, β(+) isomer, possessed high analgesic potency.

Upon acetylation of the OH grouping to give acetylisomethadol, the isomers possessing greatest activities are the α(+) and the β(−) isomers. The change in activity is clearly shown by the values for the median effective dose (ED_{50}) for the isomers of both isomethadol and acetylisomethadol (Table 2). The most potent isomethadol isomer becomes the least potent on acetylation and vice versa.

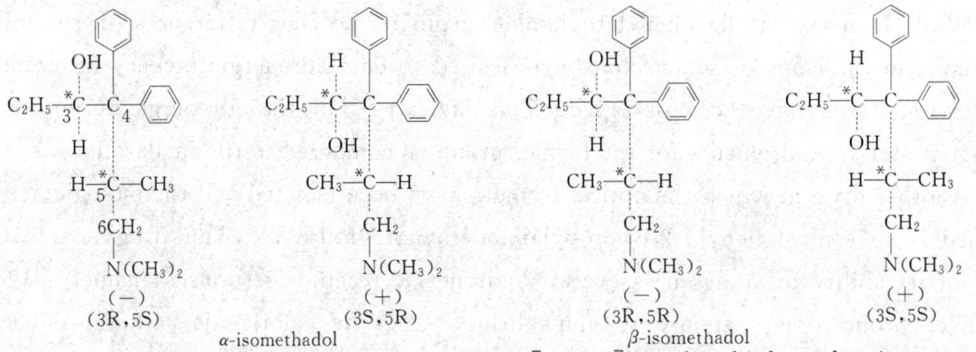

Fig. 11 Of these isomers, only the 3S, 5S, [β(+)] one has high analgesic potency.
* Indicates center of asymmetry

Table 2 Analgesic potency of isomers of isomethadol and acetylisomethadol

Isomethadol	ED_{50}(mg/kg)	Acetylisomethadol	ED_{50}(mg/kg)
α(+)	60.7	α(+)	2.7
β(−)	58.7	β(−)	10.9
α(−)	91.7	α(−)	62.7
β(+)	6.2	β(+)	70.6

Two possible explanations may account for this difference in activity. The first incorporates the suggestions that there are two sites on the same receptor but located in dissimilar topographic environments, one of which is a proton acceptor capable of binding by hydrogen bonding to the proton-donating OH group of isomethadol, and the second site is a proton donor dipole capable of binding with the proton-accepting ester molecule (acetylisomethadol). Each site is stereoselective. The second explanation is that there are two types of analgesic receptors having different stereoselectivites: one binds isomethadol, whereas the other binds acetylisomethadol.

Recent studies have demonstrated optical stereoselectivity in the calcium blockers: (−) verapamil, (−) nimodipine, and (−) D600 are the more potent enantiomers in regard to negative inotropic activity. R(+) etomidate is a potent short-acting nonbarbiturate hypnotic, while its S(−) enantiomer is devoid of hypnotic activity.

Indacrinone, a potent diuretic of long duration with only transient uricosuric activity, is an optically active indanone derivative which is used clinically as the racemate. Its diuretic activity has been shown to reside predominantly with the (−) isomer. Interestingly, the (+) enantiomer, which possesses minimal diuretic activity, has a relatively high uricosuric/ diuretic ratio. Enrichment of the isomeric ratio favoring the (+) enantiomer enables a moderate lowering of plasma uric acid, i.e., improvement of therapeutic efficacy by improving the uricosuric activity of the racemic drug by enantiomeric manipulation.

Emetine is a naturally occurring levorotatory alkaloid with four asymmetric centers. Its activity, resulting from its effect on protein synthesis, has been shown to be highly stereoselective. The synthesis of other than the naturally occurring stereoisomer has yielded products with lesser antiamebic activity. Interestingly, configurational comparisons of (−)

emetine with (−) cycloheximide (a protein synthesis inhibitor) show distinct similarities (Fig. 12) from which a steric pharmacophore for amebicidal activity and protein synthesis inhibition has been proposed.

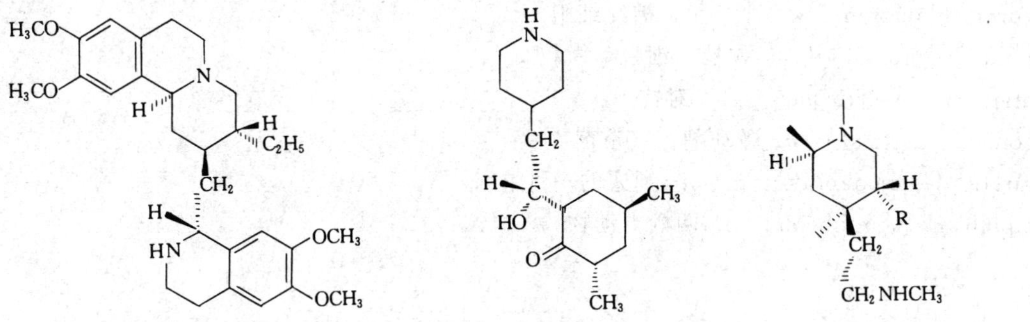

Emetine   Cycloheximide   Propsed "Pharmacophore" for protein synthesis inhibition

Fig. 12 Stereochemistry of some protein synthesis inhibitors.

Stereoselectivity has also been observed in the biologically active peptides. Naturally occurring peptides are generally composed of L-amino acids with only a few exceptions in the animal kingdom.

For example, dermorphin, an opioid peptide found in amphibian skin, contains D-alanine. In plant and bacterial peptides, however, D-configurations are more frequently found. Bacterial cell walls, for example, contain D-alanine, and D-penicillamine is found in penicillin. Substitution of the D configurational analog for the L amino acids produces conformational changes and induces resistance to enzymatic cleavage of the peptide bonds. This latter effect results in an increased duration of action of the peptide, thereby providing a potential approach to the production of longacting peptide drugs. In some instances, however, substitution of the enantiomeric amino acid produces an analog devoid of activity. For example, the naturally occurring opioid pentapeptide enkephalins possess L-tyrosine at the critical position 1 of the chain. Substitution of D-tyrosine for this amino acid inactivates this molecule in regard to morphine-like actions of the parent peptide. Replacement of other amino acids in the chain by the enantiomeric D amino acids reduces potency considerably, e. g., D-phenylalanine at position 4 and D-leucine at position 5. Assuming that the biological activity of peptides is primarily a function of the nature of the side chain interactions with receptors, an all-D analog of an all-L peptide is expected to possess overall similarity in shape and similar orientation of the side chains which would impart similar pharmacological activity. The synthesis of all-D analogs (retroanalogs) of active L peptides, e.g., D-bradykinin and D-oxytocin, however, yielded inactive compounds. The backbone of the peptide chain is thus implicated in the biological response of these compounds.

Other interesting examples of stereoselectivity in peptides have been reviewed for the ACTH neuropeptides, the luteinizing hormone-releasing hormone (LH-RH) peptide, and the arginine vasopressin (AVP) peptide.

Select from W. O. Foye, *Principles of Medicinal Chemistry*, 3rd ed., Lea & Febigen, U. S. A., 1989.

Words and Expressions

biosynthetic [ˌbaiəusin'θetik]　*a.* 生物合成的
neuron ['njuərɔn]　*n.* 神经元，神经细胞
granule ['grænju:l]　*n.* 颗粒，细粒，微粒
antagonize [æŋ'tægnaiz]　*v.* 对抗
agonist ['ægənist]　*n.* 激动剂，兴奋剂
diuretic ['daijuə'reitik]　*a.* ; *n.* 利尿的；利尿剂
amphibian [æm'fibi:ən]　*n.* 两栖类动物

Unit 3   Chemotherapy: An Introduction (I)

Chemotherapy can be defined as the use of chemical compounds to destroy infective parasites or organisms without destroying their animal host. Ancient literature describes the chemotherapeutic preparations of early times, but many of these were worthless medicines associated with superstitions and magic. Some of these compounds, however, were shown to have value through the process of trial and error over many years. In 3000 B. C. the Chinese emperor Sheng Nung[①] noted many curative substances in the *Book of Herbs*. "Ch'ang Shan" was stated to be of value against malarial paroxysms and related fevers. Since that early time, its antimalarial activity has been confirmed and its efficacy corroborated by present-day investigators.

Germ Theory of Disease

In the nineteenth century, the germ theory of disease became established. Agostino Bassi of Lodi demonstrated the transmission of silk-worm disease by a pathogenic microorganism, and proposed the transmission of certain human diseases by this mechanism. Davaine concluded that anthrax in animals was caused by bacteria, and this was later proved by Pasteur. In 1865, Lister[②] demonstrated the sterilization properties of phenol, and the medical profession started to accept the germ theory of disease. A new era in medicine began.

The influence of Paul Ehrlich[③] on the development of chemotherapy first appeared at the turn of the century. As a result of his discoveries, he is regarded as the father of chemotherapy. He first examined the distribution of dye materials in the blood and subsequently in living animals. Dyes were chosen because they were easy to see after distribution in the animal. Ehrlich found that certain dyes colored certain organs or systems selectively, whereas other dyes stained tissues generally. As the science of bacteriology developed, Ehrlich turned his attention to the staining of bacteria. He developed the acid-fast stain for the tubercle bacillus, and performed much of the early work leading to the use of the Gram stain.

Phenols

Lister applied Pasteur's germ theory to surgery in 1865. He showed that cleanliness and sterilization of wounds with phenol could prevent the dreaded putrefaction, which was common in those days. This provided the incentive for further investigations in this field. It was subsequently shown that phenols that had been alkylated or halogenated had increased anti-bacterial potency. In 1932, research on the bis-phenolic compounds began, and this resulted in the patenting of hexachlorophene in 1941.

Dyes and Arsenicals

In 1887, Rozahegyi reported that certain strains of bacteria did not grow on nutrient agar in the presence of certain dyes. In 1890, Stilling reported aniline dyes to be highly active antibacterial substances. In 1891, Ehrlich found that methylene blue stained malarial organisms, but only limited success was obtained when the dye was tried on malarial patients.

Methylene blue   Afridol violet

Because sleeping sickness was a major problem in the development of Africa by Europeans, Ehrlich attempted to find a curative dye for trypanosomiasis. Trypan red, an azonaphthalenesulfonic acid derivative, was found effective against certain species of trypanosomes, but had limited effectiveness against other species. Other dyes of this series, such as trypan blue and afridol violet, however, were later found to be of more practical value.

Resistant strains of microorganisms later developed. Resistance to drugs containing arsenic was also observed. The parasites that were resistant to one class of compounds, however, were not resistant to another class. Ehrlich explained this by his chemoreceptor theory. If the receptor of the parasite had reduced affinity for one class of drugs, it could still combine with another class. This also suggested the possibility of different types of receptors.

In 1859, Bechamp heated aniline and arsenic trioxide and obtained a compound believed to be the anilide. This is represented by equation (1).

$$\text{Ph-NH}_2 + \text{As}_2\text{O}_3 \longrightarrow \text{Ph-NHAs(OH)}_2 \uparrow O \tag{1}$$

In 1903, Ehrlich tested this compound and assumed the previous structure to be correct. He found that it was inactive in vitro against trypanosomes, but it was not tested in vivo. In 1905, it was tested against trypanosomes in vivo by Thomas and Breinl, who found that it was not only active but 40 times less toxic than potassium arsenite. They named the compound atoxyl. It was shown to be effective against sleeping sickness organisms by Koch, who was then working in Africa. Because of the demonstrated effectiveness in vivo, Ehrlich's interest in this arsenical compound was revived. He then showed the correct structure of atoxyl. In 1909, Ehrlich showed that atoxyl, when reduced to the trivalent arsenous state, did have good trypanosomicidal activity in vitro. He then proposed that the host cells reduced the pentavalent arsenic to the trivalent state, and that this was the active form of atoxyl.

Atoxyl 1   Salvarsan, R=H; Neosalvarsan, R=CH$_2$SO$_2$Na   Oxophenarsin

In 1910, Ehrlich introduced a trivalent arsenical for the treatment of syphilis; this compound, known as arsphenamine or Salvarsan, was a major triumph of chemotherapy. A less toxic derivative was Neosalvarsan; neither of these compounds could be obtained in a pure state. The corresponding arsenoxide, oxophenarsine, became more widely used.

The activity of the arsenical drugs is explained as due to a blocking of essential thiol groups. For example, lipoic acid dehydrogenase contains two cysteine molecules, which are kept near each other by folding of the molecule. As a result, an arsenical can react with these thiol groups and inactivate the molecule, as shown in equation (2).

$$RAs\begin{matrix}OH\\ OH\end{matrix} + \begin{matrix}HSR\\ HSR\end{matrix} \longrightarrow RAs\begin{matrix}SR\\ SR\end{matrix} + H_2O \qquad (2)$$

Other Heavy Metal Compounds

In addition to the arsenicals, other compounds containing heavy metals are active chemotherapeutic agents. It is considered that the bismuth compounds act against parasites as the arsenicals do, by reaction with cellular thiols.

Antimony potassium tartrate, also known as tartar emetic, was shown to be effective against leishmaniasis in 1908. Soon the treatment of this condition with this antimonial was common, but because of the high toxicity of the trivalent antimony potassium tartrate, the pentavalent antimony compounds replaced it. The arylstibonic acids were among the first pentavalent antimonials to be used.

The antimony ions are believed to combine with the mercapto groups of the microorganism's phosphofructokinase. In the host, this enzyme is apparently sufficiently different that antimony does not react to the same degree. This inhibition of phosphofructokinase results in accumulation of fructose-6-phosphate. As a result, a major source of energy is denied the infecting organism.

Antimalarials

The history of Cinchona bark as an antimalarial drug is connected with many folk tales.

A well-known story involves the discovery of the antimalarial effect of cinchona bark. A Peruvian Indian who was stricken with the fever drank from a stagnant pond into which several trees had fallen. Apparently, the alkaloids from these trees had dissolved in the water. Within hours, the Indian's fever subsided, and he eventually recovered. The news of this cure spread, and the bark of these trees was used by the natives. The Jesuit missionaries learned of the use of this bark to treat fever from malaria.

The Countess Ana de Osorio, wife of the Count of Chinchon and Viceroy of Peru, was a victim of tertian fever, and used this bark successfully. It was introduced in Europe in 1633, and its use was further spread by the Jesuit order. Early names for the bark were Countess' bark, Jesuit's bark, and Peruvian bark. Linnaeus wished to honor the Countess of Chinchon when he named the bark, but he omitted the second letter in the name. As a result, it is called cinchona bark today.

It has been reported that the Countess of Chinchon died before she got to Peru. The second wife of the Count of Chinchon never had malaria while she lived in Peru. The Count contracted the fever and was treated by bleeding, which was the customary treatment of the time; he was not cured by any drug. The story therefore remains open to question.

The alkaloid quinine was isolated from cinchona bark in 1820, and was used in the treatment of malaria until synthetic drugs were developed.

Researchers in Germany became interested in the treatment of malaria early in the century. Following the limited success reported by Ehrlich in the treatment of malaria with methylene blue, alterations of the methylene blue molecule by German workers produced no compounds of practical value, but the experience they gained was applied to other ring systems. As a result, pamaquine was reported in 1924 to be an effective anti-malarial drug. Pamaquine was first accepted with enthusiasm, but was later found to be too toxic and inferior to Quinine. It was no longer used by 1930.

$$CH_3O$$
$$NHCH(CH_3)CH_2CH_2CH_2N(C_2H_5)_2$$
Pamaquine

Quinacrine (Atabrine) was prepared by Mauss and Mietzsch in 1933. Its use became widespread during the war years of 1939 to 1945 because the Japanese controlled most of the Quinine supply. Quinacrine was found to be an effective antimalarial with low toxicity. Between 1941 and 1945, university and industrial laboratories cooperated in an antimalarial program in the United States. Nearly 13000 new organic compounds were synthesized, analyzed, and tested, and some were clinically evaluated during this period. Each compound was given a survey number, abbreviated SN. For example, Quinacrine was also known as SN 390.

$$NHCH(CH_3)CH_2CH_2CH_2N(C_2H_5)_2$$
$$OCH_3$$
Quinacrine

$$NHCH(CH_3)CH_2CH_2CH_2N(C_2H_5)_2$$
Chloroquine

Earlier, in 1939, Chloroquine was prepared by chemists at the Bayer compound in Germany. A limited amount was sent to Tunis, which was under German domination at that time. After the Anglo-American forces took control of this area in 1943, a sample of Chloroquine was turned over to them. It was found superior to Quinacrine for the treatment of malaria[4].

Schoenhofer postulated in 1942 that the possibility of tautomerism was necessary for antimalarial activity. A series of pyrimidine derivatives was prepared as potential antimalarial drugs, and their activity was attributed to their tautomeric[5] possibilities. When an amino-substituted pyrimidine ring is opened, a biguanide results, which also has the tautomeric forms regarded as desirable. High activity was found for this type of compound, which prompted the investigation of other biguanides. This led to the discovery of valuable compounds, including Chlorguanide, which was introduced as an antimalarial in 1946.

Cyclization of this biguanide produced Cycloguanil, which was also found to be a highly active antimalarial.

$$Cl-\underset{}{\text{C}_6\text{H}_4}-\text{NHCNHCNHCH(CH}_3)_2 \quad\quad \text{(Chlorguanide)}$$

$$\text{Cycloguanil}$$

Chlorguanide   Cycloguanil

Resistant strains of malarial parasites found in Vietnam have caused renewed interest in malarial chemotherapy, and new classes of antimalarials are being investigated.

Trypanosomicides

Trypan red was formerly used as a trypanosomicidal agent in the treatment of African sleeping sickness. Use of a dye was found objectionable, however, and the colorless suramin sodium replaced it.

Trypanosomes have a high rate of carbohydrate metabolism, and it was concluded that suramin sodium was trypanosomicidal because of its antagonism of carbohydrate metabolism. In 1926, it was reported that some Guanidine derivatives lowered blood sugar levels in animals. These compounds were successful as trypanosomicidal agents, but they acted at extreme dilutions, and insulin was found to be ineffective against Trypanosomes. Because of this, Lourie and Yorke believed that a Guanidine acted directly on the Trypanosomes, and its activity was independent of its hypoglycemic action.

$$R-(CH_2)_n-R, \quad R-\underset{}{\overset{NH}{C}}-NH_2, \quad -S-\underset{}{\overset{NH}{C}}-NH_2, -NH-\underset{}{\overset{NH}{C}}-NH_2,$$

$$NH_2-\underset{}{\overset{NH}{C}}-NH(CH_2)_{10}NH-\underset{}{\overset{NH}{C}}-NH_2$$

Synthalin

Large numbers of guanidines, amidines, amines, and isothioureas were then investigated as trypanosomicidal agents, the most important being Synthalin. Certain diamidines in this series, particularly Synthalin, showed a high activity both in vitro and in vivo. Because these agents were unable to penetrate to the central nervous system, they were found of little value in the treatment of late stages of sleeping sickness.

Selected from W. O. Foye, *'Principles of Medcinal Chemistry'*, 3rd ed.,
Lea & Febigen, U. S. A., 1988.

Words and Expressions

chemotherapy [ˌkeməuˈθerəpi] *n.* 化学治疗法，化疗
superstition [ˌsju:pəˈstiʃən] *n.* 迷信
paroxysm [ˈpærəksizəm] *n.* (病)发作，突发，暴发，(情感)激发
malaria [məˈlɛəriə] *n.* 疟疾
pathogenic [ˌpæθəˈdʒenik] *a.* 致病的，病源的
anthrax [ˈænθræks] *n.* 炭疽

sterilization [sterilai'zeiʃən] *n.* 消毒，杀菌
tubercle ['tju:bəkl] *n.* 结核
bacillus [bə'siləs] *n.* 杆状细菌；杆菌
tubercle bacillus 结核菌
putrefaction [ˌpju:tri'fækʃən] *n.* 腐烂，腐败，腐败物
arsenic ['ɑ:snik] *n.* 砷
nutrient ['nju:triənt] *a.*；*n.* 营养的（物），滋养的（物）
agar ['eigɑ:] （＝agaragar）*n.* 洋菜，石花菜，紫菜，细菌培养基
affinity [ə'finiti] *n.* 亲和力，嗜好
in vitro 在体外，在玻璃试管内，在玻璃容器内
in vivo 在体内，自然条件下的（实验，化验）
syphilis ['sifilis] *n.* 梅毒
Quinacrine ['kwinəkrin] *n.* 阿的平
thiol ['θaiəul] *n.* 硫醇类
tertian ['tə:ʃən] *a.* 间日的，隔日（发作）
tautomerism [tɔ:'tɔmərizm] *n.* 同质异构，互变（异构）现象，互变异构
antagonism [æn'tægənizm] *n.* 对抗（性，作用），对立性

Notes

① Sheng Nung 神农，中国神话传说中司农业、医药的神，又称炎帝神农。
② Joseph Lister (1827～1912) 英国外科医师、医学科学家，"外科消毒之父"，预防医学的先驱。
③ Paul Ehrlich (1854～1915) 德国医学家，血液学、免疫学奠基人之一。开创了化学疗法，最早促进科学研究与工业生产的合作。1908年因免疫学方面的贡献获得了诺贝尔医学奖。
④ Malaria 疟疾，是人类中一类急性或慢性复发性的严重感染病，其特征是周期性寒热发作，伴有贫血、脾肿大以及时常致死的并发症。
⑤ Tautomerism 互变异构现象，指存在一种物质，它是两种可以相互转化形态的平衡混合物，这种转化一般是由于某个氢原子的迁移，因此互变异构化合物可以产生两个系列的衍生物。

Exercises

1. Answer the following questions：
    (1) What is the mechanism of chemotherapy?
    (2) How do patients respond to specific chemotherapy?
    (3) What is the most important contribution Paul Ehrlich has made to the modern medical science?
2. Put the following into English：
    衍生物   硫醇   互变异构体   波谱
    染料   微生物   苯胺   消毒
3. Put the following into Chinese：

malarial chemotherapy bacteria in vitro
antagonism affinity parasite putrefaction

4. Fill the following blanks with proper words:

sulfonamide *bacteria* *vaccines* *cancer* *action* *effect*
chemotherapy *bacteriologist* *infection* *cell* *mode* *organism*

_____ is the treatment of disease by administering drugs that injure or kill the disease-producing organisms without damaging the host. The term is also used more loosely to mean any use of drugs in the treatment of disease, and particularly of _____. The more precise meaning given above derives from concepts introduced by the German _____ Paul Ehrlich around 1900. While working with certain chemical dyes, Ehrlich found that they have a selective action against specific kinds of disease-producing _____. Unlike _____, which destroy invading organisms indirectly (by increasing the body's natural defenses), these chemicals were found to destroy them directly. However, as Ehrlich noted, it is important that a chemotherapeutic agent have a high degree of selectivity against the invading organism if it is not to affect the body _____ of the host. Thus, a selective action is the key to successful chemotherapy.

If enough information were available on the biochemical differences between disease-producing organisms and the host's body cells, chemotherapeutic agents could be produced at will. As it happens, however, the reverse is often the case. A new drug having a curative _____ is discovered more or less by accident, and by studying the drug's _____ of action, scientists obtain new knowledge about the biochemical differences between the organism and the cell of the host. One of the best examples of this sequence of events is the history of the drugs known as _____. These drugs were generally useful in the treatment of _____ long before anything was known about their selective _____ on bacteria. Later it was found that they destroy bacteria by taking the place of paraminobenzoic acid, a growth factor essential for bacteria but not for humans. When sulfonamide molecules are present, _____ absorb them instead of paraminobenzoic acid molecules; as a result, they cannot grow and multiply.

Reading Material 3

Chemotherapy: an Introduction (II)

Sulfonamides

In 1935, Prontosil was introduced as a synthetic antibacterial agent, and a new era of bacterial chemotherapy was opened. Prontosil was inactive *in vitro* but did have good activity *in vivo*, particularly against hemolytic streptococcal infections.

The history of Prontosil goes back to earlier work on azo dyes. In 1909, it was noted that dyes containing a sulfonamide group formed stable complexes with wool proteins. In 1919, Heidelberger and Jacobs tried to increase the antibacterial properties of hydrocupreine by coupling this molecule with sulfanilamide by an azo linkage. Some activity against the pneumonia organism was seen.

Shortly after the introduction of Prontosil, Trefouel and co-workers suggested that this compound was cleaved at the azo linkage in the host tissue and yielded sulfanilamide. Further work on the bacteriostatic effect of sulfanilamide showed that it was highly active by itself. In the following years, other sulfanilamide derivatives were prepared. In 1938, Sulfapyridine was shown to be even more effective than sulfanilamide. Research in this area continues still, and new sulfonamide drugs have been introduced.

Prontosil

Suram in sodium

Antibiotics

The term antibiotic was introduced by Waksman in 1942. An antibiotic can be defined as a chemical substance produced by microorganisms that can inhibit growth of, or even destroy, other microorganisms. It has been reported in folk literature that the Chinese treated infections such as boils and carbuncles with an extract of a mold curd made from soybeans. Moldy cheese has also been used historically by Chinese and Ukrainian peasants to treat infected wounds. Antibiotic agents were not studied systematically, however, until the twentieth century.

Pasteur and Joubert noted that anthrax bacilli were killed if certain common bacteria were grown with them. Injection of a deadly dose of anthrax bacilli into a laboratory animal was rendered harmless if common bacteria were injected at the same time. In 1890, the antibacterial extract of *Pseudomonas aeruginosa* was found of value in the treatment of diphtheria and other pyrogenic coccal infections. This was the pyocyanase of Emmerich. This product contained two antibiotic substances called pyocyanase and pyocyanine. This mixture was not satisfactory, however, and its use was discontinued shortly after the turn of the century.

Interest in antibiotic substances was revived in the 1930s, after the discovery by Fleming in 1929 that a filtrate of a broth culture of a penicillium mold had distinct antibacterial properties. A culture of staphylococcus organisms was accidentally contaminated with the spores of *penicillium notatum*. Around the colonies of the mold, well-developed growth of staphylococcus appeared to be dissolving. When the mold was isolated in a pure culture, it produced a material with a powerful *in vitro* effect against many common bacteria that caused infections in humans. It had no effect against some other bacteria.

Because the mold contaminant was known as penicillium notatum, the material it produced was called Penicillin. It had an extremely low toxicity, and Fleming suggested its use as an antiseptic. Systemic use of penicillin was not attempted at this time. Subsequent attempts by other workers to concentrate this material were not successful because of the instability and low concentrations of Penicillin in the filtrates of the broth. Consequently, Penicillin remained a scientific curiosity for about 10 years.

In 1938, Florey and Chain made a systematic survey of antibiotic substances. Because of the interesting chemical and biologic properties of Penicillin, it was selected as one of the first to be studied. These workers succeeded in purifying the crude substance and demonstrated its remarkable antibiotic properties in mice and humans with staphylococcal and other infections caused by gram-positive organisms.

During World War II, England was under heavy air attack by the Germans, and this limited the development of penicillin production there. In 1941, Florey and Heatley went to the United States for experimental assistance in the production of Penicillin.

American scientists, however, had also read of Fleming's work in 1929 and had also done some research in this area. The Northern Regional Research Laboratories had even patented a procedure for the submerged fermentation production of Penicillin in 1935, six years before the visit of Florey and Heatley.

It was soon found that the Penicillin made in England and the United States were not identical. Phenylacetic acid could be obtained as a hydrolysis product of the Penicillin made in the United States but not from that made in England. Conversely, a hexenoic acid was obtained from the hydrolysis products of the British Penicillin but not from the American Penicillin. The British Penicillin became known as Penicillin I (later known as Penicillin F) and the American product as Penicillin II (later known as Penicillin G).

By 1943, only Penicillin G could be obtained in a pure state. Penicillin F contained small amounts of impurities and Penicillin G was more active. As a result, Penicillin G was produced in the United States after 1943.

After the introduction of Penicillin G, other less soluble salts were prepared to prolong the action of a single dose. Other new Penicillin derivatives that were more effective orally, or derivatives that resisted penicillinase, were also developed. In addition, Penicillin derivatives with a broader spectrum of antibacterial activity were produced. The cephalosporin relatives of these antibiotics have also been introduced in antibacterial therapy.

Searching the Actinomycetales order of microorganisms, Waksman found a valuable antibiotic in 1943. It was produced by a Streptomyces genus and was called Streptomycin. This drug has been particularly effective against mycobacteria. Neomycin was discovered in extracts of *Streptomyces fradiae* by Waksman and Lechevalier later in 1949.

In 1945, an antibiotic mixture of polypeptide substances was isolated from the infected tissues of a small girl named Margaret Tracy. This material, produced by *Bacillus subtilis*, was named Bacitracin.

Chloramphenicol, a broad-spectrum antibiotic produced by streptomycetes, was found in a Venezuelan soil sample. It was isolated from fermented media in 1947, and later was produced synthetically on a commercial basis. It has been valuable in treating typhus and typhoid fever.

The first of the broad-spectrum tetracycline family of antibiotics to be discovered was Chlortetracycline, isolated by Duggar, a retired professor, in 1947. In 1950, Oxytetracycline was isolated, and the structural resemblance to Chlortetracycline was noted. After the structures were determined, a reductive dehalogenation of Chlortetracycline was performed in 1953, producing Tetracycline. This family of antibiotics has a wider range of activity than any of those previously discovered.

Anticancer Agents

The preparation of mustard gas was described by Meyer in 1886, and its vesicant properties were noted. During World War I, mustard gas was used by the military forces, and the vesicant action on the eyes, skin and respiratory tract was described. Autopsies of soldiers killed by the gas attacks showed toxic effects on the leukocytes, bone marrow, lymph tissue, and mucosa of the gastrointestinal tract. After World War I, further research was carried on, and the closely related nitrogen mustards were developed. The activity of this type of compound in combating certain types of cancers was observed. At the close of World War II, this information was declassified, and the anticancer potential of these compounds was made public. Soon, many variations of these alkylating agents were prepared as anticancer drugs. These variations included the ethylenimines, the alkylsulfonates, and later the nitrosoureas. Many of the modern anticancer agents have been developed from these agents.

Cancer cells, like normal cells, need specific compounds for their metabolism. It was felt that certain chemicals might resemble a normally occurring, essential compound but not be able to function exactly as the normal compound should. If this false chemical were incorporated into a metabolic process, the resultant product could be inactive. A cancer cell that incorporated such a false substance would thus be inhibited or killed. Based on this assumption, many antimetabolites have been prepared as anticancer agents, e.g., folic acid and methotrexate. Folic acid is needed in the normal metabolism of a cell, and methotrexate is an analog of folic acid. It closely resembles folic acid but blocks its normal function. Methotrexate was shown to be effective against leukemias in 1948.

Purines and pyrimidines are essential components of nucleic acids. If analogs of these compounds were prepared, they might also be falsely incorporated into the nucleic acids and thus block the normal function of the cell. Purine analogs were studied by Hitchings in 1942 as potential anticancer agents. From this series, mercaptopurine was described as a clinically effective anticancer agent in 1952. Pyrimidine analogs were also described as effective anticancer drugs in 1957; 5-Fluorouracil became a clinically effective drug.

A number of antibiotics have shown some activity against various types of cancers. The actinomycins have been the most clinically effective; they are powerful bacteriostatic agents exhibiting cytostatic properties. The first of these antibiotics, Actinomycin D, was isolated from actinomycetes in 1940.

Dactinomycin
Actinomycin C1 (or D)

Vinca alkaloids
Vinblastine, R = CH₃
Vincristine, R = CHO

Colchicine, from *Colchicum autumnale*, and Podophyllotoxin, from *Podophyllum peltatum*, have long been known as inhibitors of cellular mitosis in the metaphase. These compounds have not been effective as anticancer agents, but some derivatives are promising.

Vinca rosea (commonly known as periwinkle) was originally known in folk medicine as a hypoglycemic agent. A further examination of this plant failed to substantiate this type of activity but did show anticancer activity. As a result, two alkaloids from this plant, Vinblastine and Vincristine, are presently used as anticancer agents.

The beneficial effect of an enzyme, L-asparaginase, as a cancer chemotherapeutic agent was seen in 1963. Malignant cells need L-asparagine for their normal growth. Normal mammalian cells do not. In malignant cells, L-Asparaginase converts L-asparagine to aspartic acid and ammonia. As a result, the normal amounts of L-asparagine are not available to the malignant cells, and their growth is suppressed. The L-Asparaginase can be adequately produced by *Escherichia coli*. Hence, a new type of anticancer agent became available.

Miscellaneous Agents
As the knowledge of antibiotic drugs was increasing, synthetic drugs with chemotherapeutic properties were also being developed. In the nineteenth century, tuberculosis was a dreaded disease. The early treatment involved a long rest in a sunny tuberculosis sanatorium. Then, in 1944, Streptomycin was introduced in the treatment of the disease. Large doses were required, however, and toxicity appeared. other compounds were required to augment its antitubercular activity and permit a smaller dose of streptomycin.

The effects of p-Aminosalicylic acid were observed on the metabolism of the tuberculosis organism in 1946. Soon afterward, it was used clinically in the treatment of the disease.

Thiacetazone was reported as an antitubercular agent in 1950; thilosemicarbazone derivatives of various other aldehydes were then prepared for antituberculosis testing. An intermediate in the preparation of isonicotinaldehyde, isonicotinic acid hydrazide, was tested for antitubercular activity. It was found to be a highly active compound with a wide margin of safety. This compound became known as Isoniazid and is still used as an antitubercular drug. Combination therapy of tuberculosis involving Streptomycin, p-Aminosalicylic acid, and Isoniazid has also been commonly used.

In 1961, the antitubercular activity of a series of ethylenediamine derivatives was observed, leading to the drug known as Ethambutol. In addition, a semisynthetic derivative of a macrocyclic antibiotic known as Rifampin was prepared in 1966. The bacterial inhibition of this substance against the tuberculosis organism was noted in 1968. Now, the combined use of Isoniazid, Ethambutol, and Rifampin constitutes a major weapon against tuberculosis.

The presence of a nitro group in any medicinal agent was formerly considered to cause toxicity, because many cases of methemoglobinemia were found among workers in munitions plants where trinitrotoluene was used. This compound was absorbed through the skin and reduced to aniline derivatives internally. In 1946, however, Doll introduced a series of nitrofuran drugs that showed good chemotherapeutic activity toward bacteria. In 1952, nitrofurantoin was introduced as an orally active urinary antiseptic, effective against both Gram-positive and Gram-negative organisms, and a new series of chemotherapeutic agents came into use.

Nitrofurantoin   Metronidazole   Nalidixic acid

Metronidazole was patented in 1960 as a highly effective chemotherapeutic substance for the treatment of vaginal trichomoniasis. It was active orally and relatively free of side effects. This drug has also opened new research concerning the nitroheterocyclic drugs.

The antiseptic activity of some quaternary ammonium salts was reported by Jacobs and Heidelberger in 1915. They introduced an alkyl group into the hexamethylenetetramine nucleus in an attempt to increase its antibacterial effectiveness. Quaternary amines that are more closely related to the present-day compounds were prepared by Hartmann and Kagi in 1928. Their series showed strong antiseptic activity.

The use of benzalkonium chloride as a detergent and germicidal agent was reported in 1935. Since that time, many cationic surfactants that are active as germicidal agents have been reported. These compounds can affect the enzymes and proteins of certain organisms, with the possible destruction of their cell walls.

Another drug that has shown good activity against urinary tract infections is Nalidixic acid. It was introduced in 1962 as a chemotherapeutic agent highly active against Gram-negative organisms. Even though the compound is inactive against Gram-positive organisms, it is important clincally and has opened up another area in the search for chemotherapeutic drugs.

Although past research has given us many good drugs for the treatment of infections, a number of parasitic infections remain for which no good chemotherapeutic agents are available. It is hoped that the search for agents against these infections, primarily tropical in their incidence, will be maintained to an extent commensurate with the occurrence of such infections in humans.

Selected from W. O. Foye, *'Principles of Medcinal Chemistry'*,
3rd ed., Lea & Febigen, U. S. A., 1988.

Words and expressions

soybean ['sɔi'bi:n] *n*. 大豆，黄豆
moldy ['məuldi] (=mouldy) *a*. 发(生)霉的，霉烂的
spectrum ['spektrəm] (*pl*. spectra) *n*. 谱图
mustard ['mʌstəd] *n*. 芥(禾)，芥子气
mustard-gas *n*. 芥子气
vesicant ['vesikənt] *a*. 起疱的(剂)，腐烂性的
respiratory ['respirətɔ:ri] *a*. 呼吸(作用)的
autopsies ['ɔ:təpsais] *n*. (*pl*.) 尸体解剖(检验)
incorporate [in'kɔ:pəreit] *v*. (使)合并(并加)
malignant [mə'lignənt] *a*. 有恶意的，恶毒的
asparagine [ə'spærədʒi:n] *n*. 天冬酰胺
miscellaneous [misi'leiniəs] *a*. 多方面的，其它的
augment [ɔ:g'ment] *v*. 增大(加，长)，扩大(张)
tuberculosis [tju(:)bə:kju'ləusis] *n*. 结核(病)，肺结核
munition [mju:'niʃən] *n*. (*pl*.) 军需(用)品，军火，弹药
urinary ['juərinəri] *a*. (泌)尿的
antiseptic [ænti'septik] *a*.; *n*. 防腐(消毒，杀菌)的；防腐(抗菌，消毒)剂
detergent [di'tə:dʒnt] *n*. 洗涤剂
germicidal [dʒə:mi'saidl] *a*. 杀菌的

Unit 4　Novel Analgesics

Pain is a major problem. Apart from the human dimension, it costs blllions of dollars in lost productivity and medicine. The search is now on for new painkillers.

Pain is a problem that has plagued mankind for thousands of years. Evidence of this can be found in the ancient writings of Egypt, India and China. Shen Nung, the Red Emperor, is credited with the earliest recorded attempts at using naturally occuring substances including mandragora and poppy for pain relief. Pain has had an astounding social impact on civilization. The association of pain with religious penance and cultural rights of passage confers a mystical quality to the experience.

While medical science seeks to demystify the phenomena of pain, the burden of pain on society has become enormous. Economically, the direct and indirect costs associated with the experience of chronic pain has reached disastrous proportions. Each year, billions of dollars are allocated towards treating pain. These expenditures take the form of medical costs, disability, lost productivity and days lost from work. Medical treatment is directed to help decrease the social and economic burden of pain.

Understanding pain

While pain is ubiquitous, and each individual who reads this article has probably experienced pain many times, it is challenging to define. The International Association for the Study of Pain defines pain as an unpleasant sensory and emotional experience associated with actual or potential tissue damage, or described in terms of such damage. This definition is important because it describes pain as an experience. It is not a sensation - pain includes components of environment and personality combined with sense.

To understand the tangible aspects of pain, a basic knowledge of the nervous system is needed. The peripheral nervous system (PNS) consists of nerves, which are akin to telephone wires, running throughout the body. These wires carry information from our environment to our brain via the spinal cord. The brain and spinal cord make up the central nervous system (CNS), which processes this information. The sensory experience of pain commonly begins with trauma to the skin, for example chemical, mechanical or thermal energy could create a tissue injury. This damage starts the release of several irritating substances around the site of the injury. These substances - prostaglandins, bradykinin, serotonin and hydrogen ions - lead to inflammation①[1].

The inflammatory substances sensitize or stimulate the firing of special pain nerve fibers called the primary afferents, which transmit information to the spinal cord. In the dorsal horn, a specialized area of the spinal cord, the primary afferents release glutamate (an amino acid), substance P, calcitonin gene-related protein, neurokinin A, and other small proteins, all known as neurotransmitters. These traverse the synapse②, a small space between the peripheral nerves and spinal cord nerves, binding and interacting with excitatory receptors located on the surface of various cells within the spinal cord[2]. Additional inhibitory receptors within the spinal cord modulate the signal as it is transmitted to the higher processing centers in the brain stem and brain.

After the information is processed within the brain, a message can be sent back to the region of the spinal cord where the primary afferent first made contact, and diminish or inhibit further transmission of pain signals. Modulation of signal transmission to and from the brain is analogous to the volume control on a stereo. It occurs via the interaction of endogenous and exogenous substances, or ligands, with the various receptors in the spinal cord. Through the pharmacologic manipulation of these receptors, it is possible to alter pain by decreasing the transmission of pain signals to the brain, or by increasing the inhibitory signals from the central nervous system.

The discovery of these receptors has increased our knowledge of the mechanisms by which current analgesics work. In addition, the have allowed new medications to be invented to assist in the war against pain. Further research has identified that these receptors have other subcellular elements necessary to create the sensory component of the pain signal. Some of these elements are ion channels. The receptors can become decreasingly responsive with prolonged drug exposure, a phenomenon known as pharmacological tolerance. In contrast, ion channels appear to remain responsive. The opportunity to influence neurotransmitter and ion channel activities with medication has created much of the current direction in analgesic development.

The sites of action for analgesics

Combating pain

The available analgesic medications such as aspirin, ibuprofen, acetaminophen and morphine work at various locations throughout the nervous system (see Fig. 1 and Fig. 2). Aspirin and Ibuprofen are non-steroidal anti-inflammatory drugs (NSAIDs). These inactivate the enzyme cyclo-oxygenase which decreases prostaglandin production. Prostaglandins may enhance the release or effect of substance P, bradykinin and other pain evoking chemicals from inflammatory cells near the site of injury. Blocking prostaglandin synthesis decreases inflammation and pain transmission from the PNS (see Fig. 1).

Acetaminophen is a non-opioid analgesic and fever preventative. Its mechanism of action has not been fully defined; however, it does decrease prostaglandin levels within the brain. Acetaminophen is commonly used alone or in combination with weak opiates.

Opium has been used to control pain for thousands of years. It is derived from the poppy seed of the plant *Papaver somniferum*. In 1803 Serturner, a German pharmacist, isolated a pure active substance from opium and called it Morphine[3]. Morphine has become the standard by which other natural and synthetic opiates and other non-opioid analgesics are measured.

Opiates produce analgesia by binding to receptors found throughout the peripheral and central nervous system. In the peripheral nervous system, opiate receptors are mainly

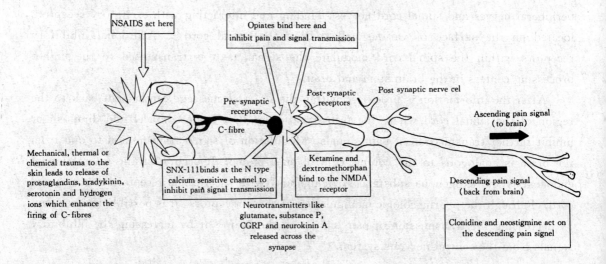

Fig. 1 The sites action for analgesics

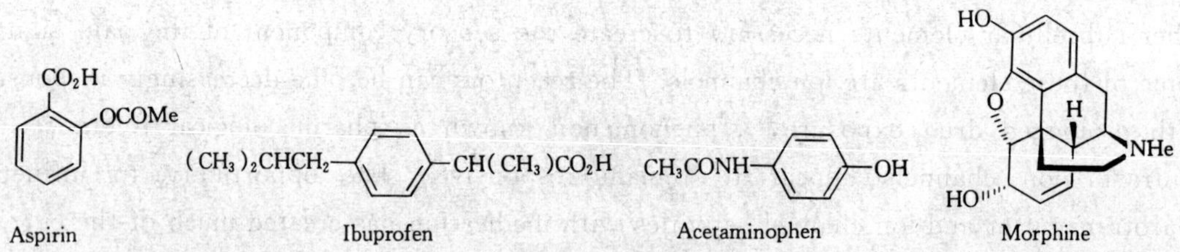

Fig. 2 Common analgesics

located on the pre-synaptic terminal ends of primary afferents, and on the post-synaptic membranes of nerves within the dorsal horn of the spinal cord. When morphine binds to the pre-synaptic receptor, it decreases the C-fiber nerve cell's ability to conduct an electrical impulse. This results in the C-fiber nerve's inability to release glutamate, substance P, calcitonin gene-related protein and neurokinin A. Opiates that bind to the post-synaptic receptor also help to decrease the barrage of pain signals from the PNS. Opiate receptors are also found in the brainstem and midbrain. These interact with the descending pathways from the brain to the spinal cord to inhibit pain signals from the PNS. The mechanism of this interaction is not yet fully understood.

Opiate medications are excellent analgesics but are not without side effects. Of these, nausea, constipation, sedation and inhibition of breathing are receptor mediated, so undesired side effects can occur before the desired analgesic efficacy is reached. Additionally, the patient may develop tolerance with prolonged use. Many of the new analgesic medications bind to receptors in the spinal cord and have the potential to act synergistically with opiates (see Fig. 1).

New uses for old drugs

As our knowledge of pain receptors within the nervous system increases, so does our ability to manipulate them. With this knowledge, we have gained the ability to use 'old' drugs for the new purpose of pain management, as in the cases of Clonidine, Neostigmine and Dextromethorphan (see Fig. 3).

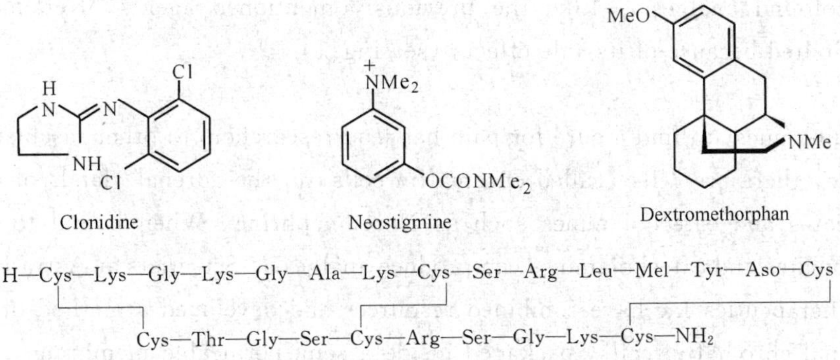

Clonidine   Neostigmine   Dextromethorphan

H—Cys—Lys—Gly—Lys—Gly—Ala—Lys—Cys—Ser—Arg—Leu—Mel—Tyr—Aso—Cys
     | | |
     Cys—Thr—Gly—Ser—Cys—Arg—Ser—Gly—Lys—Cys—NH$_2$

SNX-Ⅲ

Fig. 3 New analgesics

Clonidine and its newer, more potent cousin Dexmedetomidine, bind to pre-synaptic α_2-adrenergic receptors within the spinal cord and inhibit the release of norepinephrine. Clonidine was initially used to control blood pressure, and was later used in blunting the increased blood pressure and heart rate associated with opiate, alcohol and nicotine withdrawal syndromes[4]. It is currently under investigation as an analgesic.

When given alone orally, intravenously or spinally, Clonidine provides moderate analgesia by decreasing the release of norepinephrine and/or by promoting the release of acetylcholine within the dorsal horn of the spinal cord[5]. This increases the descending inhibitory signals from the brain to the dorsal horn of the spinal cord. Unfortunately, the higher doses needed to produce better analgesia also cause undesired side effects such as sedation, nausea, and decreased blood pressure. Clonidine and Dexmedetomidine in lower doses, combined with opiate medications, produce profound analgesia (see Fig. 1)[6,7].

Neostigmine is a drug that is commonly used in the practice of anaethesia as a reversal agent for skeletal muscle paralysis. When given intravenously or intra-spinally, it inhibits the enzyme acetylcholinesterase. This enzyme degrades acetylcholine, a neurotransmitter that relays information between nerves, as well as between nerves and muscles. Blocking acetylcholinesterase allows the acetylcholine concentration to rise, and increased spinal acetylcholine is believed to enhance the brain's ability to block pain. The spinal administration of Neostigmine in Conjunction with Clonidine enhances the analgesia provided by both drugs, without enhancing the side effects (see Fig. 1)[8].

Dextromethorphan is a common ingredient in many over the counter cough medicines[9]. Pharmacologically it is one of two clinically available antagonsists of the receptor for N-methyl-D-aspartate (NMDA). This receptor is located in the dorsal horn of the spinal cord and has been implicated in pain transmission[10]. Glutamate, an excitatory amino acid released from primary afferents, binds to the NMDA receptor and increases pain signal transmission to the brain[11]. NMDA receptor antagonists bind to the receptor and prevent being activated by Glutamate. Theoretically, this should decrease the transmission of pain.

Unfortunately, this has not been the case with Dextromethorphan[12]. It has, however, been implicated in the reversal of opiate tolerance, and could prove useful in patients that are receiving long term opiate therapy[13]. Ketamine, the other marketed NMDA antagonist, provides profound analgesia. Like the previously mentioned agents, Ketamine's use is somewhat limited because of its side effects (see Fig. 1).

New sources

The continuing quest to find a cure for pain has lead researchers to other fascinating places. For example, there are cells (called chromaffin cells) in the adrenal glands of cows which produce opiates and catecholamines such as Norepinephrine. When bound to appropriate receptors, opiates and catecholamines can produce analgesia. Scientists at Astra Pain Control and Cyto Therapeutics Inc have combined resources and developed a method of implanting bovine adrenal chromaffin cells, packaged inside a semi-permeable membrane, into human spinal fluid. The membrane allows nutrients in and cell products out, and also protects the bovine cells from the human immune system. The procedure has performed successfully in early clinical studies in patients suffering from intractable pain secondary to cancer[14]. Placebo controlled studies are still needed.

Meanwhile, in the Philippines, there are over 500 varieties of killer snails (of the genus *Conus*) whose venom contains a large number of small peptides which bind to various receptors throughout the nervous system[15]. After prolonged study of the snail venom, several protentially therapeutic peptides have been synthesized. Of these ω-conopeptides have great potential as analgesic medications.

At Neurex Corp, researchers have developed a synthetic ω-conopeptide called SNX-III (see Fig. 3). This binds selectively to N-type voltage sensitive calcium channels in mammals[16]. Found on the pre-synaptic never terminals in the dorsal horn of the spinal cord, these ion channels mediate the release of certain neurotransmitters. If calcium flows into the cell, then neurotransmitters like glutamate and calcitonin gene-related protein are released, enhancing the pain signals to the spinal cord. Blocking the influx of calcium into the cells decreases the release of these neurotransmitters, resulting in a lower pain input to the spinal cord, and this is how SNX-III works[17,18].

SNX-III is a relatively safe analgesic when given spinally in both animal models and in humans. It has been used in individuals with severe cancer pain, unresponsive to potent opiates, with promising results. Clinical trials are currently under way.

One of the most promising attributes of SNX-III is that its analgesic effect is by way of ion-channel modulation rather than receptor binding and antagonism. So, in contrast to the other analgesics reviewed, there appears to be little or no development of pharmacological tolerance with SNX-III. Other animals such as the venomous spider *Segestria florentina*, also produce ω-conopeptides which may lead to useful therapies in the future[19].

Pain management is still in its infancy. Each year we increase our understanding of the nervous system and the mechanisms of pain transduction, transmission and modulation. By understanding these mechanisms, and their mediators, we can develop new approaches to pain alleviation.

Acknowledgements I would like to express my thanks to Nacy Tish, Dawn McGuire and Scott Browersox for their assistance with this project.

References
1. Cousins, M. J., *Neural blockade*, 2nd edition., Philadelphi, PA: J. B. Lippincott Company, 1998, 740~742.
2. Wall, P. D. & Melzack, R., *Textbook of pain*, 3rd edition, New York: Churchill Livingstone, 1994, 234~237.
3. Katzung, B. G., *Basic and clinical pharmacology*, 4th edition, East Norwalk, Connecticut: Appleton and Lange, 1989, 368.
4. Jasinski, D., et al., *Arch. gen. Psychiat.*, 1985, **42**, 1063.
5. Klimscha, W., Tong, C., Tommasi, E. & Eisenach, J. C., *Anesthesiology*, 1995, **83**, A793.
6. Flacke, J., 'Opioid anesthesia and apha-2 agonsits', given at the 'Annual refresher course lectures', *American Society of Anesthesiology*, Lecture, 235, 1990.
7. Murkin, J. M., *J. Cardiothorac. Vasc. Anesth.*, 1991, **3**, 268~277.
8. Hood, D., Mallak, K., Eisenach. J. & Tong, C., *ibid*, 1996, **85**, 315~325.
9. Virtanen, R., *Acta Vet. Scand. Suppl.*, 1985, **42**, 1063.
10. Dickenson, A. H., *Treds Pharmacol. Sci.*, 1990, **11**, 307~309.
11. Dickenson, A. H. & Sullivan, A. F., *Neuropharmacology*, 1987, **26**, 1235~1238.
12. McQuay, H. J., et al., *Pain*, 1994, **59**, 127~133.
13. Elliott, K., Hynansky, A. & Inturrisi, C., *Pain*, 1994, **59**, 361~368.
14. Buchser, E., et al., *Anesthesiology*, 1996, **85**, 1005~1012.
15. Olivera, B., Rivier, J. & Clark, C., *Science*, 1990, 257~263.
16. Cruz, L., Johnson, D. & Olivea, B., *Biochem.*, 1987, 26, 820~824.
17. Browersox, S. S., Valentino, K. L. & Luther, R. R., *Drug News and Perspectives*, 1994, **7**, 261~268.
18. Malmberg, A. B. & Yaksh, T. L., *Pain*, 1995, **60**, 83~90.
19. Newcomb. R., et al., *Biochemistry*, 1995, **34**, 8341~8347.

Selected from N. C. Law, W. Brose, *Chem. Ind. (London)*, 1997, (21), 306~309.

Words and Expressions

analgesic [ˌænæ'dʒiːsik] *n.* 止痛药,镇痛剂; *a.* 止痛的,不痛的
painkiller ['pen‚kilə] *n.* 止痛药
poppy ['pɔpi] *n.* 罂粟,鸦片,麻醉品
chronic ['krɔnik] *a.* 慢性的,长期的
ubiquitous [juː'bikwitəs] *a.* 无所不在的,到处都有的
akin [ə'kin] *a.* 类似的
be akin to 与……相似
peripheral [pə'rifərəl] *a.* 外围的,周围的

the peripheral nervous system (PNS) 外周神经系统
the central nervous system (CNS) 中枢神经系统
spinal ['spainl] a. 针的；脊骨的，脊柱的
spinal cord 脊髓
trauma ['traumə] n. 外伤，创伤
bradykinin [,brædi'kainən] n. 缓激肽
serotonin ['sɛrə,tɔnin] n. 5-羟色胺（一种神经递质）
afferent ['æfərənt] a. 传入的，输入的
dorsal ['dɔ:sl] a. 背面的，背部的
calcitonin [,kælsə'tɔnin] n. 降血钙素
synapse ['sinæps] n. 突触
inhibitory [in'hibi,tɔri] a. 抑制的
endogenous [en'dɔdʒənəs] a. 内生的，内源的
exogenous [ek'sɔdʒinəs] a. 外生的，外源的
ligand ['laigənd, 'ligənd] n. 配体
manipulation [mə,nipju'leiʃən] n. 触诊；改造，操作法
Aspirin ['æspirin] n. 阿司匹林
inflammation [,inflə'meiʃən] n. 怒火，燃烧，发炎
pharmacist ['fɑ:məsist] n. 药剂师，配药师
nausea ['nɔ:siə] n. 恶心，反胃，晕船
constipation [,kɔnstə'peiʃən] n. 便秘
Dextromethorphan [,dekstrə'neθəfen] n. 右美沙芬（镇痛药）
adrenergic [,ændrə'nedʒik] a. 肾上腺素
syndrome ['sin,drɔm] n. 并发症状，综合症
analgesia [,ænæl'dʒiziə] n. 无痛觉，镇痛
glutamate ['glutə,meit] n. 谷氨酸盐（酸式根）
skeletal ['skɛlətəl] a. 骨骼的
adrenal [æd'rinl] n.；a. 肾上腺
gland [glænd] n. 腺体，腺
catecholamine [,kæti'kəuləmi:n] n. 儿茶酚胺
norepinephrine [,nɔrepi'nefrin] n. 去甲肾上腺素
intractable [in'træktəbl] a. 难处理的，难治的，难控制的
bovine ['bəuvain] n. 牛科动物；a. 似牛的，笨拙的

Notes

① Inflammation：炎（症），活体组织对损伤或感染的反应，由于充血、淋巴渗出和血细胞扩散到组织内而发生局部的红、热、疼痛和肿胀。

② Synapse：突触。两种经细胞发生功能联系的部位，神经冲动可以通过小量特异性传递质（如乙酰胆碱、去甲肾上腺素）从突触前神经细胞经过狭窄间隙弥散到突触后细胞进行传递，这些传递质由突触前神经末梢释放而作用于突触后神经细胞膜。

Exercises

1. Answer the following questions:
   (1) How is pain produced? Can you give a definition of pain?
   (2) What can be done in the treatment of pain? Please list some of analgesics.
2. Put the following into English:
   止痛药   发烧   鸦片   机理
   亲电试剂   放热反应   杂环化合物   分子内氢键
3. Put the following into Chinese:
   analgesic   synapse   pain transduction   syndrome
   manipulation   ligand   receptor   peripheral nerve
4. Fill in the blanks with the following words:
   modification   derivative   salicylate   addiction   impulse
   nonirritating   fever   mechanism   analgesic   symptom

   _____ is a drug that relieves pain by raising the pain threshold (the point at which a stimulus causes a feeling of pain) without disturbing consciousness. The _____ by which various analgesics raise the pain threshold are not clearly understood. Some seem to act by blocking pain _____ as they are carried over sensory nerve tracts. Many analgesics also act to reduce _____. Analgesics are usually divided into two classes: *narcotic analgesics* and *nonnarcotic analgesics*.

   Narcotic Analgesics. Among the narcotic analgesics are opium and its _____, including morphine and codeine, obtained from the opium poppy (*Papaver somniferum*). Synthetic derivatives and related drugs including diacetylmorphine (heroin), dihydromorphinone (Dilaudid), meperidine (Demerol), and many others. Narcotic drugs are very useful to relieve pain, but generally they are not used when lesser measures will suffice because they cause drug _____, produce drug tolerance when used for a long time, or mask _____ and obscure diagnosis.

   Nonnarcotic Analgesics. Nonnarcotic analgesics are used in enormous quantities for a variety of aches and pains. The _____ are among the oldest remedies, and they still occupy an important place in modern medicine. Some, such as salicin and methyl salicylate (oil of wintergreen), occur naturally in many trees and plants, notably the willow (genus *Salix*). The first synthetic salicylates were too irritating for internal use, but further _____ have resulted in the syntheses of acetyl salicylic acid (aspirin), salicylamide, and some salicylic acid salts that are effective and _____.

Reading Material 4

Mild Analgesics-Antipyretics

1. Mild Analgesics-Antipyretics

Antipyretics are drugs that reduce hyperthermania associated with illness. They affect the thermal centers in the brain to increase peripheral body heat loss by increasing the rate of blood circulation and of perspiration. However, they do not increase the metabolic rate; hence, normal body temperature is not decreased by therapeutic doses of antipyretics.

Most antipyretics also have analgesic activity and are widely used in the treatment of neuralgic and arthritic pain. They are often combined with strong analgesic, such as Codeine. Even so, these combinations are not as effective as the analgesics, such as Morphine or Meperidine. The mild analgesics are used primarily for relief of mild to moderate pain.

Aspirin and Acetaminophen have become the most widely used of the mild analgesic-antipyretic drugs because of their general effectiveness and lack of significant adverse reactions inmost patients.

1.1 Salicylates

Salicylates are effective as Antipyretics and mild analgesics, and in addition have useful anti-inflammatory activity. They are used widely to abate mild fever and to treat nerve and muscle pain and headache. They often the drugs of choice for treating mild or slow onset arthritis (→ Anti-inflammatory-Antirheumatic Drugs). They are well tolerated by most patients, even in large doses. Salicylates have low toxicity, but they can cause gastrointestinal blood loss and kidney damage with prolonged heavy use. Aspirin has been implicated as a possible cause of Renee's syndrome in children. Some patients are allergic to salicylates and develop skin rash and asthmatic symptoms after ingesting them.

Acetylsalicylic Acid [50-78-2], 2-Acetoxybenzoic acid, aspirin, $C_9H_8O_4$, Mr 180.16, mp 135 ℃, (for properties and synthesis, →Salicylic Acid), is one of the most widely used of the mild analgesic-antipyretic-anti-inflammatory drugs. It is effective, although not as potent as other drugs, in all three of these pharmacologic areas, and most patients can tolerate quite high doses. Aspirin is used as a component of a great many combination drug preparations.

The lithium, magnesium, calcium, and aluminum salts of acetylsalicylic acid are used in some special preparations.

Trade name: Aspirin (Bayer, FRG)

Diflunisal [22494-42-4], 2′,4′-difluoro-4-hydroxy-(1,1′-biphenyl)-3-carboxylic acid, $C_{13}H_8F_2O_3$, Mr 250.21, mp 210∼211℃.

Synthesis: treatment of 2,4-difuorobiphenyl, which is acetylated under Friedel-Crafts conditions to give 4′-acetyl-2,4-difluorobiphenyl. Baeyer-Villiger oxidation affords the corresponding acetoxy compound, which is saponified to give the sodium salt of 2,4-difluoro-4′-hydroxybiphenyl.

Carboxylation via the Kolbe-Schmitt reaction followed by acidification yields diflunisal. Diflunisal has greater analgesic and anti-inflammatory activity than aspirin, a longer duration of action, and less tendency to cause gastrointestinal irritation, It does not have useful antipyretic activity.

Trade name: Dolobid (Merck).

1.2 Aniline Derivatives

The most important of the aniline derivatives is Acetaminophen, which rivals Aspirin as a widely used mild analgesic-antipyretic with low toxicity. Acetanilide, the first of the aniline derivatives to be introduced (as Antifbrin), is no long used because it produces methemoglobinuria and cyanosis. The related Phenacetin (acetophenetidine) also produces these adverse effects, although to a lesser degree than Acetanilide, and has been largely supplanted by Acetaminophen.

Acetaminophen [103-90-2], p-hydroxyacetanilide, $C_8H_9NO_2$, Mr 151.17, mp 168~169 °C.

Synthesis: nitro benzene is electrolytically reduced to p-aminophenol, which is acetylated with acetic anhydride.

Acetaminophen is comparable to Aspirin as an antipyretic and analgesic but does not have significant anti-inflammatory activity. It is less likely than Aspirin to provoke gastrointestinal irritation. It is also useful for patients who are sensitive to salicylates because it does not produce the allergenic effects that such patient experience with Aspirin. Like Aspirin, it is used both alone and in many combinations with other drugs, including Codeine.

Trade names: Tylenol (McNeil), Ben-u-ron (Bene-Chemie, FRG); There are many combination preparations.

Phenacetin [62-44-2], acetophentidine, p-ethoxyacetanilide, $C_{10}H_{13}NO_2$, Mr 179.21, mp 134~135 °C.

Synthesis: p-phenetidine is acetylated with acetic anhydride in a hydrocarbon solvent. Although phenacetiin is an effective mild analgesic -antipyretic, it is no longer widely used alone because on prolonged administration it can cause methemoglobinuria, cyanosis, and kidney damage. Its principal use is with Aspirin and Caffeine (Aspirin-Phenacetin-Caffeine, APC), and continues to be a constituent of combination analgesic drugs.

2. Anti-inflammatory Analgesics

The nonsteroidal anti-inflammatory drugs have been developed for their activity in treating inflammatory disease, particularly various forms of arthritis (→ Anti-inflammatory-Antirheumatic Drugs). This class of drugs began with pyrazolidine-3,5-dione phenylbutazone in the 1940s and has been elaborated into several other types of chemical structures. Both the effectiveness of these drugs and types and the severity of their side effects vary widely among patients. For this reason and because of the prevalence of inflammatory diseases, research aimed at the discovery and development of new classes of nonsteroidal anti-flammatory drugs continues to be very active.

The nonsteroidal anti-inflammatory drugs also have analgesic and antipyretic activity. They are used primarily to alleviate the swelling and pain that manifests in arthritis and related diseases. They are used less frequent as analgesics for pain from other causes, although some are used rather widely for short-term alleviation of pain from sprains and similar injuries.

Examples of the principal classes of nonsteroidal anti-inflammatory-analgesic drugs are listed in this chapter, for details of their *synthesis* and *clinical applications*, and additional examples, →Anti-inflammatory-Antirheumatic Drugs.

2.1 Acidic Enolic Compounds

This chemical classes includes a number of potent anti-inflammatory agents with analgesic and antipyretic activity, of which phenylbutazone and oxyphenbutazone are particularly important. They are generally used for short-term medication because they can cause gastric irritation, gastric damage, and blood dyscrasias on prolonged administration.

Pyrazolidine-3,5-diones

Phenylbutazone [50-33-9], 4-butyl-1,2-diphenylpyrazolidine-3,5-dione, $C_{19}H_{20}N_2O_2$, Mr 308.38, mp 105 ℃.

Trade Names: Butazolidin (Ciba-Geigy), Azolid (USV Laboratories).

Oxyphenbutazone [129-20-4], 4-butyl-1-(4-hydroxyphenyl)-2-phenylpyrazolidine-3,5-dione, $C_{19}H_{20}N_2O_3$, Mr 324.38, mp 124~125 ℃.

Trade Names: Tanderil (Ciba-Geigy), Oxalid (USV Laboratories).

2.2 Arylpropionic Acids

Ibuprofen [15687-27-1], 2-(p-isobutylphenyl)-α-methylbenzeneacetic acid, $C_{13}H_{18}O_2$, Mr 206.29, mp 75~77 ℃.

Trade names: Motrin (Upjohn, USA), Rufen (Boots, USA), Brufen (UCB Chemie, Sindorf).

Naproxen [22204-53-1], (+)-6-methoxy-α-methyl-2-naphthaleneacetic acid. $C_{14}H_{14}O_3$, Mr 230.27, mp 155.3 ℃; sodium salt [26159-34-2], $C_{14}H_{13}NaO_3$, Mr 252.26.

Trade Names: Naprosyn (Syntex), Anaprox (sodium salt, Syntex).

Ketoprofen [22071-15-4], 3-benzoyl-α-methyl-benzeneacetic acid, $C_{16}H_{14}O_3$, Mr 254.29, mp 94 ℃.

Trade Name: Orudis (Rhone-Poulenc).

Fenoprofen [31879-05-7], α-methyl-3-phenoxybenzeneacetic acid, $C_{15}H_{14}O_3$, Mr 242.28, viscous oil, bp 169~171 ℃(0.015 kPa); calcium salt dihydrate [34579-40-5], $C_{30}H_{26}CaO_6$, Mr 522.62.

Trade Name: Nalfon (Eli Lilly).

Selected from W. Gerhartz, *Ullmann's Encyclopedia of industrial Chemistry*, VCH, 5th completely rev. ed., 1985, vol. A2 271

Words and Expressions

ischemia [isˈkiːmiə] n. 局部缺血，局部贫血
Diflunisal [daiˈfluːnisæl] n. 二氟苯水杨酸，二氟尼柳
saponify [səˈpɔnifai] vt & vi （使）皂化
hyperthermia [ˌhaipə(ː)ˈθmiːə] n. 体温过高，高热
carboxylation [kɑːˌbɔksiˈleiʃən] n. 羧化（作用）
methemoglobinuria [metˌhiməˌgləubiˈnjuəriə] n. 正铁血红蛋白尿
Antifebrin [ˌæntiˈfebrin] n. 乙酰苯胺
perspiration [ˌpəːspəˈreiʃən] n. 排汗，汗
cyanosis [ˌsaiəˈnəusis] n. 青紫
neuralgic [njuəˈrældʒik] a. 神经痛
Phenacetin [fiˈnæsitin] n. 非那西汀
arthritic [ɑːˈθritik] a. 关节炎的
supplant [səˈplɑːnt] vt. 代替，取代
codeine [ˈkəudiːn] n. 可待因（碱）
Meperidine [məˈperidi(ː)n] n. 哌替啶
allergenic [ˈælədʒenik] a. 过敏原的
administration [ədˌminiˈstreiʃən] n. （药的）服法，用法，给予
abate [əˈbeit] vt. 减少，减轻
Phenylbutazone [ˌfiːnilˈbjuːtəzəun] n. 苯基丁氮酮，保泰松
prevalence [ˈprevələns] n. 流行，盛行
nonsteroidal [ˈnɔnsteˈrɔidl] a. 非甾族化合物，非类固醇的
rash [ræʃ] n. 皮疹
sprain [sprein] n. & vt. 扭，扭伤
Naproxen [nəˈprɔksən] n. 萘普生
Ketoprofen [ˌkiːtəuˈprəufən] n. 酮洛芬
asthmatic [æsˈmætik] a. 气喘的，患气喘病的
dyscrasia [disˈkreizjə] n. 体液疾病，体液不调

Unit 5   Drug Development (I)

1. Introduction

Drug Development is a very complex process requiring a great deal of coordination and communication between a wide range of different functional groups. It is expensive, particularly in the later phases of clinical development, where studies involve hundreds of patients. It is currently estimated that the development of a new drug costs about $230 million (1987 dollars) and takes somewhere between 7 and 10 years from initiation of preclinical development to first marketing (excluding regulatory delays). Drug development is a high-risk business; although the rate is increasing, only about ONE out of every TEN new chemical entities studied in human beings for the first time will ever become a product. As a drug candidate progresses through development the risks of failure decrease as 'hurdles' are overcome along the way. Typical reasons for failure include unacceptable toxicity, lack of efficacy, or inability to provide advantages over competitive products (Fig. 1).

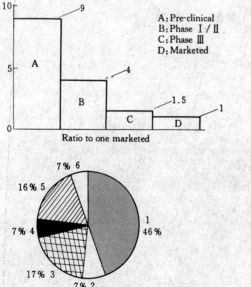

A: Pre-clinical
B: Phase I / II
C: Phase III
D: Marketed

Attrition Rate of New Chemical Entities (NCE's) entering development. On average only about 1 in 400~1000 compounds synthesized enters development.
Reasons for termination of development of NCE's (excluding anti-infectives)
1: Lack of efficacy
2: Pharmacokinetics
3: Animal toxicity
4: Miscellaneous
5: Adverse effects in man
6: Commercial reasons

Fig. 1   Attrition rates and reasons for terminations

2. Planning for development

Assessment of whether a drug candidate is likely to provide competitive advantages highlights the need first to have in place a set of product 'goals' or target product profile. Particular attention should be paid to the differentiation from competitors. This is becoming more and more critical with the increasing emphasis on limited formularies, healthcare costs, and pharmacoeconomics (discussed later in the chapter).

A target profile will define the indication(s) that a drug candidate will be developed for, along with goals such as once a day dosing, faster onset of action, better side effect profile than a major competitor. The target profile can be refined and revised as a drug candidate moves through development and new data on the drug candidate or competitors become available. The logical next steps are to define the development strategy, for example, which indications to develop first, which countries to aim to market the drug in and then to define the core clinical studies necessary to achieve regulatory approval and commercial success.

This chapter will describe the main activities required for successful development of a new drug. All these activities, many of which are interdependent, need to be carefully planned and co-ordinate. Speed to market with collection of high quality data is critical for success. The path of activities which determine the time it will take to get to registration is called, in project management terms, the critical path. It is vital to plan and prepare before studies begin and to monitor and manage problems so as to ensure that the critical path remains on schedule. With increased economic pressures and competitive intensity it is important for companies to explore ways to shorten this critical path. Running activities in parallel, or overlapping studies which would usually run sequentially, often involves an increase in risk but the dividends in time-saving can make such strategies worthwhile.

The critical path for development of a new drug generally runs through the initial synthesis of compound, subacute toxicology studies, and then the clinical program. A chart showing the critical path activities for a typical drug candidate is shown in Fig. 2.

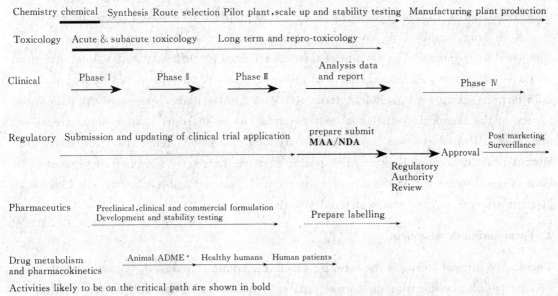

Fig. 2 The major processes in new drug development

The following sections highlight the objectives and activities of drug development work. Activities within each technical discipline are described broadly in chronological order. At any one time, work in all these disciplines may be proceeding in parallel. The timing and outcome of much of the work has direct impact on work in other disciplines.

The major phases of drug development are Preclinical (studies required before the compound can be dosed in humans), Phase I (clinical studies usually in healthy human volunteers), Phase II (initial efficacy and safety and dose finding studies in patients), and Phase III (studies in several hundred patients). There then follows assembly of a marketing application dossier for subsequent review by country regulatory authorities.

3. Chemical development

Rapid development of a drug candidate is dependent on the availability of sufficient quantity of the compound. The purity of compound needs to reach certain standards in order for it to be used in safety (toxicology), pharmaceutical, and clinical studies. Initially, chemists will work on a small to medium scale to investigate production of the compound by several different methods so as to identify the optimum route for synthesizing the compound. 'Optimum' here may mean a combination of several factors, for example, most efficient, cheapest safe, or that producing minimal waste. Analysis of the final product as well as intermediates and impurities plays a key role in identifying the best method of synthesis. Development and validation of analytical methods are necessary to support process development and guarantee the purity of the drug substance.

In some cases levels of impurities may be unacceptably high and either improved purification procedures will need to be developed or the synthetic process may require significant alterations. The main aim is to ensure that the composition of compound is understood and that ultimately the material that is prepared is as pure as possible.

As a drug candidate progresses through development, larger and larger amounts of compound are required. The amount of material required for different tests will often depend on the actual potency and dosage form of the compound. A pilot plant can be regarded as a mini-manufacturing set-up. Before transferring to a pilot plant, extensive evaluation and testing of the chemical synthesis is undertaken to ensure that any changes and hazards are minimized. Procedures are optimized, particular attention being paid to developing environmentally acceptable ways of disposing of waste products. Commercial production of bulk drug substance for production of a drug, once approved and marketed, will likely take place on a larger scale or at a registered manufacturing plant.

4. Formulation development

The dosage form of a drug is the form by which it is administered to the patient. There are a vast array of possible dosage forms ranging from transdermal patches to inhalers to intranasal medicines. The more common dosage forms include oral tablets or capsules, oral liquids, topical ointments or creams, and injectables. The dosage form or forms chosen for a particular drug candidate will be defined in the target profile.

Sometimes a more simple dosage form, for example an oral solution, is chosen for early clinical studies in human beings. This may save time and upfront costs at an early, high-risk stage of the drug development process. Later clinical studies would use the expected marketed dosage form.

Whatever the dosage form, the combination of drug and other materials which constitute it must fulfil certain criteria. One of the most important is that of adequate stability. That means a predetermined potency level must remain after, for example, two or three years. The stability data generated on a dosage form will determine its shelf-life and recommended storage conditions. Early in development the shelf-life may be limited to several months. This will not be a problem provided it is sufficient to cover use of the drug over the duration of the clinical study or studies.

5. Pharmacology[①]

Before a drug candidate is given to man, its pharmacological effects on major systems are often investigated in a number of species. The body systems studied include cardiovascular, respiratory, and nervous systems; the effects on gross behavior can also be studied.

Experiments are sometimes conducted to see whether the drug candidate interferes with the actions of other medicines which, because of their specific effects or because of their common use, are likely to be taken concurrently with the drug candidate. Any synergism or antagonism of drug effects should be investigated, and any necessary warning issued to clinical investigators. (It may be judged necessary to investigate such effects further in clinical studies, and any potential or proven drug interactions are likely to be noted in the product labeling for the drug.)

It may also be appropriate to identify a substance for possible use in the management of overdosage, particularly if the therapeutic margin of the drug candidate is small.

6. Safety evaluation

The objective of animal toxicology testing, carried out prior to the administration of a drug to man, is to reject compounds of unacceptable toxicity and to identify potential target organs and timings for adverse effects of the drug. This means that in early human studies these organs and tissues can be monitored with particular attention. It is important to establish whether toxic effects are reversible or irreversible, whether they can be prevented and, if possible, the mechanism of the toxicological effects. It is also important to interrelate drug response to blood levels in humans and blood levels in various animal species.

The toxicological studies required for the evaluation of a drug candidate in man will be relevant to its proposed clinical use in terms of route of administration and duration of treatment of the clinical studies. The size and frequency of the doses and the duration of the toxicology studies are major determinants of permissible tests in man. Countries, including UK, USA, Australia, and Nordic countries, have regulatory guidelines which relate the duration of treatment allowed in man to the length of toxicity studies required in two species. Points from the guidelines are referenced in the subsequent sections.

Initially, the pharmacological effects of increasing doses of the test substances are established in acute toxicity studies in small numbers of animals, generally using two routes of administration (one being that used in man). Results provide a guide to the maximum tolerated doses in subsequent chronic toxicity tests, aid selection of dose levels, and identify target organs.

The main aim of the subsequent sub-acute toxicity tests is to determine whether or not the drug candidate is adequately tolerated after administration to animals for a prolonged period as a guide to possible adverse reactions in man. Two to four week (daily dosing) studies are required, using the same route of administration as in man, in two species (one non-rodent) prior to administration of the compound to man. Three dose levels are usually necessary: the low daily dose should be a low multiple of the expected therapeutic dose, and the highest dose should demonstrate some toxicity.

A general guide for the evaluation of new chemical entities would be that toxicology studies of a minimum duration of 14 days are required to support single-dose exposure of a new drug candidate in normal volunteers in Phase I. Toxicology studies of 30 days duration are required to support clinical studies of 7 to 10 days duration. Clinical studies of greater than 7 to 10 days up to 30 days duration require the support of at least 90 days toxicology studies. These requirements illustrate the need to plan ahead in drug development. The duration and approximate timings for future clinical trials need to be considered well in advance in order to schedule and conduct the appropriate toxicology studies to support the clinical program and avoid any delays.

Two types of safety test are used to detect the ability of the drug candidate to produce tumours in man. The first are short-term *in vitro* genotoxicity tests, for example bacterial tests. The second are long-term animal carcinogenicity studies which are conducted in mice and rats; their length of often 2 years covers a large part of the lifespan of the animal. Mice and rats are used because of their relatively short life span, small size, and ready availability. Also, knowledge, which has accumulated concerning spontaneous diseases and tumours[2] in particular strains of these species, helps greatly in the interpretation of results.

Long-term toxicology and carcinogenicity studies are conducted in order to obtain approval to test and finally to market a product for chronic administration to man. These studies may need to start during the late preclinical/ early clinical phase in order to 'support' the subsequent clinical program. Long-term toxicity studies will normally include toxicity studies of six and twelve months duration in two species (one non-rodent). Any toxicity previously detected may be investigated more closely, for example extra enzymes looked at in blood samples.

Reproductive toxicology is that part of toxicology dealing with the effect of compounds on reproduction-fertility, foetal abnormalities, post-natal development. Prior to clinical studies in women of child-bearing age, regulatory authorities require teratology data from two species (normally rat and rabbit) as well as clinical data from male volunteers. No reproductive data are required prior to clinical studies in male subjects. The effects of compounds on reproduction differ with the period of the reproductive cycle in which exposure takes place and studies are designed to look at these phases. Teratology[3] studies are designed to detect foetal abnormalities, fertility studies to investigate the compounds' effect on reproductive performance, and peri- and post-natal studies to study the development of pups.

Selected from F. D. King, *'Medicinal Chemistry Principles and Practice'*, the Royal Society of Chemistry, Thomas Graham House, G. B., 1994.

Words and Expressions

clinical ['klinikəl]   a. 临床的，临诊的
entity ['entəti]   n. 实体
hurdle ['hə:dl]   vt. 用篱笆围住，跳过（栏栅），克服（障碍）
attrition [ə'triʃən]   n. 摩擦，磨损
pharmacokinetics [ˌfɑ:məkəuki'netiks]   n. 药物动力学
adverse ['ædvə:s]   a. 不利的，相反的
onset ['ɔnset]   n. 发作
regulatory ['regjulətəri]   n. 调整的，调节的
reimburse [ˌri:im'bə:s]   v. 偿还，偿付
interdependent [ˌintədi'pendənt]   a. 互相依赖的，相倚的
subacute [ˌsʌbə'kju:t]   a. 亚急性的
dividend ['dividend]   n. 股份红利，股息
chronological [ˌkrɔnə'lɔdʒikəl]   a. 按年代顺序排列的
preclinical [pri'klinikəl]   a. 潜伏期的，临症前期的
optimum ['ɔptiməm]   a. 最好的，最佳的，最有利的
impurity [im'pjuəriti]   n. 杂质
pilot [pailət]   a. 试验性
repro ['ri:prəu]   n. 复制品
submission [səb'miʃən]   n. 屈从，降服
surveillance [sə:'veiləns]   n. 监视，看守
excretion [eks'kri:ʃən]   n. 排泄，分泌
dermal ['də:məl]   a. 皮肤的，真皮的
inhaler [in'heilə]   n. 吸入器
capsule ['kæpsju:l]   n. 胶囊
cardiovascular [ˌkɑ:diəu'ræskjulə]   a. 心脏血管的
rodent ['rəudənt]   n. 啮齿动物
tumour ['tju:mə]   n. 瘤，肿瘤，肿块
foetal ['fi:tl]   a. 似胎儿的，胎儿的
teratology [ˌterə'tɔlədʒi]   a. 畸形学，怪异研究

Notes

① Pharmacology 药理学，医学分支科学之一，研究药物和动物生命过程和系统功能之间的相互作用，尤其是对各种药物的作用机制、治疗效果及其他用途的研究。
② Tumor （肿）瘤，任何肿胀或病理性肿大，现指新生物由无生理功能的新生细胞增殖形成的非炎性肿块，良性肿瘤为孤立的、有被膜、能压迫而不侵入附近组织；恶性肿瘤（癌、肉瘤）侵入附近组织，有复发和转移到身体其他部位的倾向。
③ Teratology 畸形学，是研究畸形以助于理解正常发育的科学。

Exercises

1. Answer the following questions:
   (1) Why do people consider the discovery of the novel drug is a long, expensive and tortuous process with no guarantee of success?
   (2) How many major processes are there in new drug development?
   (3) What has been achieved in the novel drug development in the past century?
   (4) Please list the disadvantages or barriers in Chinese novel drug development.
2. Put the following into English:
   杂质   胶囊   毒性   致癌物   畸形学
   内服药   共轭   杂化   蒸馏   中和反应
3. Put the following into Chinese:
   pharmacokinetics   assessment   optimum   highlight   regulatory approval
   preclinical   pharmacology side effect excretion   safety evaluation
4. Fill the blanks with the following words:
   pharmacodynamics   toxicology   pharmacognosy
   pharmacotherapeutics   pharmacokinetics   pharmacy

   _____ is a descriptive science concerned with the physical characteristics of natural drugs, primarily those derived from plants and animals. _____ is the art and science of preparing, compounding, and dispensing medicines. _____ is the study of the way drugs are absorbed into the body, their metabolism by the body, and the way they are excreted. _____ is the study of the actions of drugs on living organisms and can itself be further subdivided. It borrows freely from the experimental techniques of physiology, biochemistry, microbiology, pathology, genetics, immunology and cellular and molecular biology. Research in this area of pharmacology is at the very frontier of medical knowledge. It studies the ways in which drugs interact with the molecular structures (such as enzymes, cell receptors, and genetic material) that make up the machinery of living tissue. As knowledge has expanded, several of these subareas have developed specialized journals, such as the *Journal of Molecular Pharmacology* and the *Journal of Biochemical pharmacology*. Knowledge of precisely how drugs affect the chemistry of the cell has permitted the deliberate design of new drugs to treat formerly untreatable diseases. _____ deals with the use drugs in the prevention and treatment of disease, while _____ deals with the adverse effects of drugs.

Reading Material 5

Drug Development (II)

Drug metabolism and pharmacokinetics

Drug metabolism and pharmacokinetic (DMPK) studies are required to build a knowledge of metabolism of a compound together with the way in which the levels of the compound and its metabolites vary according to the dose administered and the length of time from when it was administered.

There is rarely a definitive regulatory requirement for metabolism data at the preclinical/early clinical stage of drug development. However, metabolism studies aid interpretation of toxicological results and study design and help in the extrapolation of animal safety and efficacy data to man.

Development of assays is required to measure drug and major metabolite levels in biological fluids or tissues. Aims are to develop rapid and reproducible methods. HPLC is normally used for separation although other techniques such as GLC may be used where suitable. Detection may be UV, flurometric, electrochemical, mass spectroscopy, to give some examples. When the activity of the compound is very high and consequently only trace amounts of material will actually be present in body fluids or tissues, detection problems may arise. RIA (radio-immuno assay) may provide greater sensitivity as well as giving the potential to analyze a greater number of compounds in a given time. However, an RIA is likely to take longer to develop and lack of specificity can be a problem.

Information on plasma concentrations of compound and/or metabolites is required in support of toxicology studies and to aid selection of dose levels. There is an initial need to establish the region of pharmacokinetic linearity, *i.e.* range in which dose *vs.* AUC (area under the curve-from concentration-time curves) may be regarded as linear. Identification of causes of non-linearity such as metabolic saturation of absorption/elimination processes will help in the understanding of toxicological or pharmacological events.

Clinical

Once adequate animal studies have been completed and analyzed, the pharmaceutical company will decide whether or not to take the drug into the human phase of research. This step often involves approval from company experts, clinical investigators and their Ethics Committees, and in some countries, for example USA, review by a government agency-in this example, the FDA (US Food and Drugs Administration). A new drug is first reviewed by the FDA when a sponsoring company submits a new drug investigation application (IND) to FDA. Within 30 days the FDA must let the sponsor know whether in its judgement the proposed clinical study is sufficiently safe. If so, the IND is considered to be 'in effect' and the clinical study may proceed. If not, the FDA may place the clinical study 'on hold' until their concerns are satisfactorily addressed.

In planning the clinical program it is important to refer to the target profile and explore the potential clinical benefits of new drug candidates as early as possible so as to reject drug candidates which fail to meet the desired goals.

The main objectives of the initial investigations of a new drug candidate in man are to:
- Determine the safety and tolerance in man;
- Determine the pharmacokinetics and bioavailability for a range of doses;
- Determine the pharmacological profile.

Well designed and well conducted early studies in man are important because results from these enable studies later in development to be better designed in terms of dose range and frequency, and better monitoring of side effects and toxicity. Initial clinical trials should be designed so as to ensure that the maximum information can accrue from studies in minimal numbers of subjects, thus reducing the spread of risk.

To begin with, single, increasing doses of the drug candidate are administered to a small number of subjects, who are monitored intensively. In this way an indication of the maximum tolerated dose is obtained. The subjects are usually young, healthy male volunteers. One advantage of using healthy volunteers is that it is much easier to define the cause of any adverse reactions. Adverse reactions include both 'toxic effects' (unwanted actions of the substance on organs or tissues of the body sufficient to impair their function or to cause cell death) and 'side effects' (unexpected and unwanted effects caused by known or expected pharmacological actions of the substance at or around the therapeutic dose). Female volunteers of childbearing potential are not used in clinical trials until the results of adequate reproductive toxicology tests are available in animals. Usually these tests are not available prior to Phase I and volunteers studies are invariably conducted in males. Clinical trials can be conducted in males without any reproductive data in animals, in countries including USA and UK. In contrast, in Japan, male fertility studies in animals are required prior to volunteer Phase I studies. Although the majority of initial clinical studies are conducted in normal healthy (male) subjects, there are instances where this is inappropriate, for example, products indicated for cancer chemotherapy or AIDS. In these cases initial clinical studies may be undertaken in patients.

During a phase I trial, in addition to safety data, pharmacokinetic data can be obtained by sampling body fluids from single-dose and subsequent repeat-dose studies. Half-life, area under the curve, clearance, and accumulation can be determined. Studies using radio abelled material are often performed to establish the metabolite profile and routes of excretion in man, and to compare with the data obtained in toxicology species. Therapeutic effects can seldom be measured in Phase I, although pharmacological action may be detectable. Such data, if available, can provide valuable indications of clinical usefulness and of therapeutic dose ranges and can help in the planning and design of later clinical trials. In some instances pharmacological activity of potential benefit in disease can be demonstrated in non-patient volunteers by the treatment of induced effects.

The route of administration in man should be the same as that used in the toxicology studies. The formulation used should ideally be the simplest presentation consistent with the objectives of the study. The starting dose in man can be derived in different way; from the animal data: for example, 1% of the dose (unit weight) which has produced any effect on animals, 10%~20% of the maximum tolerated dose in animals, or alternatively scrutiny of effective and safe doses in man of closely related compounds.

When satisfactory single-dose human data are available, repeated-dose Phase I studies may be conducted. The number of doses given to volunteers should be the minimum that will yield the required information and will be constrained by the duration of the completed two species animal toxicology studies. In multiple dose studies the interval between doses is usually approximately one half-life -'rounded-up' to a convenient dosing regimen, for example, once daily or 8 hourly.

Placebo administration acts as a control in phase1 studies and a randomized, controlled study provides a strong design in that it removes bias in allocation of subjects to a control or drug group, provides comparable groups, and allows valid statistical tests.

The cut-off points between the Phase I, II, and III clinical trials are somewhat subjective and arbitrary. Phase II studies are designed to evaluate safety and efficacy in patients for whom the drug is intended. They provide confirmation on the effective dose and the therapeutic ratio. Dosing usually begins with a single dose lower than the expected therapeutic dose, taking into account any differences in the absorption, distribution, and metabolism, which might arise from abnormalities resulting from disease process.

The initial studies are usually small and patients are monitored intensively for therapeutic and adverse effects. Often, the initial studies are conducted on hospital patients, inpatients rather than outpatients. Later phase II studies entail a more rigorous demonstration of a drug's efficacy. These studies are often controlled against placebo or a competitor compound (the latter to establish the comparative advantages and disadvantages of the new medicinal product). In the first instance, subjects with incompetence of any target organs which are expected to be affected by the pharmacological action of the drug candidate, or of any other important organs (especially the liver and kidney), must be excluded unless this type of abnormality is an integral part of their disease process.

In the UK, clearance for studies in patients is required from the Medicine's Control Agency (Committee for Safety of Medicines -CSM) of the Department of health. A pharmaceutical company will require a Clinical Trial Exemption (CTX) or Certificate (CTC) for which information is required on the chemistry, pharmacy, and preclinical safety of the compound. Permission or refusal of a CTX comes through in 35 days after application, unless an extension is requested by the MCA.

Multiple-dose studies will involve a decision on the dosing frequency or interval between individual doses. The half-life of the compound in the blood and/or the duration of the pharmacological effect will determine the dosing frequency.

There may be some constraint here imposed by the target product profile such that dosing which is more frequent than once a day is not competitive. A decision may have to be made about the viability of the drug candidate if pharmacokinetic / pharmacodynamic data point to a need for bid (twice daily) or tid (three times daily) dosing.

Phase III studies are large studies, in terms of patient numbers. Their aim is to establish the efficacy and safety of a treatment in order to substantiate the best method of treatment for patients. The duration of treatment should be long enough to induce a satisfactory response of the target disease and be related to the probable use by patients. The trials often include direct comparison with other available treatments. Thus the data address not only how efficacious and safe is the drug candidate but what is its relative efficacy and safety *versus* other medicines. Such comparative data are not only useful in marketing the drug but also increasingly in assessing the costbenefit/pharmacoeconomics of the drug candidate *versus* other treatments. Whether placebo or another drug is used as a comparator will also depend on the disease being treated and the ethics of the trial. In the UK and Europe it is generally considered unethical to use a placebo in a chronic study if an effective therapy is available. The FDA, however, still require at least one well-designed placebo-controlled study to gain registration approval. Placebos should 'match' the active drug in all physical respects such that the patient and clinical investigator cannot tell them apart.

Numbers of patients in the Phase III studies are based on the need to demonstrate differences in efficacy and/or safety in the drug candidate group *versus* the active comparator or placebo group. For active comparator trials it is necessary to have a good understanding of the expected safety and efficacy in order to predict the differences expected with the drug candidate and thus the required sample size. Transnational companies will usually carry out Phase III trials on a multi-national basis. Additional clinical studies are conducted in parallel to the Phase II and III studies. These may include interaction studies with drugs which are likely to be prescribed concurrently, food interactions studies and special populations, for example elderly or renally or hepatically impaired patients. The results from these studies will be reflected in the labeling (prescribing information) for the drug as, for example, contraindications warnings, adverse reactions.

The task in Phase I to III is to try and establish the degree of efficacy and the degree of side effects of a new drug candidate. The purpose of conducting all the preclinical and clinical studies is to enable the placement of new drugs on the market. In each major country there is a Government department (Regulatory Authority) which reviews the data, to determine whether the product should be granted a license. Although guidelines on the information necessary for approval differ throughout the world, three basic criteria must be met; products must be of proven quality, safety, and efficacy. Each regulatory dossier or marketing approval application (MAA) contains volumes of data. Providing the data in a user friendly manner is very important. To date most MAAs have been provided as hard copy but increasingly some companies are implementing electronic submissions. The regulatory dossier is the culmination of many years work; the quality of the data together with the therapeutic need for the targeted disease will to a significant extent determine the approval times for marketing of the drug.

A point worth highlighting is that pharmacoeconomics data are increasingly needed at the time of product registration and when negotiating product pricing and reimbursement. Data that measure the value of the benefit of a new drug in terms of better health and the value of cost saving, for example, in terms of need for surgical interventions or residential care, need to be collected In the future, the concern about value for money is unlikely to subside. Cost-containment for healthcare expenditure is a worldwide issue. Pharmaceutical companies now need to provide evidence to decision-makers, regulators, healthcare providers, formulary holders, insurers, doctors, pharmacists, and patients, of the value of new products.

At time of marketing usage of the drug may still be limited to 1000~2000 patients and attention is now being drawn to the limitations of this in terms of rarer side effects. Also, once the drug has been marketed it is available for widespread use and such use is not always in accordance with the manufacturer's recommendations. These aspects often produce reports, sometimes anecdotal, of new effects either advantageous or, more often, disadvantageous.

The aim of post-marketing stage of drug evaluation, in addition to continuing clinical trials, is to conduct long-term surveillance of the efficacy and safety of the drug in general use. Post-marketing clinical trials usually involve collection of a smaller amount of clinical data per patient than for Phase II or III studies. However, the trials must be of adequate scientific standard and sufficiently well documented to be compiled into a report which could be expected to be publishable in a medical journal. All adverse reactions notified to pharmaceutical companies should be kept in an appointed register. Documentation of unusual effects should be extensive enough so that any retrospective analysis of the files would allow consideration of any possible causes or contributory factors.

In summary, drug development requires effective integration and execution of many activities from diverse groups, under demanding cost, schedule, and performance requirements. It is important to set product goals at the start of development and to explore these 'advantages' as early as possible so as to reject drug candidates which fail. The plan for development of a new drug candidate provides an important road-map for organizing multi-disciplinary activities towards desired results. It should also indicate a series of checkpoints at which data will be reviewed to assess if the product goals are likely to be met. This will be pivotal to ensuring that any new drug candidate justifies the investment in its development and offers benefits in the healthcare of its target patients.

Selected from F. D. King, *Medicinal Chemistry Principles and Practice*, the Royal Society of Chemistry, Thomas Graham House, G. B., 1994.

Words and Expressions

extrapolation [ˌekstrəpəuˈleiʃən] *n.* 外推法，推断

spectroscopy [spek'trɔskəpi] n. 光谱学，波谱学，分光镜使用
ethics ['eθiks] n. 道德规范
sponsor ['spɔnsə] n. 发起人，主办者，保证人，主办人
accrue [ə'kru:] n. 自然增加，产生
regimen ['redʒimən] n. 食物疗法，养生法
impair [im'pɛə] n. 损害，使弱
scrutiny ['skru:tini] n. 详细审查
placebo [plə'si:bəu] n. 安慰剂
entail [in'teil] vt. 使必需，使蒙受，使承担，遗传给
viability [ˌvaiə'biliti] vt. 生存力
substantiate [səb'stænʃieit] vt. 证实
efficacious [ˌeifi'keiʃən] a. 有效的，灵验的
versus ['və:səs] prep. 与……相对
renal ['ri:nl] a. 肾的，肾脏的
hepatical ['hepətikə] a. 肝的
contraindication [ˌkɔntrə'indikeiʃən] n. 禁忌症
dossier ['dɔsiei, dəu'siei] n. 卷宗，档案
culmination [ˌkʌlmi'neiʃən] n. 巅峰，最高点，累积
intervention [ˌintə'venʃən] n. 干涉
subside [səb'said] vi. 下沉，沉淀，平息，减退，衰减
pivotal ['pivətl] a. 枢轴的，关键的

PART 2　BIOCHEMICAL PHARMACEUTICALS

Unit 6　Isolation of Caffeine from Tea

In this experiment, Caffeine will be isolated from tea leaves. The major problem of the isolation is that caffeine does not occur alone in tea leaves, but is accompanied by other natural substances from which it must be separated. The major component of tea leaves is cellulose[①], which is the major structural material of all plant cells. Cellulose is a polymer of glucose. Since cellulose is virtually insoluble in water, it presents no problems in the isolation procedure. Caffeine, on the other hand, is water soluble and is one of the major substances extracted into the solution called "tea." Caffeine comprises as much as 5 percent by weight of the leaf material in tea plants. Tannins also dissolve in the hot water used to extract tea leaves. The term tannin does not refer to a single homogeneous compound, or even to substances which have similar chemical structure. It refers to a class of compounds which have certain properties in common. Tannins are phenolic compounds having molecular weights between 500 and 3000. They are widely used to "tan" leather. They precipitate alkaloids[②] and proteins from aqueous solutions. Tannins are usually divided into two classes: those which can be hydrolyzed and those which cannot. Tannins of the first type which are found in tea generally yield glucose and gallic acid when they are hydrolyzed. These tannins are esters of gallic acid and glucose. They represent structures in which some of the hydroxyl groups in glucose have been esterified by digalloyl groups. The non-hydrolyzable tannins found in tea are condensation polymers of catechin. These polymers are not uniform in structure, but catechin molecules are usually linked together at ring positions 4 and 8.

　　When tannins are extracted into hot water, the hydrolyzable ones are partially hydrolyzed, meaning that free gallic acid is also found in tea. The tannins, by virtue of their phenolic groups, and gallic acid by virtue of its carboxyl groups, are both acidic. If calcium carbonate, a base, is added to tea water, the calcium salts of these acids are formed. Caffeine can be extracted from the basic tea solution with chloroform, but the calcium salts of gallic acid and the tannins are not chloroform soluble and remain behind in the aqueous solution.

　　The brown color of a tea solution is due to flavonoid pigments and chlorophylls, as well as their respective oxidation products. Although chlorophylls are somewhat chloroform soluble, most of the other substances in tea are not. Thus, the chloroform extraction of the basic tea solution removes nearly pure caffeine. The chloroform is easily removed by distillation (bp 61℃) to leave the crude caffeine. The caffeine may be purified by recrystallization or by sublimation.

Caffeine

Glucose if R=H
A Tannin if some R=Digalloyl

A Digalloyl Group

Catechin

Gallic Acid

In a second part of this experiment, Caffeine will be converted to a derivative. A derivative of a compound is a second compound, of known melting point, formed from the original compound by a simple chemical reaction. In trying to make a positive identification of an organic compound, it is often customary to convert it into a derivative. If the first compound, Caffeine in this case, and its derivative both have melting points which match those reported in the chemical literature (e.g., a handbook), it is assumed that there is no coincidence and that the identity of the first compound, Caffeine, has been definitely established.

Caffeine is a base and will react with an acid to give a salt. Using salicylic acid, a derivative salt of Caffeine, Caffeine salicylate, will be made in order to establish the identity of the Caffeine isolated from tea leaves.

Special Instructions Be careful when handling chloroform. It is a toxic solvent, and you should not breathe it excessively or spill it on yourself. When discarding spent tea leaves, do not put them in the sink because they will clog the drain. Dispose of them in a waste container.

Procedure Place 25g of dry tea leaves, 25g of calcium carbonate powder, and 250ml of water in a 500ml three neck round bottom flask equipped with a condenser for reflux. Stopper the unused openings in the flask and heat the mixture under reflux for about 20 minutes. Use a Bunsen burner to heat. While the solution is still hot, filter it by gravity through a fluted filter using a fast filter paper such as E & D No. 617 or S & S No. 595. You may need to change the filter paper if it clogs.

Cool the filtrate (filtered liquid) to room temperature and, using a separatory funnel, extract it twice with 25ml portions of chloroform. Combine the two portions of chloroform in a 100ml round bottom flask, Assemble an apparatus for simple distillation and remove the chloroform by distillation. Use a steam bath to heat. The residue in the distillation flask contains the caffeine and is purified as described below (crystallization). Save the chloroform that was distilled. You will use some of it in the next step. The remainder should be placed in a collection container.

Crystallization (**Purification**) Dissolve the residue obtained from the chloroform extraction of the tea solution in about 10ml of the chloroform that you saved from the distillation. It may be necessary to heat the mixture on a steam bath. Transfer the solution to a 50ml beaker. Rinse the flask with an additional 5ml of chloroform and combine this in the beaker. Evaporate the now light-green solution to dryness by heating it on a steam bath in the hood.

The residue obtained on evaporation of the chloroform is next crystallized by the mixed solvent method. Dissolve it in a small quantity (about 2 to 4ml) of hot benzene and add just enough highboiling (60℃ to 90℃) petroleum ether (or ligroin) to turn the solution faintly cloudy. Alternatively, acetone may be used for simple crystallization without a second solvent. Cool the solution and collect the crystalline product by vacuum filtration using a Hirsch funnel. Crystallize the product the same way a second time if necessary, and allow the product to dry by allowing it to stand in the suction funnel for a while. Weigh the product. Calculate the weighty percentage yield based on tea and determine the melting point. If desired, the product may be further purified by sublimation as described in the next experiment.

The Derivative Dissolve 0.20g of Caffeine and 0.15g of salicylic acid in 15ml of benzene in a small beaker by warming the mixture on a steam bath. Add about 5ml of high boiling (60℃ to 90℃) petroleum ether and allow the mixture to cool and crystallize. It may be necessary to cool the beaker in an ice water bath or to add a small amount of extra petroleum ether to induce crystallization. Collect the crystalline product by vacuum filtration using a Hirsch funnel. Dry the product by allowing it to stand in the air, and determine its melting point. Check the value against that in the literature. Submit the sample to the instructor in a labeled vial.

Selected from Pavia Donald L. *Introduction to Organic Laboratory Techniques: a Contemporary Approach*. W. B. Saunders Company, 1976.

Words and Expressions

isolation [aisə'leiʃən] *n.* 分离
caffeine ['kæfi:n] *n.* 咖啡因，咖啡碱
glucose ['glu:kous] *n.* 葡萄糖
extract [iks'trækt] *vt.* 榨出，萃取，提取，蒸馏（出）
　　　　['ekstrækt] *n.* 萃取物，提取物
tannin ['tænin] *n.* 丹宁，丹宁酸，鞣酸
homogeneous [ˌhɔmə'dʒi:njəs] *a.* 均一的，均相的，均匀的，同质的
phenolic [fi'nɔlik] *a.* 酚的
precipitate [pri'sipiteit] *vt.* 使沉淀；*vi.* 沉淀
　　　　　[pri'sipitit] *n.* 沉淀物
hydrolyze ['haidrɔlaiz] *vi.* 水解
gallic acid　五倍子酸

hydroxyl group 羟基
esterify [es'terifai] v. （使）酯化
digalloyl group 鞣酰基
non-hydrolyzable a. 不可水解的
catechin ['kætitʃin] n. 儿茶酸
hydrolyzable ['haidrəlaizəbl] a. 可水解的
carboxyl group 羧基
acidic [ə'sidik] a. 酸的，酸性的
calcium carbonate 碳酸钙
base [beis] n. 碱
chloroform ['klɔːrəfɔrm] n. 氯仿
flavonoid pigment 黄酮类颜料
chlorophyll ['klɔːrəfil] n. 叶绿素
distillation [disti'leiʃən] n. 蒸馏
recrystallization ['riːˌkristəlai'zeiʃən] n. 重结晶
sublimation [ˌsʌbli'meiʃən] n. 升华
derivative [di'rivətiv] n. 衍生物；a. 衍生的
salicylic acid 水杨酸
salicylate [sæ'lisileit] n. 水杨酸盐，水杨酸酯
three neck round bottom flask 三口烧瓶
condenser [kən'densə] n. 冷凝器
reflux ['riːflʌks] n. 回流
stopper ['stɔpə] v. 塞住 n. 塞子
Bunsen burner 本生灯
filtrate ['filtrit] n. 滤（出）液
        ['filtreit] v. 过滤
filter paper 滤纸
separatory funnel 分液漏斗
steam bath 蒸气浴
distillation flask 蒸馏瓶
beaker ['biːkə] n. 烧杯
rinse [rins] v. 冲洗，漂洗；n. 漂清，冲洗
petroleum ether 石油醚
ligroin ['ligrouin] n. 轻石油，石油英，粗汽油
acetone ['æsitoun] n. 丙酮
Hirsch funnel 赫尔什漏斗
suction funnel 吸入漏斗
ice water bath 冰水浴
vial ['vaiəl] n. 小瓶，小玻璃瓶；vt. 放……于小瓶中

Notes

① cellulose 纤维素。D-葡萄糖以 β-1,4-糖苷键连接而成的链状高分子。具有 $(C_6H_{10}O_5)_n$ 的

组成。是维管束植物、地衣植物以及一部分藻类细胞壁的主要成分。

② alkaloid 生物碱。亦称植物碱。系含氮的碱性有机化合物，常以较小的量而对人或动物呈现显著的药理作用。多数具有吡啶、喹啉、异喹啉、吡咯烷、六氢吡啶、吲哚、托品烷、嘌呤等的环状结构。大部分为无色结晶性固体，在植物液泡内可与酸形成盐。

Exercises

1. Answer the following questions:
   (1) Can you list several plants that contain caffeine?
   (2) What kind of method can be used to isolate caffeine from tea?
   (3) How does man use caffeine in the daily life?

2. Competing the following paragraph. Choose **Not More Than Three Words** from the passage for each answer.

   The active ingredient that makes tea and coffee valuable to man is [1]_____. Caffeine is an [2]_____, a class of naturally occurring compounds containing nitrogen and having the properties of an organic amine base. Tea and coffee are not the only plant sources of caffeine. Others include: kola nuts, mate leaves, guarana seeds, and in smaall amount, cocoa beans.

   Place 35g of ground coffee, a boiling stone, and 125ml of water into a 500ml [3]_____ round bottom flask equipped with a [4]_____ for reflux. [5]_____ the unused openings in the flask and heat the mixture under [6]_____ for about 20 minutes. Use a [7]_____ to heat. During the heating period, assemble a vacuum filtration apparatus. When boiling action has stopped and the coffee grounds have settled somewhat, but while the solution is still hot, filter the solution through a [8]_____ by vacuum filtration.

3. Put the following into Chinese:

cellulose	glucose	chloroform	beaker
crystallization	purification	apparatus	filter paper
hydroxyl group	carboxyl group	benzene	acetone
evaporation	insoluble	condensation	residue

4. Put the following into English:

蒸馏	重结晶	升华	过滤
酸	碱	盐	水杨酸
水杨酸钙	水杨酸甲酯	冷凝器	塞子
分液漏斗	水解	可水解的	三口烧瓶

Reading Material 6

Medicinal of Plant Origin: Historical Aspects

The use of plants or plant extracts for medicinal purposes has been going on for thousands of years, and herbalism and folk medicine, both ancient and modern, have been the source of much useful therapy. Some of the plant products currently used, either in their natural form or as derivatives, were often used originally for other purposes, such as arrow poisons, as part of religious or other rituals, or even as cosmetics. Many drugs originally used as folk remedies, on the other hand, have been abandoned. The intent, in this brief review, is to present some of the more important drugs, of both the past and present, derived from herbs and nonwoody plants.

Perhaps the earliest recorded use of a plant medicinal is that of the herb called "Ma Huang," a species of *Ephedra* used medicinally in China for over 5000 years. The important constituent of this plant is ephedrine, which has been used successfully in the treatment of bronchial asthma, hay fever[1], and other allergic conditions. Probably the major use of ephedrine and other ephedra alkaloids today is as antitussives and oral decongestants for the common cold.

Ephedra occupies a peculiar position in the vegetable kingdom, since it belongs to a very small class of Gymnospermae, the Gnetales. In the gymnosperms, the seeds are situated on an open scale, common to the conifers, instead of in a seed vessel, as in the true flowering plants, or angiosperms. The Gnetales number about 40 living species, 35 belonging to *Ephedra*. They occur in temperate and subtropical regions of Asia, America, and the Mediterranean; most of the American species, however, are devoid of the alkaloidal drugs. They have marked resemblances to the angiosperms and are considered by some to be relatives of those transitional plant types that existed during the Cretaceous[2] before the advent of the true flowers.

Related alkaloids (nitrogen-containing basic organic molecules) having structures similar to that of ephedrine and of medicinal importance today are found in a number of plants. For example, β-phenethylamine, a pressor amine (which increases blood pressure), occurs in mistletoe . Hordenine, a derivative of β-phenylethylamine, occurs in barley and in the cactus , and Dopamine, another relative of β-phenethylamine, is found in the banana. The latter compound, under slightly alkaline conditions, undergoes atmospheric oxidation with ease, giving rise to a black pigment.

An alkaloidal drug having a much more complicated chemical structure, but part of which is a β-phenylethylamine moiety, is Morphine, a major constituent of opium. Morphine was first isolated from opium by Serturner in 1805 and was the first plant alkaloid to be isolated in relatively pure form. Opium consists of the dried latex from the unripe fruit of *Papaver somniferum*, a species of poppy. Opium has been produced commercially in Asia Minor, Turkey, Bulgaria, Yugoslavia, Iran, India, and China for extraction of morphine; the clandestine production, which is considerable, is probably more widespread.

Morphine is used mainly for the relief of pain, but it has hypnotic (sleep-producing) and cough-suppressing properties as well. Codeine and Noscapine are used extensively today as antitussives in anticold preparations. The early Egyptians were aware of the sleep-producing properties of Opium. In regard to its use as a narcotic, the habit of opium eating was established in Eastern Europe in the seventeenth century. Despite this ultimately harmful tendency, Morphine is still one of the most important drugs of today. Thomas Sydenham, the noted seventeenth century physician and founder of the clinical method, remarked that "without Opium I would not care to practice medicine." Actually, 25 alkaloids have been isolated from Opium, but with the exception of morphine and Codeine (Morphine methyl ether), the other alkaloids are of limited medicinal importance.

A number of species of the family Solanaceae contain some therapeutically useful alkaloids, including belladonna, henbane, thornapple, and mandrake. All of these plants contain alkaloids composed of a common base, tropine, combined with various organic acids. Cocaine, found in the leaves of the coca plant, is also a tropine derivative, containing two organic acids. The solanaceous alkaloids produce hallucinations and were the sorcerer's drugs of the Middle Ages.

The working model on which the organic structures of today's local anesthetics are based is cocaine, an alkaloid found in the leaves of the coca plant. The Indians of South America chew the dried leaves of the shrub after mixing them with slaked lime or plant ash, to allay the onset of hunger and fatigue. Although Cocaine of plant source is used to a limited extent today as a local anesthetic, its use by addicts is considerable. Cocaine addiction results in physical ill health and the wildest hallucinations. Cocaine addiction became one of the common forms of narcotic addiction during the trench warfare of World War I. Chewing the leaves, however, does not lead to addiction or ill effects. Cocaine addicts generally sniff a few milligrams of the ground leaf powder up one nostril.

Cocaine was not used in medicine until the latter half of the nineteenth century. In 1882, Koller and Freud, in Vienna, discovered the anesthetic effect of Cocaine on the eye, making eye surgery possible. Cocaine was also used for operations on the throat and larynx and for extraction of teeth. Cocaine and other local anesthetics are frequently injected with adrenaline, a β-phenylethylamine derivative, which contracts the blood vessels and localizes the anesthetic action and also reduces the toxic effects on the central nervous system. Cocaine is still considered superior to the synthetic local anesthetics for operations involving the nasal septum.

Selected from William O. Foye. *Principles of Medicinal Chemistry*. Henry Kenry Kimpton Publishers, London, 1981, 697~700

Word and expressions

herbalism [ˈhəːbəlizəm] *n.* 草药医术学
arrow poison   箭毒
ritual [ˈritjuəl] *n.* 仪式，典礼；*a.* 仪式的，典礼的
cosmetic [kɔzˈmetik] *n.* 化妆品；*a.* 化妆用的
herb [həːb] *n.* 草本植物，药草，香草
nonwoody plants   非木本植物

Ma Huang 麻黄
ephedra [iˈfedrə] n. 麻黄
constituent [kənˈstitjuənt] n. 成分，要素；a. 组成的
ephedrine [eˈfedrin] n. 麻黄碱，麻黄素
bronchial asthma 支气管哮喘
allergic [əˈləːdʒik] a. 过敏的，患过敏症的
antitussive [ˌæntiˈtʌsiv] n. 止咳药，镇咳药；a. 能止咳的，能防咳的
decongestant [diːkənˈdʒetənt] n. 减轻充血药
Gymnospermae 裸子植物纲
Gnetales 买麻藤目
gymnosperm [ˈdʒimnəspəːm] n. 裸子植物
conifer [ˈkounifə] n. 松类植物，针叶树（如松、枞等）
seed vessel 果皮
angiosperm [ˈændʒiəspəːm] n. 被子植物
β-phenethylamine β-苯乙基胺
amine [ˈæmiːn] n. 胺
mistletoe [ˈmisltou] n. 槲寄生（西俗用作基督教圣诞节的装饰物）
hordenine 大麦芽碱，对二甲氨乙基苯酚
barley [ˈbɑːli] n. 大麦
cactus [ˈkæktəs] n. 仙人掌
dopamine [ˈdəupəˌmiːn] n. 多巴胺
alkaline [ˈælkəlain] a. 碱的，碱性的，含碱的
oxidation [ˌɔksiˈdeiʃən] n. 氧化
alkaloidal [ˌælkəˈlɔidl] a. 生物碱的
morphine [ˈmɔːfiːn] n. 吗啡
opium [ˈoupjəm] n. 鸦片
latex [ˈleiteks] n. 乳液，胶乳，橡胶浆
Papaver somniferum 罂粟
poppy [ˈpɔpi] n. 罂粟，深红色
extraction [iksˈtrækʃən] n. 提取（法），萃取（法），抽出物
clandestine [klænˈdestin] a. 秘密的
hypnotic [hipˈnɔtik] n. 催眠药；a. 催眠的，易被催眠的
cough-suppressing 镇咳的
codeine [ˈkoudiːn] n. 可待因
noscapine [ˈnɔskəpiːn] n. 那可丁
anticold [ˈæntikould] n. 抗感冒，抗伤风
narcotic [nɑːˈkɔtik] n. 麻醉药，致幻毒品，镇静剂；a. 麻醉的，麻醉剂的，催眠的
clinical [ˈklinikəl] a. 临床的，病房用的
morphine methyl ether 吗啡甲基醚
Solanaceae [ˌsəuləˈneisiiː] n. 茄科

therapeutically [ˌθerə'pju:tikəli] *ad.* 治疗（学）地，疗法地
belladonna [belə'dɔnə] *n.* 颠茄，莨菪，颠茄制剂
henbane ['henbein] *n.* 天仙子（茄科的药用植物）
thornapple ['θɔ:n'æpl] *n.* 曼陀罗
mandrake ['mændreik] *n.* 曼德拉草（根）
tropine ['trəupi:n] *n.* 莨菪碱，托品
solanaceous alkaloids 茄科生物碱
hallucination [həlu:si'neiʃən] *n.* 幻觉，幻想
sorcerer ['sɔ:sərə] *n.* 男巫士，魔术师
anesthetic =anaesthetic [ˌænis'θetik] *n.* 麻醉剂，麻药；*a.* 麻醉的
larynx ['læriŋks] *n.* 喉
adrenaline [ə'drenəlin] *n.* 肾上腺素
nasal septum 鼻隔膜
Cephaelis ipecacuanha Rich. 头九节波状吐根属
emetine ['eməti:n] *n.* 吐根碱，吐根素，依米丁
Ipecacuanha [ˌipikækju'ænə] *n.* 吐根，吐根的根茎和根，吐根制剂
expectorant [eks'pektərənt] *a.* 化痰的，祛痰的，助咳的；*n.* 除痰剂，祛痰剂，助咳药
bronchitis [brɔŋ'kaitis] *n.* 支气管炎
whooping cough 百日咳
emetic [i'metik] *n.* 催吐剂；*a.* 引起呕吐的

Notes

① hay fever 花粉热，枯草热。指主要由豚草属（*Ambrosa*）、一枝黄花（*Solidago*）等牧草的花粉引起的鼻旁窦炎、哮喘以及相伴出现的低热。因出现在家畜用牧草干制的季节，故名枯草热。现在多被称作花粉病（pollen disease）。

② cretaceous 白垩纪，白垩系。地质年代的名称。是中生代三纪中最新的一纪。在欧洲由于此年代的地层多由白垩构成的，故有此名。该纪大约相当于距今1.3亿年到6500万年前这一时期。白垩纪是处于整个地质年代中地球海洋最广阔的一个时期，但到该纪的末期，海洋从世界范围退缩，陆地开始上升。在植物界中，被子植物从白垩纪中期开始迅速地繁盛起来，植物区系向近代结构转变。

Unit 7 Developing Drugs from Traditional Medicinal Plants

Over three quarters of the world's population relies mainly on plants and plant extracts for health care. Approximately one third of the prescription drugs in the US contain plant components, and more than 120 important prescription drugs are derived from plants. Most of these drugs were developed because of their use in traditional medicine. Economically, this represents \$8000～10,000M of annual consumer spending. Recent World Health Organization (WHO) studies indicate that over 30 per cent of the world's plant species have at one time or another been used for medicinal purposes. Of the 250,000 higher plant species on Earth, more than 80,000 species are medicinal. Although traditional medicine is widespread throughout the world, it is an integral part of each individual culture. Its practice is based mainly on traditional beliefs handed down from generation to generation for hundreds or even thousands of years. Unfortunately, much of this ancient knowledge and many valuable plants are being lost at an alarming rate. The scientific study of traditional medicines and the systematic preservation of medicinal plants are thus of great importance.

For quite a long time, the only way to use plant medicines was either direct application or the use of crude plant extracts. With the development of organic chemistry at the beginning of this century, extraction and fractionation techniques improved significantly. It became possible to isolate and identify many of the active chemicals from plants. In the 1940s, advances in chemical synthesis enabled the synthesis of many plant components and their derivatives. In western countries, it was thought that chemical synthesis of drugs would be more effective and economical than isolation from natural sources. Indeed, this is true in many cases. However, in many other cases, synthetic analogues are not as effective as their natural counterparts. In addition, some synthetic drugs cost many times more than natural ones. Inspired by these realisations, coupled with the fact that many drugs with complex structures may be totally impossible to synthesise, there is now a resurgent trend of returning to natural resources for drug development.

Important prescription drugs from plants

Ephedrine is the oldest and most classic example of a prescription drug developed from a traditional medicinal plant. It is derived from Ma Huang, a leafless shrub. Used to relieve asthma and hay fever in China for over 5000 years, it was introduced into western medicine in 1924 by Chen and Schmidt. Ephedrine is an alkaloid closely related to adrenaline, the major product of the adrenal gland. Pharmacologically, Ephedrine is used extensively to stimulate increased activity of the sympathetic nervous system. It is used as a pressor agent to counteract hypotension associated with anaesthesia, and as a nasal decongestant. The drug action of this medicine is based both on its direct effect on α and β adrenergic receptors and on the release of endogenous noradrenaline.

Digitalis is one of the most frequently used medications in the treatment of heart failure and arrhythmia. It increases the contractility of the heart muscle and modifies vascular resistance. It also slows conduction through the atrioventricular node in the heart, making it useful in the treatment of atrial fibrillation and other rapid heart rhythms.

Digitalis is found in the leaves and seeds of Digitalis purpurea and Digitalis lanata, commonly known as the foxglove plant. Foxglove has been used in traditional medicine in many parts of the world——by African natives as arrow poisons, by the ancient Egyptians as heart medicine, and by the Romans as a diuretic, heart tonic, emetic and rat poison. The Chinese, who found this ingredient not only in plants but also in the dry skin and venom of the common toad, used it for centuries as a cardiac drug. In the western world, the foxglove was first mentioned in 1250 in the writing of a physician, Walsh, and it was described botanically in the 1500s.

Digitalis is a glycoside containing an aglycone, or genin, linked to between one and four sugar molecules. The pharmacological activity resides in the aglycone, whereas the sugar residues affect the solubility and potency of the drug. The aglycone is structurally related to bile acids, sterols, sex hormones and adrenocortical hormones.

d-Tubocurarine and its derivatives are the most frequently used drugs in operating rooms to provide muscle relaxation and prevent muscle spasm. These agents interrupt the transmission of the nerve impulse at the skeletal neuromuscular junction. Curare, the common name for South American arrow poisons, has a long and interesting history. It has been used for centuries by Indians along the Amazon and Orinoco rivers for hunting. It causes paralysis of the skeletal muscles of animals and finally results in death. The methods of curare preparation were a secret entrusted only to tribal doctors. Soon after their discovery of the American continent, European explorers became interested in curare. In the late 16th century, samples of native preparations were brought to Europe for investigation. Curare, an alkaloid, was found in various species of Strychnos and certain species of Chondrodendron. The first use of curare for muscle relaxation was reported in 1942 by Griffith and Johnson. This drug offers optimal muscular relaxation without the use of high doses of anaesthetics. It thus emerged as the chief drug for use in tracheal intubation and during surgery.

Vinblastine and Vincristine are two of the most potent antitumour drugs. They are obtained from Catharanthus roseus, commonly known as the rosy periwinkle. This plant, indigenous to Madagascar, is also cultivated in India, Israel and the US. It was originally examined for clinical use because of its traditional use in treating diabetes. The leaves and roots of this plant contain more than 100 alkaloids. Fractionation of these extracts yields four active alkaloids: Vinblastine, Vincristine, Vinleurosine and Vinresidine. These alkaloids are asymmetric dimeric compounds referred to as vinca alkaloids, but of these, only Vinblastine and Vincristine are clinically important antitumour agents. These two alkaloids are cell-cycle[①] specific agents that block mitosis[②] (cell division). Vincristine sulphate is used to treat acute leukaemia in children and lymphocytic leukaemia. It is also effective against Wilm's tumour, neuroblastoma, rhabdomyosarcoma (tumour of voluntary or striped muscle cells), reticulum cell③ sarcoma and Hodgkin's disease④. Vinblastine sulphate is used in the treatment of Hodgkin's disease, lymphosarcoma, choriocarcinoma, neuroblastoma, carcinoma of breast, lung and other organs, and in acute and chronic leukaemia.

Emerging plant medicines

Artemisinin is the most recent anti-malaria drug developed from plant-based traditional medicine. It is isolated from the leaves and flowers of Artemisia annua L. (Compositae), commonly known as the sweet wormwood, a cousin of tarragon. Indigenous to China, the extract of this plant is traditionally known as the Qinghao⑤. It has been used to treat malaria in China for over 2000 years. Its active component, Artemisinin, was first isolated in the 1970s by Chinese scientists. Unlike Quinine and Chloroquine, this compound is non-toxic rapid in effect, and safe for pregnant women. Furthermore, it is effective against chloroquine-resistant Plasmodium falciparum malaria and in patients with cerebral malaria. It kills the parasites directly so parasitemia is quickly controlled. This work was confirmed by the WHO in Africa and other parts of Southeast Asia.

Artemisinin is an endoperoxide of the sesquiterpene lactone. The structure of this compound is too complex to be synthesised effectively. Artemisia is also found in many parts of the US, abundantly along the Potomac River in Washington DC, but the drug content of these varieties is only about half that of the Chinese variety. Currently, the WHO and the US are jointly engaged in the cultivation of Chinese Artemisia for worldwide use. This recent development offers renewed hope for using traditional medicine to provide new drugs for future medicines.

Selected from Paul L Huang, Philip L Huang, Peter Huang et al., *Chem. Ind.* (*London*), 1992, 290~293

Word and expressions

prescription [pri'skripʃən] *n.* 处方，药方，规定
World Health Organization 世界卫生组织（缩写为 WHO）
adrenergic [ˌædrə'nəːdʒik] *a.* 肾上腺素的，类似肾上腺素的，释放肾上腺素的
Artemisinin 青蒿素
antimalaria [ˌæntimə'lɛəriə] *n.* 抗疟疾，防疟疾
fractionation [ˌfrækʃə'neiʃən] *n.* 分馏
counterpart ['kauntəpɑːt] *n.* 配对物，副本，极相似的人或物
resurgent [ri'səːdʒənt] *a.* 复活的，苏醒的，恢复活力的
asthma ['æsmə] *n.* 哮喘
adrenal [ə'driːnəl] *n.* 肾上腺 *a.* 肾上腺的
gland [glænd] *n.* 腺
pharmacologically [ˌfɑːməkə'lɔdʒikəli] *ad.* 药理地，药学地，药用地
pressor ['presə] *n.* 升高血压的物质 *a.* 有使血压增高的，收缩血管的

hypotension [ˌhaipou'tenʃən] n. 低血压
anaesthesia [ˌænis'θi:zjə] n. 麻醉（法），感觉缺乏，麻木
nasal ['neizəl] a. 鼻的，护鼻的，鼻音的 n. 鼻音，鼻音字
endogenous [en'dɔdʒinəs] a. 内生的，内长的
noradrenaline [ˌnɔ:rə'drenəlin] n. = norepinephrine 去甲肾上腺素
digitalis [didʒi'teilis] n. 洋地黄
arrhythmia [ə'riðmiə] n. 心律不齐
contractility [kənˌtræktə'biliti] n. 收缩性，缩小性，伸缩力
vascular ['væskjulə] a. 脉管的，血管的，有脉管的
atrioventricular a. 房室的，心房与心室的
node [nəud] n. 结
atrial ['ɑ:triəl] a. 心房的，有关心房的
fibrillation [ˌfaibri'leiʃən] n. 纤维性颤动
Digitalis purpurea 紫花毛地黄
Digitalis lanata 毛花洋地黄
foxglove ['fɔksglʌv] n. 毛地黄
diuretic [daijuə'retik] n. 利尿剂；a. 利尿的
a heart tonic 强心药
venom ['venəm] n. 毒液
toad [təud] n. 蟾蜍，癞蛤蟆
cardiac ['kɑ:diæk] n. 强心剂，强胃剂；a. 心脏的，（胃的）贲门的
botanically [bə'tænikəli] ad. 植物（学）地
glycoside ['glaikəˌsaid] n. 苷，配糖类，配糖物
aglycone [ə'glaikəun] n. 配质，配基，（苷的）非糖部
genin ['dʒenin] n. 配质，配基
solubility [ˌsɔlju'biliti] n. 溶（解）度，溶（解）性，（可）溶性
potency ['poutənsi] n. 效力，效验，能力，潜力，力量
bile acid 胆汁酸
sterol ['sterɔl] n. 甾醇，固醇
sex hormone 性激素
adrenocortical hormone [ədri:nəu'kɔtikəl] n. 肾上腺皮质激素
digoxigenin [didʒɔksi'dʒenin] n. 异羟基洋地黄毒苷，地谷新配质
digitoxigenin [didʒtɔksi'dʒenin] n. 毛地黄毒苷配基，β-(丁烯酸内酯)-14-羟甾醇
d-tubocurarine [tju:bəukju'rɑ:rin] n. d-管箭毒碱
relaxation [ri:læk'seiʃən] n. 松弛，缓和，减轻，放宽
spasm ['spæzəm] n. 痉挛，一阵发作
skeletal ['skelitl] a. 骨骼的，骸骨的
neuromuscular [ˌnjuərou'mʌskjulə] a. 神经肌肉的
curare [kju'rɑ:ri] n. 箭毒，马钱子属植物，马钱子（也叫番木鳖）
paralysis [pə'rælisis] n. 瘫痪，麻痹

entrusted [in'trʌst] vt. 委托，托管，信托
Strychnos ['striknɔs] n. [S-] 马钱子属，毒鼠碱
Chondrodendron [ˌkɔndrə'dendrɔn] n. 南美防己属
tracheal [trə'kiːəl] a. 气管的，导管的，呼吸管的
intubation [ˌintju'beiʃən] n. 插管，插管法
Vinblastine [vin'blɑstiːn] n. 长春碱
Vincristine ['vinkristiːn] n. 长春新碱
antitumour [ˌænti'tjuːmə] n. 抗癌的，抗肿瘤的
Catharanthus roseus 长春花
periwinkle ['periwiŋkəl] n. 长春花属的植物，玉黍螺
indigenous [in'didʒinəs] a. 本土的
Madagascar [ˌmædə'gæskə] n. 马达加斯加岛（非洲岛国）
diabetes [daiə'biːtiːz] n. 糖尿病，多尿症
Vinleurosine n. 环氧长春碱
Vinresidine n.（=leurosidine） 异长春碱，洛诺西丁
asymmetric [æsi'metrik] a. 不对称的，不均匀的
dimeric [dai'merik] a. 二聚的，形成二聚物的
vinca ['viŋkə] n. 长春花
Vincristine sulphate 硫酸长春新碱
acute [ə'kjuːt] a. 急性的，敏锐的
chronic ['krɔnik] a. 慢性的，延续很长的
leukaemia [ljuː'kiːmiə] n. 白血病
lymphocytic ['limfə'sitik] a. 淋巴球的，淋巴细胞的
neuroblastoma [ˌnjuərəblæs'təumə] n. 成神经细胞瘤
rhabdomyosarcoma n. 横纹肌肉瘤
striped [straipt] a. 有斑纹的
sarcoma [sɑː'kəumə] n. 肉瘤，恶性毒瘤
lymphosarcoma [ˌlimfəusɑː'kəumə] n. 淋巴肉瘤
choriocarcinoma [ˌkəuriəuˌkɑːsi'nəumə] n. 绒膜癌
carcinoma [ˌkɑːsi'nəumə]（[复] carcinomas 或 carcinomata [ˌkɑːsi'nəumətə]）n. 癌
anti-malaria [aːnti mə'lɛəriə] n. 抗疟疾
Artemisia annua L. 黄花蒿属植物，青蒿属植物
Compositae n. 菊科
wormwood ['wəːmwəːd] n. 蒿属植物（尤指洋艾），苦艾
tarragon ['tærəgən] n. 龙蒿，龙蒿叶
malaria [mə'lɛəriə] n. 疟疾，瘴气
Quinine [kwi'niːn] n. 奎宁
Chloroquine [ˌklɔːrə'kwiːn] n. 氯喹
Plasmodium falciparum 恶性疟原虫，镰状疟原虫
cerebral ['seribrəl] a. 脑的，大脑的

parasite ['pærəsait] n. 寄生虫，食客
parasitemia [ˌpærəsaiˈtiːmiə] n. 寄生虫血症
endoperoxide [ˌendoupəˈrɔksaid] n. 桥过氧化物
sesquiterpene [ˌseskwiˈtəːpiːn] n. 倍半萜烯
lactone [ˈlæktoun] n. 内酯

Notes

① cell-cycle 细胞周期，亦称细胞分裂周期。是指各细胞的生活周期。增殖中的体细胞，其细胞周期分为分裂期（M期）和间期。分裂期又进一步分为前期、中前期、后期和末期五个时期，间期中间夹着一个进行 DNA 合成的时期（S期），所以它可以分为 G_1 期、S 期、G_2 期三个时期。一个细胞周期及其各期所需要的时间可用活体细胞的直接观察、分裂指数和放射自显术等方法求出。

② mitosis 有丝分裂，指真核生物细胞核的一般的分裂方式。而在病态细胞和退化中的细胞所进行的特殊分裂称为无丝分裂。有丝分裂有两种，一种为在体细胞繁殖中见到的体细胞有丝分裂；另一种是在生物生活史的特定时期所进行的减数有丝分裂（通常称为减数分裂）。

③ reticulum cell 网状细胞。形成骨髓、脾脏、淋巴结、胸腺等造血组织或作为淋巴系组织的网状结缔组织（reticular connective tissue）的细胞。呈纺锤形或星形的细胞，突起部分互相牵连构成网眼状，内有血球和淋巴球。网状细胞具有吞噬能力，作为固定的巨噬细胞而存在着。

④ Hodgkin's disease 何杰金病，淋巴网状细胞瘤。1832年英国医生何杰金（T. Hodgkin 1796～1866年）所报道的疾病。亦称淋巴肉芽肿（lymphogranulomatosis）或何杰金肉瘤（Hodgkin's sarcoma）。根据恶性度和宿主的免疫状态，分类不断在变化。本病是一种以淋巴结系统的肿胀为特征的重症疾病，多见于 30～40 岁的男性。

⑤ qinghao 即 '青蒿' 的拼音。

Exercises

1. Answer the following questions:
   (1) Can you give a definition for drugs from traditional medicinal plants?
   (2) Do you have any idea about the difference between drugs from traditional medicinal plants and drugs from syntheses?
   (3) Can you list drugs that are derived from traditional medicinal plants?
   (4) Do you think that all diseases can be treated by plant medicines?

2. Competing the following paragraph. Choose **Not More Than Three Words** from the passage for each answer.

   An interesting compound developed from traditional Chinese medicine is the antimalarial compound artemisinin. Originally called Qing hao'su, it comes from [1] _____. This plant was recorded in old manuscripts as useful in treating fevers ang [2] _____. Tests to identify the [3] _____ compound present resulted in [4] _____ artemisinin. This acts against the malaria parasite in [5] _____ way from quinine and most of the synthetic quinoline antimalarials.

3. Put the following into Chinese:

biology	botanically	anaesthesia	cardiac
anti-malaria	diabetes	fractionation	asymmetric
antimalaria	antitumer	antiviral	decongestant
a heart tonic	sesquiterpene	sterol	lactone

4. Put the following into English:

处方	生物学	急性的	慢性的
对称的	不对称的	氨基酸	蛋白
多肽	基因	肾上腺素的	肾上腺的
苷	配基	免疫缺陷	心律不齐

Reading Material 7

Naturally Occurring Flavans Unsubstituted in the Heterocyclic Ring

Introduction The term flavan is applied, collectively, to a large group of naturally occurring compounds possessing a 3,4-Dihydro-2-phenyl-2H-1-benzopyran (2-phenylchroman) nucleus. Flavans substituted in the heterocyclic ring (3 and 4-positions, e.g. catechins) are frequently encountered in nature, but the unsubstituted flavans have rarely been found due, presumably, to their instability in solution leading to polymeric products. The Scientific literature on this latter class of compounds is scattered. There has been so far no comprehensive report on the phytochemistry and biological properties of this class of compounds. The present review records the distribution, spectral and biological properties of this class of flavan.

Extraction and Separation Extraction of naturally occurring flavans (free and glycosylated) is usually carried out on dried plant materials. The classical method of continuous extraction using increasingly polar solvents (light petrol, chloroform, methanol) has proved to be efficient. Strongly polar solvents (acetone, ethanol, methanol) are also directly employed for extraction of dried and milled plant materials followed by solvent-gradient fractionation of the polar extractives. Flavans of varying polarities are often separated by column chromatography on silica gel using solvents of graded polarity (hexane, benzene, ethyl acetate and different proportions of mixtures thereof) as eluants. Preparative TLC on silica gel (using EtOAc-MeOH-H_2O, 18:1:1; MeOH-$CHCl_3$-HOAc, 8:1:1) is employed in instances of molecules difficult to separate. In a number of cases the isolation is accomplished after derivatization, because of instability of the parent compounds, into permethyl[①] ethers or acetates followed by column chromatography. Strongly polar compounds are occasionally obtained after passing the methanol solutions over Sephadex LH20 using methanol as eluant. Strongly polar flavans are also separated by HPLC on ODS hypersil (5μm) column using elution with 35% methanol in 5% formic acid as well as on reversed phase columns using methanol-water (4:1, 7:3) as solvent.

The thin layer chromatoplates are viewed in UV light (λ=254nm), and after keeping the chromatoplates in I_2 vapour when reddish-purple colours are developed. This forms a basis for their detection even when admixed with a number of unrelated phenolic constituents. Spraying plates with dilute methanolic sulphuric acid (2%) produces reddish-brown colorations. Flavan glycosides having free phenolic groups respond to ferric reagent and Feigels test. A yellow coloration is developed when chromatograms are sprayed with diazotized p-nitroaniline. The purity of the isolated flavans can also be tested by analytical HPLC.

The hydrolysis of glycosides is carried out by warming methanol solutions with dil[2] hydrochloric acid according to procedures followed for flavonoids. Enzymatic hydrolysis (with emulsion) is also of interest in case of glucosides. Aglucones are separated by column chromatography or preparative TLC on silica gel (C_6H_6-EtOAc, 3:1; or C_6H_6-$CHCl_3$, 1:1). The glycone moieties are identified as their alditol acetates by GC.

Pharmacological Activity Auriculoside was the first flavan glycoside to be investigated pharmacologically. The initial results with auriculoside, as reported by Sahai et al, revealed only a minor CNS depressant activity. However, subsequent studies with related glucosyloxy flavans showed pronounced adaptogenic (anti-stress/anti-anxiety) activity. Thus, diffutin isolated from *Canscora diffusa*, was initially found to produce a mild CNS depressant action (potentiation of barbiturate hypnosis and morphine analgesia in laboratory animals, in doses of 20~5 mg/kg ip). While elucidating the mechanism of this CNS depressant action of diffutin, it was found to be associated with anti-stress and anti-anxiety activities (collectively termed 'adaptogenic activity') in the battery of tests designed for such activities in laboratory animals. Diffutin also exhibited a marked positive inotropic effect in perfused frog heart in doses of 10~30 mcg (no arrhythmogenic property). It further potentiated the contractile responses of guinea-pig vas deferens to catechol amines (by a process other than the uptake inhibition of adrenaline). Diffutin was found to be non-toxic up to 500mg/kg in dog. In summary, these results provide a reasonable explanation for the therapeutic use of *Canscora diffusa* in some mental disorders, e.g. melancholia, in the Indian system of medicine. The plant extract is used as a substitute of *C. decussata* Schult, the latter contains xanthone glucosides as its active principle.

Selected from Kulwant S Saini and Shibnath Ghosal. *Phytochemistry*, 1984, 23(11): 2415~2421

Words and Expressions

flavan ['fleivən] n. 黄烷
unsubstitute [ʌn'sʌbstitjuːt] v. 无取代
heterocyclic [ˌhetərə'saiklik] a. 杂环的
3,4-dihydro-2-phenyl-2H-1-benzopyran n. 3,4-二氢-2-苯基-2H-1-苯并吡喃

2-phenylchroman n. 2-苯基色满
catechin ['kætikin] n. 儿茶酸
polymeric [ˌpɔli'merik] a. 聚合的，聚合体的
phytochemistry [ˌfaitou'kemistri] n. 植物化学
glycosylate ['glaikəsileit] vt. 糖基化
polar solvent 极性溶剂
light petrol ['petrəl] n. 轻气油
extractive [iks'træktiv] n. 萃取物，抽出物，精；a. 萃取的，抽取的
polarity [pou'læriti] n. 极性
column chromatography 柱色谱法
silica gel 硅胶
hexane ['heksein] n. 己烷
eluant ['eljuənt] n. 洗提（脱）液，展开剂
derivatization n. (=derivation) 衍生（作用），导出
acetate ['æsiteit] n. 醋酸盐（酯）
elution [i'lju:ʃən] n. 洗提
formic acid 甲酸，蚁酸
thin layer chromatoplate 薄层色谱板
chromatoplate ['krəumətəˌpleit] n. （薄层）色谱板
admix [əd'miks] v. (使) 混合，掺和
dilute [dai'lju:t] a. 淡的，稀释的，弱的；v. 稀释，变淡，冲淡
methanolic sulphuric acid 含甲醇硫酸
coloration [ˌkʌlə'reiʃən] n. 染色，着色
chromatogram ['krouməcərgræm] n. 色谱，层析谱
diazotize [dai'æzətaiz] v. 使重氮化
p-nitroaniline [naitrou'ænilin] n. 对硝基苯胺
enzymatic [ˌenzai'mætik] a. 酶的，酶促的
emulsin [i'mʌlsin] n. 苦杏仁酵素，杏仁酪
aglucone [ə'glu:kəun] n. 配基，（葡糖苷的）非糖部
glycone ['glaikəun] n. (= glycerin suppository) 甘油栓
alditol acetate 乙酸醛醇酯
pharmacological [ˌfɑ:məkə'lɔdʒikəl] a. 药理学的
auriculoside [ɔːˌrikjulə'said] a. 心房侧的，从属心房的
depressant [di'presənt] n. 镇静剂；a. 有镇静作用的
glucosyloxy flavan 葡糖氧基黄烷
adaptogenic [əˌdæptə'dʒenik] a. 适应原的
anti-anxiety [æŋg'zaiəti] a. 抗焦虑的
Canscora diffusa 多枝叶穿心草属
potentiation [pəutenʃi'eiʃən] n. 增效作用，增强作用
barbiturate [bɑː'bitjurit] n. 巴比妥酸盐

hypnosis [hip'nousis] n. 催眠，催眠状态
analgesia [ænæl'dʒi:ziə] n. 无痛觉，痛觉丧失，镇痛
inotropic [inəu'trɔpik] a. 影响收缩力的，变力的（心神经纤维）
arrhythmogenic [əriðmə'dʒenik] a. 致心律不齐的
potentiate [pə'tenʃieit] v. 加强
contractile [kən'træktail] a. 有收缩性的
guinea-pig ['ginipig] n. 豚鼠，天竺鼠
catechol amine 儿茶酚胺
mental disorder 精神障碍
melancholia [ˌmelən'kəuliə] n. 精神忧郁症
xanthone ['zænθoun] n. 呫吨酮

Notes

1. permethyl 全甲基。即分子中所有的羟基均甲基化为甲氧基。
2. dil 为 dilute 的缩写，意为稀（释）的；其反义词是 conc 为 concentrated 的缩写，意为浓（缩）的。

Unit 8 The Chemistry of Insulin

Insulin was isolated in crystalline form by Abel in 1926, and its chemical structure was elucidated by Sanger and his co-workers in the early 1950s. Sanger found that the insulin molecule is composed of two polypeptide chains, an A chain, consisting of 21 amino acid residues, and a B chain, containing 30 residues. The two chains are connected by two disulfide bonds, and there is an additional disulfide linkage within the A chain.

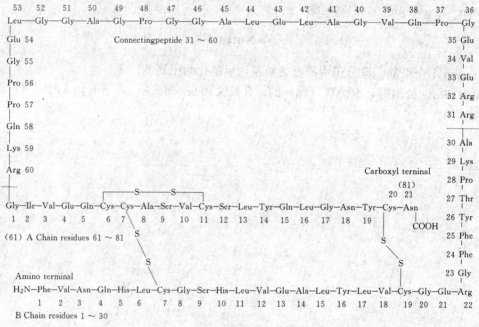

Bovine proinsulin

The amino acid sequences of insulin for at least 28 species have been reported. Although most of these insulins are remarkably similar in amino acid composition and molecular weight, insulin from hagfish has been found to differ from human insulin in almost 50% of the residues. The two types of insulin of greatest importance to us, due to their therapeutic role, are those isolated from the pig and cow. Porcine insulin differs from human insulin in that it contains a C-terminal alanine in the B chain, whereas human insulin has a C-terminal threonine. Because they are so similar in structure, it is possible to convert porcine insulin into human insulin. The sequential differences between bovine insulin and human insulin are more striking in that, in addition to the porcine change, there are amino acid differences at positions 8 and 10 of the A chain. At position A-8, alanine replaces threonine, and at A-10, valine is substituted for isoleucine. Although the biologic activity is retained with these amino acid changes, it should be kept in mind that the more dissimilar the sequences, the greater is the potential for antigenicity. Predictably, bovine insulin is more antigenic[①] than porcine insulin in humans.

The three-dimensional arrangement of atoms in insulin has been determined by X-ray crystallography. From this work we can appreciate that insulin looks like a typical globular protein, despite its small size. Insulin crystallized at neutral pH is composed of six molecules of insulin organized into three identical dimers. The three dimers are arranged around two zinc ions, each of which is coordinated to the imidazole nitrogens of three B-10 histidines. Presumably, insulin is stored in granules in the β-cell as the hexamer, but the physiologically active form of insulin is the monomer.

The chemical synthesis of insulin was achieved independently by three groups during the mid-1960s. All three used the method of separate synthesis of the A and B chains followed by random combination. The process involved more than 200 steps and took several years to accomplish. Using the modern-day methods of solidstate synthesis developed by Merrifeld and Marglin, the same results have been obtained in just a few days.

The major difficulty encountered in the synthesis of insulin was the correct positioning of the three disulfide bonds. This was because of the many ways in which the sulfhydryl groups could combine. The problem of poor yields was partially resolved by treating the sulfhydryl form of one chain with the S-sulfonated derivative of the other. Proper positioning of the disulfide bonds has been further facilitated through conformational-directed disulfide bond formation. By reversible cross-linking of amino acids known to be in juxtaposition in the three-dimensional structure, the formation of the correct disulfide bonds can be enhanced.

Another novel approach to the synthesis of insulin has been to circumvent the problem of disulfide bond formation. The appropriate disulfide bond was first formed between fragments of the A and B chains. Then the fragments, with the disulfide bonds correctly positioned, were condensed in an orderly fashion so as to obtain the final product. Human insulin synthesized in this manner has been shown to be biologically equivalent to the natural hormone. Although the fragment condensation approach is a significant improvement over other methods for synthesizing proteins containing disulfide bonds, it is not likely to become a commercial source of insulin in the near future. Natural sources of insulin still appear to be sufficiently large and are cheaper to obtain.

Besides, concern over the future adequacy of insulin supplies may soon become academic. Advances in recombinant DNA[2] technology have moved us closer to the synthesis of insulin by bacteria. Ullrich and co-workers have successfully incorporated the gene for rat insulin into bacterial plasmids; Gilbert's team from Harvard has reported the successful synthesis of rat proinsulin from another bacterial clone; and investigaters from Genentech reportedly have bacterial strains that synthesize either the A chain or the B chain of insulin. Although none of these advances are commercially feasible at the present time, the stage has been set for the construction of bacterial plasmids containing human insulin genes. Such an achievement would assure an almost limitless supply of insulin for the world's 60 million diabetics.

The availability of insulin analogs and chemically and enzymatically modified insulin derivatives has provided a means of studying the relationship between the chemical structure and the biologic activity of the insulin molecule. Neither the A chain nor the B chain is active in the fully reduced form.

There is no apparent loss of activity in the insulin molecule when the C-terminal alanine is removed from the B chain of porcine or boving insulin, but the biologic activity is diminished appreciably when both the C-terminal alanine and the C-terminal asparagine are removed. The removal of the second and third amino acids from the C-terminus of the B-chain decreases the potency slightly, and desoctapeptide insulin (insulin minus eight amino acids from the C-terminal end of the B chain) has almost no activity and retains little ability to dimerize. Removing or chemically modifying the N-terminal glycine of the A chain substantially decreases biologic activity, but activity is retained if the B chain N-terminal phenylalanine is deleted. Chemical modification of the side chain carboxyl groups or the tyrosine residues also leads to inactivity.

The information obtained from studies such as these has confirmed that the conformation of the insulin molecule is critical to its activity, and has provided a basis for Pullin and collaborators to propose a receptor-binding region within the insulin molecule. The receptor-binding region, as proposed, consists largely of invariant amino acids located both in the A chain (residues A-1 gly, A-5 gln, A-19 tyr, and A-21 asn) and in the B chain (residues B-24 phe, B-25 phe, B-26 tyr, B-12 val and B-16 tyr). Modification of insulin or the receptor may decrease biologic activity by reducing the hormone: receptor affinity or by decreasing the ability of the complex, once formed, to elicit a response.

Selected from William O. Foye, *Principles of Medicinal Chemistry*, Henry Kenry Kimpton Publishers, London, 1981

Words and Expressions

insulin ['insjulin] *n.* 胰岛素
crystalline ['kristəlain] *a.* 结晶的，水晶的
polypeptide [ˌpɔli'peptaid] *n.* 多肽
chain [tʃein] *n.* 链，链条
disulfide [dai'sʌlfaid] *n.* 二硫化物
bond [bɔnd] *n.* 键
hagfish ['hægfiʃ] *n.* 八目鳗类鱼
therapeutic [ˌθerə'pju:tik] *a.* 治疗的，治疗学的；*n.* 治疗剂，治疗学家
porcine ['pɔ:sain] *a.* 猪的
alanine ['æləni(:)n] *n.* 丙氨酸
threonine ['θri:əni(:)n] *n.* 苏氨酸，羟丁氨酸
bovine ['bouvain] *a.* 牛的，牛一般的
valine ['væli:n] *n.* 缬氨酸

isoleucine [ˌaisou'ljuːsiːn] n. 异白氨酸，异亮氨酸
antigenicity [ˌæntidʒə'nisiti] n. 抗原性
crystallography [kristə'lɔgrəfi] n. 结晶学
globular ['glɔbjulə(r)] a. 球状的
dimer ['daimə] n. 二聚物
zinc [ziŋk] n. 锌
ion ['aiən] n. 离子
imidazole [ˌimi'dæzoul] n. 咪唑，1,3-二氮杂茂
histidine ['histidiːn] n. 组氨酸
hexamer ['hekseimə] n. 六聚物
physiologically [ˌfiziə'lɔdʒikəli] ad. 生理学地，生理地
monomer ['mɔnəmə] n. 单体
synthesis ['sinθisis] n. 合成
solidstate ['sɔlid'steit] a. 固态的
sulfhydryl [sʌlf'haidril] n. 硫氢(基)，巯(基)
sulfonate ['sʌlfəneit] (= sulphonate) n. 磺酸盐；vt. 使磺化
conformational [ˌkɔnfɔː'meiʃənəl] a. 构象的
juxtaposition [ˌdʒʌkstəpə'ziʃən] n. 并列，毗邻，并置
condense [kən'dens] v. 缩合，(使)浓缩，(使)凝结
synthesize ['sinθisaiz] v. 合成，综合
condensation [kɔnden'seiʃən] n. 缩合，浓缩，凝结
recombinant [ri'kɔmbinənt] n. 重组细胞，重组体
bacterial [bæk'tiəriə] a. 细菌的
plasmid ['plæzmid] n. 质体，质粒
proinsulin [ˌprəu'insjulin] n. 胰岛素原
clone [kloun] n. 克隆，无性繁殖，无性系；v. 复制，无性繁殖
bacterial strain 细菌(菌)株
diabetic [daiə'betik] n. 糖尿病患者；a. 糖尿病的
analog ['ænəlɔːg] n. 类似物，相似体
enzymatically [ˌenzai'mætikəli] ad. 酶地，促酶地
gene [dʒiːn] n. (遗传)因子，(遗传)基因
asparagine [ə'spærədʒiːn] n. 天门冬酰胺，门冬酰胺
desoctapeptide [diˌzɔktə'peptaid] n. 脱八肽
dimerize ['daiməraiz] vt. 使聚合成二聚物
glycine ['glaisiːn, glai'siːn] n. 甘氨酸
phenylalanine [ˌfenil'æləniːn] n. 苯丙氨酸
tyrosine ['taiərəsiːn] n. 酪氨酸
gly = glycine 甘氨酸
gln = glutamine 谷酰胺
tyr = tyrosine 酪氨酸

asn = asparagine 天冬酰胺
phe = phenylalanine 苯丙氨酸
val = valine 缬氨酸
hormone ['hɔːmoun] n. 激素，荷尔蒙

Notes

① antigenic ['ænti'dʒenik] a. 抗原的。能引起抗原体反应及免疫反应的物质，总称为抗原。大多是分子量约为 1000 以上的蛋白质和多糖类及其复合物，脂类及其复合物等。

② DNA 即 deoxyribonucleic acid（脱氧核糖核酸）。

Exercises

1. Answer the following questions：
   (1) What actions does insulin have ?
   (2) Can you tell the materials that contain insulin ?
   (3) Are there any differences between human insulin and other animal insulin ?
   (4) What components is insulin composed of ?

2. Competing the following paragraph. Choose **Not More Than Three Words** from the passage for each answer.

   The structure of insulin is more complex than that of the peptide hormones. It has ^{1} _____, the A chain, consisting of ^{2} _____, and the B chain, having 30. The chains are joined by ^{3} _____ between residues A_7 and B_7 and between A_{20} and B_{19}. The A chain has a third ^{4} _____ connecting residues A_6 and A_{11}. The ^{5} _____ of insulin was determined by the pioneering effort of Sanger. His development of fluorodinitrobenzene as a reagent for determining amino acids of the amino terminal aided greatly. The structure has been confirmed by ^{6} _____, a monumental effort carried out independently in the United States, mainland China, and Germany.

   Human and hog insulin differ in only one ^{7} _____, having threonine or alanine, respectively, at the C-terminal end of ^{8} _____. ^{9} _____ patients, who have been treated with hog ^{10} _____ for a long time, may produce ^{11} _____ against this type of insulin, caused either by impurities, e.g., proinsulin, or by the presence of the wrong amino acid in the B-chain.

3. Put the following into Chinese：

polypeptide	sulfonate	hormone	alanine
glycine	herapeutic	construction	diabetic
complex	activity	protein	phenylalanine
histidine	gene	residue	synthesis

4. Put the following into English：

中性的	酸性的	碱性的	氨基酸序列
二硫键	三维结构	固态合成法	组成
生物活性	酶地	结晶	单体

二聚物　　　六聚物　　　脱氧核糖核酸　缩合

Reading Material 8

Steroid Saponins

Introduction The saponins are plant glycosides which have the property of forming a soapy lather when shaken with water. The cardiac glycosides also possess this property but these are classified separately because of their specific biological activity. The saponins are classified as steroid or triterpenoid saponins depending upon the nature of the aglycone. The aglycone of a steroid saponin is usually a spirostanol or its modification. A third group of saponins which are called basic steroid saponins contain nitrogen analogues of steroid sapogenins as aglycones. Some natural products may produce froth with water but only exhibit some of the properties of saponins.

Isolation The methods of isolation of steroid saponins are essentially the same as those of triterpenoid saponins. The classical methods of isolation of triterpenoid saponins have been reviewed. The separation of a saponin mixture into individual components is a formidable task. The development of recent chromatographic techniques has provided valuable means for isolation of pure saponins and their derivatives. A convenient method of separation of steroidal glycosides has been described by Nohara *et al*.

Sephadex LH-20 chromatography and droplet countercurrent chromatography (DCC)

Sephadex LH-20 has successfully been used for the separation of steroidal saponins. A typical isolation procedure involving Si gel CC and Sephadex LH-20 for the separation of furostanol oligosides of *Asparagus cochinchinensis* has been described by Konishi and Shoji. The technique of DCC has been applied successfully for the separation of saponins. The technique is based on the difference of the partition coefficients of compounds in liquid-liquid phases such as countercurrent distribution. Those solvent systems which form two immiscible layers are selected for the separation of the compounds by this method. In the case of Sephadex LH-20 chromatography, plant extracts are partially purified by the usual Si gel CC methods before subjecting them to DCC. This technique is useful for the small scale and semi-micro qualitative and quantitative determination of saponins. Nevertheless, it requires a longer time, viz., a period of four days to a week even for effective semi-micro separation. The molluscacidal saponins from *Cornus florida* have been separated by Hostettman *et al*. The methanol extract of the plant was first fractionated by Sephadex LH-20 CC followed by the separation. of pure saponins by DCC. This method has also been applied for the separation of the dammaranetype saponins of *Panax ginseng* by Tanaka *et al*. The separation of the major saponins of *Bupleurum radix* has been achieved using the DCC technique by Otsuka *et al*.

High performance liquid chromatography (HPLC)

The very efficient newer technique of HPLC is increasingly being used for the separation of various compounds including saponins. The technique has been described in a recent book by Simpson. Rapid, selective, and highly sensitive separation of saponins can be effected by HPLC using a variety of stationary and mobile phases. Successful separation of the major saponin components in liquorice has been achieved using HPLC. Tanaka *et al* have analysed the saponin constituents of *Bupleurum radix* on a column of octadecylsilylated (ODS) Si gel LS-410 with a mixture of methanol, water, acetic acid and triethylamine as the mobile phase. Anthracene was used as an appropriate int. standard for quantitative analysis. The saponin mixture obtained from *Tribulus terrestris* was separated on a column of μ-Bondapak C_{18} using methanol as the mobile phase. The very complex mixtures of saponins which were not amenable to separation previously can now be effectively separated by a combination of silica gel CC, gel chromatography on Sephadex LH-20 and HPLC on a reversed phase column.

Structure Elucidation The conventional method of structure elucidation of steroidal saponins starts with acid hydrolysis which yields the aglycone and the sugar moieties which are separately investigated. Extensive chemical studies on the aglycones revealed that they are almost exclusively spirostane derivatives. But furostanol glycosides, which according to Marker and Lopez are precursors of spirostane glycosides, have also been isolated and characterized. A simple qualitative test for furostanol glycoside has been developed by Kawasaki *et al*. The furostanol glycosides with some exceptions, show a characteristic red colour on a TLC plate when sprayed with *p*-dimethylaminobenzaldehyde and hydrochloric acid. Moreover, the furostane skeleton does not exhibit the characteristic IR absorptions of spirostane derivatives. Confirmatory evidence for the furostane structure is obtained by examination of the products of Marker's degradation or Baeyer-Villiger oxidation followed by hydrolysis. The first isolation of a furostanol glucoside, jurubine, was announced by Schrieber and Ripperger and later Tschesche *et al* isolated and characterized a furostanol bisglycoside, sarsaparilloside, corresponding to the spirostanol glycoside, parillin. Moreover, some glycosides have been isolated whose aglycones are not spirostanol but a modification. In general, the sugar moieties of steroidal saponins are oligosaccharides which consist of 2-4 kinds of sugar units, e. g. D-glucose, D-galactose, D-xylose and L-rhamnose. D-Xylose and L-rhamnose generally occur at the terminal positions. Arabinose-containing steroidal saponins are also known. In a very few cases, quinovose occurs as the carbohydrate moiety. Trillenoside A, a novel 18-norspirostanol glycoside, contains xylose, rhamnose, arabinose and apiose as the sugar constituents. Another unusual saponin consisting of kammogenin and five molecules of 2-deoxyribose has been reported by Backer *et al*. The furostanol bisglycosides so far isolated contain a glucose unit attached to the C-26 hydroxyl.

In the classical method, the structure of the sugar moieties of the saponins is determined by identification of the monosaccharides obtained on acid hydrolysis by PC and GLC, quantitative determination of monosaccharides by GLC, partial hydrolysis followed by isolation and characterization of prosapogenins and also, where possible, by characterization of oligosaccharides. The points of attachment of different sugar units are revealed by permethylation of the saponins followed by hydrolysis or methanolysis and identification of the methylated sugars by PC or GLC. The mode of sugar linkage in saponins is determined by enzymic hydrolysis with α- and β-glycosidases or by the application of Klyne's rule on molecular rotation difference. However, both of these methods are not always applicable, particularly in the case of complex glycosides.

Biological Activity

Action on the cardio-vascular system The cardiotonic actions of g-strophanthin, α-solanine and T. T. saponin were studied on a comparative basis. g-Strophanthin and T. T. saponin decreased the frequency of cardiac contraction whereas α-solanine had no effect. Cardiotonic activity of some glycoalkaloids, when compared with K-strophantoside by the use of isolated frog heart, is found to be directly related to the nature of the aglycone and the number of sugar units. Saponin isolated from the seeds of *Achyranthes aspera* is found to increase the force of contraction of isolated frog heart, guinea-pig heart and rabbit heart. Two new steriodal saponins ruscoside A (ruscogenin + glc + 1 gal + 2 rha) and ruscoside B (ruscogenin + 1 gal + 1 glc + 2 rha + 1 ara) exhibit various biological activities. They decrease the cholesterol content of the blood, lipid deposition in the aorta and liver arterial tension. They also slow down the cardiac rhythm and respiration of humans and rabbits suffering from arteriosclerosis.

Antimicrobial Activity Saponins are generally good antifungal and antibacterial agents. The antifungal activity is found to be more effective with saponins than the sapogenins and the acetylated saponins, the activity being highly influenced by the number of component monosaccharides and their sequence.

Action on the Reproductive System Saponins from *Costus speciosus* have shown varied and interesting biological activities. They have a stimulating effect and anti-inflammatory activity on uterus and they produced proliferative changes in both vagina and uterus showing a similar effect to that produced by stilbesterol.

Selected from S B Mahato, A N Ganguly and N P Sahu, *Phytochemistry*, 1982, 21(5):959~978

Words and Expressions

steroid ['sterɔid] *n.* 甾族化合物，类固醇，甾体
saponin ['sæpənin] *n.* 皂草苷，皂角苷
soapy lather   肥皂泡
triterpenoid [ˌtraiˈtəːpəˌnɔid] *n.* 三萜（烯）化合物
spirostanol   *n.* 螺甾烷醇
codification [ˌkɔdifiˈkeiʃən] *n.* 整理，编纂，法典编纂
sapogenin [ˌseipəˈdʒenin] *n.* 皂草配质，皂角苷配质
froth [frɔːθ] *n.* 泡，泡沫，废物；*vt.* 使生泡沫；*vi.* 发泡
formidable ['fɔːmidəbəl] *a.* 可怕的，强大的，艰难的，令人敬畏的

chromatographic [ˌkroumə'tɔgrəfik] a. 色谱分离法的，层析的
chromatography [ˌkroumə'tɔgrəfi] n. 色谱（分离）法，层析
droplet ['drɔplit] n. 小滴
countercurrent ['kauntəˌkʌrənt] ad. 相反地；n. 逆流
Si gel 硅胶
furostanol ['fjuərəstənəl] n. 呋甾醇
Asparagus cochinchinensis 天冬草，天门冬
partition coefficient 分配系数
immiscible [i'misibəl] a. 不能混合的，不融和的
semi-micro 半微（量）
qualitative ['kwɔlitətiv] a. 定性的
quantitative ['kwɔntitətiv] a. 定量的，数量的
molluscacidal [mɔlʌskə'saidl] a. 灭螺的，灭软体动物的
Cornus florida 佛罗里达的山茱萸
fractionate ['frekʃəneit] vt. 使分馏
dammarane ['dæmərein] n. 达玛烷
Panax ginseng 高丽参
Bupleurum radix 柴胡属植物的根
high performance liquid chromatography 高压液相色谱（简写 HPLC）
stationary phase 固定相
mobile phase 流动相
liquorice ['likəris] n. (= licorice) 甘草，甘草属植物
octadecylsilylated a. 十八烷基硅烷基化的
triethylamine [traieθi'læmi:n] n. 三乙胺
anthracene ['ænθrəsi:n] n. 蒽
Tribulus terrestris 刺蒺藜
amenable [ə'mi:nəbəl] a. 有责任的，应服从的，有服从义务的
spirostane n. 螺旋甾烷
p-dimethylaminobenzaldehyde p-二甲胺基苯甲醛
degradation [ˌdegrə'deiʃən] n. 降解，递降分解，降级，降格，退化
Baeyer-Villiger oxidation 拜耳-维列格氧化反应
jurubine n. 圆椎茄碱
bisglycoside n. 双糖苷
sarsaparilloside n. 葡萄糖洋菝葜皂苷
parillin n. 杷日灵，副菝葜皂角苷
oligosaccharide [ˌɔligou'sækəraid] n. 低聚糖
D-galactose [gə'læktəus] n. D-半乳糖
xylose ['zailous] n. 木糖，戊醛糖
L-rhamnose ['ræmnəus] n. L-鼠李糖
arabinose [ə'ræbənəus] n. 阿戊糖，阿（拉伯）糖

quinovose ['kwinəvəus] n. 奎诺糖，鸡纳糖，6-去氧葡糖
carbohydrate [ˌkɑːbou'haidreit] n. 碳水化合物，醣类
18-norspirostanol n. 18-降螺甾烷醇
kammogenin ['kæməˌdʒənən] n. 茨摸配质，茨摸皂苷元
2-deoxyribose 2-脱氧核糖
hydroxyl [hai'drɔksil] n. 羟基
monosaccharide [ˌmɔnə'sækəraid] n. 单糖
prosapogenin n. 前皂配基
permethylation n. 全甲基化
methanolysis [ˌmeθə'nɔlisis] n. 甲醇分解作用
methylate ['meθileit] vt. 使甲基化，向……导入甲基
glycosidases [glai'kəusideis] n. 糖苷酶
cardio-vascular [kɑːdiə'væskjulə] a. 心血管的
cardiotonic [ˌkɑːdiəu'tɔnik] n. 强心剂；a. 强心的
g-strophanthin n. g-羊角拗质
solanine ['səuləˌniːn] n. 茄碱
glycoalkaloid [ˌglaikou'ælkəlɔid] n. 配糖（生物）碱
k-strophantoside n. k-羊角拗糖苷，绿毒羊角拗苷
Achyranthes aspera 倒扣草，土牛膝
ruscoside n. 鲁士可宁苷
ruscogenin n. 鲁士可宁
cholesterol [kə'lestərɔl] n. 胆固醇
aorta [ei'ɔːtə] n. 大动脉
respiration [ˌrespə'reiʃən] n. 呼吸，呼吸作用
arteriosclerosis [ɑːˌtiəriəuˌskliə'rəusis] n. 动脉硬化（症），闭塞性动脉硬化
antifungal ['ænti'fʌŋgəl] a. 杀真菌的，抗真菌的
Costus speciosus 闭鞘姜
anti-inflammatory 抗炎的
uterus ['juːtərəs] n. 子宫
proliferative [prou'lifəreitiv] a. 增殖的，增生的，多育的，扩散的，激增的
vagina [və'dʒainə] n. 叶鞘，鞘；阴道
Stilbesterol [stil'bestrɔl] n. 己烯雌酚

Unit 9 Multidrug-Resistant Bacterial Infections: Driving the Search for New Antibiotics

Throughout recorded history, bacterial infections have periodically exacted heavy tolls on the human population. During the "Black Death" bubonic plague episode of 1347~1351, *Yersinia pestis* killed an estimated 25 million people in Asia and Europe. US Public Health Service statistics for 1910 and 1920 show that early in this century tuberculosis killed one in every 1000 US residents. Even today, mainly in developing countries, *Mycobacterium tuberculosis* remains the leading cause of death attributable to a single infectious agent, killing over three million people worldwide every year.

Such unremitting microbial attack throughout the course of vertebrate evolution has provoked the evolution of an amazingly complex protective immune system. With the appearance of the humans, there eventually arrived a species which could devise ways to assist the innate and acquired immune systems for staving off infection. By exploiting microbial antigenic components (yielding vaccines and horse-serum antitoxins), and then microbial secondary metabolites (antibiotics), humans have become adept at preventing and curing many previously fatal microbial diseases.

Within just a few decades, the availability of an anti-infective pharmacopoeia suddenly provided humans with the potential to circumvent Nature's time-tested, live-or-die evolutionary paradigm for enhancing their survival prospects under constant microbial barrage. Those members that previously would have succumbed could now survive longer with the help of vaccines and antibiotics — auxiliary agents which work alongside the immune system to fight infection. In effect, humans' employment of these auxiliaries can be looked upon as exemplifying a self-contrived evolution in their immunological defence system.

Once the usefulness of Sir Alexander Fleming's[①] penicillin discovery had been demonstrated, a flurry of other antibiotics unearthed from natural sources followed. Some of these proved suitable for treating disease, usually after chemical modification to improve the natural compound's potency, safety or pharmacokinetic profiles.

For most of the past 50 years, it seemed that medical science had gained a strong upper hand over bacterial disease. Some pharmaceutical houses and funding agencies decided to cut back on antibiotic discovery efforts, as it appeared that the physician's antibacterial arsenal was well stocked. But the nature of the diseases has proved otherwise.

The rapid escalation in the incidence of multiple-antibiotic-resistant pathogens is now raising very serious concerns worldwide. This development underscores the powerful evolutionary capabilities of bacterial populations under the selective pressure imposed by antibiotic therapy.

Antibiotic resistance   Resistance problems are seen with both Gram-negative[2] (for example *Escherichia coli*) and Gram-positive bacteria[3] (such as *Staphylococcus aureus*), but most of the current concerns are with the latter group of pathogens. *Streptococcus pneumoniae* is a respiratory Gram-positive pathogen responsible for 40,000 deaths a year in the US alone. A rapidly rising prevalence of penicillin-resistant *S. pneumoniae* infections is now problematic in many countries. One of the worst situations is in Hungary, where 70% of the *S. pneumoniae* isolates from children tested in 1988~1989 were resistant to penicillin.

Bacteria have evolved numerous ploys for defeating antibiotic action——they inactivate the antibiotic by hydrolysis, acylation, phosphorylation or nucleotidylation reactions; alter the antibiotic's target site; or reduce the intracellular drug concentration by decreasing membrane permeability and/or actively pumping the drug out of the cell. With improved understanding of these mechanisms of resistance through molecular biology and biochemical techniques, medicinal chemists have been provided with the targets for attempting to circumvent some of the resistance problems.

A predominant resistance mechanism against the β-lactam drugs (such as Penicillin) involves enzymatic cleavage of the β-lactam ring. While the drug Methicillin was developed because it could withstand such action, strains of Methicillin-resistant S. aureus (MRSA) emerged in 1961, just two years after the drug first went into wide use. MRSA strains evolved so that they had an additional drug-target protein involved with cell wall biosynthesis, and this altered protein has a very low affinity for virtually all β-lactams. To make matters worse, most MRSA strains are also resistant to many other classes of antibiotics, with the exception of the glycopeptide Vancomycin. Now seen around the globe, MRSA strains are very problematic in Japan (where in some hospitals 60% of *S. aureus* isolates are MRSA), as well as in Spain, France, Italy and the US, each with a greater than 30% incidence.

A particularly disturbing milestone was the 1988 emergence of Vancomycin-resistant enterococci (VRE). Some VRE now don't respond to any available antibiotics. The enterococci have become the second most frequently encountered hospital acquired pathogen in the US, where the incidence of VRE strains is now about 15% of all clinical enterococcal isolates. Resistance to Vancomycin arises because a D-alanine-D-lactate residue (which vancomycin binds to only poorly) has been substituted for the D-alanine-D-alanine residue normally found at the terminus of a pentapeptide precursor involved in the bacteria's cell wall biosynthesis.

There is now a great concern that the genes conferring resistance in VRE to glycopeptides like Vancomycin will be naturally transferred to *S. aureus*, as has been experimentally demonstrated feasible by William Noble at St Thomas' Hospital, London. As Vancomycin is the drug of last resort for treating MRSA infections, the anticipated natural acquisition of Vancomycin resistance in this virulent pathogen would result in the sobering return to pre-antibiotic era therapeutic failures, should no alternate effective therapy become available.

Conclusions

Man's use of antibiotics has rapidly accelerated the dynamic evolutionary interplay between humans and bacteria. The recent rapid rise in multidrug-resistant Gram-positive bacterial infections worldwide has sounded a loud claxon for the need of new, effective therapies. The newer agents described here may provide physicians with a refurbished arsenal.

The discovery of new bacterial drug targets through genomic research, as well as improvements in our understanding of bacterial resistance mechanisms, hold promise for the discovery of new means of treating multidrug-resistant bacterial infections. Given enough time, bacteria will eventually be able to develop resistance to any new antibacterial agent. Those drugs that can attack the pathogen through a novel mechanism may have reduced propensities to rapid resistance development.

Selected from Steven J Brickner, *Chem.Ind.*(*London*), 1997, (4) 131~135

Words and Expressions

multidrug   *n.* 多药物
infection   [in'fekʃən]   *n.* 传染,传染病,感染,影响
antibiotic   ['æntibai'ɔtik]   *n.* 抗生素,抗菌素; *a.* 抗生的,抗菌的
toll   [tɔl]   *n.* 费,代价
Black Death   黑死病(14世纪蔓延于亚欧两洲的鼠疫)
bubonic   [bju:'bɔnik]   *a.* 腹股沟腺炎的
plague   [pleig]   *n.* 鼠疫,瘟疫,灾祸; *vt.* 使得灾祸,折磨
episode   ['episoud]   *n.* (一系列事件中的)一个事件,一段情节
Yersinia pestis   耶尔森菌属鼠疫,耶尔森菌属瘟疫
tuberculosis   [tju:,bə:kju'lousis]   *n.* 肺结核
Mycobacterium tuberculosis   结核丝杆菌(缩写为 M. tuberculosis)
infectious   [in'fekʃəs]   *a.* 有传染性的,易传染的,有感染力的
unremitting   [,ʌnri'mitiŋ]   *a.* 不间断的,持续的,不停的,不懈的
microbial   [ma'ikroubiəl]   *a.* 微生物(或细菌)的,由细菌(或微生物)引起的
vertebrate   ['və:tibreit]   *n.* 脊椎动物; *a.* 脊椎动物的,有椎骨的,有脊椎的
provoke   [prə'vouk]   *vt.* 驱使,惹起,激怒,挑拨,煽动
immune   [i'mju:n]   *a.* 免疫的
innate   [i'neit]   *a.* 先天的,天生的
stave off   避免,避开,延缓
antigenic   ['ænti'dʒenik]   *a.* 抗原的
vaccine   ['væksi:n]   *n.* 疫苗; *a.* 疫苗的,牛痘的
serum   ['siərəm]   *n.* 血清,免疫血清,浆液
antitoxin   [ænti'tɔksin]   *n.* 抗毒素
metabolite   [me'tæbəlait]   *n.* 代谢物
anti-infective   抗传染的,防传染的

pharmacopoeia [ˌfɑːməkəˈpiːə] n. 药典，（一批）备用药品
evolutionary [ˌiːvəˈljuːʃənəri] a. 进化的，发展的
paradigm [ˈpærədaim] n. 范例
succumb [səˈkʌm] vi. 屈从，屈服
immunological [ˌimjuˈnɔlədʒikəl] a. 免疫学的
Penicillin [peniˈsilin] n. 青霉素
flurry [ˈflʌri] n. 阵风，飓风
modification [ˌmɔdifiˈkeiʃən] n. 修改，改变，更改
pharmacokinetic [ˌfɑːməkəkaiˈnetik] a. 药动力学的
arsenal [ˈɑːsinl] n. 军火库，兵工厂
antibacterial [ˈæntibækˈtiəriəl] n. 抗菌药；a. 抗菌的
β-lactams n. β-内酰胺类抗生素
glycopeptide [ˌglaikəuˈpeptaid] n. 糖肽
pharmaceutical [ˌfɑːməˈsjuːtikəl] a. 药物的，药学的，药用的
escalation [ˌeskəˈleiʃən] n. 逐步上升，逐步升级，增加，扩大
pathogen [ˈpæθədʒən] n. 病菌，病原体
therapy [ˈθerəpi] n. 治疗
Escherichia coli 大肠杆菌，埃（舍利）希杆菌，大肠埃希杆菌（缩写为 E. coli）
Staphylococcus aureus 金黄色酿脓葡萄球菌（缩写为 S. aureus）
Streptococcus pneumoniae 肺炎链球菌，肺炎双球菌（缩写为 S. pneumoniae）
respiratory [riˈspirətəri] a. 呼吸的
prevalence [ˈprevələns] n. 流行
problematic [ˌprɔbləˈmætik] a. 问题的，有疑问的
ploy [plɔi] n. 策略，趣味，工作
inactivate [inˈæktiveit] v. 使钝化，使失去活性，使不活泼，阻止
phosphorylation [fɔˌsfəriˈleiʃən] n. 磷酸化（作用）
nucleotidylation n. 核苷酸化作用
intracellular [ˌintrəˈseljulə] a. 细胞内的
membrane [ˈmembrein] n. 膜，隔膜
permeability [ˌpəːmjəˈbiliti] n. 渗透，渗透性
biochemical [ˈbaiouˈkemikəl] a. 生物化学的
cleavage [ˈkliːvidʒ] n. 分裂，裂开，避开，断裂
Methicillin [meθiˈsilin] n. 美替西林，二甲氧基苯青霉素
biosynthesis [ˌbaiouˈsinθisis] n. 生物合成
affinity [əˈfiniti] n. 亲合力，吸引力，密切关系
Vancomycin [ˌvænkəˈmaisin] n. 万古霉素
incidence [ˈinsidəns] n. 发生，发生率
enterococcus [ˌentərəuˈkɔkəs] n. （复 enterococc [ˌentərəuˈkɔksai]）肠球菌
enterococcal [ˌentərəuˈkɔkəl] a. 肠球菌的
lactate [lækˈteit] n. 乳酸盐（酯）；v. 分泌乳汁

pentapeptide [ˌpentəˈpeptaid] n. 五肽
acquisition [ˌækwiˈziʃən] n. 获得，获得物
virulent [ˈvirjulənt] a. 剧毒的，有病毒的，毒害的
sober [ˈsoubə] a. 清醒的，适度的，庄重的，合理的；vt. 使清醒，使严肃
pre-antibiotic era 指使用抗生素之前的时期
versus [ˈvəːsəs] prep. 与……相对
efficacy [ˈefikəsi] n. 功效，效验
bactericidal [bækˌtiəriˈsaidl] a. 杀菌的，杀菌性的
interplay [ˈintəplei] n.；v. 相互影响
claxon [ˈklæksn] n. 电气警笛，电器喇叭
refurbish [riːˈfəːbiʃ] vt. 刷新，再磨光
genomic [ˈdʒiːnəumik] a. 染色体组的，基因组的
propensity [prəˈpensiti] n. 倾向

Notes

① Alexander Fleming 阿力山大·弗莱明。1881.8.6～1955.3.11。英国细菌学家。曾求学于伦敦圣玛丽医院附属医学校，在伦敦大学获得学位（1908）。后在圣玛丽医院疫苗研究所担任以调理素学说闻名的赖特（J. H. Wright）的助手。他一生在此研究所从事研究工作。在培养葡萄球菌的变异研究中，观察到细菌因混入霉菌而死亡，作为其活性物质而发现了青霉素（1929）。在1945年他和合作者牛津小组的弗洛里（H. W. Flory）、秦（E. B. Chain）一起获得诺贝尔生理医学奖。

② Gram-negative bacteria 革兰阴性菌。指用革兰染色法可被复染染色剂染色的细菌。细胞壁薄（约10nm），很多在其外侧有脂多糖。因此，除非用EDTA（乙二胺四乙酸）将该层损伤，对溶菌酶不敏感。它包括大肠杆菌、沙门氏菌和赤痢菌等，一般产生内毒素。

③ Gram-positive bacteria 革兰阳性菌。指用革兰染色法染上最先被染色的细菌。有较厚的细胞壁（15～80nm），但其外层缺少脂多糖，对溶菌酶有极高的敏感性。包括葡萄球菌、链球菌、枯草杆菌、巨大杆菌等，一般产生外毒素。

Exercises

1. Answer the following questions：
   (1) Do you think that one antibiotic can treat all infections?
   (2) Can you list classes of antibiotics or antibacterials?
   (3) Why is the search for new antibiotics drived by multidrug-resistant bacterial infections?
   (4) What is the future of antibiotics or antibacterials?
2. Competing the following paragraphs. Choose **Not More Than Three Words** from the passage for each answer.

The introduction of penicillin and similar β-lactam [1] _____ had a dramatic effect on the mortality rate in consequence of [2] _____. However, the introduction of penicillin was historically preceded by a different class of [3] _____, the sulfonamides, which were introduced for the treatment of staphylococcal infections in the 1930s.

Sulfonamides have a broad spectrum of [4]_____ and their introduction meant a revolution in the treatment of [1]_____. Unfortunately, the widespread use of these agents resulted in the appearance of numerous sulfonamide resistant strains of [5]_____, and they have largely been replaced by penicillins and other [6]_____. However, the importance of sulfonamides to the concept of rational drug development must not be underestimated, as these compounds were some of the first examples of drug to which a molecular mechanism of action could be assigned.

Soon after the introduction of β-lactam antibiotics, bacterial enzymes capable of hydrolyzing the amide bond in the β-lactam ring, [7]_____, were recognized. The β-lactamases serve as a bacterial defense mechanism against penicillins and cephalosporins containing [8]_____. Their production is controlled by either chromosomal or plasmid genes, and may be induced by the presence of an antibiotic. The plasmid-mediated [9]_____ are the major determinants of bacterial tesistance to [10]_____, as plasmid transfer of genetic material is a widespread bacterial phenomenon. Resistance to antibiotics is a growing and serious problem in the clinic.

3. Put the following into Chinese:

microbial	infection	immune	antigenic
pharmacopoeia	β-lactam	cephalosporin	β-lactamase
macrolide	lactate	virulent	efficacy
vaccine	cleavage	inactivate	semi-synthetic

4. Put the following into English:

在体内	使沉淀	革兰阴性的	革兰阳性的
生物合成	青霉素	滤纸	代谢物
成分	抗菌药	抗生素	回流
病菌	治疗	药品	键

Reading Material 9

Beta-Lactams Past and Present

A cavity in the foundation stone laid for the North West Extension to St Mary's Hospital Medical School in Paddington, London, contains some memorabilia connected with famous employees of the Hospital. One item is a stopwatch recording the time of the first sub-four-minute mile run by Dr Roger Bannister; also contained in the stone is a replica of the culture plate that led Sir Alexander Fleming to the discovery of penicillin. Bannister's achievement was a tribute to his dedication, training and supreme physical fitness, while Fleming's discovery of the first antibiotic is a classic example of a scientist finding an unusual, at the time possibly annoying, outcome in a standard experiment and carefully following up the observation to reveal a major scientific breakthrough.

Isolation from natural sources

It was in September 1928 that fungal spores gained access to Fleming's laboratories (either from the street below or from an adjacent mycobiological laboratory) and settled on an agar[①] plate containing *Staphylococcus* bacteria. In Fleming's own words "when next observed, the mould spores which had gained access had developed into a large colony... what was surprising was that the staphylococcal colonies in the neighbourhood of the mould, which had been well developed, were observed now to be showing signs of dissolution···" The mould was identified as *Penicillium notatum* (the name was coined from the Latin word for paintbrush, due to the brush-like composition of the mould) and the active ingredient was called Penicillin.

While luck played a part in this observation of the lysis of the bacterial cells, Fleming used his experience and acumen to capitalise on his good fortune. However, the next 10 years showed unexpectedly slow progress towards the use of Penicillin in the treatment of bacterial infections. There are probably a number of reasons for this hiatus in developments. For a start, obtaining dilute aqueous solutions of penicillin from the mould proved difficult and nonreproducible. In addition, the *in vivo* stability of Penicillin was regarded as unsatisfactory. However, it was probably other scientists, some clinicians and certain medical doctors, suspicious of using a fungal broth[②] to cure infections, who were mainly responsible for the loss of momentum. Nevertheless, some treatments were noted in this period. For example, a medical student at St Mary's contracted pneumococcal conjunctivitis which Fleming successfully treated with a Penicillin broth.

The outbreak of the Second World War revealed a need for a safe antibacterial substance for the treatment of infected deep wounds. A great deal of work was undertaken in the UK and the USA to prove that Penicillin was an ideal substance for such therapy. In Oxford, Florey and Chain et al continued to develop production, isolation and assay methods for Penicillin. They also demonstrated the potential of Penicillin by the successful treatment of experimentally infected animals.

In the North Regional Research Laboratory, Peoria, Illinois, strains of Penicillium which gave higher yields of Penicillin than Fleming's original culture were discovered (highly productive moulds were found on a piece of cheese and on an over-ripe melon). The American group showed that the mould could be grown in submerged culture with a consequent decrease in the number of other products formed. Better yields of Penicillin were obtained on adding corn steep liquor to the brew.

In the mid-1940s, the structure of Penicillin was elucidated. Significant contributions were made by Dorothy Hodgkin and Robert Robinson in Britain, and by the young American chemist R. B. Woodward. The bicyclic structure of a Penicillin contains a β-lactam ring that is readily cleaved; the endocyclic amide bond is the susceptible linkage. Simple β-lactams, first made by Staudinger in the early years of this century, are considerably more stable than Penicillin. The instability of the antibiotic was attributed to the steric strain imposed by the presence of the second sulphur-containing ring.

Since this period, other naturally occurring compounds possessing a β-lactam ring and exhibiting anti-bacterial properties have been isolated. In 1961, a strain of *Cephalosporium* growing near the outlet of a Sardinian sewer was shown to produce Cephalosporin C. For many years it seemed that the Penicillins and cephalosporins were the only β-lactams to possess potent anti-bacterial properties. However, the isolation of Thienamycin, a very active and broad spectrum antibiotic, from *Streptomyces* and the discovery of the less active monocyclic compound Nocardicin from some strains of Nocardia dispelled this idea. The more interesting monocyclic compounds, called mono-bactams for example, Aztreonam have been described recently. The first members of the latter series of compounds were produced from bacteria found in soil samples taken from pine forests in the U.S.A.

Preparation of semi-synthetic and synthetic beta-lactams
Left to its own devices, the Penicillium fungus will produce isopenicillin N and Penicillin F. Supplying and additional carboxylic acid to the fermentation broth gave modified penicillins. For example, addition of phenoxyacetic acid gave Penicillin V, while the presence of phenylacetic acid in corn steep liquor in the brew gave rise to Penicillin G.

Although of major importance in the clinic for a time, penicillins V and G became increasingly ineffective against a number of important pathogenic bacteria. The main reason for the developing immunity of some bacteria was their ability to produce an enzyme (a beta-lactamase) which was able to destroy the β-lactam before it could interact with and kill the bacterium. The production of penicillins with increased antibacterial activity was made possible by modification of the readily available natural products. First, scientists at the Beecham Laboratories found that the parent substance, 6-aminopenicillanic acid or 6-APA, could be obtained from some fermentations. Slightly later, 6-APA became available in bulk quantities by enzymic or chemical hydrolysis of the natural penicillins.

A vast range of semi-synthetic penicillins became available by chemical derivatisation of the free amino group. In this way, β-lactams were obtained that possessed broad spectra of activity against Gram-positive and Gram-negative organisms. The penicillins Amoxycillin and ampicillin are of this type and still in widespread use. These new penicillins could be administered orally just like penicillins G and V, and they had a little extra stability against the β-lactamase enzymes. Other penicillins were prepared, with different side-chains at C-6, which conferred respectable antibacterial activity coupled with good β-lactamase stability on these molecules.

Another strategy has been developed recently to enhance the chance of success of Penicillin treatment against invasive, β-lactamase-producing bacterial organisms. This strategy involves administration of the Penicillin (for example, Amoxycillin) together with a second compound that inhibits the action of the β-lactamase enzyme. The β-lactamase inhibitor presently in use in the clinic is the β-lactam Clavulanic acid.

The chemistry of the penicillins and cephalosporins has been investigated in depth and a large number of intriguing transformations have been reported. Certain Penicillin derivatives can be transformed readily into the corresponding cephalosporin derivative lacking the acetoxy group linked through a carbon atom to the 3-position. Selective functionalisation of the 3-methyl group is difficult and some attempts to accomplish straightforward transformations have led to unexpected rearrangements.

In short, chemical production of a wide range of cephalosporins from readily available penicillins is not attractive from a commercial standpoint. Furthermore, no simple enzymatic or fermentation process is available to modify the 7-amino side-chain of the cephalosporins in a similar fashion to that described above for the penicillin system. Production of semi-synthetic cephalosporins has been accomplished by making cephalosporin C by fermentation, chemical removal of the acyl side chain to give 7-aminocephalosporanic acid or 7-ACA (usually with the carboxylic acid group protected as an ester) followed by acylation of the amino group and modification of the 3-substituent.

A wide variety of cephalosporins have been produced in this manner. Note that the 7-acylamino side-chains of the active cephalosporins differ in structure from the preferred 6-acylamino side-chains in the penicillin series. As few cephalosporins are active after oral administration, research in this field has been directed at finding broad spectrum agents for use by injection. Recently, the anti-bacterial agent Ceftazidime has been prepared. This cephalosporin is a powerful, broad spectrum, injectable antibiotic for use in the hospital environment and it is of particular value in the treatment of serious and life-threatening infections.

Selected from Stanley M Roberts, *Chem. Ind. (London)*, 1984, (9), 162~166

Words and Expressions

memorabilia [ˌmeməˈbiliə] [复] n. 大事记，值得纪念的事
stopwatch [ˈstɔpwɔtʃ] n. 秒表，跑表
tribute [ˈtribjuːt] n. 颂词，礼物，贡品
dedication [dediˈkeiʃən] n. 贡献，奉献
fungal [fʌŋɡəl] a. (=fungous) 真菌的
spore [spɔː] n. 孢子; vi. 长孢子
mycobiological [ˈmaikouˌbaiəˈlɔdʒikəl] a. 真菌生物学的
staphylococcus [ˌstæfilouˈkɔkəs] [复] staphylococci [ˌstæfilouˈkɔksai] n. 葡萄球菌
mould [mould] n. 霉，霉菌
colony [ˈkɔləni] n. (生物) 群体
staphylococcal [ˌstæfilouˈkɔkəl] a. 葡萄球菌的
penicillium notatum 青霉菌，特异青霉，点青霉
paintbrush [ˈpeintbrʌʃ] n. 画笔，漆刷
ingredient [inˈɡriːdiənt] n. 成分，因素
lysis [ˈlaisis] [复] lyses [ˈlaisiːz] n. (病的) 渐退，消散，细胞溶解
acumen [əˈkjuːmen] n. 敏锐，聪明

hiatus [hai'eitəs] *n.* 脱落，裂缝
nonreproducible [ˈnɔnˌriːprəˈdjuːsəbl] *a.* 不能繁殖的，不能再生产的
clinician [kliˈniʃən] *n.* 临诊医师，门诊医师
momentum [mouˈmentəm] *n.* 要素，动力
pneumococcal [ˌnjuːməˈkɔkəl] *a.* 肺炎双球菌的
conjunctivitis [kənˌdʒʌŋktiˈvaitis] *n.* 结膜炎
melon [ˈmelən] *n.* （各种的）瓜
corn steep liquor　玉米浸液
bicyclic [ˌbaiˈsaiklik] *a.* 双环的
endocyclic [ˌendouˈsaiklik] *a.* 桥环的
sulphur [ˈsʌlfə] *n.* 硫，硫磺
cephalosporium [ˌsefələuˈspɔːriəm] *n.* （复 cephalosporia [ˌsefələuˈspɔːriə]）假头状孢子头
Sardinian [sɑːˈdinjən] *n.* 撒丁岛人，撒丁岛语；*a.* 撒丁岛的，撒丁岛人的
Thienamycin　*n.* 硫霉素
Streptomyces　*n.* 链霉菌素
monocyclic [ˌmɔnəˈsaiklik] *a.* 单环的
Nocardicin　诺卡杀菌素，诺卡地菌素
nocardia [ˈnəuˈkɑːdiə] *n.* 诺卡氏菌属，土壤细菌属
mono-bactams　单内酰胺化合物
Aztreonam [ˈæztriənæm] *n.* 氨曲南
semi-synthetic　半合成的
fungus [ˈfʌŋgəs] *n.* 真菌（包括霉菌、酵母菌和伞菌等）
isopenicillin [ˌaisəˌpeˈnisilin] *n.* 异青霉素
carboxylic acid　羧酸
fermentation [ˌfəːmenˈteiʃən] *n.* 发酵
phenoxyacetic acid　苯氧基乙酸
phenylacetic acid　苯基乙酸
6-aminopenicillanic acid　6-氨基青霉烷酸
Amoxycillin　*n.* 阿莫西林
Ampicillin [æmpiˈsiliːn] *n.* 氨苄西林
side-chain　侧链
invasive [inˈveisiv] *a.* 侵略的，侵害的，侵袭的
Clavulanic acid　克拉维酸
intriguing　*a.* 引起兴趣（或好奇心）的，有迷惑力的
transformation [ˌtrænsfəˈmeiʃən] *n.* 变化，转化，转换，蜕变
acetoxy group　乙酰氧基
3-methyl group　3-甲基
straightforward [ˌstreitˈfɔːwəd] *a.*；*adv.* 简单的（地），易懂的（地），坦率的（地）
rearrangement [ˈriːəˈreindʒmənt] *n.* 重排
acyl [ˈæsil] *n.* 酰基

7-aminocephalosporanic acid　7-氨基头孢烷酸
acylamino ［ˌæsi'læminəun］　n. 乙酰氨基
Ceftazidime ['sefteizidi:n]　n. 头孢他啶
depict ［di'pikt］　vt. 描述，描写

Notes

① agar　琼脂，冻粉。以1,3-糖苷键结合的D-吡喃半乳糖（52个）长链的C（1）端，与L-吡喃半乳糖-C（6）-硫酸酯（1个）的C（4）相结合，按此比例形成的半乳聚糖硫酸酯的Ca盐或Ca-Mg盐的多糖衍生物。除食用和工业用外，常用作细菌的培养基等。

② broth　肉汁，亦称肉汤。为兽肉或鱼肉的浸出物。主要用于培养腐生性异养菌。通常用市售的肉汤，或将细菌学研究专用的肉膏配成0.3%的溶液，在其中加入0.5%的蛋白胨，有时还加入0.5%酵母膏、0.8%食盐等，调节pH至7左右制成基础培养基。在其中加入1.5%的琼脂制成的固体培养基，称为普通琼脂培养基。

Unit 10   Preparation and Purification of Heparin

In the 1950's there was a gradual shift to other tissues as a source of Heparin. A number of factors influenced this change. Aside from lungs being difficult to handle, most basic processes autolyzed the lung tissue as the first step. Not only was the tissue degraded, but in some instances the Heparin as well. Bacterial as well as enzymatic treatment uncontrolled can degrade Heparin. Also, the odor of rotting lungs created problems with surrounding communities. Very few, if any of the procedures included the methodology to remove extraneous Heparin-like compounds, and also the processing conditions utilized in many instances, partially degraded the heparin.

Intestinal mucosa of bovine or porcine origin was found to be a better and cleaner source. The mucosa is a side product of manufacturing sausage casings. In the U.S. there are few bovine casings made, hence porcine mucosa became the primary source. Most Heparin used today is of porcine origin. Aside from higher potencies gained, manufacturers were able to reduce the price of the finished material.

Basic processes today fall into four general classifications. The alkaline treatment usually frees most of the Heparin from the gross tissue and the salts aid in splitting bonds and to keep them from reforming. The salts present and the coagulation step in the first two processes removes much protein. The third process frees the Heparins, but at the same time releases amino acids, peptides, peptones[①], etc., which can complicate extraction procedures. Also, there is the possibility of partial heparin degradation. The fourth process aims for the total digestion of the raw material. A digestion on the acid side, and then digestion under alkaline conditions. Actually most processes today employ a combination of the different steps to obtain a filtrate with the desired characteristics.

The methodology of the isolation of the heparins from the filtrate has undergone the greatest changes. With the discovery of metachromasia[②] and the Heparin complexing qualities of quaternaries, conditions for isolating Heparin have become more mild. The quaternaries have proven to be the most popular to isolate the small quantities of Heparin present in the large quantities of tissue or filtrate. Particular ion exchange resins can act in the same manner as the quaternaries. Normally, one can expect approximately 5 pounds of finished heparin from 40,000 pounds of mucosa, which is a tank truck load.

These complexes can then be extracted with solvents or the use of salt solutions of varying concentrations to dissociate the Heparin complex. Alcohols, some ketones, or most any water miscible organic solvent can then effect precipitation of the crude Heparin. Depending on the basic process used, and how well they can be fractionated, these crude Heparins can carry U.S.P. anticoagulant potencies from 30 to 160 units per mg.

The basic crude process that had been employed for extraction and the accompanying extraneous factors determines the purification process. The purification process should be designed to purify and decolorize the Heparins in as gentle a manner as possible, and to minimize alterations in the molecule.

The oxidizing agents used in scheme 1, and the conditions employed should not in themselves react with heparin, but only act on color bodies or to remove unwanted impurities. Alkaline conditions have been shown to have no effect on potency.

CRUDE HEPARIN PREPARATION

INTESTINAL MUCOSA COLLECTION OR WHOLE INTESTINES

PRESERVATION (Bisulfite and/or Phenol)

HEPARIN MANUFACTURING PROCESSES

HIGH ALKALINE TREATMENT   MODERATE ALKALINE   HEAT & PRESSURE   PROTEOLYTIC DIGESTION

(pH 11~12)	(pH 8~9)		
Neutralization	Salts : Chlorides,	Hydrolysate	Acid Conditions
Salts : chlorides,	Sulfates, Nitrates,	Salts	(pH 2.5~4.0)
Nitrates, Phosphates	Phosphates	Filtration	Alkaline Conditions
Coagulation (95 C)	Coagulation		Filtration and/or Concentration
Filtration	Filtration		

AQUEOUS SOLUTION OF HEPARIN

COMPLEXING AGENTS

Quaternary NH_4 Cpds.

Primary or Sec. Amines

Ion Exchange Resins

Metachromatic Dyes

ISOLATION OF COMPLEX

Extraction or breaking of Complex with Solvents or Salt Solutions

(varying concentrations)

Precipitation with Alcohols-Ketones

(water miscible organic solvents)

CRUDE HEPARIN

Reducing agents are infrequently used. These compounds are primarily useful for removal of metallic salt contamination.

The use of complexing agents or ion exchange resins in a purification scheme serves to still further purify the crude Heparins. The crudes are almost always still contaminated with not just other heparin-like compounds such as chrondroitin sulfate, heparin sulfate, and dermatan sulfate, but protein residues (peptides, peptones, amino acids, etc.).

HEPARIN PURIFICATION
CRUDE HEPARIN

OXIDATION	REDUCING AGENTS	COMPLEXING AGENTS	ISOLATION COMPLEX
Permanganates	Hydrosulfites	Quaternary NH_4 Cpds.	a) Fractionation with Salts
Peroxides	Bisulfites	Primary or Sec. Amines	b) Extraction with water
Ozone		Simple Proteinsi	mmiscible solvents
Hypochlorites		Metachromatic Dyes	
Highly Alkaline	Acidic		Extraction of active
(pH 9~11)			principles with aqueous
Acidic-Alkaline			salt solutions OR highly
(pH 4~9)			alkaline conditions

FRACTIONATE & PRECIPITATE WITH WATER MISCIBLE SOLVENTS
PURIFIED HEPARIN

The purification scheme should also provide for the fractionation and the removal of very low molecular weight heparins as well as very high molecular weight materials in a consistent manner. There should be vary few variations from batch to batch. Selective salts and water miscible solvents allow one to gain the desired purity and potency.

As with the basic extraction from raw materials, there is a crossover by manufacturers of these three outlined processes. Most manufacturers use parts 1, 2, and 3 to obtain their purified material.

The extraction and the purification process should be designed to protect the Heparin that is present from the time of slaughter, as well as the differentiation and separation of Heparin and nonheparin components during purification.

In 1950 the U.S.P. heparin unit and the first international unit were listed as being the same. Since then there has been International Standard II and now International III. There have been numerous U.S.P. standards as well, and there has been a shift to heparins of different tissues as standards. Also, tests used to determine the unit have been varied, with many other types of assays included in international collaborative studies. It is highly probable that with all of these changes, that the continuity of the basic anticoagulant unit has been lost. The present U.S.P. compendial assay recognizes only the delay of clotting of the recalcified sheep plasma. There is no regard for any of the other factors in the plasma, or any of the other effects of Heparin, whether the product be an unfractionated or fractionated product.

The U.S.P. is in the process of considering changes in definitions of Heparin, contaminants such as dermatan, extraneous cations, and molecular weight limitations. It was noted years ago that as galactosamine went up, potency dropped.

This is based only on the present knowledge and state of recognized assays of Heparin. There is ongoing work to bring the international unit and the U.S.P. unit closer together. Presently there is an approximate 7 percent difference in the standards. As mentioned, the international unit is based on the average of a number of different types of clotting assays, whereas the current U.S.P. standard unit is the average of only U.S.P. type assays which were carried out in the international collaborative study.

Heparin will probably never be isolated as a homogeneous molecule, for if it exists in the native state as a proteoglycan, the individual chain lengths need not all to be of the same size. However, the most highly active, or a special specific activity function may exist as a definite entity.

The chemical and structural analysis of Heparin has proceeded rapidly, and for example the active site of action with antithrombin is known. However, there are many more valuzable effects of Heparin still to be determined by the peculiarities of the structure; action on thrombin, etc. We can now determine the amount of uronic acids, that is, the iduronic and glucuronic acids, hexosamines, acetyl content, and degree of sulfation which does have an effect on activity.

We still do not know the entire cause of side effects such as thrombocytopenia and platelet aggregation, or many of the other ill effects. It's possible that some of these side effects may be caused by a contaminant, but at the same time there are enough chemical differences between the different species of Heparin to possibly get varying effects. Also, within a given species there can be differences in structure depending on the particular manufacturing process.

For the future, the basic processes will remain about the same as today, with perhaps a more gentle extraction process by some manufacturers. Crude Heparin in the purification steps or perhaps the purified Heparin of today will be fractionated to a much higher degree, with the subsequent isolation of these fractions designed for particular effects. Whether these separations will be carried out utilizing ion exchange resins, charge density separations quaternary factionation, solvent partition, gel filtration or affinity chromatography will be the option of the manufacturer.

The identification and characterization of these Heparins coupled with assays of a specific nature, perhaps utilizing the chromogenic substances will enable these compounds to be designed for a particular therapeutic or prophylactic use and also covering different methods of administration for a desired effect. These newer compounds will enable not only injectable Heparins to be utilized, but the oral, intratracheal and topical use to be common for a beneficial effect.

Selected from Roger L. Lundblad, W. Virgil Brown, Kenneth G. Mann et al. ,*Chemistry and Biology of Heparin*, Elsevier North Holland, Inc, New York 1981, 9~17

Words and Expressions

heparin ['hepərin] *n.* 肝素
digestion [di'dʒestʃən] *n.* 消化力，消化作用，蒸煮（作用），煮解，加热浸提
plasma ['plæzmə] *n.* 血浆，乳浆
coagulation [kouˌægju'leiʃən] *n.* 凝结，凝结物

clot [klɔt] n. (血液等的) 凝块; v. (使) 凝结
autolyze [ˌɔːtəˈlaiz] v. 自溶, 自体溶解
decolorize [diːˈkʌləraiz] vt. 使脱色, 将……漂白
glucuronic acid 葡糖醛酸
anticoagulant [ˈæntikouˈægjulənt] n. 抗凝血剂
precipitation [priˌsipiˈteiʃən] n. 沉淀 (作用)
methodology [meθəˈdɔlədʒi] n. 方法论, 方法学
extraneous [eksˈtreniəs] a. 外部裂化, 新异反射; 外来的, 无关系的
intestinal [inˈtestinl] a. 肠的, 肠内的
mucosa [ˈmjuːkəusə] n. (复 mucosae [ˈmjuːkəusiː], -s) 粘膜 (粘液膜)
sausage [ˈsɔsidʒ] n. 香肠, 腊肠, 香肠状物
casing [ˈkeisiŋ] n. 包装, 保护性的外套
nitrate [ˈnaitreit] n. 硝酸盐 (酯)
phosphate [ˈfɔsfeit] n. 磷酸盐 (酯)
hydrolysate [haiˈdrɔliseit] n. 水解产物, 水解液
proteolytic [ˌproutiəˈlitik] a. (分) 解肮的, 水解蛋白质的
metachromatic [ˌmetəˈkroumətik] a. (温度变化引起的) 变色反应的
gross [grous] n. 总额; a. 总的, 毛重的
degrade [diˈgreid] v. (使) 降解, (使) 退化
degradation [ˌdegrəˈdeiʃən] n. 降解, 退化, 递降分解
permanganate [pəˈmæŋgənit] n. 高锰酸盐
peroxide [pəˈrɔksaid] n. 过氧化物
ozone [ˈouzoun] n. 臭氧
hypochlorite [ˌhaipəˈklɔːrait] n. 次氯酸盐
bisulfite [baiˈsʌlfait] n. 重亚硫酸盐, 酸性亚硫酸盐
chrondroitin n. 软骨素
dermatan sulfate 硫酸软骨素 B
crossover [ˈkrɔsouvə] n. 交叉, 天桥, 转线路
differentiation [difərenʃiˈeiʃən] n. 区别, 分化, 变异
compendium [kəmˈpendiəm] ([复] compendiums 或 compendia [kəmˈpendiə]) n. 概要, 概略
recalcify 再钙化
galactosamine [gəˌlækˈtəusəˌmiːn] n. 半乳糖胺, 氨基半乳糖
proteoglycan [proutiəˈglaikæn] n. (含) 蛋白多糖
antithrombin [ˈæntiˈθrɔmbin] n. 抗凝血酶
thrombin [ˈθrɔmbin] n. 凝血酶
uronic acid n. 糖醛酸
iduronic acid n. 艾杜糖醛酸
hexosamine [hekˈsɔsəmiːn] n. 氨基己糖, 己糖胺
thrombocytopenia [ˌθrɔmbəusaitəuˈpiːniə] n. 血小板减少 (症)

platelet ['pleitlit] *n.* 血小板，小板，小盘
aggregation [ægri'geiʃən] *n.* 聚合，集合，集合体
chromogenic [ˌkroumə'dʒenik] *a.* 发色的，发色体的
prophylactic [prɔfi'læktik] *n.* 预防药，避孕药；*a.* 预防疾病的
intratracheal [intrə'treikiəl] *a.* 气管内的

Notes

① peptone ['peptoun] *n.* 胨。蛋白质被酶、酸、碱等部分水解得到的非结晶性的、双缩脲反应阳性的多肽和寡肽类的混合物之总称。胨可作为培养异养细菌的氮源使用。

② metachromasia 异染性。指在用单一染料染细胞和组织时，染色部分被染成与染料色调不同的颜色。异染性染料有甲苯胺蓝、天青B、硫堇（碱性染料）和刚果红系染料（酸性染料）等。如单指异染性时，通常是指由碱性染料染色的，异染性与染料溶液和浓度有关，也可由于混杂了其他物质而引起。

Exercises

1. Answer the following questions:
    (1) What's the use of heparin?
    (2) Do you know in which organ exists heparin?
    (3) Do you have any idea that how many raw materials should be there for 1 pound of purified heparin?

2. Competing the following paragraph. Choose **Not More Than Three Words** from the passage for each answer.

Water is added to lung or liver homogenate and 2% NaOH and 3.6% $(NH_4)_2SO_4$ are added. The mixture is warmed to extract ^{1} _____ from the cells. Diluted H_2SO_4 is then added to pH 2.5, and the precipitation is suspended in water, pH 8.0, and digested with trypsin. Ethanol is added to 67 vol% and crude heparin is ^{2} _____ by adjusting the pH to 6. Crude heparin is then dissolved in weakly alkaline water, and the pH of the solution is adjusted to 5 with acetic acid. When adding 10% cadmium chloride to the solution, proteins precipitate and are removed by ^{3} _____. Upon addition of acetone to the filtrate and adjustment of the pH with acetic acid, heparin ^{4} _____. After redissolution and precipitation of the heparin complex with brucin, ^{5} _____ is set free by adding ammonia. It is then treated with a mixture of barium acetate and acetic acid to obtain the barium salt of heparin. The crystalline heparin barium is heated with Na_2CO_3 solution and precipitated $BaCO_3$ is filtered off. Ethanol is added to the solution to crystallize heparin sodium. The crystals are washed with ethanol and ether, and then dried.

A highly sultated mucopolysaccharide isolated from mammalian (chiefly beef) tissues, with blood ^{6} _____ activity. Heparin was first found in abundance in ^{7} _____, hence the name, but it is present in substantial amounts in the spleen, muscle, and lung as well.

Heparin is a complex organic acid (mucopolysaccharide) present in mammalian tissues and a strong ⁸ _____ of blood coagulation. Although the precise formula and structure of heparin are uncetain, it has been suggested that the formula for sodium heparinate, generally the form of the drug used in ⁹ _____, is $(C_{12}H_{16}NS_2Na_3)_{20}$ with a molecular weight of about 12,000. The commercial drug is derived from animal livers or lungs.

3. Put the following into Chinese:

clot	purification	digestion	precipitation
filtration	evaperation	extraction	peroxide
acidification	degradation	coagulation	adsorption
rearrangement	transformation	derivatization	distillation

4. Put the following into English:

羧酸	胰岛素	硝酸盐	磷酸盐
硫酸盐	次氯酸盐	柠檬酸盐	碳酸钠
乳酸盐	磺酸盐	酰基	硫磺
乙酸乙酯	酮	甲醇	羟基

Reading Material 10

Deoxyribonucleic Acid

Each DNA strand is a long polymeric molecule consisting of many individual nucleotides linked end to end. The great size and complexity of DNAs are indicated by their molecular weights, which commonly range in the hundreds of millions. DNA is the chemical constituent of the genes of an organism, and is thus the ultimate biochemical object of the study of genetics. Information is contained in the DNA in the form of the sequence of nucleotide building blocks in the nucleic acid chain.

Nucleotides The number of nucleotide building blocks in DNA is relatively small——only four nucleotides constitute the vast majority of DNA polymeric units. These are deoxyadenylic, deoxyguanylic, deoxycytidylic, and deoxythymidylic acids. For purposes of brevity, these nucleotides are symbolized by the letters A, G, C, and T, respectively. Each of these nucleotides consists of three fundamental chemical groups: a phosphoric acid group, a deoxyribose 5-carbon sugar group, and a nitrogenous base which is a derivative of either purine or pyrimidine. Some nucleotides contain the purine groups adenine (6-aminopurine) or guanine (2-amino-6-oxypurine), and some contain the pyrimidine groups cytosine (2-oxy-5-aminopyrimidine) or thymine (2,6-dioxy-6-methyl-pyrimidine). These are the only major bases found in most DNA, although in specific sequences certain methylated derivatives of these bases, such as 5-methyl cytosine or N^6-methyl adenine, can also be detected. In each nucleotide, these subunits are linked together in the following order: purine or pyrimidine base-ribose sugar-phosphoric acid. Removal of the phosphoric acid group leaves a base-sugar compound which is called a nucleoside. In each nucleoside the base is attached to the sugar through a bond from nitrogen at position 9 (for purines) or 3 (for pyrimidines) to carbon at position 1 of the sugar ring. The nucleosides and nucleotides are named for the base they contain as follows:

Base	Nucleoside	Nucleotide
Adenine	Adenosine	Adenylic acid
Guanine	Guanosine	Guanylic acid
Cytosine	Cytidine	Cytidylic acid
Thymine	Thymidine	Thymidylic acid
Uracil	Uridine	Uridylic acid

It is necessary to denote the position of the phosphoric acid residue when describing nucleotides. Nucleotides synthesized by cells for use as building blocks in nucleic acids all have phosphoric acid residues coupled to the $5'$ position of the ribose sugar ring, as shown for deoxyadenylic acid (deoxyadeno-sine-$5'$-phosphate). Upon hydrolysis of DNA, however, nucleotides can be produced which have phosphoric acid coupled to the $3'$ position of the sugar ring.

When DNA is hydrolyzed by using the enzyme deoxyribonuclease I. prepared from bovine pancreas, the principal products are oligonucleotides ending with $3'$-hydroxyl groups and $5'$-phosphoric acid groups. In contrast, when DNA is hydrolyzed by using the enzyme micrococcal nuclease, prepared from *Staphylococcus aureus*, the principal products are nucleotides or oligonucleotides ending with $3'$-phosphoric acid groups and $5'$-hydroxyl groups. Studies such as these led very early to the conclusion that in intact DNA the nucleotides were linked via phosphoryl groups which join the $3'$ position of one sugar group to the $5'$ position of the next sugar group. This $5'$-to-$3'$ linkage of nucleotides imparts a polarity to each DNA strand which is an important factor in the ability of DNA to form the three-dimensional structures necessary for its ability to replicate and to serve as a genetic template.

Sequences The sequence of nucleotide pairs in the DNA determines all of the hereditary characteristics of any given organism. The DNA acts as a template which is copied, through the process of transcription to make RNA. The RNA in turn serves as a template in a process by which its encoded information is translated to determine the amino acid sequences of proteins. Each amino acid in a protein chain is specified by a triplet of nucleotides (in RNA) or nucleotide pairs (in DNA) known as a codon. The set of correlations between the amino acids and their specifying codons is called the genetic code. Each gene which codes for a protein thus contains a sequence of triplet codons which corresponds to the sequence of amino acids in the polypeptide. This sequence of codons may be interrupted by intervening DNA sequences so that the entire coding sequence is not continuous. In addition to coding sequences, there also exist regulatory sequences, which include promoter and operator sequences involved in initiating gene transcription and terminator sequences involved in stopping transcription. Regulatory sequences are not necessarily made up of triplets, as are the codons. In order to study the regulation of a given gene, it is necessary to determine its nucleotide sequence.

There are several methods for sequencing DNA. Most of these methods employ radioactive end-labeling of one or both DNA strands, followed by either cleavage or extension of labeled strands to produce end-labeled fragments which terminate at nucleotides with specific bases. For example, one commonly used method involves labeling the 5' end of a DNA strand with ^{32}P-phosphate by using the enzyme polynucleotide kinase and γ-^{32}P-adenosinetriphosphate as a phosphate donor. Procedures are then used to end-labeled strands at each of the four nucleotides in turn. Polyacrylamide gel electrophoresis is then used to size the radioactive fragments, and the sequence of nucleotides from the labeled 5' end can be deduced.

The complete DNA sequences of several different genes, together with adjacent regulatory sequences, are now known. The first entire genome of any organism to be sequenced was that of the single-strand DNA phage ϕX174. This sequence of 5386 nucleotides was worked out by Fred Sanger and coworkers. One interesting aspect of this sequence is that it reveals the presence of overlapping genes coding for proteins. A single nucleotide sequence can code for more than one amino acid sequence, depending on the phasing with which the sequence is grouped into triplet codons during the process of protein synthesis. Specific start and stop signal codons are required to specify the phasing.

Selected from Sybil P Parker, *McGraw-Hill Encyclopedia of Chemistry*, 2nd ed., McGraw-Hill, Inc., 1992, 723~727

Words and Expressions

deoxyribonucleic acid　脱氧核糖核酸（即 DNA）
genetic　[dʒi'netik]　*a*. 遗传的，起源的
nucleotide　['njuːkliətaid]　*n*. 核苷酸
nucleic acid　核酸
deoxyadenylic acid　脱氧腺苷酸，脱氧腺嘌呤核苷酸
deoxyguanylic acid　脱氧鸟苷酸
deoxycytidylic acid　脱氧胞苷酸
deoxythymidylic acid　脱氧胸腺嘧啶核苷酸
phosphoric acid　磷酸
deoxyribose　[diːˈɔksiˌraibous]　*n*. 脱氧核糖
purine　['pjuəriːn]　*n*. 嘌呤
pyrimidine　[pai'rimidiːn]　*n*. 嘧啶
adenine　['ædəniːn]　*n*. 腺嘌呤（也即 6-aminopurine 6-氨基嘌呤）
guanine　['gwɑːniːn]　*n*. 鸟嘌呤（也即 2-amino-6-oxypurine 2-氨基-6-氧代嘌呤）
cytosine　['saitəsiːn]　*n*. 胞（核）嘧啶（也即 2-oxy-5-aminopyrimidine 2-氧-5-氨基嘧啶）
thymine　['θaimiːn]　*n*. 胸腺嘧啶（也即 2,6-dioxy-6-methyl-pyrimidine 2,6-二氧-6-甲基嘧

啶)

subunit [sʌb'juːnit] n. 子（分，亚）组，子（亚，次一级的）单位，子单元，副族
ribose sugar n. 核糖
nucleoside ['njuːkliəsaid] n. 核苷
adenosine [ə'denəsiːn] n. 腺苷，腺嘌呤核苷
adenylic acid 腺苷酸，腺嘌呤核苷酸
guanosine ['gwɑːnəsin] n. 鸟嘌呤核苷，鸟苷
guanylic acid 鸟苷酸
cytidine ['saitədin] n. 胞啶，胞嘧啶核苷
cytidylic acid 胞苷酸
thymidine ['θaimidiːn] n. 胸腺嘧啶核苷
thymidylic acid 胸腺嘧啶核苷酸
uracil ['juərəsil] n. 尿嘧啶，二氧嘧啶
uridine [juəridi(ː)n] n. 尿苷
uridylic acid 尿苷酸
deoxyribonuclease [diːˈɔksiˌraibouˈnjuːkliːis] n. 脱氧核糖核酸酶
template ['templeit] n. 模板
bovine pancreas 牛胰腺
oligonucleotide [ɔligəuˈnjukliːətaid] n. 低（聚）核苷酸，寡核苷酸
micrococcal nuclease 微球菌核酸酶
Staphylococcus aureus 金黄色葡萄球菌
genome ['dʒiːnoum] n. 基因组，染色体组
encode [inˈkəud] n. 把（电文等）译成电码（或密码），编（译）码
codon ['koudən] n. 密码子，基码
kinase ['kaineis] n. 激酶，致活酶
adenosinetriphosphate n. 三磷酸腺苷
polyacrylamide n. 聚丙烯酸酰胺
electrophoresis [iˈlektroufəˈriːsis] n. 电泳现象
phage [feidʒ] n. 噬菌体

PART 3 INDUSTRIAL PHARMACY

Unit 11 Tablets (The Pharmaceutical Tablets Dosage Form)

Role in Therapy

The oral route of drug administration is the most important method of administering drugs for systemic effects[①]. Except in cases of Insulin therapy, the parenteral route is not routinely used for self-administration of medication[②]. The topical route of administration has only recently been employed to deliver drugs to the body for systemic effects, with two classes of marketed products: Nitroglycerin for the treatment of angina and scopolamine for the treatment of motion sickness[③]. Other drugs are certain to follow, but the topical route of administration is limited in its ability to allow effective drug absorption for systemic drug action. The parenteral roue of administration is important in treating medical emergencies in which a subject is comatose or cannot swallow, and in providing various types of maintenance therapy for hospitalized patients. Nevertheless, it is probable that at least 90% of all drugs used to produce systemic effects are administered by the oral rote. When a new drug is discovered, one of the first questions a pharmaceutical company asks is whether or not drug can be effectively administered for its intended effect by the oral route. If it cannot, the drug is primarily relegated to administration in a hospital setting or physician's office. If patient self- administration cannot be achieved, the sales of the drug constitute only a small fraction of what the market would be otherwise. Of drugs that are administered orally, solid oral dosage forms represent the preferred class of product. The reasons for this preference are as follows. Tablets and capsules represent unit dosage forms in which one usual dose of the drug has been accurately placed. By comparison, liquid oral dosage forms, such as syrups, suspensions, emulsions, solutions, and elixirs, are usually designed to contain one dose of medication in 5 to 30 ml. The patient is then asked to measure his or her own medication using a teaspoon, tablespoon, or other measuring device. Such dosage measurements are typically in error by a factor ranging from 20% to 50% when the drug is self-administered by the patient[④].

  Liquid oral dosage forms have other disadvantages and limitations when compared with tablets. They are much more expensive to ship (one liquid dosage weighs 5 g or more versus 0.25 to 0.4 g for the average tablet), and breakage or leakage during shipment is a more serious problem with liquids than with tablets. Taste masking of the drug is often a problem (if the drug is in solution even partially). In addition, liquids are less portable and require much more space per number of doses on the pharmacist's shelf. Drugs are in general less stable (both chemically and physically) in liquid form than in a dry state and expiration dates tend to be shorter. Careful attention is required to assure that the product will not allow a heavy microbiologic burden to develop on standing or under normal conditions of use once opened (preservation requirements). There are basically three reasons for having liquid dosage forms of a drug: (1) The liquid form is what the public has come to expect for certain types of products (e. g. cough medicines). (2) The product is more effective in a liquid form (e. g. , many adsorbents and antacids). (3) The drug(s) are used fairly commonly by young children or the elderly, who have trouble swallowing the solid oral dosage forms.

Properties

The objective of the design and manufacture of the compressed tablet is to de liver orally the correct amount of drug in the proper form at or over the proper time and in the desired location, and to have its chemical integrity protected to that point. Aside from the physical and chemical properties of the medicinal agent(s) to be formulated into a tablet, the actual physical design, manufacturing process, and complete chemical makeup of the tablet can have a profound effect on the efficacy of the drug(s) being administered.

A tablet (1) should be an elegant product having its own identity while being free of defects such as chips, cracks, discoloration, contamination, and the like; (2) should have the strength to withstand the rigors of mechanical shocks[5] encountered in its production, packaging, shipping, and dispensing; and (3) should have the chemical and physical stability to maintain its physical attribute over time. Pharmaceutical scientists now understand that various physical properties of tablets can undergo change under environmental or stress conditions, and that physical stability, through its effect on bioavailability in particular, can be of more significance and concern in some tablet systems than chemical stability.

On the other hand, the tablet (1) must be able to release the medicinal agent(s) in the body in a predictable and reproducible manner and (2) must have a suitable chemical stability over time so as not to allow alteration of the medicinal agent(s). In many instances, these sets of objectives are competing. The design a of tablet that emphasizes only the desired medicine effects may produce a physically inadequate product. The design of a tablet emphasizing only the physical aspects may produce tablets of limited and varying therapeutic effects. As one example of this point, Meyer and associates present information on 14 Nitrofurantoin products, all of which passed the compendia physical requirements, but showed statistically, significant bioavailability differences.

Selected from Lachman Leon et al. , *The Theory and Practice of Industrial Pharmacy*, 3 rd ed. , Lea and Febiger, Philadelphia, 1986.

Words and Expressions

therapy ['θerəpi]   *n.* 治疗
administration [ədminis'treiʃən]   *n.* 管理，（药的）服法
Insulin ['insju:lin]   *n.* 胰岛素

parenteral [pæˈrentərəl] a. 非肠道的
topical [ˈtɔpikəl] a. (医) 局部的
Nitroglycerin [ˈnaitrəuˈglisərin] n. 硝酸甘油,三硝酸甘油酯
angina [ænˈdʒainə] n. (医) 心绞痛
scopolamine [skəuˈpɔləmin] n. 莨菪胺
comatose [ˈkəumətəus] a. 昏迷的,麻木的
swallow [ˈswɔləu] n. 吞咽,咽喉,食道; vt. vi 吞下,咽下
relegate [ˈreligeit] vt. 驱逐的,使降级,把……归类
tablet [ˈtæblit] n. 药片,片剂
capsules [ˈkæpsjuːls] n. 胶囊,囊
dosage [ˈdəusidʒ] n. 配药,剂量,用量,一剂,一服,一次分发量
syrup [ˈsirəp] n. 糖浆
suspension [səsˈpenʃən] n. 悬浮液
emulsion [iˈmʌlʃən] n. 乳浊液,乳剂
elixir [iˈlikə] n. (药) 甘香酒剂
versus [ˈvəːsəs] prep. 与……相对
breakage [ˈbreikidʒ] n. 破损
leakage [ˈliːkidʒ] n. 漏,泄漏,漏出物
taste masking [teist mɑːskiŋ] n. 味觉模糊
expiration [ekspaiəˈreiʃən] n. 呼气,吐气
microbiologic [ˈmaikrəubaiɔlədʒik] a. 微生物学的
preservation [prezəːˈveiʃən] n. 保存,储藏,防腐
contamination [kɔnˈtəmineiʃən] n. 污染
rigor [ˈraigə] n. 僵硬
dispens [ˈdispens] vt. 分配 调剂,配药
bioavailability [baiəuəˈveiləbiliti] n. 生物利用度
therapeutic [θerəˈpjuːtik] a. 治疗学的
nitrofurantoin [naitrəufjuəˈrætɔin] n. 硝化呋喃妥英

Notes

① systemic effects 系统效应(全身效应)。
② self-administration of medication 自我服药。
③ motion sickness 运动病,眩晕病。
④ …by the Patient. Such dosage measurements are typically in error by… 全句可译为:
"病人自己服药时,采用这种服药方法是典型的,误差范围20%到50%"。
⑤ …to withstand the rigors of mechanical shocks… 经得住机械撞击的考验。

Exercise

1. Answer the following questions.

(1) How many kinds of the route of drug administration are there?

(2) Can you present these usual dosage forms of the drug that are administered orally?

　　(3) How is an evaluation of a tablet's properties made?

2. Complete the passage below.

　　Solid _____ dosage forms are delivery systems presented as solid dose units readily administered by mouth. The group includes _____, _____, _____, and _____, as well as bulk or unit-dose powder and granules. The group constitutes the most popular form of presentation, and tablets and capsules account for the greatest number of preparations in this category. The prime reasons for this popularity includes: easy of accurate (yet versatile) _____, good _____ and _____ stability, competitive unit production costs, and an elegant distinctive appearance resulting in a high level of patient acceptability. Among the potential disadvantages are irritant effects on the gastrointestinal mucosa by some solids and the possibility of bioavailability problems caused by the fact that both _____ (in most causes) and _____ must take place before the drug is a available for absorption.

3. Put the following into Chinese.

absorption	action	treat	medication
medicine	pharmaceutical	compress	quality
quantity	uniformity	measure	composite

4. Put the following into English.

片剂	胶囊	糖浆	悬浮液
乳剂	溶液	酊剂	丸剂
稀释剂	黏合剂	崩介剂	润滑剂
香味剂	甜味剂		

Reading Material 11

Evaluation

To design tablets and later monitor tablet production quality, quantitative evaluations and assessments of a tablet's chemical, physical, and bioavailability properties must be made. Not only could all three property classes have a significant stability profile, but the stability profiles may be interrelated, i.e. chemical breakdown or interactions between tablet components may alter physical tablet properties, greatly changing the bioavailability of a tablet system.

　　General Appearance. The general appearance of a table, its visual identity and overall "elegance." Is essential for consumer acceptance, for control of lot-to-lot uniformity and general tablet-to-tablet uniformity[①], and for monitoring trouble-free manufacturing. The control of the general appearance of a tablet involves the measurement of a number of attributes such as a tablet's size, shape, color, presence or absence of an odor, taste, surface texture, physical flaws and consistency, and legibility of any identifying markings.

Size and Shape. The size and shape of the tablet can be dimensionally described, monitored, and controlled. A compressed tablet's shape and dimensions are determined by the tooling during the compression process. The thickness of a tablet is the only dimensional variable related to the process. At a constant compressive load, tablet thickness varies with changes in die fill, with particle size distribution and packing of the particle mix being compressed, and with tablet weight, while with a constant die fill, thickness varies with variations in compressive load. Tablet thickness is consistent batch-to-batch[2] or within a batch only if the tablet granulation or powder blend is adequately consistent in particle size and size distribution, if the punch tooling is of consistent length, and if the tablet press is clean and in good working order.

Hardness and Friability. Tablets require a certain amount of strength, or hardness and resistance to friability, to withstand mechanical shocks of handling in manufacture, packaging, and shipping.

In addition, tablets should be able to withstand reasonable abuse when in the hands of the consumer, such as bouncing about[3] in a woman's purse in a partially filled prescription bottle. Adequate tablet hardness and resistance to powdering and friability are necessary requisites for consumer acceptance. More recently, the relationship of hardness to tablet disintegration, and perhaps more significantly, to the drug dissolution release rate, has become apparent. The monitoring of tablet hardness is especially important for drug products that possess real or potential bioavilability problems or that are sensitive to altered dissolution release profiles as a function of the compressive force employed.

Weight variation. With a tablet designed to contain a specific amount of drug in a specific amount of tablet formula the weight of the tablet being made is routinely measured to help ensure that a tablet contain the proper amount of drug. In practice, composite samples of tablets (usually 10) are taken and weighed throughout the compression process. The composite weight divided by 10, however, provide an average weight but contains the usual problems of averaged values. Within the composite sample that has an acceptable average weight, there could be tablets excessively overweight or underweight. To help alleviate this problem the United States Pharmacopoeia (USP)/National Formulary (NF)[4] provides limits for the permissible variations in the weights of individual tablets expressed as a percentage of the average weight of the sample[5]. The USP weight variation test is run by weighing 20 tablets individually, calculating the average weight, and comparing the individual tablet weights to the average. The tablets meet the USP test if no more than 2 tablets are outside the percentage limit and if no tablet differs by more than two time the percentage limit[6]. The weight variation tolerances for uncoated tablets differ depending on average tablet weight.

The weight variation test would be a satisfactory method of determining the drug content uniformity of tablets if the tablets were all or essentially all (90%~95%) active ingredient, or if the uniformity of the drug distribution in the granulation or powder from which the tablets were made were perfect. For tablets such as Aspirin, which are usually 90% or more active ingredient, the +/−5% weight variation should come close to defining true potency and content uniformity (95%~105% of the label strength)if the average tablet weight is close to the theoretic average weight. The weight variation test is clearly not sufficient to assure uniform potency of tablets of moderate or low-dose drugs, in which excipients make up the bulk of the tablet weight.

The potency of tablets is expressed in terms of grams, milligrams, or micrograms (for some potent drugs) of drug per tablet and is given as the label strength of the product. Official compendia or other standards provide an acceptable potency range around the label potency. For highly potent. Low-dose drugs such as Digitoxin, this range is usually not less than 90% and not more than 110% of the labeled amount. For most other larger-dose drugs in tablet form, the official potency range that is permitted is not less than 95% and not more than 105% of the labeled amount.

Disintegration. A generally accepted maxim is that for a drug to be readily available to the body, it must be in solution. For most tablets, the first important step toward solution is break down of the tablet into smaller particles or granules, a process known as *disintegration*. The time that it takes a tablet to disintegrate is measured in a device described in the USP/NF.

Research has established that one should not automatically expect a correlation between disintegration and dissolution. However, since the dissolution of a drug from the fragmented tablet appears to control partially or completely the appearance of the drug in the blood, disintegration is still used as a guide to the formulator in the preparation of an optimum tablet formula and as an in-process control test to ensure lot-to-lot uniformity.

Selected from Lachman Leon et al. *The Theory and Practice of Industrial Pharmacy*, 3 rd ed., Lea and Febiger, Philadelphia, 1986.

Words and Expressions

friability ['fraiə'biliti] n. 易碎性，脆性
shock [ʃɔk] n. 冲击，打击，休克，中风
abuse [ə'bju:z] vt. 滥用
bouncing [bausiŋ] a. 强壮的，肌肉丰满的
prescription [priskri'pʃən] n. 药方，处方
disintegration [dis'intigreiʃən] n. 崩解
compressive [kəm'presiv] a. 压缩的；n. 有压力的
weight variation [weit vɛəri'eiʃən] n. 重量差异
overweight a. 过重的
underweight a. 过轻的
alleviate [ə'li:vieit] vt. 减轻，缓和
permissable [pə:'misəbl] a. 可允许的，许可的

maxim ['mæksim] n. 格言，准则，谚语
breakdown [breikdaun] n. 崩解～into～
granule ['grænju:l] n. 颗粒
optimum ['ɔptiməm] n. 最适条件；a. 最适的
in-process control 过程中控制
uniformity [ju:ni'fɔ:miti] n. 一样，一致(性)，均匀(性)

Notes

① lot-to-lot uniformity 批与批的均一性。
   tablet-to-tablet uniformity 片与片的均一性。
② batch-to-batch 生产批号间。
③ bounce about 蹦蹦跳跳。
④ United States Pharmacopoeia (U.S.P) 美国药典。
   National Formulary (NF) （美国）国家处方集。
⑤ expressed as a percentage of the average weight of the sample 以样品的平均重量百分比表示。
⑥ …if no more than 2 tablets are outside the percentage limit and if no tablet differs by more than 2 times the percentage limit. 如果超出平均限量的药片只不过2片，并且片重不大于平均限量的2倍……

Unit 12 Manufacture of Tablets

Tablet Design and Formulation
The three basic methods of tablet manufacture have been previously detailed, the desirable proper ties and required features of granulations and tablets defined, and the interrelationships between many of these properties and the processing and machine variables noted. Regardless of how tablets are manufactured, conventional oral tablets for ingestion usually contain the same classes of components in addition to the active ingredients, which are one or more agents functioning as (1) a diluent, (2) a binder or an adhesive, (3) a disintegrant, and (4) a lubricant. Some tablet formulations may additionally require a flow promoter. Other more optional components include colorants, and in chewable tablets[①], favors and sweeteners. All nondrug components of a formula are termed excipients.

Tablet Granulations
Basic Characteristics

The characteristics of a tablet that make it a popular dosage form, e.g., compactness, physical stability, rapid production capability, chemical stability, and efficacy, are in general dictated primarily by the qualities of the granulation from which it is made. Basically stated, materials intended for compaction into a tablet must possess two characteristics: fluidity and compressibility. To a great extent, these properties are required by the compression machine design. As previously discussed, good flow properties are essential for the transport of the material through the hopper, into and through the feed frame, and into the dies. Tablet materials should therefore be in a physical form that flows smoothly and uniformly. The ideal physical form for this purpose is spheres, since these offer minimum contact surfaces between themselves and with the walls of the machine parts. Unfortunately, most materials do not easily form spheres; However, shapes that approach spheres improve flowability. Therefore granulation is in part the pharmaceutical process that attempts to improve the flow of powdered materials by forming spherelike or regularly shaped aggregates called granules. The need to assess the shape of particles and their relative regularity or approximation to spheres has led to the development of equations whereby certain "factors" can be calculated to provide quantitative comparisons of different particle shapes. By measuring particle surface area (S), volume (V) and a projected equivalent diameter (d_p), a volume shape factor (a_v), a surface shape factor (a_s), and a shape coefficient (a_{vs}) can be calculated using equations (1) to (3) for quantitative work.

$$a_s = S/d_p^2 \tag{1}$$

$$a_v = V/d_p^2 \tag{2}$$

$$a_{vs} = a_s/a_v \tag{3}$$

The shape coefficient for a sphere is 6. As a particle becomes more irregular in shape, the value of a increases. For a cube, a is equal to 6.8.

The other desirable characteristic, compressibility, is the property of forming a stable, compact mass when pressure is applied. The requisite physical properties and the forces that hold the tablet together are discussed in Chapter 4. "Compression and Consolidation of Powdered Solids." The consideration of compressibility in this discussion is limited to stating that granulation is also the pharmaceutical process that converts a mixture of powders, which have poor cohesion, into aggregates capable of compaction.

Manufacture of Granulations

Dry Manufacturing Methods

The manufacture of granulations for tablet compression may follow one or a combination of three established methods: the dry methods of direct compression, compression granulation, and wet granulation[2].

Wet Granulation

The wet granulation technique uses the same preparatory and finishing steps (screening or milling, and mixing) as the two previously discussed granulation techniques. The unique portions of wet granulation process involve the wet massing of the powders, wet sizing or milling, and drying.

The theory, equipment, and methods associated with drying are discussed in Chapter 3. Methods. Wet granulation forms the granules by binding the powders together with an adhesive, instead of by compaction. The wet granulation technique employs a solution, suspension, or slurry containing a binder, which is usually added to the powder mixture; however, the binder may be incorporated dry into the powder mix, and the liquid may be added by itself.

The method of introducing the binder depends on its solubility and on the components of the mixture. Since, in general, the mass should merely be moist rather than wet or pasty, there is a limit to the amount of solvent that may be employed. Therefore, when only a small quantity is permissible, the binder is blended in with the dry powders initially; when a large quantity is required, the binder is usually dissolved in the liquid. The solubility of the binder also has an influence on the choice of methods, since the solution should be fluid enough to disperse readily in the mass.

The wet screening process involves converting the moist mass into coarse, granular aggregate by passage through a hammer mill or oscillating granulator, equipped with screens having large perforations. The purpose is to further consolidate granules, increase particle contact points, and increase surface area to facilitate drying. Overly wet material dries slowly and forms hard aggregates, which tend to turn to powder during subsequent dry milling. There are many instances in which wet milling may be omitted, with considerable saving of time. The formulator should be alert these opportunities and not follow the old method blindly.

A drying process is required in all wet granulation procedures to remove the solvent that was used in forming the aggregates and the reduce the moisture content to an optimum level of concentration within the granules. During drying, interparticulate bonds result from fusion or recrystallization and curing of the binding agent, with van der Waals forces playing a significant role.

After drying, the granulation is screened again. The size of the screen depends upon the grinding equipment used and the size of the tablet to be made.

Selected from Lachman Leon et al. The Theory and Practice of Industrial Pharmacy,
3rd ed., Lea and Febiger, Philadelphia, 1986.

Words and Expressions

granulation ['grænjuːleiʃən] n. 成粒，制粒
ingestion [in'dʒestʃən] n. 咽下，吸收，摄取
ingredient [in'griːdjənt] n. 组分，配料，成分
diluent ['diljuənt] a. 稀释的；n. 稀释剂
binder ['baidə] n. 粘合剂
adhesive [əd'hiːsiv] n. 胶粘剂，粘合剂
disintegrant [dis'intigrənt] n. 崩释剂
lubricant ['ljuːbrikənt] n. 润滑剂
colorant ['kʌlə'rənt] n. 颜料，着色剂
flavor ['fleivə] n. 调味剂，香味剂
sweetener ['swiːtenə] n. 甜味剂
excipient [ik'sipiənt] n. 赋形剂
dictate [dik'teit] n. 指令，指示
fluidity [fljuː'iditi] n. 流动性
compressibility [kəmpresi'biliti] n. 可压缩性
hopper ['hɔpə] n. 漏斗
die [dai] n. 冲磨，磨具
flowability [fləuebiliti] n. 可流动性
aggregate ['ægrigit] n. 聚集；a. 聚集的
screening [skriːniŋ] n. 筛网，过筛
unique [juː'niːk] a. 唯一的，均一的，独特的
mass [mæs] vt. 聚集；n. 团
sizing [saiziŋ] n. 填料，上浆
compaction [kɔm'pækʃən] n. 压紧
slurry [sləːri] n. 浆
pasty [peisti] a. 面糊的
planetary mixer a. 齿轮的
chopper n. 粉碎机
hydraulic bowl a. 水压的，液压的
perforations [pəfə'reiʃən] n. 穿孔
overly ['əuvəli] adv. 过度地，极度地
fusion [fjuːʒən] n. 熔化，熔解

Notes

① chewable tablets 咀嚼片。
② 1) direct compression 直接压片法（包括结晶或粉末直接压片）。它们对原辅料的流动性和可压性有一定要求。
   2) compression granulation 挤压制粒法，如干法制粒（一般应用于对湿热不稳定的药物）。
   3) wet granulation 湿法制粒，常用的生产方法之一。（一般包括制软材，制湿颗粒，干燥和整粒等生产过程）。

Exercise

1. Answer the following questions:
   (1) Have you ever known the general methods and processes of the manufacture of tablet?
   (2) What is the importance of manufacture granulation which tables are made from?
   (3) What components are included in general excipients in a tablet's formula?
   (4) Have you understood the principle of tablet compression operation?

2. Complete the passage below

   One of the commonly used dosage forms oral is _____, the components in tablet's formulation include in general _____, _____, _____, _____, and _____ the granulation is an important process of tablet's manufacture, the characteristics of a tablet depend basically on the qualities of the granulation, _____ must possess two characteristic: _____ and _____. The _____ is a commonly used method of granulation, which involves _____ of the powders, _____ or _____ and _____. The ideal physical form of tablet materials is _____. Unfortunately, most materials do not easily form _____, which must be processed by granulation for forming sphere like or regularly shaped _____.

3. Put the following into Chinese.

   formulation   design   fluidity   compressibility
   screening   mill   mix   dry
   adherive   compaction

4. Put the following into English

   粒子   形状   不规则的   固化
   成团   聚集   挤压   压片

5. There are three essential methods of the manufacture of granulation for tablet compression, what are they?

Reading Material 12

Solids Mixing and Drying

Mixing

The theory of solids mixing has not advanced much beyond the most elementary of concepts and, consequently, is far behind that which has been developed for fluids. This lag can be attributed primarily to an incomplete understanding of the ways in which particulate variables influence such systems and to the complexity of the problem itself.

When viewed superficially, such multiparticulate solids as pharmaceutical bulk powders or tablet granulations are seen to behave somewhat like fluids. That is, to the casual observer, they appear to exhibit fluid-like flow when they are poured from one container to another and seem to occupy a more or less constant bulk volume. Dissimilar powders can be intimately mixed at the particulate level much like miscible liquids, at least in principle. Contrary to these similarities with fluids, however, the mixing of solids presents problems that are quite different from those associated with miscible liquids. The latter, once mixed, do not readily separate and can be poured, pumped, and otherwise subjected to normal handling without concern for unmixing. In addition, they can be perfectly mixed in any standard equipment, with the primary concerns being power efficiency and time required. In contrast, well-mixed powders are often observed to undergo substantial segregation during routine handling following the mixing operation. Such segregation of particulate solids can occur during mixing a s well and is perhaps the central problem associated with the mixing and handling of these materials.

Drying

There is hardly a pharmaceutical plant engage in the manufacture of tablets or capsules that does not contain dryers. Unfortunately, the operation of drying is so taken for granted that efforts for achieving increased efficiency in the production of tablets do not include a study of drying. This chapter introduces the industrial pharmacist to the theory and fundamental concepts of drying.

Definition. For the purpose of this discussion, drying is defined as the removal of a liquid from a material by the application of heat, and is accomplished by the transfer of a liquid from a surface into an unsaturated vapor phase. This definition applies to the removal of a small amount of water from moisture-bearing table salt as well as to the recovery of salt from the sea by evaporation. Drying and evaporation are distinguishable merely by the relative quantities of liquid removed from the solid.

There are, however, many nonthermal methods of drying. For example, the expression of a solid to remove liquid(the squeezing of a wetted sponge),the extraction of liquid from a solid by use of a solvent, the adsorption of water from a solvent by the use of desiccants (such as anhydrous calcium chloride), the absorption of moisture from gases by passage through a sulfuric acid column, and the desiccation of moisture from a solid by placing it in a sealed container with a moisture-removing material (silica gel in a bottle).

Purpose. Drying is most commonly used in pharmaceutical manufacturing as a unit process in the preparation of granules, which can be dispensed in bulk or converted into tablets or capsules. Another application is found in the processing of materials, e. g.. The preparation of dried aluminum hydroxide, the spray drying of lactose, and the preparation of powdered extracts. Drying also can be used to reduce bulk and weight, thereby lowering the cost of transportation and storage. Other uses include aiding in the preservation of animal and vegetable drugs by minimizing mold and bacterial growth in moisture-laden material and facilitating comminution by making the dried substance far more friable than the original, water-containing drug.

Tablet compression operation

Tablet compression machines

Tablets are made by compressing a formulation containing a drug or drugs with excipients on stamping machines called *presses*. Tablet compression machines or tablet presses are designed with the following basic components:

1. Hopper(s) for holding and feeding granulation to be compressed.
2. Dies that define the size and shape of the tablet.
3. Punches for compressing the granulation within the dies.
4. Cam tracks for guiding the movement of the punches.
5. A feeding mechanism for moving granulation from the hopper into the dies.

Tablet presses are classified as either single punch or multi-station rotary presses.

Multi-station presses are termed *rotary* because the head of the tablet machine that holds upper punches, dies, and lower punches in place rotates. As the head rotates, the punches are guided up and down by fixed cam tracks, which control the sequence of filling, compression, and ejection. The portions of the head that hold the upper and lower punches are called the upper and lower puncher turrets respectively, and the portion holding the dies is called the die table. At the start of compression cycle granulation stored in a hopper (not shown), empties into the feed-fame (A), which has several interconnected compartments. These compartments spread the granulation over a wide area to provide time for the dies (B) to fill. The pull-down cam (C) guides the lower punches to the bottom of their vertical travel, allowing the dies to overfill. The punches then pass over a weight control cam (E), which reduces the fill in the dies to the desired amount. A wipe-off blade (D) at the end of the feed-frame removes the excess granulation and directs it around the turret and back into to the front of the feed-frame. Next, the lower punches travel over the lower compression roll (F) while simultaneously the upper punches ride beneath the upper compression roll (G). The upper punches enter a fixed distance into the dies, while the lower punches are raised to squeeze and compact the granulation within the dies. To regulate the upward movement of the lower punches, the height of the lower pressure roll is changed. After the moment of compression, the upper punches are with-dawn as they follow the upper punch raising cam (H); the lower punches ride up the cam (1), which brings the tablets flush with or slightly above the surface of the dies. The exact position is determined by a threaded bolt called the ejector knob. The tablets strike a sweep-off blade affixed to the front of the feed-frame (A) and slide down a chute into a receptacle. At the same time, the lower punches re-enter the pulldown cam (C), and the cycle is repeated.

In-Process Quality Control

During the compression of tablets, in-process tests are routinely run to monitor the process, including tests for tablet weight, weight variation, hardness, thickness, disintegration, and various evaluations of elegance. The in-process tests are performed by production and/or quality control (QC) personnel. In addition, many in-process tests are performed during product development by the formulator. Such testing during development has become increasingly important in recent years for process validation purposes. The data supplied by the formulator is usually employed by QC personnel to establish the test limits. At the start-up of a tablet compression operation, the identity of the granulation is verified, along with the set-up of the proper tabletting machine and proper tooling.

Selected from Lachman Leon et al. *The Theory and Practice of Industrial Pharmacy*, 3rd ed., Lea and Febiger, Philadelphia, 1986.

Words and Expression

multiparticulate [mʌltipə'tikjulit] n. 多颗粒
intimately [intimitəli] ad. 密切地
miscible [misibl] a. 易溶合的
segregation ['segrigeiʃən] n. 分离
unsaturated [ʌn'seitjuretid] a. 不饱和的
evaporation [ivæpə'reiʃən] n. 蒸发
nonthermal a. 无热量的
extraction [iks'trækʃən] n. 提取，萃取
desiccant [desi'kənt] n. 干燥剂
desiccation [desi'keiʃən] n. 干燥
dispense ['dispens] vt. 分发，分配
friable [fraiəbl] a. 易碎的，脆的
validation [væli'deiʃən] n. 确认

Unit 13   Sterile Products

Sterile Products

Sterile products are dosage forms of therapeutic agents that are free of viable microorganisms. Principally, these include parenteral, ophthalmic, and irrigating preparations. Of these, parenteral products are unique among dosage forms of drugs because they are injected through the skin or mucous membranes into internal body compartment. Thus, because they have circumvented the highly efficient first line of body defense, the skin and mucous membranes, they must be free from microbial contamination and from toxic components as well as possess an exceptionally high level of purity. All components and processes involved in the preparation of these products must be selected and designed to eliminate, as much as possible, contamination of all types, whether of physical, chemical, or microbiologic origin.

Preparations[1] for the eye, though not introduced into internal body cavities, are placed in contact with tissues that are very sensitive to contamination. Therefore, similar standards are required for ophthalmic preparations[2].

Irrigating solutions[3] are now also required to meet the same standards as parenteral solutions because during an irrigation procedure, substantial amounts of these solutions can enter the bloodstream directly through open blood vessels of wounds or abraded mucous membranes. Therefore, the characteristics and standards presented in this chapter for the production of large-volume parenteral solutions apply equally to irrigating solutions.

Sterile products are most frequently solutions or suspensions, but may even be solid pellets for tissue implantation. The control of a process to minimize contamination for a small quantity of such a product can be achieved with relative ease. As the quantity of product increases, the problems of controlling the process to prevent contamination multiply. Therefore, the preparation of sterile products has become a highly specialized area in pharmaceutical processing. The standards established, the attitude of personnel, and the process control must be of a superior level.

vehicles

By far the most frequently employed vehicle for sterile products is water, since it is the vehicle for all natural body fluids. The superior quality required for such use is described in the monograph on Water for Injection in the USP. Requirements may be even more stringent for some products, however.

One of the most inclusive tests for the quality of water is the total solids content, a gravimetric evaluation of the dissociated and undissociated organic and inorganic substances present in the water. However, a less time-consuming test, the elevtrolytic measurement of conductivity of the water, is the one most frequently used. Instantaneous measurements can be obtained by immersing electrodes in the water and measuring the specific conductance, a measurement that depends on the ionic content of the water. The conductance may be expressed by the meter scale as conductivity in micromhos, resistance in megohms[4], or ionic content as parts per million (ppm)[5] of sodium chloride. The validity of this measurement as an indication of the purity of the water is inferential in that methods of producing high-purity water, such as distillation and reverse osmosis, can be expected to remove undissociated substances along with those that are dissociated. Undissociated substances such as pyrogens, however, could be present in the absence of ions and not be disclosed by the test. Therefore, for contaminants other than ions, additional tests should be performed.

Additional tests for quality of Water for Injection with permitted limits are described in the USP monographs. When comparing the total solids permitted for Water for Injection with that for Sterile Water for Injection, one will note that considerably higher values are permitted for Sterile Water for Injection. This is necessary because the latter product has been sterilized, usually by a thermal method, in a container that has dissolved to some extent in the water. Therefore, the solids content will be greater than for the nonsterilized product. On the other hand, the 10 ppm total solids officially permitted for Water for Injection may be much too high when used as the vehicle for many products. In practice, water for Injection normally should not have a conductivity of more han 1 micromho (1 megohm, approximately 0.1 ppm NaCl).

Added Substances.
Substances added to a product to enhance its stability are essential for almost every product. Such substances include solubilizers, antioxidants, chelating agents, buffers, tonicity contributors, antibacterial agents, antifungal agents, hydrolysis inhibitors, antifoaming agents, and numerous other substances for specialized purposes. At the same time, these agents must be prevented from adversely affecting the product. In general, added substances must be nontoxic in the quantity administered to the patient. They should not interfere with the therapeutic efficacy nor with the assay of the active therapeutic compound. They must also be present and active when needed throughout the useful life of the product. Therefore, these agents must be selected with greatcare, and they must be evaluated as to their effect upon the entire formulation. An extensive review of excipients used in parenteral products and the means for adjusting pH of these products has recently been published and should be referred to for more detailed information.

Formulation
The formulation of a parenteral product involves the combination of one or more ingredients with a medicinal agent to enhance the convenience, acceptability, or effectieness of the product. Rarely is it preferable to dispense a drug singly as a sterile dry powder unless the formulation of a stable liquid preparation is not possible.

On the other hand, a therapeutic agent is a chemical compound subject to the physical and chemical reactions characteristic of the class of compounds to which it belongs. Therefore, a careful evaluation must be made of every combination of two or more ingredients to ascertain whether or not adverse interactions occur, and if they do, of ways to modify the formulation so that the reactions are eliminated or minimized. The formulation of sterile products is challenging, therefore, to the knowledge and ingenuity of the persons responsible.

The amount of information available to the formulator concerning the physical and chemical properties of a therapeutic agent, particularly if it is a new compound, is often quite meager. Information concerning basic properties muse be obtained, including molecular weight, solubility, purity, colligative properties, and chemical reactivity, before an intelligent approach to formulation can begin. Improvements in formulation are a continuing process, since important properties of a drug or of the total formulation may not become evident until the product has been stored or used for a prolonged time. However, because of the extensive test documentation required by the U. S. Food and Drug Administration (FDA), only outstanding formulations can be justified for continuance to the state of a maketed product.

Production

The production process includes all of the steps from the accumulation and combining of the ingredients of the formula to the enclosing of the product in the individual container for distribution. Intimately associated with these processes are the personnel who carry them out and the facilities in which they are performed. The most ideally planned processes can be rendered ineffective by personnel who do not have the right attitude or training, or by facilities that do not provide an efficiently controlled environment.

To enhance the assurance of successful manufacturing operation, all process steps must be carefully reduced to writing after being shown to be effective. These written process steps are often called standard operating procedures (SOPs)[6]. No extemporaneous changes are permitted to be made in these procedures; any change must go through the same approval steps as the original written SOP. Further, extensive records must be kept to give assurance at the end of the production process that all steps have been performed as prescribed, an aspect emphasized in the FDA's Good Manufacturing Practices. Such in-process control is essential to assuring the quality of the product, since these assurances are even more significant than those from product release testing. The production of a quality product is a result of the continuous, dedicated effort of the quality assurance, production, and quality control personnel within the plant in developing, performing, and confirming effective SOPs.

Selected from Lachman Leon et al. *The Theory and Practice of Industrial Pharmacy*, 3rd ed., Lea and Febiger, Philadelphia, 1986.

Words and Expression

sterile ['sterail]　*a.* 无菌的
ophthalmic [ɔf'θelmik]　*a.* 眼的; *n.* 眼药

irrigate ['irigeit] vt. 冲洗
mucous ['mju:kəs] a. 粘液的；n. 粘膜
contamination [kəntæmi'neiʃən] n. 污染物
cavity ['kæviti] n. 洞，腔
abrade [ə'breid] vt. 磨，擦，擦伤
pellet ['pelit] n. 药丸，小球
implantation [im'plɑ:nteiʃən] n. 对端植入法
vehicles ['vi:ikl] n. 赋形剂，运载工具
gravimetric [grævi'metrik] a. 重量分析的，重量的
instantaneous [instən'teinjəs] a. 瞬间的，即刻的
inferential [infə'renʃəl] a. 推论的，推理的
osmosis [ɔz'məusis] n. 渗透，渗透作用
dissociate [disəusieit] vt. 使分离，使离解
pyrogen [paiərədʒən] n. 致热质，热原
solubilizing ['sɔljubilaiziŋ] a. 增溶的
antioxidants [æntiɔksidənts] n. 抗氧剂
buffer [bʌfə] vt. 缓冲；n. 缓冲剂
tonicity [tə'nisiti] n. 强壮，强健
antifungal [ænti'fʌŋgəl] a. 抗真菌的
inhibitor [in'hibitə] n. 抑制剂
antifoaming [ænti'fəmiŋ] a. 防沫的，消沫的
colligative [kɔligeitiv] a. 综合的，概括的
accumulation [ə'kju:mjuleiʃən] n. 积累，积聚物
aseptic [æ'septik] n. 防腐剂；a. 无菌的
wrap [ræp] vt. 包装
extemporaneous [eksdempə'reinjəs] a. 即席的，临时的
specification [spesifi'keiʃən] n. 说明书，规范，规格

Notes

① preparation 此处作制剂解释。
② ophthalmic preparation 眼用制剂。
③ irrigating solution 冲洗液。
④ megohm 兆欧姆，micromhos 微欧姆。
⑤ parts per million (ppm) 百万分之一 (10^{-6})。
⑥ Standard Operation Procedures (SOP) 标准操作规程。

Exercise

1. Answer the following questions：
    (1) Can you tell the difference in quality control between the oral tablet and sterile products injected.

(2) How is the quality of sterile products assured in-process?

(3) What is the standard operating procedure (SOPs)?

(4) How is the water for injection usually prepared?

2. Complete the passage below:

Sterile product are dosage forms of therapeutic agent that are free of viable _____, these include _____ _____ and _____, because they are injected through the _____ or _____ membranes into internal body, parenteral products must be free from _____ and from _____.

Sterile products are most frequently _____ or _____, the most frequently employed _____ for sterile product is _____ the quality of water for injection (WFI) is required by pharmacopeia, which is superior quality required, the natural water contain generally dissociated and undisssciated _____ and _____ substances which they must be essentially removed and set a permitted limits, _____ are products of matabolism of microorganisms, the removal of _____ is very important for water for injection.

Water for injection is prepared by _____ or _____.

3. Put the following into Chinese:

parenteral   ophthalmic   irrigating   microoganisms

contamination   specialize   conductivity   pycogens

4. Put the following into English

灭菌产品   反相渗透   蒸馏   测量仪

电极   比电导   微生物   组织

5. Why the removal of pycogens is very important for WFI?

Reading Material 13

Processing

The initial processing step is the procurement of acceptable components. In a plant, the majority of components are requisitioned from tested and approved stock, and are then subjected to whatever processing steps are required to prepare them for use. A few components, such as Water for Injection, are manufactured to specifications as needed.

Water for Injection.

Water for Injection (WFI)[①] usually is prepared by distillation in a still specifically designed to produce the high-quality water required. Reverse osmosis[②], however, is a method that is now approved by the USP, and it is receiving increasing attention and use. The specifications for the quality of the water required have been discussed under the heading "Vehicles." Earlier in this chapter.

The specifications for a still should include (1) prepurification of feed water by chemical softening, deionization, or filtration to improve the quality of the distillate and reduce the frequency of required cleaning due to insoluble scale in the boiler, (2) removal of entrained contaminants from the vapor before it is condensed by passage through an efficient baffle system[3], (3) ejection of volatile constituents from the top of the system before the vapor is cooled so that they will not redissolve and appear in the condensate, (4) construction of all surfaces that will come incontact with the vapor and condensate of a material that will not dissolve in even trace amounts, preferably pure tin, 304 stainless steel, or borosilicate glass.

In addition to conventional stills, "two types of stills frequently used for the production of large volumes of water are the vapor compression stills" and the multiple effect stills. While they operate on somewhat different principles, both utilize initially heated feed water and steam to conserve on energy consumption and cooling water. Both types are capable of producing highpurity water at rates of 50 to 1000 or more gallons per hour.

A reverse osmosis system functions by applying pressure (usually 200 to 400 psi) to raw water sufficient to force the permeation of water through a select semipermeable membrane[4] in the opposite direction from natural osmosis[5]. The membranes most commonly used are composed of cellulose esters or polyamides (nylon) and are effective in retaining all macromolecules and 85% or more of small ions such as Na^+ and Cl^- Since pyrogens are macromolecules, they should be retained as well as such viable particles as microorganisms. Greater efficiency and reliability are achieved by passing the water through two membranes in series. The acceptance of reverse osmosis for the preparation of Water For Injection is increasing as experience is gained with the system and its characteristics are understood more fully.

Cleaning Equipment and Containers.

Equipment and containers to be used in the processing of a sterile product must be scrupulously clean. New, unused containers and equipment are contaminated principally with dust, fibers, and chemical films, which usually are relatively easy to remove, often by rinsing only. Debris that is more dangerous and more difficult to remove may be present as a residue from a previous use. Such debris usually must be removed by vigorous treatment with hot detergents.

In general, equipment used previously should be scrubbed by hand immediately after use with an effective detergent that does not leave a residue of its own. Whenever possible, equipment should be disassembled so that each part can be thoroughly scrubbed and cleaned with particular attention given to screw threads, joints, and other dirt-collecting structures. Live steam can sometimes be used to loosen debris effectively, particularly in areas that are not easily accessible. After cleaning, the equipment should be rinsed several times, with a final rinse with WFI. Just prior to reuse, large clean tanks and similar equipment should be rinsed thoroughly with WFI. Reserving equipment for use with only one type of product reduces cleaning problems.

Filling Equipment for Liquids.

Certain fundamental features are found on all machines used for filling containers with liquids. A means is provided for repetitively forcing a measured volume of the liquid through the orifice of a delivery tube designed to enter the constricted opening of a container. The size of the delivery tube is governed by the opening in the container to be used, the viscosity and density of the liquid, and the speed of delivery desired. The tube must freely enter the neck of the container and deliver the liquid deep enough to permit air to escape without sweeping the entering liquid into the neck of the container. To reduce the resistance to the flow of the liquid, the tube should have the maximum possible diameter. Excessive delivery force causes splashing of the liquid and troublesome foaming, if the liquid has a low surface tension.

The delivery of relatively small volumes of liquids is usually obtained from the stroke of the plunger of a syringe. The stroke of the syringe forces the liquid through a two-way valve that provides for an alternate filling of the syringe from a reservoir and delivery to a container. For heavy, viscous liquids a sliding piston valve provides more positive action.

Filling Equipment for Solids.
Sterile solids, such as antibiotics, are more difficult to subdivide accurately and precisely into individual dose containers than are liquids. The rate of flow of solid material tends to be slow and irregular, particularly if finely powdered. Small, granular particles flow most evenly. Containers with a relatively large opening must be used; even so, the filling rate is slow, and the risk of spillage is ever present. For these reasons, the tolerances permitted for the content of such containers must be relatively large. Suggested tolerances may be found tabulated in the USP.

Sterile solids can be subdivided into containers by individual weighting. The operation can use a scoop that holds a volume approximately equal to the weight required, but the quantity filled into the container is finally weighed on a balance. This is a slow process.

When the solid is obtainable in a relatively free-flowing form, machine methods of filling may be employed. In general, these methods involve the measurement and delivery of a volume of the solid material, which has been calibrated in terms of the weight desired. Among the major problems in the use of such machines are stratification of particles due to varying particle sizes, the development of electrostatic charge within the mass of dry solid particles, the formation of air pockets, and uneven flow due to clumping of the particles. These all result in uneven filling of the container. The problems usually can be minimized in uniform particle size of the solid is achieved and a small electric current is used to neutralize the developing charge.

Selected from Lachman Leon et al. *The Theory and Practice of Industrial Pharmacy*, 3rd ed., Lea and Febiger, Philadelphia, 1986.

Words and Expressions

injection [in'dʒekʃən]   *n.* 注射，注射剂
procurement [prɔ'kjuəment]   *n.* 获得
baffle [bæfl]   *n.* 挡板

prepurification [priːpjurifiˈkeiʃən] n. 预纯化
scale [skeil] n. 锅垢
ejection [iːdʒekʃən] n. 排斥，喷出
volatile [ˈvɔletil] a. 易挥发的
borosilicate [bɔrəsilikeit] n. 硼硅酸盐
still [stil] n. 蒸馏器，蒸馏
consumption [kənˈsʌmpəʃən] n. 消耗，肺结核
raw water n. 生水
permeation [pəːmiˈeiʃən] n. 渗透，充满
cellulose [seˈljulous] n. 纤维素
polyamide [pɔlimaide] n. 聚酰胺
macromolecules [mækrəuˈmɔlikjuːl] n. 大分子
reliability [rilaiəˈbiliti] n. 可靠度
scrupulously [ˈskruːpjuləsli] adv. 审慎地，严格地
debris [ˈdebri] n. 碎片
scrub [skrʌb] vt. 擦净
disassemble [disəˈsembl] vt. 拆卸，分解
screw [ˈskruː] n. 螺丝，螺孔；vt. 调节，拧紧
thread [θred] n. 针，丝，罗纹
orifice [ˈɔrifis] n. 孔，口
viscosity [visˈkɔsiti] n. 粘性，粘滞性
splash [splæʃ] vt. 溅污
troublesome [trʌblsəm] a. 令人烦恼的
foaming [fɔmiŋ] n. 发泡，起泡
syringe [sirindʒ] n. 注射器，注射
subdivide [sʌbdiˈvaid] vt. 把……再分，分装
spillage [ˈspilidʒ] n. 溢出，洒落
tolerance [ˈtɔlərəns] n. 忍受，容限，耐受性，耐（药）性
stratification [strætifiˈkeiʃən] n. 分层
clump [klʌmp] vi. 结块，结团

Note

① Water For Injection (WFI)　注射用水。
② reverse osmosis　反向渗析。
③ an efficient baffle system　有效的挡板系统。
④ a select semipermeable membrane　选择性的半渗透膜。
⑤ the opposite direction from natural osmosis　与自然渗透相反的方向。

Unit 14　Sustained Release Dosage Forms

With many drugs, the basic goal of therapy is to achieve a steady-state blood or tissue level[①] that is therapeutically effective and nontoxic for an extended period of time. The design of proper dosage regimens is an important element in accomplishing this goal. A basic objective in dosage form design is to optimize the delivery of medication so as to achieve a measure of control of the therapeutic effect in the face of uncertain fluctuations in the in vivo environment[②] in which drug release takes place. This is usually accomplished by maximum drug availability[③], i. e., by attempting to attain a maximum rate and extent of drug absorption; however, control of drug action through formulation also implies controlling bioavailability to reduce drug absorption rates. In this chapter, approaches to the formulation of drug delivery systems, based on the deliberate control of drug availability, are considered with emphasis on peroral dosage forms.

The Sustained Release Concept

Sustained release, sustained action, prolonged action, controlled release[④], extended action, timed release, depot, and repository dosage forms are terms used to identify drug delivery systems that are designed to achieve a prolonged therapeutic effect by continuously releasing medication over an extended perior of time after administration of a single dose. In the case of injectable dosage forms, this period may vary from days to months. In the case of orally administered forms, however, this period is measured in hours and critically depends on the residence time of the dosage form in the gastrointestinal (GI) tract[⑤]. The term "controlled release" has become associated with those systems from which therapeutic agents may be automatically delivered at predefined rates over a long period of time. Products of this type have been formulated for oral, injectable, and topical use, and include inserts for placement in body cavities as well.

The pharmaceutical industry provides a variety of dosage forms and dosage levels of particular drugs, thus enabling the physician to control the onset and duration of drug therapy by altering the dose and/or mode of administration. In some instances, control of drug therapy can be achieved by taking advantage of beneficial drug interactions that affect drug disposition and elimination, e. g., the action of Probenecid, which inhibits the excretion of Penicillin, thus prolonging its blood level. Mixtures of drugs might be utilized to potentiate, synergize, or antagonize given drug actions. Alternately, drug mixtures might be formulated in which the rate and/or extent of drug absorption is modified. Sustained release dosage form design embodies this approach to the control of drug action, i.e., through a process of either drug modification or dosage form modification, the absorption process, and subsequently drug action, can be controlled.

Physicians can achieve several desirable therapeutic advantages by prescribing sustained release forms. Since the frequency of drug administration is reduced, patients compliance can be improved, and drug administration can be made more convenient as well. The blood level oscillation characteristic of multiple dosing of conventional dosage forms is reduced, because a more even blood level is maintained. A less obvious advantage, implicit in the design of sustained release forms, is that the total amount of drug administered can be reduced, thus maximizing availability with a minimum dose. In addition, better control of drug absorption can be attained, since the high blood level peaks that may be observed after administration of a dose of a high availability drug can be reduce by formulation in an extend action form. The safety margin of high potency drugs can be increased and the incidence of both local and systemic adverse side effects can be reduced in sensitive patients. Overall, administration of sustained release forms enables increased reliability of therapy.

Product Evaluation and Testing

In Vitro Measurement of Drug Availability

It is not possible to simulate in a single in vitro test system the range of variable that affect drug release during the passage of sustained release medication through the GI tract. Properly designed *in vitro* tests for drug release serve two important functions, however. First, data from such tests are required as a guide to formulation during the development stage, prior to clinical testing. Second, *in vitro* testing is necessary to ensure batch-to-batch uniformity in the production of a proven dosage form. Different methods are usually required by these two distinctly different testing situations. Although attempts to correlate in vitro release profiles with clinical performance are useful once sufficient clinical testing has been completed, in-vitro/in-vivo correlation must not be assumed. In vitro studies are not sufficient to establish the efficacy of a new preparation.

Tests developed for the purpose of quality control are generally limited to USP dissolution testing methods, using either the rotating basket, the paddle, or the modified disintegration testing apparatus. In many instances in which USP test procedures are followed, upper and lower limits are specified for drug release in simulated gastric and/or intestinal fluid. Measurements are made at specified time intervals appropriate to the specific product. Complete release profiles are not measured unless automated techniques are used. At present, there are no specific USP specifications for sustained release dosage forms. Procedures are determined by nature of the dosage form (e. g., tablet or capsule), the principle utilized to control drug release (e. g., disintegrating or nondisintegrating), and the maintenance period.

During formulation development, testing methods should be designed to provide answers to the following questions.

1. Does the product "dump" maintenance dose before the maintenance period is complete? Sustained release products are subject to either of two modes of failure: Insufficient dose is released, or too much drug is made available too quickly.

2. What fraction of the dose remains unavailable, i.e., what fraction will not be released in the projected time of transit in the GI tract?

3. What is the effect of physiologic variables on drug release? For example, delayed gastric emptying, interaction between drug and GI constituents, composition and volume of GI fluids, and variation in intensity of agitation should be considered.

4. Is the loading dose (id present) released immediately? Is release of the maintenance dose delayed? If so, is the delay time within the desired range?

5. What is the unit-to-unit variation? How predictable is the release profile?

6. What is the sensitivity of the drug release profile to process variables?

7. What is the stability of the formulation with respect to its drug release profile?

8. In short, does the observed release profile fit expectations?

The methods used to measure drug release profiles should have the following characteristics. The analytic technique should be automated so that the complete drug release profile can be directly recorded. Allowance should be made for changing the release media from simulated gastric to simulated intestinal fluid at variable programmed time intervals, to establish the effect of retention of the dosage form in gastric fluid as well as to approximate more closely the pH shifts that the dosage form is likely to encounter *in vivo*. In addition, the hydrodynamic state in the dissolution vessel should be controllable and capable of variation. The apparatus should be calibrated using a nondisintegrating dissolution standard (e. g., salicylic acid compacts).

Selected from Lachman Leon et al. *The Theory and Practice of Industrial Pharmacy*,
3rd ed., Lea and Febiger, Philadelphia, 1986.

Words and Expressions

regiment ['redʒimənt] n. 一大群，大量
optimize ['ɔptimaiz] vt. 优化
fluctuation ['flʌktju'eiʃən] n. 波动
availability [ə'veilə'biliti] n. 有效性，效力
deliberate [di'libərit] a. 审慎地
peroral ['perərei] a. 经口的
depot ['depəu] n. 仓库
sustain [səs'tein] vt. 维持
gastrointestinal (GI) [gæstrəuin'testinəl] n. 肠胃道的
predefine [pri:di'fain] vt. 预先确定
cavity ['kæviti] n. 腔，窝
onset [ɔn'set] n. 开始，反应
Probenecid [prə'benisid] n. 丙磺舒（抗痛风药）
excretion [eks'kriʃən] n. 排泄，分泌
potentiate [pə'tenʃieit] vt. 加强，更有效
synergies [si'nə:dʒiz] n. 药的协同作用
antagonize [ænt'ægənaiz] vt. 拮抗

embody [im'bɔdi] vt. 体现，包含
compliance [kəm'plaiəns] n. 顺从
oscillation [ɔsi'leiʃən] n. 震动，摇动
implicit [im'plisit] a. 含蓄的，固有的
margin [mɑ:dʒin] n. （时间）余地，界限
simulate ['simjuleit] vt. 模拟
tract [trækt] n. 系统，道束（医）
clinical [klinikəl] a. 临床的
proven [pru:ven] a. 证实的
distinctly [dis'tiŋktli] adv. 清楚地
efficacy ['efikəsi] n. 功效，效验
paddle [pædl] vt. 搅打；n. 桨，搅拌器
intestinal [in'testinl] a. 肠的
interval [in'təvəl] n. （时间的）间隔

Notes

① a steady-state blood or tissue level 稳定态的血液或组织水平。
② in vivo/in vitro environment 在体内的/在体外的环境。
③ maximizing drug availability 达到最大的药物利用度。
④ sustained release 缓释；controlled release 控释。
⑤ gastrointestinal (GI) tract 肠胃系统。

Exercises

1. Answer the following questions：
   (1) What is the sustained release concept?
   (2) What are the advantages of sustained release dosage forms?
   (3) What methods are employed for in vitro measurement of drug availability?
2. Complete the passage below.
   The effectiveness of drug's therapy correlate in general with _____ of in vivo drugs, which are influenced by _____, _____, _____, _____ and _____ of drug in internal body.
   _____ and _____ are terms used to identity drug delivery system that are designed to _____ therapeutic effect by continuously releasing medication over an extended period of time.
   Term "_____" has associated to deliverance automatic predefined _____ over a long period of _____.
   During the development stage, the effect of sustained release is simulated by in vitro testing with the _____ permissible of pharmacopoeia.
3. Put the following into Chinese.
   therapy   delivery   function   clinical

procedure   control   sustain   extend

4. Put the following into English.

    吸收   分布   代谢   排泄
    消除   释放   稳定态   利用率
    胃液   肠液

5. Please compare sustained release dosage forms with a general dosage forms and give out the advantage of sustained release dosage forms.

Reading Material 14

Tabletted Slow Release Granulations

Compression of timed-release[①] granulations into tablets is an alternate to encapsulation. Such tablets should be designed to disintegrate in the stomach so as to simulate the administration of a capsule form having the advantages associated with sustained release encapsulations, while retaining the advantages of the tablet dosage form. Three examples, each utilizing a different process, illustrate this type of formulation. The first is a tabletted mixed release granulation in which binders with different retardant properties are used to prepare three different granulations, which are color coded for identification, blended, and tabletted. The first is a conventional nonsustained release granulation prepared using gelatin as a binder; the second uses vinyl acetate, and the third uses shelae as binders. Drug release is controlled by erosin of the granulation in intestinal fluid[②]—the vinyl acetate granulation disintegrates at a faster rate than the shellac granulation.

    The second example is illustrated by a sustained release aspirin formulation based on the microdialysis cell principle. Aspirin crystals are microencapsulated in a retardant barrier and are compressed to form a tablet that rapidly disintegrates into sustained release granules. The barrier approach is particularly advantageous for formulation of high-milligram-potency drugs such as aspirin, since only a relatively small amount of retardant is required in the formulation. The third example is represented by a sustained release form of theophylline, which is claimed to release drug zero-order[③] for a 12-hour dosiing interval. The table is formulated as a matrix of loading dose of theophylling pellets encapsulated in a semipermeable coating. Disintegration of the matrix in the stomach releases the extended action pellets. The loading dose granulation should have physical characteristics, e. g., size, similar to the maintenance dose pellets to ensure homogeneous mixing of the two granulations during compression.

Controlled Release Technology
Controlled release dosage forms are designed to release drug in vivo according to predictable rates that can be verified by in vitro measurements. Of the many approaches to formulation of sustained-release medication described in this chapter, those fabricated as insoluble matrix

tablets come closest to realization of this objective. Since release of water-soluble drug from this form should be independent of in vivo variables. Controlled release technology implies a quantitative understanding of the physicochemical mechanism of drug availability to the extent that the dosage form release rate can be specified. Potential developments and new approaches to oral controlled release drug delivery include hydrodynamic pressure controlled systems[④], intragastric floating tablets, transmucosal tablets and microporous membrane coated tablets.

One example of a dosage form design that illustrates the application of controlled release technology to pharmaceutical formulation is the orally administered elementary osmotic pump. This device is fabricated from a tablet that contains water-soluble osmotically active drug[⑤] or that is blended with an osmotically active diluent, by coating the tablet with a cellulose tracetate barrier, which functions as a semipermeable membrane. A laser is used to form a precision orifice in the barrier. Since the barrier is permeable only to water, initial penetration of water dissolves the outer part of the core, resulting in the development of an osmotic pressure difference across the membrane. The system imbibes water at a rate proportional to the water permeability and effective surface area of the membrane and to the osmotic gradient of the core formulation. The device delivers a volume of saturated solution equal to the volume of water uptake through the membrane. After an initial lag time (approximately 1 hour) during which the delivery rate increases to its maximum value, drug release is zero-order, until all solid material is dissolved. Thereafter, the delivery rate decreases parabolically to zero.

Selected from Lachman Leon et al. *The Theory and Practice of Industrial Pharmacy*, 3rd ed., Lea and Febiger, Philadelphia, 1986.

Words and Expression

blend [blend] v. 混合
gelatin ['dʒelətin] n. 凝胶，白明胶
shellac [ʃə'læk] n. 虫胶
aspirin ['æspərin] n. 阿司匹林
microdialysis [maikrəu'dailisis] n. 微量渗析
barrier [bæriə] n. 障碍物
theophylline [θiə'filin] n. 茶叶碱
matrix [meitriks] n. 模式，基质，骨架
verify ['verifai] v. 验证，核实
hydrodynamic [haidrəudai'næmik] a. 流体动力学的
intragastric [intə'gæstrik] a. 胃内的
float [fləut] v. 漂浮，浮动
transmucosal a. 透过粘膜的
microporous [maikrə'pɔ:rəs] a. 多微孔的

cellulose triacetate   *n.* 三醋酸纤维素
penetration [peni'treiʃən]   *n.* 穿过，渗透
gradient [greidjəut]   *n.* 梯度
saturated [sætʃəreit]   *a.* 饱和的
parabolically [pærə'bɔlikəli]   *a.* 抛物线地

Notes

① timed-release　定时释放。
② intestinal fluid　肠内液体。
③ release drug zero-order　药物零级释放。
④ hydrodynamic pressure controlled systems　流体动力学的压力控制系统。
⑤ water-soluble osmotically active drug　水溶性渗透型活性药物。

Unit 15 Kinetic Principles and Stability Testing

The importance of stability testing in the development of pharmaceutical dosage forms is well recognized in the pharmaceutical industry. Increased fillings of Abbreviated New Drug Applications (ANDA)[①] and Paper New Drug Applications (PNDA)[②] by generic and nongeneric drug manufacturers have resulted in an increase in submissions of stability data to the Food and Drug Administration (FDA). With the coming of the biotechnologic age, and as bioengineered products become ready for testing in humans, stability test data for these compounds are required as part of the submissions of Investigational New Drug Applications (INDs)[③] to the FDA to assure their quality and safety. This increase in stability testing has come at a time in which the empiric methods have, for the most part, been replaced by a more scientific approach to stability evaluation using various appropriate physical and chemical principles.

From a regulatory consideration, there are several sections of the Federal Food and Drug and Cosmetic Act[④] that relate to the stability of pharmaceutical products, Section 505 (b)(4) concerns itself with preservation of the characteristics of the new drug and it the basis for requiring stability data in the new drug application. Section 501(a)(2)(B) concerns itself with drug adulteration. A drug is considered adulterated if it does not meet the quality and purity characteristics that it is represented to possess. Section 505(h) states that a drug shall be deemed to be misbranded if found bu the Health Education and Welfare Agency[⑤] to be liable to deterioration unless it is packaged in such form and manner, with its label bearing a statement of such precautions, as are necessary for the protection of the public health.

Of the three sections mentioned, the one that pertains most directly to stability testing of drugs is Section 505(b)(4). The FDA Regulation dealing with this Section is 314.1(8) (p) under New Drug Applications, and requires " a complete description of and data derived from studies of the stability of the drug, including information showing the suitability of the analytical method used". It further states that stability data should be submitted for the new substance, for the finished dosage form in the container in which it is to be marketed, and, if it is reconstituted at the time of dispensing, for the solution so prepared. It requires that an expiration date appear on the label to preserve the identity, strength, quality, and purity of the drug until it is used. In fact it states, "if no expiration date is proposed, the applicant must justify its absence".

Further, the FDA current Good Manufacturing Practices (GMP)[⑥] regulations under sections 211.166 and 211.167 set forth basic guidelines for stability for all drugs, and the requirement for expiration dates on pharmaceutical products. No drug product in a container-closure system is indefinitely stable, and the manufacturer or packer of a drug product is responsible for determining the stability characteristics for each of the products. In the preamble to the Good Manufacturing Guidelines published in the Federal Register of September 29, 1978, the Commissioner of the FDA indicated that valid expiration dates[7] must be established for all drug products.

In a 1983 FDA survey of regulatory actions, it was reported that 22% of GMP violations involved problems with laboratory controls, and that the most common deficiencies involved stability testing requirement of section 211,166. Deficiencies included failures to have written stability testing protocols, inability to support product expiration dates, inadequate number of stability test batches, and use of assays that were not stability-indicating.

The application of certain physicochemical principles in the performance of stability studies has proved to be of considerable advantage in the development of stable dosage forms. Only through this approach is it possible to accurately and adequately make use of data obtained from exaggerated storage conditions for the purposes of predicting the stability at normal shelf storage for extended periods of time. It is extremely important that the pharmaceutical manufacturer accurately predict the shelf stability of a new product from accelerated storage data, because of the considerable economic advantage gained in marketing a new product as soon as possible after formulation. A sound stability testing program is possible only if personnel are skilled in employing these principles and if appropriate equipment is available.

Chemical and Physical Stability Testing of Pharmaceutical Dosage Forms
Chemical Stability.
The information presented thus far has illustrated that it is possible, through the use of chemical kinetic principles to study the degradation of an active drug in solution accurately, as well as determine the mechanism responsible for the degradation. A more complicated situation arises when one attempts to study the stability of one or more drugs in a liquid pharmaceutical dosage form. Because of the multiplicity of ingredients in most pharmaceutical formulations, there exists the possibility of interactions taking place, as well as each ingredient having different degradative characteristics. The ideal situation would be to study the degradation pattern of each ingredient in the mixture individually. This is, of course, difficult, time-consuming, and expensive to accomplish. Fortunately, it is not necessary for purposes of stability prediction to determine the mechanisms of degradation. In general, it is possible to evaluate the stability of any component of a pharmaceutical preparation by determining some property of the degradation as a function of time. If this function can be linearized in accordance with chemical kinetic reaction orders, the temperature dependency of the degradation can be obtained. Information of this type, obtained from exaggerated test conditions of short duration, permits the determination of the chemical stability of an active ingredient or ingredients, colorants, and antimicrobial preservatives for extended shelf storage.

The color stability of a multisulfonamide preparation was determined in this fashion. By the use of colormetric measurements of samples subjected to thermally accelerated degradation, it was possible to predict the color stability of the preparation at room temperature, with data obtained in about 25 days.

Physical Stability

Although there are a considerable number of reports in the literature concerned with chemical stability testing of active ingredients in pharmaceutical dosage forms, there is a conspicuous scarcity of reports dealing with physical stability testing. From both pharmaceutical and therapeutic standpoints, physical changes in the dosage form upon storage can be as serious as chemical instability of the active ingredients, sometimes more so. Examples of physical changes that can take place are crystal growth, change in crystal form, increase or decrease in dissolution rate and disintegration time, cracking of emulsions, caking of suspension, color fading, color development, and sediment or swirl development in solution. Crystal growth in a suspension can result in a change in the rate of absorption and possibly in ineffective therapeutic levels. Crystal growth in an ointment or cream can cause skin irritation as well as poorer absorption. A change in crystal form of a steroid in suspension can result in the formation of a therapeutically inactive form of the drug.

Selected from Lachman Leon et al. *The Theory and Practice of Industrial Pharmacy*, 3rd ed., Lea and Febiger, Philadelphia, 1986.

Words and Expressions

filing [filing] *n.* 提出申请
biotechnologic ['baiəutek'nɔlədʒik] *a.* 生物技术的
bioengineered [baiəu'endʒi'niərid] *a.* 生物工程的
empiric [em'pirik] *a.* 经验性的
regulatory [regjulətəri] *a.* 调整的
adulteration [ədʌtə'reiʃən] *n.* 掺杂
misbrand [mis'brænd] *n.* 贴错标签
deterioration [ditiəriə'reiʃən] *n.* 变坏,退化
pertain [pə:'tein] *v.* 适合,属于
submit [səb'mit] *v.* 服从,顺从
expiration [ekspaiə'reiʃən] *n.* 截止
justify [dʒʌstifai] *v.* 证明……是正当的
guideline [gaidəlin] *n.* 方针
preamble [pri:'æmbl] *n.* 导言
violation [vaiə'leiʃən] *n.* 违反,妨碍
exaggerate [igz'ædʒəreit] *v.* 夸大,夸张
degradation [degrə'deiʃən] *n.* 退化,降级,降解
linearize ['liniəraiz] *v.* 使……线性化
preservative [pri'zə:vətiv] *a.* 防腐的,保存的; *n.* 防腐剂,保存剂

multisulfonamide n. 多磺酰胺
colorimetric [kʌləri'metrik] a. 比色的
conspicuous [kən'spekjuəs] a. 明显的，显著的
scarcity ['skɛəsiti] n. 缺乏，不足
crack [kræk] n. 裂缝，破裂
sediment ['sedimənt] n. 沉淀
ointment ['ɔintmənt] n. 软膏，药膏，油膏
cream ['kri:m] n. 霜剂
steroid ['sterɔid] n. 甾体化合物

Notes

① Abbreviated New Drug Application（ANDA） 简要的新药申请。
② Paper New Drug Application（PNDA） 书面新药申请。
③ Investigational New Drug Application（INDA） 研究性新药申请。
④ Federal Food and Drug and Cosmetic Act 联邦食品药物和化妆品条例。
⑤ Health Education and Welfare Agency 卫生教育和福利机构。
⑥ Good Manufacture Practices（GMP） 药品生产质量管理规范。
⑦ valid expiration dates 有效截止日期。

Exercise

1. Answer the following questions:
   (1) Why the stability testing in the development of pharmaceutical dosage forms is important?
   (2) What is the principle content of the stability testing?
   (3) Which pathway occurs the decomposition of active ingredients in pharmaceutical dosage forms? What is those most frequently encountered?

2. Complete the passage below.
   One of the principal problems studied of stability testing in pharmaceutical dosage forms is _____, another is _____. Chemical stability study principally the _____ of an active drug in a formulation and mechanism of _____. Because of each ingredient in a formulation having different degradative characteristics, _____ is often complicated.
   The factors influenced on degradation include in general _____, _____ and _____ etc.
   Physical changes that can take place are _____, change in _____, _____ and _____ etc. For example, crystal growth in a suspension can result in _____ in the rate of absorption and possibly in _____.

3. Put the following into Chinese.

stability testing	regulation	precaution
protection	description	justify
determination	survey	exaggerate

4. Put the following into English.

生物工程产品	基因药物	降解反应
机理	相互作用	测定
评价	总结	动力学的

Reading Material 15

Degradative Pathways

Although the decomposition of active ingredients in pharmaceutical dosage forms occurs through several pathways, i.e., hydrolysis, oxidation-reduction, racemization, decarboxylation, ring cleavage, and photolysis, those most frequently encountered are hydrolysis and oxidation-reduction. Consequently, this section treats these two important degradation processes in detail and only briefly reviews the others.

Hydrolysis

Many pharmaceuticals contain ester or amide functional groups, which undergo hydrolysis in solution.

A number of reports in the literature deal with detailed kinetic studies of the hydrolysis of pharmaceutical ingredients containing an ester group in the molecule. Probably one of the earliest and most thorough studies was performed on aspirin by Edwards. He studied the degradation of aspirin in various buffer solutions and treated the overall reaction as pseudo-first-order.

The pH of optimum stability is at 2.4. At a pH of 5 to 7, the degradation reaction was essentially pH-independent, and at a pH above 10, the stability of aspirin was found to decrease rapidly with increase in pH. In the area in which the degradation is pH-independent, there are several reactions going on, each causing an effect of its own resulting in a cancellation of the effect of its own resulting in a cancellation of the effect of H^+ and OH^-, which gives a uniform rate over this pH range.

Although the use of pseudo-first-order kinetics is sufficient to define and study the degradation of aspirin, the hydrolysis of aspirin proceeds through a complex mechanism over the pH range sudied, consisting of six different degradative pathways as shown below.

Oxidation-Reduction

The oxidative decomposition of pharmaceutical compounds is responsible for the instability of a considerable number of pharmaceutical preparations. For example, steroid, vitamins, antibiotics, and epinephrine undergo oxidative degradation. These reactions are mediated either by free radicals or by molecular oxygen. Because of the complexity of oxidative processes and their sensitivity to trace metal and other impurities, it is difficult to reproduce them and to establish mechanisms for the reactions. Consequently, many reports dealing with oxidation reduction reactions are qualitative in nature rather than quantitative.

For the most part, oxidative degradations of pharmaceutical compounds follow first-order or second-order kinetic expressions. Guttman and Meister studied the base-catalyzed degradation of prednisolone and found that the degradation exhibited a first-order dependency on steroid concentration. The rate of prednisolone disappearance from aqueous solutions increased with an increase in hydroxyl ion concentration under both aerobic and anaerobic conditions; however, the reaction mixture exposed to air showed more rajpid degradation of prednisolone. For example, at a hydroxide ion concentration of 0.01N, the rate constant for the overall degradation obtained under anaerobic conditions was approximately half the value of that obtained when no precautions were taken to exclude air from the system.

Trace metal impurities in buffer salts caused an accelerated decomposition of prednisolone, which was first thought to be due to buffer concentration. By studying the oxidative degradation with and without 0.1% disodium salt of ethylenediamine tetraacetic acid at different buffer concentrations, it was found that the solutions not containing any chelating agent degraded more rapidly as the buffer concentration increased, while the buffered solutions containing chelating agent showed that therate of degradation was independent of concentration of buffer.

Selected from Lachman Leon et al. *The Theory and Practice of Industrial Pharmacy*, 3rd ed., Lea and Febiger, Philadelphia, 1986.

Words and Expressions

decomposition [di:kɔmpə'ziʃən] n. 分解（作用）
racemization [ræsimaizeiʃən] n. 消旋化
decarboxylation [di:'kɑ:bɔksileʃən] n. 脱羧
cleavage ['kli:veidʒ] n. 裂解
photolysis [fəu'tɔlisis] n. 光分解
degradation [degrə'deiʃən] n. 降解
ester [estə] n. 酯
amide [æmaid] n. 酰胺
kinetic ['kainetik] a. 动力学的
postulate ['pɔstjuleit] v. 要求，假定，假设
cancellation [kænsə'leiʃən] n. 删除，取消
vitamin ['vitəmin] n. 维生素，维他命
epinephrine [epi'nefrin] n. 肾上腺素
mediate [mi:dieit] v. 调停，调解，中介
radical [rædikəl] a. 基本的，基的
sensitivity [sensi'tiviti] n. 敏感性，灵敏度
prednisolone [prəd'nisələun] n. 强的松
aerobic ['ɛərəubik] a. 需氧的
ethylenediamine tetraacetic acid 乙二胺四乙酸（EDTA）
chelating ['ki:leitiŋ] a. 螯合的

PART 4 PHARMACEUTICAL ENGINEERING

Unit 16 Reactor Technology

Reactor technology comprises[①] the underlying principles of chemical reaction engineering (CRE) and the practices used in their application. The focuses of reactor technology are reactor configurations, operating conditions, external operating environments, developmental history, industrial application, and evolutionary change. Reactor designs evolve from the pursuit of new products and uses, higher conversion, more favorable reaction selectivity, reduced fixed and operating costs, intrinsically safe operation, and environmentally acceptable processing.

Besides stoichiometry and kinetics, reactor technology includes requirements for introducing and removing reactants and products, efficiently supplying and withdrawing heat, accommodating phase changes and material transfers, assuring efficient contacting of reactants, and providing for catalyst replenishment or regeneration. Consideration must be given to physical properties of feed and products (vapor, liquid, solid, or combinations), characteristics of chemical reactions (reactant concentrations, paths and rates, operating conditions, and heat addition or removal), the nature of any catalyst used (activity, life, and physical form), and requirements for contacting reactants and removing products (flow characteristics, transport phenomena, mixing requirements, and separating mechanisms).

All the factors are interdependent and be considered together. Requirements for contacting reactants and removing products are a central focus in applying reactor technology; other factors usually are set by the original selection of the reacting system, intended levels of reactant conversion and product selectivity, and economic and environmental considerations.

Reactor Types and Characteristics

Specific reactor characteristics depend on the particular use of the reactor as a laboratory, pilot plant, or industrial unit. All reactors have in common selected characteristics of four basic reactor types: the well-stirred batch reactor, the semibatch reactor, the continuous-flow stirred-tank reactor, and the tubular reactor (Fig. 1).

Batch reactor

A batch reactor is one in which a feed material is treated as a whole for a fixed period of time. Batch reactors may be preferred for small-scale production of high priced products, particularly if many sequential operations are employed to obtain high product yields, e. g., a process requiring a complex cycle of temperature-pressure-reactant additions. Batch reactors also may be justified when multiple, low volume products are produced in the same

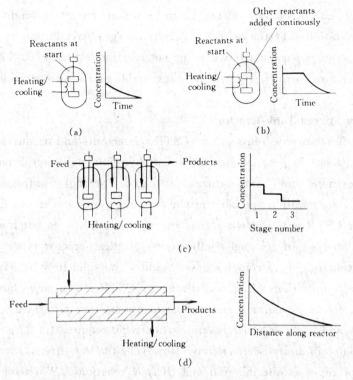

Fig. 1 Reactor types: (a) batch, (b) semibatch, (c) continues-flow stirred-tank, and (d) tubular

equipment or when continuous flow is difficult, as it is with highly viscous or sticky solids-laden liquids, e.g., in the manufacture of polymer resins where molecular weight and product quality are markedly affected by increasing viscosity and heat removal demands. Because residence times can be more uniform in batch reactors, better yields and higher selectivity may be obtained than with continuous reactors. This advantage exists when undesired reaction products inhibit the reaction, side reactions are of lower order than that desired, or the product is an unstable or reactive intermediate.

Batch reactors often are used to develop continuous processes because of their suitability and convenient use in laboratory experimentation. Industrial practice generally favors processing continuously rather than in single batches, because overall investment and operating costs usually are less. Data obtained in batch reactors, except for very rapid reactions, can be well defined and used to predict performance of large scale, continuous-flow reactors. Almost all batch reactors are well stirred; thus, ideally, compositions are uniform throughout and residence times of all contained reactants are constant.

Semibatch Reactor

The semibatch reactor is similar to the batch reactor but has the additional feature of continuous addition or removal of one or more components. For example, gradual addition of chlorine to a stirred vessel containing benzene and catalyst results in higher yields of di- and trichlorobenzene than the inclusion of chlorine in the original batch. Similarly, thermal decomposition of organic liquids is enhanced by continuously removing gaseous products.

Constant pressure can be maintained and chain-terminating reaction products removed from the system. In addition to better yields and selectivity, gradual addition or removal assists in controlling temperature particularly when the net reaction is highly exothermic. Thus, use of a semibatch reactor intrinsically permits more stable and safer operation than in a batch operation.

Continuous-Flow Stirred-Tank Reactor

In a continuous-flow stirred-tank reactor (CSTR), reactants and products are continuously added and withdrawn. In practice, mechanical or hydraulic agitation is required to achieve uniform composition and temperature, a choice strongly influenced by process considerations, i.e., multiple specialty product requirements and mechanical seal pressure limitations. The CSTR is the idealized opposite of the well-stirred batch and tubular plug-flow reactors. Analysis of selected combinations of these reactor types can be useful in quantitatively evaluating more complex gas-, liquid-, and solid-flow behaviors.

Because the compositions of mixtures leaving a CSTR are those within the reactor, the reaction driving forces, usually reactant concentrations, are necessarily low. Therefore, except for zero- and negative-order reactions, a CSTR requires the largest volume of the reactor types to obtain desired conversions. However, the low driving force makes possible better control of rapid exothermic and endothermic reactions. When high conversions of reactants are needed, several CSTRs in series can be used. Equally good results can be obtained by dividing a single vessel into compartments while minimizing back-mixing and short-circuiting. The larger the number of stages, the closer performance approaches that of a tubular plug-flow reactor.

Tubular Reactor

The tubular reactor is a vessel through which flow is continuous, usually at steady state, and configured so that conversion and other dependent variables are functions of position within the reactor rather than of time. In the ideal tubular reactor, the fluids flow as if they were solid plugs or pistons, and reaction time is the same for all flowing material at any given tube cross section; hence, position is analogous to time in the well-stirred batch reactor. tubular reactors resemble batch reactors in providing initially high driving forces, which diminish as the reactions progress down the tubes.

Flow in tubular reactors can be laminar, as with viscous fluids in small-diameter tubes, and greatly deviate from ideal plug-flow behavior, or turbulent, as with gases, and consequently closer to the ideal. Turbulent flow generally is preferred to laminar flow, because mixing is introduced in the direction of flow. For slow reactions and especially in small laboratory and pilot-plant reactors, establishing turbulent flow can result in inconveniently long reactors or may require unacceptably high feed rates. Depending on the consequences in process development and impact on process economics, compromises, though necessary, may not prove acceptable.

Multiphase Reactors

The overwhelming majority of industrial reactors are multiphase reactors. Some important

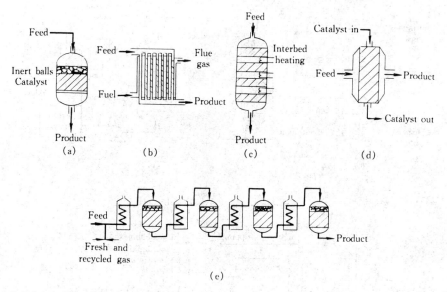

Fig. 2 Multiple fixed-bed configurations: (a) adiabatic fixed-bed reactor, (b) tubular fixed beds, (c) staged adiabatic reactor with interbed heating (cooling), (d) moving radial fixed-bed reactor, and (e) trickle beds in series

reactor configurations are illustrated in Fig. 2 and Fig. 3. The names presented are often employed, but are not the only ones used. The presence of more than one phase, whether or not it is flowing, confounds analyses of reactors and increases the multiplicity of reactor configurations. Gases, liquids, and solids each flow in characteristic fashions, either dispersed in other phases or separately. Flow patterns in these reactors are complex and phases rarely exhibit idealized plug-flow or well-stirred flow behavior.

A fixed-bed reactor is packed with catalyst. If a single phase is flowing, the reactor can be analyzed as a tubular plug-flow reactor or modified to account for axial diffusion. If both liquid and gas or vapor are injected downward through the catalyst bed, or if substantial amounts of vapor are generated internally, the reactors are mixed-phase, downflow, and fixed-bed reactors. If the liquid and gas rates are so low that the liquid flows as a continuous film over the catalyst, the reactors are called trickle beds. Trickle beds have potential advantages of lower pressure drops and superior access for gaseous reactants to the catalyst; however restricted access can also be a disadvantage, e. g., where direct gas contact promotes undesired side reactions.

At higher total flow rates, particularly when the liquid is prone to foaming, the reactor is a pulsed column. This designation arises from the observation that the pressure drop within the catalyst bed cycles at a constant frequency as a result of liquid temporarily blocking gas or vapor pathways. The pulsed column is not to be confused with the pulse reactor used to obtain kinetic data in which a pulse of reactant is introduced into a tube containing a small amount of catalyst.

Downflow of reactants is preferred because reactors are more readily designed mechanically to hold a catalyst in place and are not prone to inadvertent excessive velocities,

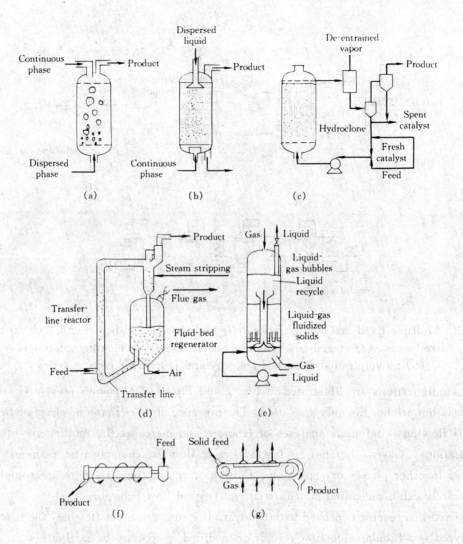

Fig. 3 Multiphase fluid and fluid-solids reactors: (a) bubble column, (b) spray column, (c) slurry reactor and auxiliaries, (d) fluidization unit, (e) gas-liquid-solid fluidized reactor, (f) rotary kiln, and (g) traveling grate or belt drier

which upset the beds. Upflow is used less often but has the advantage of optimum contacting between gas, liquid, and catalyst over a wilder range of conditions. Mixed-phase, upflow, and fixed-bed reactors offer higher liquid holdups and greater assurance of attaining uniform catalyst wetting and radial flow distribution, the consequences of which are more uniform temperature distribution and greater heat transfer.

At high liquid flow rates in these co-current fixed-bed reactors, gas becomes the dispersed phase and bubble flow develops; flow characteristics are similar to those in countercurrent packed-column absorbers. At high gas rates, spray and slug flows can develop. Moving beds are fixed-bed reactors in which spent catalyst or reactive solids are slowly removed from the bottom and fresh material is added at the top. A fixed bed that collects solids impurities present in the feed or produced in the early reaction stages is a guard bed. If catalyst deposits are periodically burned or otherwise removed, the operation is cyclic, and the catalyst remaining behind the combustion front is regenerated.

In bubble column reactors, gas bubble flow upward through a slower moving liquid. The bubbles, which rise in essentially plug flow, draw liquid in their wakes and thereby induce back-mixing in the liquid with which they have come in contact. Analogously, in spray columns, liquid as droplets descend through a fluid, usually gas. Both bubble and spray columns are used for reactions where high interfacial areas between phases are desirable. Bubble column reactors are used for reactions where the rate-limiting step is in the liquid phase, or for slow reactions where contacting is not critical. An important variant of the bubble column reactor is the loop reactor, commonly used for both multiphase and highly viscous systems. Loop reactors are distinguishable by their hydraulically or mechanically driven fluid recirculation, which offers the benefits of the well-stirred behavior of CSTRs and high average reactant concentrations of tubular reactors.

Reactors are termed fluidized or fluid beds if upward gas or liquid flows, alone or in concert, are sufficiently high to suspend the solids and make them appear to behave as a liquid. This process is usually referred to as fluidization. The most common fluid bed is the gas-fluidized bed. With gas feeds, the excess gas over the minimum required for fluidization rises as discrete bubbles, through which the surrounding solids circulate. At higher gas rates, such beds lose their clearly defined surface, and the particles are fully suspended. Depending on the circumstances, these reactors are variously called riser, circulating-fluidized, fast-fluidized, or entrainment reactors. In ebullating-bed or gas-liquid-solid reactors, the solids are fluidized by liquid and gas, with gas primarily providing lifting power in the former, and liquid in the latter. These become slurry bubble column reactors (less precisely, slurry reactors) at high rates when the beds begin to lose their defined surfaces. Slurry bubble column reactors that contain finely powdered solids are often termed and treated as bubble column reactors because such suspensions are homogeneous.

A reactor is termed a radial or panel-bed reactor when gas or vapor flow perpendicular to a catalyst-filled annulus or panel. These are used for rapid reactions to reduce stresses on the catalyst or to minimize pressure drops. Similar cross-flow configurations also are used for processing solids moving downward under gravity while a gas passes horizontally through them. Rotary kilns, belt dryers, and travelling grates are examples. Cross-flow reactors are not restricted to solids-containing systems. Venturis, in which atomized liquids are injected across the gas stream, are effective for fast reactions and similarly for generating small gas bubbles in downward-flowing liquids where mass transport across the gas-liquid interface is limiting.

Selected from R. E. Kirk &. D. F. Othmer, Encyclopedia of Chemical Technology,
4th ed., vol. 20, 1996, John Wiley &. Sons, New York.

Words and Expressions

stoichiometry [stɔiki'ɔmitri] *n.* 化学计算，化学计量（法，学），理想配比法

replenishment [ri'pleniʃmənt] n. （再）补给（充），充实，供给
pilot-plant 中试工厂，小规模试验性工厂（设备）
batch [bætʃ] a. 间歇的，分批的；n. 一批，批料，一次的份量
tubular ['tjubjulə] a. 管（状，形）的，有管的，筒式的
residence time 滞留时间
exothermic [eksəu'θɔːmik] a. 放热的，发热的
endothermic [endɔ'θəːmik] a. 吸热的，内热的
short circuit 短（捷）路，短接
laminar ['læminɑː] a. 层（式，状，流）的，分层的，片（状）的
regime [rei'ʒiːm] n. 方式，方法，规范
adiabatic [ædiə'bætik] a. 绝热的，不传热的
radial [reidiəl] a. 径向的，（沿）半径的，放射的；n. 径向，光（射）线
slurry ['sləːri] n. 稀（泥，沙）浆，淤（矿）浆，悬浮体（液）；v. 使变成泥浆
kiln [kiln] n. （砖，瓦）窑，（火）炉，干燥器；vt. （窑内）烘干，窑烧
entrainment [in'treimənt] n. 挟带，夹带，带去，传输
ebullating-bed 沸腾床
annulus ['ænjuləs] n. 环（带，形，状）物，环形套筒，环状空间
delineate [di'linieit] vt. 描外形，刻划，描绘

Notes

① Comprise 可以是"包含和包括"，也可以解释为"构成"。它可以表示一个整体由若干部分组成，也可表示若干部分组成一个整体。是一个双向的动词，因此没有被动语态。例如：The committee comprises seven persons. 委员会由七人组成。Nineteen articles comprise Book One. 十九篇文章组成了第一卷。

Compose 表示若干部分组成一个整体，所以如果要表示一个整体由若干部分组成就要用被动语态了。Five elements compose this compound. 或 This compound is composed of five elements.

Consist of 表示一个整体由若干部分组成。由于 consist 是一个不及物动词，所以没有被动语态。Water consists of hydrogen and oxygen. 水由氢和氧组成。

Exercise

1. Answer the following questions:
   (1) What kinds of the reactor are often used in pharmaceutical factories?
   (2) What are the advantages and disadvantages of the Continuous-Flow Stirred-Tank reactor?
   (3) Could you give some production examples that use multiphase reactors?
   (4) What kind of the reactor does a jacked fermentor belong to?
2. Translate the "Tubular Reactor" section into Chinese.
3. Write a short essay to describe the multiplicity of multiphase reactor.

Reading Material 16

Fermentation

Components of Fermentation Processes

With few exceptions, such as biotransformations, most existing fermentation processes can be broken down into several distinct operations. First, there is the formulation of the culture medium used to grow the microorganism during inoculum propagation and production fermentation. This is followed by the preparation of sterile medium, fermentors, and related equipment. Then there is propagation of a pure and active culture to seed the production fermentor. Fourth is the culyuring of the microorganism in the production fermentor under optimum conditions for product formation. Then the product is separated from the fermentation broth and subsequently purified. Lastly, there is the treatment and disposal of the cellular and effluent by-products of the process.

All microorganisms require water, sources of carbon, energy, nitrogen, and minerals. Certain vitamins and growth factors are often required as well. Additionally, oxygen is necessary for all aerobic fermentations. Chemically defined or semidefined media are often used up to the seed stage of a fermentation to ensure rapid and reproducible growth. However, on a large scale, economics play a key role in determining the components. The material cost and availability, location of fermentation plant and commodity pricing are key variables. In the case of the ICI pressure cycle fermentor for single-cell proteins the whole fermentation process was essentially designed around the availability of a relatively inexpensive and abundant raw material, i.e., methanol derived from methane gas. Generally, the nutritional requirements for most conventional fermentations can be met by formulating a medium having, eg, molasses, cereal grains, starches, glucose, sucrose, and lactose as carbon sources. Corn steep liquor, soybean meal, cottonseed flour, slaughterhouse waste, fish meal, ammonia, ammonium salts, and fermentation residues often serve as the nitrogen base.

Soya bean oil, lard, and cotton seed oil serve to control foam in aerated fermentations as well as providing carbon for nutrition. Often, other more traditional defoamers such as silicone oils and polypropylene glycol are necessary as well. Brewer's yeast is frequently used as a combination nitrogen, vitamin, and growth factor source. The overall contribution of the cost of the medium may be very high in some commodity-type fermentations; thus the producer microorganism is often selected or engineered to use components it traditionally would not, but which are available at a reasonable price.

With few exceptions, the nutrient medium is charged or batched into the fermentor in a sterile form or is sterilized in the fermentor. Sterilization inactivates the indigenous fauna present including water that would foul up the fermentation of interest. Sterilization of the batch medium is usually accomplished by heating to 121~125 C under pressure of 103~124 kPa (15~18 psig) for at least 15 minutes. Heat is supplied by directly injecting live clean steam into the fermentor or into the fermentor jacket. Continuous sterilization of various feed components and often the initial batch charge itself is accomplished by pumping the medium through heat exchangers using an appropriate holdup time. Smaller amounts of various components may be autoclaved and heat-sensitive components are filter-sterilized under aseptic conditions prior to addition. The bioconversion of D-sorbitol [50-70-4][1] to L-sorbose [87-79-6] by *Gluconobacter suboxydans* can be accomplished using partial sterilization because the process only takes 24 h and the high concentration of D-sorbitol (20% w/w) inhibits the growth of most contaminating microorganisms. In the formation of lactic acid by *Lactobacillus delbruekii*, the fermentation occurs at 50 C, and this combined with a high substrate concentration guards against contamination. Apart from these few exceptions, any material must be sterilized prior to entering a fermentor. Air is routinely sterilized by passage through various filters such as packed columns of glass wool, stainless-steel mesh, or 0.2 micrometer hydrophobic (so-called absolute) bacteriological filters. A few companies prefer to heat sterilize air or heat sterilize the air in addition to a downstream filter, thus minimizing any chance of contamination. Following sterilization, the fermentor medium is adjusted in terms of pH and temperature prior to being seeded or inoculated with an actively growing culture of the producer microorganism. Inocula are typically developed in several stages and the final volume is usually 1%~10% of the fermentation volume. Actively growing cultures are preferred because those that have entered stationary phase may lead to undesirable process changes and variations as a result of metabolic and genetic variations. It is particularly important to use actively growing cultures of sporulating bacteria. Sporulation leads to an excessivly long lag phase. On the other hand, fermentations employing fungi and streptomycetes often have an inoculum development protocol that employs spores.

Once the culture is actively growing, the environment in the fermentor changes in part because of the depletion of medium components and in part because of the production of metabolites by the fermenting mass. In order to maximize productivity, a number of parameters must be maintained within close predetermined limits. The temperature is usually maintained at ± 0.5 C from the set point. Thermocouples (TC) or platinum resistance thermometer devices (RTD) are typically used to measure the temperature. The set point for the large portion of the fermentation is often a few degrees lower than that used to grow the culture, and such changes or profiles are typically controlled by a computer or microprocessor based on time or some off-line measurement such as culture density, oxygen uptake rate, or carbon dioxide evolution rate. Experience has show that in very large (250 m^3) fermentors when the culture is actively growing, such fine control is not normally possible and transient temperatures of a few degrees above the set point can be attained because the fermentation broth produces heat at a greater rate than can be removed by the cooling process employed. Cooling is achieved by pumping chilled water through coils submerged inside the vessel or by the half-pipe design using external coils. Cooling jackets are rarely employed on large-scale production fermentors.

In part because of the enormous cost of cooling large-scale production fermentors, much attention has been paid to the design and operation of both internal and external cooling coils. Also, because cooling water is not sterile, it has a tremendous potential to contaminate the fermentation if hairline fractures ever occur in internally located coils. A novel method of cooling is use of a heat exchanger located external to the fermentor. This technique is employed in the Vogel-Busch deep-jet system for smaller (<10 m^3) volumes of fast growing *E. coli* fermentations producing genetically engineered products at high cell densities.

Other than temperature, pH is the second most important variable that must be controlled within defined limits. The actual pH used is, of course, a function of the microorganism employed. Control is usually achieved to within ± 0.20 pH unit in large-scale operations through the use of steam sterilizable electrodes.

Aerobic fermentations must be supplied with an adequate supply of sterile air. Because of the low solubility of oxygen in water (10 mg/L) it must be constantly replenished. The amount of air supplied is typically $0.5 \sim 1.0$ fermentor broth volume per minute. For an industrial-scale fermentor (350 m^3) the enormous amount of sterile air needed lends itself to a significant operating expense. The air is typically introduced into the fermentor through a perforated pipe or sparger located at the bottom of a stainless steel draft tube. To maximize transfer of oxygen into the liquid phase, many design changes to the traditional ring assembly sparger have been proposed and used. The open pipe or ring spargers dominate design features as of this writing.

Aeration by sparging alone can be insufficient to meet the demands of an active culture and oxygen starvation is often the limiting factor in both culture growth and productivity. The use of a stirrer or agitator (ca $40 \sim 70$ rpm) having multiple impellers in combination with internal baffles and tank-over pressure helps overcome this problem to a large extent. The design and testing of impellers to improve both oxygen transfer and mixing of viscous fermentations broths is seemingly paying off with the use of hydrofoil mixers in conjunction with traditional Rushton turbines. However, in many fermentations, despite the use of stirrer motors of several hundred horsepower, oxygen transfer is still insufficient to provide an optimally aerated culture.

On a laboratory scale and in smaller (<1.5 m^3) fermentors the air can be enriched with oxygen and speeds (up to 600 rpm) can largely offset oxygen deprivation. Oxygen enrichment and high speed agitation (>100 rpm) is prohibitive from both safety and cost perspectives on a large scale. Because of mechanical simplicity and the ability to provide reasonable aeration and good mixing, air-lift fermentors and their draft-tubeless counterparts, ie, the bubble-columns, are increasingly being used at the largest end of the scale. Steam sterilizable probes provide real time information with respect to the oxygen tension in the fermentor. The more expensive, but more reliable, polarographic-type probe is preferred over the galvanic type. The probe output is usually referred to as important indictor of both culture growth and productivity, care is needed to make sure that the reading is an indication of what is really happening in the bulk phase of the fermentation broth rather than just a localized phenomenon.

Selected from R. E. Kirk & D. F. Othmer, *Encyclopedia of Chemical Technology*, 4th ed., vol.10, 1993, John Wiley & Sons, New York.

Words and Expressions

culture medium　（细菌的）培养基
inoculum [i'nɔkjuləm] n. 培养液，接种体
sterile ['sterail] a. 无菌的，消过毒的
broth [brɔθ] n. 肉汤，清汤
effluent ['efluənt] a.; n. 发出（的），流出（的，物，液），污水，溢流
molasses [mə'læsiz] n. （废）糖浆，糖蜜
cereal [siəriəl] n.; a. 谷类（的），谷子（的），谷物
starch [stɑːtʃ] n. 淀粉，浆（糊）
glucose ['gluːkəus] n. 葡萄糖，右旋糖
sucrose ['sjuːkrəus] n. 蔗糖，砂糖
lactose ['læktəus] n. 乳糖
indigenous [indi'dʒinəs] a. 本土的，土（国）产的，固有的
fauna [fɔːnə] n. 动物群，动物区系
foul up　搞糟，弄乱，做坏
aseptic [æ'septik] a. 无菌的，防腐的；n. 防腐剂
sorbitol ['sɔbitəl] n. 山梨醇
sorbose ['sɔːbəus] n. 山梨糖
autoclave ['ɔːtəkleiv] vt. 用高压锅蒸（消毒），压煮；n. 高压锅（釜）
lactobacillus [læktoubə'siləs] n. 乳酸杆菌
metabolic [metə'bɔlik] a. 变化（形）的，（新陈）代谢的
sporulate ['spɔrjuleit] vi. 形成孢子
spore [spɔː] n. 孢子
depletion [di'pliːʃən] n. 用尽，损耗，缺乏，亏损
perforate ['pəːfəreit] v. 穿（钻，打，冲）孔，打眼
sparger ['spɛədʒə] n. 分布器，喷雾器
impeller [im'pelə] n. 叶轮，涡轮，推进器
baffle ['bæfl] n. 隔板，导流片，折流板；v. 挫败，阻碍
hydrofoil ['haidrəfɔil] n. 水叶，着水板，水翼
turbine ['təːbin] n. 涡轮（机），透平（机）
deprivation [depri'veiʃən] n. 脱除，剥夺，免职
galvanic [gæl'vænik] a. （流）电的，（电池）电流的，电镀的
polarographic [pəulærə'græfik] a. 极谱（法）的

Notes

① D-sorbitol[50-70-4]方括号中的数码表示化学物质登记号。美国化学文摘服务社给化学成分明确,结构及化学键清楚的每种化学物质编一个登记号,即每一个号码代表一种物质,所以可由登记号查出 CA(Chemical Abstract)选用名。登记号由三部分组成,用短线连接。第一部分最多可有六位数,第二部分为两位数,第三部分为一位数。

Unit 17 Distillation

Distillation columns are vertical, cylindrical vessels containing devices that provides intimate contacting of the rising vapor with the descending liquid. This contacting provides the opportunity for the two streams to achieve some approach to thermodynamic equilibrium. Depending on the type of internal devices used, the contacting may occur in discrete steps, called plates or trays, or in a continuous differential manner on the surface of a packing material. The fundamental requirement of the column is to provide efficient and economic contacting at a required mass-transfer rate. Individual column requirements vary from high vacuum to high pressure, from low to high liquid rates, from clean to dirty systems, and so on. As a result, a large variety of internal devices has been developed to fill these needs. The column devices discussed herein are used for absorption (qv) and stripping, the gas flowing up the column is primarily a noncondensable phase at column conditions, whereas in distillation the gas phase is a condensable vapor.

Plate Columns

There are two general types in use: crossflow and counterflow. These names refer to the direction of the liquid flow relative to the rising vapor flow. On the cross-flow plate the liquid flows across the plate and from plate to plate via downcomers. On the counterflow plate liquid flows downward through the same orifices used by the rising vapor.

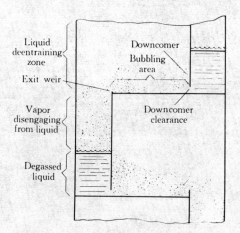

Fig. 1 Flow pattern in a crossflow plate distillation column

Crossflow Plates. As indicated in Fig. 1, liquid enters a crossflow plate from the bottom of the downcomer of the plate above and flows across the active or bubbling area where it is aerated zone where most of the vapor-liquid mass transfer occurs. The aerated mixture flows over the exit weir into a downcomer. A vapor-liquid disengagement takes place in the downcomer and most of the trapped vapor escapes from liquid and flows back to the interplate vapor space. The liquid, essentially free of entrapped vapor, leaves the plate by flowing under the downcomer to the inlet side of the next lower plate. The vapor, disengaging from the aerated mass on the plate, rises to the next plate above.

The pressure drop incurred by the vapor as it passes through the orifices of the plate is fundamental to plate operation. In most plate designs, the pressure drop prevents the crossflowing liquid from falling through the plate. The pressure drop also results from the energy consumed to disperse the vapor-liquid mixture, e. g., to atomize a portion of the liquid to provide increased interfacial area for mass transfer. Diameters of commercial crossflow plate columns range from 0.3 to 15m and plate spacings range from 0.15 to 1.2. The total pressure drop per plate is often in the range of 0.25 to 1.6 kPa (2~12 mmHg).

The principal vapor-liquid contacting devices are used in current crossflow plate design: the sieve plate, the valve plate, and the bubble cap plate. These devices provide the needed intimate of vapor and liquid, requisite to maximizing transfer of mass across the interfacial boundary.

Sieve Plates. The conventional sieve or perforated plate is inexpensive and the simplest of the devices normally used. The contacting orifices in the conventional sieve plate are holes that measure 1 to 12mm diameter and exhibit ratios of open area to active area ranging from 1 : 20 to 1 : 7. If the open area is too small, the pressure drop across the plate is excessive; if the open area is too large, the liquid weeps or dumps through the holes.

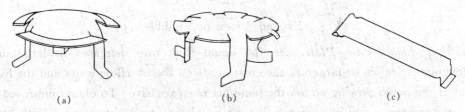

Fig. 2 Individual valve units used in valve plates: (a) Koch Flexitray valve, (b) Glitsch Ballast valve, (c) Nutter Float valve

Valve Plates. Valve plates are categorized as proprietary and details of design vary from one vendor to another. These represent a variation of the sieve plate in which the holes are large and are fitted with liftable valve units such as those shown in Fig. 2. The principal advantage over sieve plates is the ability to maintain efficient operation over a wider operating range through the use of variable orifices (valves) which open or close depending on vapor rate. The most common valve units consist of flat disks having attached legs that allow the valve to open or close. Sometimes two weights of valves are used on a single plate to extend operating range and improve vapor distribution. The valve units usually have a tab or indentation that provides a minimum open area of vapor flow, even when the valve is closed, and also prevents the valve from sticking under corrosive or fouling conditions. Details on valve plate geometry, along with methods for valve plate design, are available.

Bubble Cap Plates. Until the early 1950s, bubble caps were the standard design in the chemical industry. Usage in newer installations is limited to low liquid flow rate applications, or to those cases where the widest possible operating range is desired. A typical bubble cap is shown in Fig. 3. The vapor flows through a hole in the plate floor, through the riser, reverses direction in the dome of the cap, flows downward in the annular area between the riser and the cap, and exits through the slots in the cap. commercial caps range from 50 to 150 mm in diameter and many slot design variations have been used. Bubble cap trays are more expensive and have lower capacity than sieve or valve plates, therefore, use has dropped to a very small percentage of newer column designs.

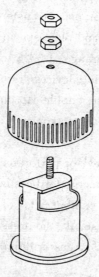

Fig. 3 Expanded view of a bubble cap

Multiple Liquid-Path Plate. As the liquid flow rate increases in large diameter crossflow plates (ca 4m or larger), the crest heads on the overflow weirs and the hydraulic gradient of the liquid flowing across the plate become excessive. To obtain improved overall plate performance, multiple liquid-flow-path plates may be used, with multiple downcomers. These designs are illustrated and discussed in detail in the literature.

Counterflow Plates. Counterflow plates are used frequently than crossflow plates. The liquid flows downward and the plate does not have downcomers. The opening are round holes (dualflow tray) or slots (Turbogrid tray). A variation of the fashion. Counterflow plates are used advantageously in fouling services because for each hole vapor and liquid flow alternately, providing a self-cleaning action that is quite effective. The dualflow and Turbogrid plates have similar operating characteristics, and typical operating data have been published.

Another important plate which has characteristic similar to a counterflow plate is the Multiple Downcomer (MD) plate. This is a plate where the active are occupies the full column cross section but with a plurality of small downcomers interspersed among the perforations. The downcomers are specially sealed to prevent upflow of vapor through them. The plate has been used successfully in many high liquid flow cases.

Packed Columns.

In packed columns, the vapor-liquid contacting takes place in continuous beds of solid packing elements rather than in discrete individual plates. The contacting can be visualized as occurring in differential increments across the height of packing; thus packing are knowns as counterflow device rather than stagewise devices. Mechanically, the packed column is a relatively simple structure.

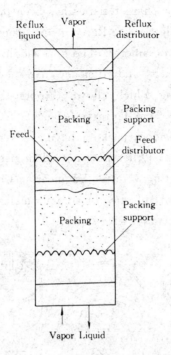

Fig. 4 Packed column shell and internal. Column shown has single packed beds above and below the feed. For separations requiring a large number of stages, additional beds, separated by redistribution devices, are likely tube needed

In its simplest form the packed column comprises a vertical shell having dumped or carefully arranged packing elements on an opentype support, together with a suitable liquid distribution device above the packed bed. A packed column having two packed beds and a midcolumn feed is shown in Fig. 4. The vapor enters column below the bottom bed and flows upward through the column. The liquid (reflux or other liquid stream) enters at the top through the liquid distributor and flows downward through the packing countercurrently to the rising vapor. The height of the individual packed beds is limited to $2 \sim 9m$ by the mechanical strength of the packing or by the need to redistribute the liquid so that good mass-transfer efficiency can be maintained.

Packings. For many years packed columns consisted of randomly dumped packings almost exclusively, with occasional applications of regularly stacked packing or pad of woven or knitted wire. In the late 1960s a partial trend away from random packings began when a special structured packing made of wire gauze was introduced by Sulzer Brothers in Switzerland. The indicated advantages of the structured packings were high mass-transfer efficiency and very low pressure drop. These devices appeared to be ideal for high vacuum distillations. However, cost of fabrication was very high and they were considered mainly for the vacuum distillation of specialty chemicals. In 1997, a lower cost sheet metal version was introduced, and since that time a large business in structured sheet metal packings has arisen. At the same time, improved random packings have been developed and a comprehensive discussion of their characteristics has been published. Some of the common random packings are shown in Fig. 5. The Raschig ring, one of the oldest of packings, is an open cylinder of equal height and diameter. The Berl saddle and the ceramic Intalox saddle (Norton Co.) have a higher capacity and efficiency than the Rascig ring. The Pall ring is a modification of the Raschig ring which allows through-flow of liquid and vapor, with consequent lower pressure drop amd better efficiency. The newer Intalox metal saddle (IMTP) is an example of a random packing having a very high void fraction and low resistance to the flowing phases. Other newer random packings, include the CMR ring (Glitsch, Inc.) and the Nutter ring (Nutter Engineering Co). The random-type packings can generally be made from metal, plastic, or ceramic materials; the approximate nominal size range for the individual elements is 12~75mm.

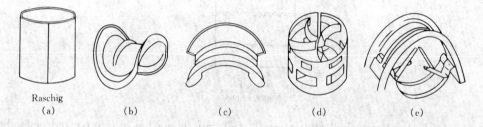

Fig. 5 Random packing elements for distillation columns: (a) Raschig ring (metal), (b) Berl saddle (ceramic), (c) Intalox saddle (ceramic), (d) Pall ring (metal), and (e) Intalox saddle (metal)

Packed Column Internals. In order to ensure good packed column mass-transfer efficiency, the liquid must be distributed uniformly over the surface of the packing. As a general rule there should be at least 100 pour points per square meter (10points/ft^2), although fewer points may be used for random packings of the bluff-body type such as Raschig rings and Berl saddles. Although they have capacity and pressure drop limitations, the bluff-body packing elements are able to divide the downflowing liquid and thus improve on an initially marginal distribution. On the other hand, the through-flow type random packings, e.g., Pall rings and Intalox metal tower packings, as well as the structured packings, are not able to correct the initial distribution and in fact allow some deterioration of distribution if the bed heights are greater than about five meters.

Considerable research is in progress on methods for ensuring good liquid distribution in large diameter column, and the packing manufacturers maintain large test stands where a particular design of distributor can be tested using water before being installed in the column. The distributor design problem becomes more severe at low, i.e., $<700cm^3/(s \cdot m^2)$ (1 gal/min. ft^2)[1] liquid rates or in large ($>$3 m) diameter towers. An example of a more fundamental study of liquid distribution is available as are typical liquid distributor designs and typical packing supports.

Selected from R. E. Kirk & D. F. Othmer, *Encyclopedia of Chemical Technology*, 4th ed., vol. 8, 1993, John Wiley & Sons, New York.

Words and Expressions

discrete [dis'kri:t] *a.* 不连续（接）的，分离（散）的，个别的
tray [trei] *n.* 分馏塔盘，塔板
strip [strip] *v.* 汽提，解吸
orifice ['ɔrifis] *n.* （小）孔，小洞，喷嘴，孔板
weir [wiə] *n.* 堰，溢流堰，低坝；*v.* 用坝挡住
downcomer 泄水管，下气道
atomize ['ætəmaiz] *vt.* 使雾化，喷雾，散布
requisite ['rekwizit] *a.* 必需的，必不可少的；*n.* 必须品，必要条件，要素
valve [vælv] *n.* 阀（门），活门，气门，闸门
sieve [siv] *n.* 筛，筛子，滤网
bubble cap 泡罩
proprietary [prə'praitəri] *a.* 专利的，有专利权的，独占的；*n.* 所有（权），所有人，业主
indentation [inden'teiʃən] *n.* 刻（压）痕，凹槽，缺口
dome [doum] *n.* 园（拱，穹）顶，圆顶帽，穹面
slot [lɔt] *n.* 缝，隙，槽，条板
crest [krest] *n.* （峰）顶，脊，振幅，齿顶
gradient ['greidiənt] *n.* 坡度，斜率，梯度变化曲线
corrugate ['kɔrugeit] *v.* 成波（纹）状，起皱
precipitous [pri'sipitəs] *a.* 险峻的，陡峭的，突然的，急转直下
abscissa [æb'sisə] *n.* 横（坐）标，横线
ordinate ['ɔ:dinit] *n.* 纵坐标，竖标距；*a.* 有规则的
heuristics [hjuə'ristiks] *n.* 直观推断，试探法
pseudo ['sju:dəu] *a.* 假的，伪的
gauze [gɔ:z] *n.* （线、纱、滤、金属丝）网，纱布，铁砂
nominal ['nɔminl] *a.* 标（公）称，标定的，规定的，名义上的
emboss [im'bɔs] *vt.* 使浮凸于（表面）上，使凸起，作浮雕
lance [lɑ:s] *v.* 切开，刺破，投，急走前进；*n.* （长）枪，矛（装器具），喷枪，喷水器
bluff [blʌf] *a.* 陡峭的；*n.* 悬崖，天然陡坡
deterioration [ditiəriə'reiʃən] *n.* 变坏，降低（品质），损坏

Notes

① [gal/min·ft²] 是英制单位。gal—gallon，加仑（液量单位，1 美加仑=3.785 升，1 英加仑=4.546 升。ft—英尺，1 英尺=0.3048 米）。

Exercises

1. Answer the following questions:
   (1) What are the fundamental requirements of the distillation columns?
   (2) How does the liquid flow in a plate column?
   (3) Where does the liquid and gas contact in a packed column?
   (4) How much do you know about the supercritical fluid extraction?
2. Write a short essay to compare the value plates with the sieve plates.
3. Translate the "packing" section into Chinese.

Reading Material 17

Supercritical Fluid Extraction

Within the past decade numerous industrial and academic research and development laboratories have investigated the underlying fundamentals and process applications of supercritical fluid solvents, that is, gases or liquids above their critical points (McHugh Paulaitis et al., 1983a; Pauluitis and McHugh, 1981). When a supercritical fluid (SCF) is used as an extractive solvent, it is possible to separate a multicomponent mixture by capitalizing on both the differences in component volatilities (i.e., the salient feature of distillation) and the differences in the specific interactions between the mixture components and the SCF solvent (i.e., the salient feature of liquid extraction). The application of SCF solvents is based on the experimental observation that many gases exhibit enhanced solvating power when compressed to conditions above the critical point. Scientists and engineers have been aware of this experimental fact for more than one hundred years, but it is only in the past decade or so that supercritical fluid solvents have been the focus of active research and development programs.

Table 1 Critical Conditions for Various Supercritical Solvents

Solvents	Critical Temperature (℃)	Critical Pressure (atm)
Carbon dioxide	31.1	72.8
Ethane	32.3	48.2
Ethylene	9.3	49.7
Propane	96.7	41.9
Propylene	91.9	45.6
Cyclohexane	280.3	40.2
Isopropanol	235.2	47.0
Benzene	289.0	48.3
Toluene	318.6	40.6
p-Xylene	343.1	34.7
Chlorotrifluorlmethane	28.9	38.7
Trichlorofluoromethane	198.1	43.5
Ammonia	132.5	111.3
Water	374.2	217.6

The motivation for the development of SCF solvent technology as a viable separation technique is a result of:

1. a sharp increase in the cost of energy, which has increased the cost of traditional, energy-intensive separation techniques, such as distillation;

2. increased governmental scrutiny and regulation of common industrial solvents, such as chlorinated hydrocarbons, which has made nontoxic, environmentally acceptable supercritical fluid solvents such as CO_2 very attractive as alternative industrial solvents;

3. more stringent pollution-control legislation, which has caused industry to consider alternative means of waste treatment; and

4. increased performance demands on materials, which traditional processing techniques cannot meet.

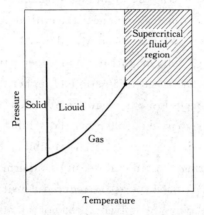

Fig. 1 Pressure-temperature diagram for a pure component

To capitalize fully on the unique solvent characteristics of supercritical fluids it is necessary to understand the phase behavior of pure SCF solvents and of SCF-solute mixtures. Let us first consider the pure SCF solvent. The critical region for a pure component is show by the crosshatched area in the pressure-temperature (p-T) diagram in Fig. 1. Table 1 lists the critical temperatures and pressures for a number of gases and liquids. A cursory inspection of this table reveals the following trends:

1. Most hydrocarbons have a critical pressure (p_c) close to 50 atm;

2. The critical temperatures (T_c) for the light hydrocarbons, such as ethylene and ethane, are around room temperature; cyclic aliphatics and aromatics have higher critical temperatures;

3. Carbon dioxide has a mild critical temperature and a slightly elevated critical pressure; and

4. The last two compounds have high critical temperatures or pressures, which is a result of polarity and hydrogen bonding.

The authors of virtually all the previously mentioned review papers suggest that, to a first approximation, the solvent power of a supercritical fluid can be related to the solvent density in the critical region. This statement can be rationalized by considering the density behavior of a pure component. For a reduced temperature (T_R) range of 0.9 to 1.2 and at reduced pressures (p_R) greater than 1.0, the reduced density (ρ_R) of the solvent can change from a value of about 0.1, a gaslike density, to about 2.5, a liquidlike density. As the reduced densities become liquidlike, the supercritical fluid begins to act as a liquid solvent. Note, however, that as the reduced temperature is increased to a value of 1.55, the supercritical fluid becomes more expanded. Therefore, if liquidlike densities are to be reached, the reduced pressure must be increased to values as high as 10.0. When operating in the critical region both pressure and temperature can now be used to regulate the density and, therefore, the solvent power of a supercritical fluid.

The unique feature of a supercritical fluid is that it displays a wide spectrum of solvent characteristics. As an example of the ability to "fine-tune" the solvent power of an SCF, consider the solubility behavior for the solid naphthalene ($T_m = 80.2$ C) supercritical ethylene ($T_c = 0.3$ C, $p_c = 49.8$ atm)[1] system near the critical point of pure ethylene (Diepen and Scheffer, 1953; Tskhanskaya, Iomtev, and Mushkina, 1964). At a temperature of 12 C ($T_R = 1.01$), the solubility of solid naphthalene in supercritical ethylene increases quite dramatically as the pressure is increased to 50 atm and higher. At pressures below 50 atm, naphthalene solubility is extremely low, as would be expected for the solubility of a solid in gas. At pressures much higher than about 90 atm, the solubilty of naphthalene in ethylene reaches a limiting value of about 1.5 mole-%. The solubility behavior along this isotherm can be interpreted by considering the reduced-density isotherm at 1.0. Note that the 12 C isotherm has the same characteristic shape as the reduced-density isotherm at 1.0. From this example, one can readily see why the solvent behavior of an SCF is related (to a first approximation) to the solvent density behavior in the critical region.

To obtain an appreciation of the enhanced solvent power of supercritical ethylene, let us compare the experimentally observed naphthalene solubility (y) at 100 atm and 12 C with the solubility that is calculated when the supercritical fluid phase is assumed to act like an ideal gas. In this instance we use the following expressing:

$$y_2 = \left[\frac{p_2^{\text{sub}}}{p}\right] \exp\left[\int_{p_2^{\text{sub}}}^{p} \frac{V_2^S}{RT} dp\right] \quad [2]$$

Where the subscript 2 represents naphthalene, p_2^{sub} represents the sublimation pressure of solid naphthalene, and V_2^S represents the molar volume of solid naphthalene (Prausnitz, 1969). At 12 C and 100 atm the sublimation pressure is equal to 0.0000303 atm (Dipen and Scheffer, 1953). For pressures up to about 1,000 atm, it can be assumed that V_2^S is a constant equal to 111.9 cc/gmol (Vaidya and kennedy, 1971). At 100 atm and 12 C, we find

$$\frac{y_2(\text{oberved})}{y_2(\text{calculated})} = 16156$$

This simple calculation, although not rigorous, does indicate the large increase in solvent capacity of supercritical ethylene relative to the capacity of ethylene considered as an ideal gas at 100 atm. The large increase in solvent power of ethylene cannot be attributes to a hydrostatic pressure effect since the pressure effect is explicitly accounted for in the exponential term in the above equation Instead, the large difference in experimental and calculated naphthalene solubility at high pressures is associated with the nonideal behavior of ethylene as it is compressed to liquidlike densities in its critical region.

Considering now the 35°C ($T_R = 1.09$) isotherm, we see that the solubility behavior is not as sensitive to pressure in the region near 50 atm as it was for the 12°C isotherm. However, at pressures greater than 100 atm, where ethylene exhibits liquidlike densities, the 35°C isotherm reaches a higher limiting solubility value (about 5 mole-%).

As further verification of the fluid density versus sublimation pressure effect, consider the change in naphthalene solubility in supercritical ethylene when the temperature is increased from 12°C to 35°C at a constant pressure of about 50 atm. Naphthalene solubility drops by more than an order of magnitude for this 23°C change in temperature[3]. This sharp decrease in solubility upon heating the mixture isobarically near the critical point of ethylene is attributed to the large decrease in ethylene density.

This SCF-solid solubility behavior may be used as a model system whose principles can be applied to many practical SCF separation problems, such as the extraction of (almost solid) oleoresins, the color and taste ingredients from spices and red peppers (Stahl et al., 1980); the separation of solid aromatic isomers (Krukonis and Kurnik, 1985); and the removal of lower-molecularweight constituents from coal at elevated temperatures using an SCF with a high critical temperature, such as toluene (Williams, 1981).

In contrast to a liquid-liquid extraction process, where the solvent in the extract phase is separated by distillation, an SCF-liquid extraction process has the advantage that the solvent can be recovered by decreasing the system pressure (Elgin and Weinstock, 1959). As an example of a single-stage SCF-liquid extraction process, let us consider the separation of ethanol from water using supercritical fluids. A variety of SCF solvents such as carbon dioxide, ethane, and ethylene have been tasted for recovering ethanol from water. For example, figure 2 shows the phase behavior for the ethanol-water-ethane system (Mchuge, Mallett, and Kohn, 1983).

One possible procedure for extracting ethanol from a 50 : 50 mixture of ethanol and water using supercritical ethane is depicted by the dashed line in Fig. 2. The 50 : 50 mixture, incidentally, is not one of industrial importance, but it is a convenient example for explaining the general behavior of ternary systems. Enough supercritical ethane is introduced into the system at a constant temperature and pressure until the overall ethanol-water-ethane composition coincides with a value well within the two-phase liquid-fluid region of the diagram (e.g., at coordinates of 30 : 30 : 40 ethanol : water : ethane). If a tie-line were drawn at this point a liquid phase of 40 mole-% ethanol, 40 mole-% water, and 20 mole-% ethane exists in equilibrium with a fluid phase of 4 mole-% ethanol, 1 mole-% water, and 95 mole-% ethane. The selectivity of supercritical ethane for ethanol relative to water as defined by

$$\text{Selectivity} = \frac{[(x_1)_F]/[(x_1)_L]}{[(x_2)_F]/[(x_2)_L]}$$

Where x denotes composition, subscripts 1 and 2 denote ethanol and water, respectively, and subscripts F and L denote the fluid and liquid phases, is approximately 2.5. The loading or amount of ethanol in the fluid phase is only 4 mole-%; therefore, large amounts of ethane are needed to recover the ethanol from the feed solution. This example indicates that the values for both the loading and the selectivity of ethanol in the supercritical fluid phase must be considered when designing an SCF extraction process. Numerous examples of SCF-liquid separations are described in a later chapter of this book.

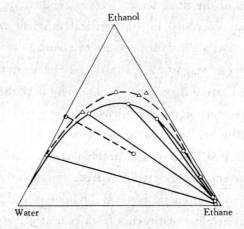

Fig. 2   Phase behavior of the ethanol-water-supercritical ethane system at 40℃. The open triangles represent the 50-atm isobar and the open circles represent the 80-atm

In addition to its unique solubility characteristics, an SCF solvent possesses certain other physicochemical properties that add to its attractiveness as a solvent. For example, even though it possesses a liquidlike density over much of the range of industrial interest, it exhibits gaslike transport properties of diffusivity and viscosity (Schneider, 1978). Additionally, the zero surface tension of supercritical fluids allows facile penetration into microporous materials.

The properties of gaslike diffusivity and viscosity, zero surface tension, and liquidlike density combined with the pressure dependent solvent power of a supercritical fluid have provide the impetus for applying SCF technology to a gamut of separation problems experienced in many segments of industry. Although the combination of properties of an SCF solvent does indeed make it a potentially attractive solvent, on occasion these properties may offer no advantage relative to the properties of conventional solvents. It is necessary to evaluate SCF technology on a case-by-case basis, as is illustrated by the numerous examples covered in this book.

Selected from Marr A. McHugh, Val J. Krukonis, *Supercritical Fluid Extraction: Principle and Practice*, 1986, Butterworth Publisher, Boston.

Words and Expressions

capitalize on (upon)　利用
salient　['seiliənt]　*a.* 凸（突）的，显著，喷射的；*n.* 凸角，突出部
viable　[vaiəbl]　*a.* 能生存的，有生存力的，可行
cross-hatch　['krɔːʃætʃ]　*vt.* 给……近交叉阴影线
cursory　['kəːsəri]　*a.* 草率的，仓促的，疏忽的
vicinity　[vi'siniti]　*n.* 附近，邻近，近处，接近，密切的关系
isotherm　['aisəuθəm]　*n.* 等温线
sublimation　['sʌblimeiʃən]　*n.* 升华（作用），凝华，精炼，提纯
hydrostatic　['haidrəstætik]　*a.* 静水利学的，流体静力（学）的
exponential　[ekspəu'nenʃəl]　*a.* 指数（标）的，幂的；*n.* 指数
verification　[verifi'keiʃən]　*n.* 检验，鉴定，核实验证
isobaric　[aisəu'bærik]　*a.* 等压（线），恒压的，等权的
microporous　['maikrəu'pɔːrəs]　*a.* 微孔性的，多孔的
diffusivity　[difju'siviti]　*n.* 扩散性（率，系数，能力），弥散性
impetus　['impitəs]　*n.* （原，推）动力，动（冲）量，激励，冲击
gamut　['gæmət]　*n.* 全部，全（整个）范围，音阶，色移

Notes

① 1atm—1 个大气压。1 [物理大气压] =101.3kPa，1 [工程大气压] =98.1kPa。

② $y_2 = \left[\dfrac{p_2^{sub}}{p}\right] \exp\left[\int_{p_2^{sub}}^{p} \dfrac{V_2^5}{RT} dp\right]$ 的读法如下：y two equals p two sub over p all multiplied by e to the power of integral of V two to the five over R times T multiplied by dp between limits p two sub and p.

③ Naphthalene solubility drops by more than an order of magnitude for this 23℃ change in temperature. an order of magnitude— 一个数量级。

Unit 18 Crystalization

Crystallization is one of the oldest unit operations in the portfolio of industrial and /or laboratory separations. Almost all separation techniques involve formation of a second phase from a feed, and processing conditions must be selected that allow relatively easy segregation of the two or more resulting phases. This is a requirement of crystallization also, and there are a variety of other properties of the solid product that must be considered in the design and operation of a crystallizer. Interactions among process function, product, and phenomena important in crystallization are illustrated in Fig. 1.

Function. Fig. 1 lists several possible functions that can be achieved by crystallization: separation, purification, concentration, solidification, and analysis. A few examples follow.

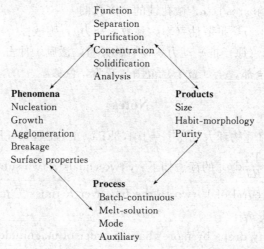

Fig. 1 Crystallization.

Separation. Sodium carbonate (soda ash) is recovered from a brine by first contacting the brine with carbon dioxide to form sodium bicarbonate. Sodium bicarbonate has a lower solubility than sodium carbonate, and it can be readily crystallized. The primary function in this process is separation; a high percentage of sodium bicarbonate is solidified in a form that makes subsequent separation of the crystals from the mother liquor economical. With the available pressure drop across filters that separation liquid and solid, the capacity of the process is determined by the rate at which liquor flows through the filter cake. That rate is set by the crystal size distribution produced in the crystallizer.

Separation of a chemical species from a mixture of similar compounds can also be achieved by melt crystallization, which is, for example, an important means of separation para-xylene (p-xylene) from the ortho and meta isomers. p-Xylene is crystallized at the top of a vertical column and crystals are moved downward countercurrently to liquid. The liquid flowing upward is generated by adding heat to melt the crystals at the bottom of the column;

a portion of the melt is removed as product and the remainder flows up the column to contact the downward-flowing crystals. Effluent mother liquor, consisting almost entirely of the orho and meta isomers of xylene, is removed from the top of the column.

Concentration. The concentration of fruit juice requires removal of solvent (water) from the natural juice. This is commonly done by evaporation, but the derived juices may lose flavor components or undergo thermal degradation during evaporation. In freeze concentration, solvent is crystallized (frozen) in a relatively pure form to leave behind a solution with a solute concentration higher than the original mixture. Significant advantages in product taste have been observed in the application of this process to concentration of certain fruit juices.

Purification. The objective of crystallization also can be purification of a chemical species. For example, L-isoleucine (an essential amino acid) is separated by crystallization from a fermentation broth that has been filtered and subjected to ion exchange. The recovered crystals contain impurities deleterious to use of the product, and these crystals are, therefore, redissolved and recrystallized to enhance purity.

Solidification. Production of a product in a form suitable for use and acceptable to the consumer also may be an objective of a crystallization process. For example, the appearance of sucrose (sugar) varies with local customs, and deviations from that custom could lead to an unacceptable product. A final crystallization may thus be called for to bring the product appearance into compliance with expectations.

Analysis. Many analytical procedures calling for determination of molecular structure are aided by crystallization or require that the unknown compound be crystalline. Methodologies coupling crystallization and analytical procedures will not be covered here.

Products. In all of the instances in which crystallization is used to carry out a specific function, product requirements are a central component in determining the ultimate success of the process. These requirements grow out of how the product is to be used and the processing steps between crystallization and recovery of the final product. Key determinants of product quality are the size distribution (including mean and spread), the morphology (including habit or shape and form), and purity. Of these, only the last is important with other separation processes.

Crystal size distribution (CSD) determines several important processing and product properties, including crystal appearance, separation of crystals from liquor, reactions, dissolution and other processes and properties involving surface area of the crystalline product, crystal transportation, and crystal storage. In fact, experience indicates that a large fraction of crystallizer trouble shouting cases have been initiated to solve problems associated with inadequate throughput of filters or centrifuges; when solutions are found they generally involve manipulation of CSD. It is often important to control the CSD of pharmaceutical compounds, e. g., in the synthesis of human insulin, which is made by recombinant DNA techniques. The most favored size distribution is one that is monodisperse, i. e., all crystals are of the same size, so that the rate at which the crystals dissolve and are taken up by the body is known and reproducible. Such uniformity can be achieved by screening or otherwise separating the desired size from a broader distribution or by devising a crystallization process that will produce insulin in the desired form. The latter of these options is preferable, and considerable effort has been expended in that regard.

Process. In each of the systems discussed above there is a need to form crystals, to cause the crystals to grow, and to separate the crystals from residual liquid. There are various ways to accomplish these objectives leading to a multitude of processes that are designed to meet requirements of product yield, purity, and, uniquely, crystal size distribution.

Phenomena. The critical phenomena in crystallization are, as shown in Fig. 1, nucleation and growth kinetics, interfacial phenomena, breakage, and agglomeration. Nucleation leads to the formation of crystals, either from a solution or a melt. Growth is the enlargement of crystals caused by deposition of solid material on an existing surface. The relative rates at which nucleation and growth occur determine the crystal size distribution; qualitatively, when the rate of nucleation is high relative to growth rate, crystals formed are small and numerous. Agglomeration is the formation of a larger particle though two or more smaller particles (crystals) sticking together. It is prevalent in many processes, and agglomeration can be essential for solid-liquid separation or it can be undesirable because it may adversely affect crystal quality. Breakage of crystals is almost always undesirable because it is detrimental to crystal appearance and it can lead to excessive fines and have a deleterious effect on crystal purity. Interfacial phenomena influence solid-liquid separation, flow characteristics of slurries, agglomeration, and crystal morphology.

Solid-liquid Equilibrium and Mass and Energy Balances

Solubility. Solid-liquid equilibrium, or the solubility of a chemical compound in a solvent, refers to the amount of solute that can be dissolved at constant temperature, pressure, and system composition; in other words, the maximum concentration of the solute in the solvent at static conditions. In a system consisting of a solute and a solvent, specifying system temperature and pressure fixes all other intensive variables. Such a system is said to form a relating rate of cooling or evaporation or addition of diluent required maintaining a specified supersaturation in the crystallizer. Contrast this to the uncontrolled situation of natural cooling in which the heat transfer rate is given by

$$Q = UA(T - T_C)$$

Where U is a heat-transfer coefficient, A is the area available for heat transfer. T is the temperature of the magma, and T_C is the temperature of the cooling fluid. If U and T_C are constants, the maximum heat transfer rate and the highest rate at which supersaturation is generated are at the beginning of the process when T is highest. These conditions can lead to excessive primary nucleation and the formation of incrustations on the heat-transfer surface.

Better product characteristics are obtained through control of the rate at which supersaturation (cooling, evaporation, and addition of a nonsolvent or precipitant) is generated. An objective of the operation may be to maintain the supersaturation at some constant prescribed value, usually below the metastable limit associated with primary nucleation. For example, the batch may be cooled slowly at the beginning of the cycle and more rapidly at the end.

Formulations of population balances on batch crystallizers have been illustrated, and a variety of operating strategies have been considered. The results are often complex and present difficult control schemes at best. For example, suppose a model is needed to guide the operation of a batch seeded crystallizer so that isothermal solvent evaporation can be accomplished at a rate that gives a constant crystal growth rate and no nucleation. It is shown that the evaporation rate required is a cubic function of time and the corresponding rate of heat input to the crystallizer must be controlled accordingly. If cooling were to be used rather than evaporation, a similar analysis would show that the dependence of crystallizer temperature on time is highly nonlinear[1]. Although the development of a strategy for generating supersaturation can be aided by such analyses, the initial conditions in the models derived are based on properties of seed crystals added to the crystallizer.

The advantages of selective removal of fines from a batch crystallizer have been demonstrated. These experimental programs showed narrowing of crystal size distributions and suggest significant reductions in the fraction of a product that would consist of fines or undersize material.

Crystallizers and Crystallization Operations

Crystallization equipment can vary in sophistication from a simple stirred tank to a complicated multiphase column, and the operation can range from allowing a vat of liquor to cool through exchanging heat with the surroundings to the complex control required of batch cyclic operations. In principle, the objectives of these systems are all the same: to produce a pure product at a high yield with an acceptable crystal size distribution. However, the characteristics of the crystallizing system and desired properties of the product often dictate that a specific crystallizer be used in a particular operating mode.

Crystallization from Solution. Crystallization techniques are related to the methods used to induce a driving force for solids formation and to the medium from which crystals are obtained. Several approaches are defined in the following discussion.

Cooling crystallizers use a heat sink to remove both sensible heats from the feed stream and the heat of crystallization released as crystals are formed. The heat sink may be no more than the ambient surroundings of a batch crystallizer, or it may be cooling water or another process stream.

Evaporative crystallizers generate supersaturation by removing solvent, thereby increasing solute concentration. These crystallizers may be operated under vacuum, and, in such circumstances, it is necessary to have a vacuum pump or ejector as apart of the unit. If the boiling point elevation of the system is low (that is, the difference between the boiling point of a pure solvent at the system pressure), mechanical recompression of the vapor obtained from solvent evaporation can be used to produce a heat source to drive the operation.

Evaporative-cooling crystallizers are fed with a liquor that is at a temperature above that in the crystallizer. As the feed is introduced to the crystallizer, which is at reduced pressure, solvent flashes, thereby concentrating the solute in the resulting solution and reducing the temperature of the magma. The mode of this operation can be degenerated to that of a simple cooling crystallizer by returning condensed solvent to the crystallizer body.

Salting-out crystallization operates through the addition of a nonsolvent to the magma in a crystallizer. The selection of the nonsolvent is based on the effect of the solvent on solubility, cost, properties that affect handling, interaction, with product requirements, and ease of recovery. The effect of adding a nonsolvent can be quite complex as it increases the volume required for a given residence time and may produce a highly nonideal mixture of solvent, nonsolvent, and solute from which the solvent is difficult to separate.

Reactive crystallization addresses those operations in which a reaction occurs to produce a crystalline solute. The concentration of the solute formed generally is greater than that corresponding to solubility. In a subset of systems, the solubility is nearly zero and, concomitantly, the supersaturation produced by reaction is large. These are often referred to as *precipitation* operations and crystal size distribution from them contain a large fraction of fine crystals.

Supercritical fluid solvents are those formed by operating a system above the critical conditions of the solvent. Solubilities of many solutes in such fluids often are much greater than those found for the same solutes but with the fluid at subatmospheric conditions. Recently, there has been considerable interest in using supercritical fluids as solvents in the production of certain crystalline materials because of the special properties of the product crystals. Rapid expansion of a supercritical system rapidly reduces the solubility of the solute throughout the entire mixture. The resulting high supersaturation produces fine crystals of relatively uniform size. Moreover, the solvent poses no purification problems because it simply becomes a gas as the system conditions are reduced below critical.

Selected from R. E. Kirk & D. F. Othmer, *Encyclopedia of Chemical Technology*, 4th ed., vol. 7, 1993, John Wiley & Sons, New York.

Words and Expressions

segragation [segri'geiʃən]　*n.* 分开，隔离，离析
brine [brain]　*n.* 盐（卤）水，海水；*v.* 用海水泡
isoleucine [aisou'lju:si:n]　*n.* 异白氨酸，异亮氨酸
deleterious [deli'tiəriəs]　*a.* 有害（毒）的，有害杂质的
compliance [kəm'plaiəns]　*n.* 符合，一致，顺从，依从，可塑性
throughput [θru:'put]　*n.* 生产量（率，能力），允许量
nucleation [ˌnju:kli'eiʃən]　*n.* 成核（现象，作用），核化，集结
agglomeration [əg'ləməreiʃən]　*n.* 团（附，凝）聚（作用），结块
prevalent ['prevələnt]　*a.* 普通的，一般的，流（盛）行的

adverse ['ædvə:s] a. 逆的，相反的，反向的，不利的，有害的
detrimental [detri'mentl] a. 有害（损）的，不利的；n. 有害的东西
hypothetical [haipou'θetikəl] n. 假设（设想）的，有前提的
magma ['mægmə] n. 岩浆，稠液，（稀）糊
incrustation [inkrʌ'steiʃən] n. 结硬壳，积垢，（建筑物）表面，装饰，镶嵌（物）
precipitant [pre'cipitənt] n. 沉淀剂（物），脱溶物；a. 头朝下，很快落下的，突然的
prescribe [pris'kraib] v. 规定，命令，开（药方），医嘱
heat sink 换热器，散热片，散热装置，冷却套
concomitant [kən'kɔmitənt] a. 伴生（随）的，相伴的；n. 伴随物

Notes

① If cooling were to be used rather than evaporation, a similar analysis would show that the dependence of crystallizer temperature on time is highly nonlinear. 这是非真实条件句，用虚拟语气。

Exercises

1. Answer the following questions
   (1) Do you know the typical applications of the main types of crystallizer?
   (2) What are the factors that determine the product quality?
   (3) Can you show the features of some basic types of drying?
   (4) What are the differences between drying and evaporation?
2. Translate the "Phenomeua" paragraph into Chinese.
3. Rewrite the "Melt Crystallization" section with not more than 250 words.

Reading Material 18

Drying

Drying is an operation in which volatile liquids are separated by vaporization from solids, slurries, and solutions to yield solid products. In dehydration, vegetable and animal materials are dried to less than their natural moisture contents or water of crystallization is removed from hydrates. In freeze drying (lyophilization), wet material is cooled to freeze the liquid; vaporization occurs by sublimation. Gas drying is the separation of condensable vapors from noncondensable gases by cooling, adsorption, or absorption. Evaporation differs from drying in that feed and product are both pumpable fluids.

Reasons for drying include user convenience, shipping cost reduction, product stabilization, removal of noxious or toxic volatiles, and waste recycling and disposal. Environmental factors, such as emission control and energy efficiency, increasingly influence equipment choices. Drying operations involving toxic, noxious, or flammable vapors employ gas-tight equipment combined with recalculating inert gas systems having integral dust collectors, vapor condensers, and gas reheaters.

Drying is an applied science; i.e., drying theory is based on the laws of physics, physics chemistry, and the principles underlying the transfer processes of chemical and mechanical engineering: heat mass and momentum transfer, vaporization, sublimation, crystallization, fluid mechanics, mixing, and material handling. Drying is one of several unit operations involving simultaneous heat and mass transfer. However, drying is complicated by the presence of solids that interfere with heat, liquid, and vapor flow and retard the transfer processes, at least during the final drying stages or when a solids phase is continuous.

Because all drying operations involve processing of solids, equipment material handling capability is of primary importance. In fact, most industrial dryers are derived from material handling equipment designed to accommodate specific forms of solids. If possible, liquid separation from solids as liquid, by dewatering in a mechanical separation operation, should precede drying. Solids handling is made easier, and liquid separation without vaporization is less costly. Evaporators, which have lower investment and operating costs than dryers, are also used to minimize dryer loads.

Several methods are employed to classify commercial dryers by process application. Mode of heat transfer is the conventional choice. The principal heat-transfer mechanisms in drying are (1) convection from a hot gas that contacts the material, used in direct-heat or convection dryers; (2) conduction from a hot surface that contacts the material, used in indirect-heat or contact dryers; (3) radiation from a hot gas or hot surface that contacts or is within sight of the material, used in radiant-heat dryers; and (4) dielectric and microwave heating in high frequency electric fields that generate heat inside the wet material by molecular friction, used in dielectric, or radio frequency, and microwave dryers. In the last group, high internal vapor pressures develop and the temperature inside the material may be higher than at the surface. Many dryers effect more than one heat-transfer mechanism, but most dryers can be identified by the one that predominates.

In order of priority, the factors that govern the selection of industrial dryers are (1) personnel and environmental safety; (2) product moisture and quality attainment; (3) material handling capability; (4) versatility for accommodating process upsets; (5) heat-and mass-transfer efficiency; and (6) capital, labor, and energy costs.

Costs are determined by energy, labor, capacity, and equipment materials of construction. Continuous dryers are less expensive than batch dryers and drying costs rise significantly if plant size is less than 500 t/yr. Vacuum batch dryers are four times as expensive as atmospheric-pressure batch dryers and freeze dryers are five times as costly as vacuum batch dryers. Once-through air dryers are half as costly as recirculating inert-gas dryers. Per unit of liquid vaporization, freeze and microwave dryers are the most expensive. The cost of difference between direct- and indirect-heat dryers is minimal because of the former's large dust recovery requirement. Drying costs for particulate solids at rates of $1 \times 10^3 \sim 50 \times 10^3$ t/yr are about the same for rotary, fluid-bed, and pneumatic conveyor dryers, although few applications are equally suitable for all three (4,5).

Terminology

Bound moisture is liquid held by a material that exerts a vapor pressure less than that of the pure liquid at the same temperature. Liquid can be bound by solution in cell or fiber walls, by homogeneous solution throughout the material, and by chemical or physical adsorption on solid surfaces.

Capillary flow is liquid flow through the pores, interstices, and over the surfaces of solids which is caused by liquid-solid molecular attraction and liquid surface tension.

Contrast rate period is the drying period during which the liquid vaporization rate remains constant per unit of drying surface.

Critical moisture content is that obtained when the constant rate period ends and the falling rate periods begin. Second critical moisture content specifies that remaining in a porous material when capillary flow dominance is replaced by vapor diffusion.

Dry basis describes material moisture content as weight of moisture per unit weight of dry material.

Dryer efficiency is the fraction of total energy consumed which is used to heat and vaporize the liquid.

Equilibrium moisture content is that which a material retains after prolonged exposure to a specific ambient temperature and humidity.

Evaporative efficiency in a direct-heat dryer compares vaporization obtained to that which would be obtained if the drying gas were saturated adiabatically.

Falling rate period is a drying period during which the liquid vaporization rate per unit surface or weight of dry material continuously decreases.

Fiber saturation point is the bound moisture content of cellular materials such as wood.

Free moisture content is the liquid content that is removable at a specific temperature and humidity. Free moisture may include bound and unbound moisture, and is equal to the total average moisture content minus the equilibrium moisture content for the specific drying conditions.

Humidity denotes the amount of condensable vapor present in a gas, expressed as weight of vapor per unit weight of dry gas; i.e., dry basis weight.

Internal diffusion occurs during drying when liquid or vapor flow obeys the fundamental diffusion laws.

Moisture is a word used commonly to describe any volatile liquid or vapor involved in drying; i.e., it is not used selectively to mean only water.

Moisture gradient is the moisture profile in a material at a specific moment during drying, which usually reveals the mechanisms of moisture movement in the material up to the moment of measurement[1].

Percent saturation is the ratio of the partial pressure of a condensable vapor in a gas to the vapor pressure of the liquid at the same temperature, expressed as a percentage. For water vapor in air this is called percent relative humidity.

Unaccomplished moisture change is the ratio of free moisture present in a material at any moment during drying to that present initially.

Unbound moisture in a hygroscopic material is moisture that exerts the same vapor pressure as the pure liquid at the same temperature. Unbound moisture behaves as if the material were not present. All moisture in a nonhygroscopic material is unbound.

Wet basis is a material's moisture content expressed as a percentage of the weight of wet material. Although commonly employed, this basis is less satisfactory for drying calculations than the dry basis for which the percentage change of moisture per unit weight of dry material is constant at all moisture contents.

Dryers

Industrial dryers may be broadly classified by heat-transfer method as being either direct or indirect heat. Dryers evolved from material handling equipment and thus most types of industrial dryers are specially suited for certain forms of material. Dryers are also classified as being batch or continuous.

A batch dryer is best suited for small lots and for use in single-product plants. This dryer is one into which a charge is placed; the dryer runs through its cycle, and the charge is removed. In contrast, continuous dryers operate best under steady-state conditions drying continuous feed and product streams. Optimum operation of most continuous dryers is at design rate and steady-state. Periods of low rate operation are energy inefficient; shutdowns and start-ups waste fuel and frequently include periods of off grade production. Continuous dryers are unsuitable for short operating runs in multi-product plants.

Direct-Heat dryers. In direct-heat dryers, steam-heated, extended-surface coils are used for gas heating up to about 200°C. Electric and hot oil or vapor heaters are added for higher temperatures. Diluted combustion products are used for all temperatures. An increasingly popular technique for producing inert gas is to recycle the dryer exit gas and vapor as secondary dilution gas for incoming combustion products. Thereby the oxygen level in the dryer gas stream is reduced to safe levels for organic materials. This is usually less than 10% oxygen, but always material-dependent. These are called self-inerting heaters.

If material must be protected from combustion product contact, gas may be heated indirectly by passing it through tubes in a furnace. A clean, high temperature gas is obtained, but fuel efficiency is 50%~70% of direct combustion gas heaters. Unless metal surfaces are protected by insulating or refractory lining, maximum usable gas temperature is about 1000°C. For low temperature operations, gas may be dehumidified. It usually is more economical to recirculate gas back through the dehumidifier after each dryer pass than to continuously dehumidify fresh gas. Polymers dried to very low moisture contents for extrusion or solid-state polymerization require very dry gas regardless of drying temperature. It is more economical to predry these materials as low as possible using ambient humidity gas before final drying in very dry or inert gas.

In most direct-heat dryers, more gas is needed to transport heat than to purge vapor. Larger dust recovery installations are needed than for indirect-heat dryers handling the same vapor load. Strict environmental regulations have eliminated the capital cost advantage of direct-heat dryers, e.g., dust recovery investment for a modern spray dryer often exceeds the dryer investment. The greater the gas velocity over, through, or impinging upon a material, the greater the convection heat-transfer coefficient. The more completely material is dispersed, i.e., greater surface-to-mass exposure, the faster the drying rate. Gas and material flowing in the same direction in a continuous dryer is called cocurrent flow; gas flow opposing material flow is countercurrent flow. Gas flow across a material is parallel flow or crossflow. Gas flow normal to material flow is impingement flow or through-circulation.

Indirect-Heat Dryers. In indirect-heat dryers, heat is transferred mostly by conduction, but heat transfer by radiation is significant when conducting surface temperatures exceed 150°C. For jacketed vessels, steam is the common heating medium because the condensing-side film resistance is insignificant compared to material-side resistance. Hot water is circulated for low temperature heating. Liquid-transfer oils or condensing organic vapors is much greater than that of condensing vapor; therefore, liquids ate better suited for simple heating jobs rather than for drying operations having high evaporative thermal loads. Indirect-heat rotary dryers and calciners operating at temperatures exceeding 200°C usually are furnace-enclosed. The cylinders are heated externally by electric or gas-fired radiant heaters and circulating combustion products. Regardless of heating medium or method, the primary heat-transfer resistance in indirect-heat drying is on the material side. The material-side heat-transfer coefficient is affected by the rapidity o material agitation, particle size, shape, porosity, density, and degree of wetness.

Selected from R. E. Kirk & D. F. Othmer, *Encyclopedia of Chemical Technology*, 4th ed., vol. 8, 1993, John Wiley & Sons, New York.

Words and Expressions

lyophilization [laiɔfilai'zeiʃən] n. （低压）冻干法，升华干燥，真空冷冻干燥
convection [kən'vekʃən] n. （热，电）对流，运流，迁移，传递
dielectric [daii'lektriʃən] a. 不导电的，绝缘的，介电的；n. （电）介质（体），绝缘材料
pneumatic [nju:'mætik] a. 气（风）动的，风力的，空气的；n. 气胎，有充胎的车辆
conveyor (=conveyer) [kən'veiə] n. 输送机（设备），传递者，交付者，让与人
terminology [tə:min'ɔlədʒi] n. 专门名词，术语，词汇
capillary [kə'pilən] a.；n. 毛细（管）的，毛细（现象）的，表面张力的
hygroscopic [haigrə'skɔpik] a. 吸湿（水）的，吸湿的，温度计的
spout [spaut] v. 喷（出，射，水，注），涌（出，流）；n. 喷口，喷嘴，喷出
pervious ['pə:vjəs] a. 透光（水）的，有孔的，能通过的，能接受的
pelletize ['pelitaiz] vt. 造球，制粒，做成丸
refractory [ri'fræktəri] a. 耐熔（火）的，难治的，顽固性的
lining [lainiŋ] n. 衬里（套，垫，层，板），镶（炉，砖，塘）衬
purge [pə:dʒ] v. 清（吹，扫，消）除，（使）清洁，清（吹）洗，催泻；n. 净化，泻药

impinge [im'pindʒ] v. 碰撞，冲（撞，打）击，侵犯
briquette [bri'ket] n. 煤饼（球，砖），坯块，模制（标准）试块
increment ['inkrimənt] n. 增加（大，长，收，益），增加物，增量，余差
turbo- （词头）涡轮，透平
drape [dreip] vt. （用布，帘，幕）覆盖（包上，挂上），悬挂，隔声，吸音，调整
festoon [fes'tu:n] n. 花彩，垂花饰；vt. 结彩
nozzle ['nɔzl] n. 喷管（嘴，口，头），管嘴，烧杯（嘴）
mount [maunt] v. 安装，装配，固定，悬挂，粘贴，测定
conserve [kən'sə:v] v. 节省，保藏，保存
permeable ['pə:miəbl] a. 可渗（穿）透的
extrusion [eks'tru:ʒən] n. 挤（压，喷，推）出，挤压，热（模）压
score [skɔ:] v. 擦伤，刻，划线，打记号，计算
fibrous ['faibrəs] a. 纤维的，含纤维的
clump [klʌmp] n. （土，铀）块，群，丛
chute [ʃu:t] n. （斜，滑，流）槽，沟，斜道（管）
tow [təu] v.；n. （丝，纤维）束，麻屑，短纤维，拖，拉，拽
dislodge [dis'lɔdʒ] vt. 移（挪，调）动，移去，取出，驱逐
splashing n. 喷溅物
peripheral [pə'rifərəl] a. 周边（围，缘）的，外围的，周围的；n. 外部设备
hopper ['hɔpə] n. 漏斗，布（给）料器，斗仓
Venturi [ven'tu:ri] n. 文氏管，文杜里管（喷嘴），缩喉管
abrasive [ə'breisiv] n. 磨料，研磨剂，摩擦；a. 磨料的，磨损的
obviate [ɔbvieit] vt. 排（消，免）除，避免，事先预防

Notes

① *Moisture gradient* is the moisture profile in a material at a specific moment during drying, which usually reveals the mechanisms of moisture movement in the material up to the moment of measurement. 此句中 profile 表示断面图。但，有时 profile 表示历程，例如 reaction profile.

Unit 19 Water and Air in the Chemical Process Industries

The chemical process industries are among the leading consumers of water and air. These two materials are used in nearly all chemical processing for a large variety of purposes. Chemical factories today use up as much as 1 million cubic meters of water per day. Water is used to produce hydrogen and oxygen, to dissolve solids, liquids and gases, as a reaction medium, an extractive agent, an absorbent or a carrier, to heat and cool materials and pieces of equipment, to form pulps and slurries, to wash products and plant items, etc. Also, it is widely used as the working fluid in hydraulic, thermal and nuclear power stations.

All water present on the Earth totals about 1500 million km^3. Our planet's hydrosphere accounts for 70.8% of the Earth's total surface area, or 361 million km^2. This is 1370 million km^3 in volume. The greater proportion of this water is in a continuous movement through the hydrologic cycle under the action of the heat coming from the sun and from the planet's insides.

Usable fresh water from water bodies accounts for a mere 0.3% of the hydrosphere by volume. More important economically is river water. This is because, above all, the rivers carry fresh water and span huge distances. Historically it has so happened that most cities, towns and other communities are situated at the river banks. The instantaneous reserves of water in all of the globe's rivers is about $1200 km^3$, and this volume is renewed every 12 days on the average.

At this writing, a total of up to 170 km^3 of water per year is used up in the world for the various needs (irrecoverable losses).

Natural water is usually classed into atmospheric, surface, and ground (subsurface or subterranean).

Atmospheric water falls out as rains or snow and carries negligible amounts of impurities. These impurities mainly are dissolved gases (O_2, CO_2, N_2, etc.), salts, bacteria, etc. Atmospheric water is the source of water supply in arid regions.

Surface water refers to the water flowing in rivers and canals and held in oceans, seas, lakes, and water reservoirs. It contains a wide range of inorganic and organic substances, depending on the climatic, geomorphological, soil, and geological conditions, man's agricultural and hydraulic-engineering activities, the impact of industry, and some other factors.

Special mention should be made of seawater. It is a multicomponent solution of electrolytes and contains all the elements present in seawater are many salts (up to 2.6% by mass sodium chloride, magnesium chloride and sulfate, etc.) and also atmospheric gases (nitrogen, oxygen, and carbon dioxide). Water from one sea or ocean differs from that from any other in both the overall concentration and make-up of salts.

Groundwater is that which comes from artesian wells, water-table wells, springs, and geysers. It carries appreciable amounts of mineral salts leached out of soil and sedimentary rock, and small amounts of organic substances.

Another way to class water is according to its salt content. Thus we have fresh water which carries up to 1g of salts per kilogram of water ; brackish water with 1 to 10 grams of salts per kilogram, and saline water with over 10g of salts per kilogram.

Still another way to differentiate between various kinds of water is according to the anion is HCO_3^- or the sum of HCO_3^- and CO_3^{2-} anions; sulfate water ; chloride water, etc.

Natural water is a complex dynamic system which contains gases, inorganic and organic substances present in true solution form, in colloidal form , or in suspension.

Those present in true solution form are mainly the inorganic salts that enrich water with the Ca^{2+}, Mg^{2+}, Na^+ and K^+ cations and the SO_4^{2-}, CO_3^{2-}, HCO_3^-, and Cl^- anions. These ions find their way into water from soil and rock. Some organic compounds and dissolved gases (CO_2, O_2, H_2S, etc.) may be present as undissociated molecules. The solubility of gases in water depends on temperature, pressure, and ionic makeup of the other substances dissolved.

Those present in colloidal form are undissociated or slightly dissociated compounds of alumosilicates, iron silicates, iron hydroxide, silicic acid, and various organic substances. Organic colloids mainly consist of humic acids, fulvic acids, lignin, protein, cellulose, various resins, and other complex compounds. Those present in suspension are particles of clay, sand, limestone and gypsum. Natural water may also carry some living organisms, such as bacteria, fungi, algae, etc.

Natural water is continuously changing in composition. This is favored by redox reactions, by mixing of water from different sources, by the fact that the dissolved salts may be precipitated due to changes in temperature and/or pressure, the coarse particles may be allowed to settle or be stirred up again, the soil and water may exchange ions, and the microbiological processes may enrich water with microelements.

There is a further arbitrary subdivision of water into industrial and drinking or potable. The impurity content of each category is subject to applicable regulations.

Water quality is determined by physical, chemical, and bacteriological tests. It is customary to destribe water quality in terms of smell, taste, clarity (or turbidity), colour, temperature, suspended solids content, total solids content, total and constituent alkalinity, chemical oxygen demand, and pH value.

The suspended solids test tells us what fraction of the total solids present in a water sample is present as suspensions of clay, sand, and soil. Numerically it is expressed in milligrams per liter on a dry mass basis.

The total solids test quantifies all the solids in a water sample, both inorganic and organic, suspended and dissolved, in true solution and in colloidal form. This parameter is found by evaporating a water sample to dryness and weighing the residue. The total quantity is expressed as milligrams per liter on a dry-mass-of-solids basis.

Once a sample has been dried and measured, the organic content of both total and suspended solids can be determined by firing the residue at a specified temperature and for a specified span of time. The remaining material will represent the inorganic residue, and the driven-off balance will represent its organic fraction.

Total alkalinity, A_{tot}, is a measure of the total concentration of the OH^-, HCO_3^-, CO_3^{2-}, PO_4^{3-}, $HSiO_3^-$ and SiO_3^{2-} anions and some salts of weak organic acids (humates) in a water sample. It is expressed in mmol litre^{-1}.

Since all of the above substances react with acids, the total alkalinity of a water sample is determined by the quantity of acid used for the titration of a water sample to the methyl orange end point. By far the most common constituents of alkalinity are bicarbonate (HCO_3^-), carbonate (CO_3^{2-}) silicate ($HSiO_3^-$), hydroxide (OH^-), and phosphate ($H_2PO_4^-$, HPO_4^{2-}, PO_4^{3-}), respectively designated as A_b, A_c, A_s, A_h and A_p. Obviously,

$$A_{tot}=A_b+A_c+A_s+A_h+A_p$$

As a rule, natural water contains noticeable quantities of only bicarbonate ions. Therefore, the total alkalinity of natural water is

$$A_{tot}=A_b$$

Hardness. This is among the most important indicators of water quality. It is due to the presence of calcium and magnesium salts in natural water. It is expressed in millimoles of Ca or Mg ions per litre or in millimoles per kilogram of water. Hardness may be temporary, permanent, and total.

Temporary (carbonate or removable) hardness, H_c, is mainly due to the presence of calcium and magnesium bicarbonates, $Ca(HCO_3)_2$ and $Mg(HCO_3)_2$, which are sensitive to heat and precipitate readily on boiling to form a dense residue commonly known as boiler scale or simply scale:

$$Ca(HCO_3)_2 \longrightarrow CaCO_3+H_2O+CO_2$$
$$2Mg(HCO_3)_2 \longrightarrow MgCO_3+Mg(OH)_2+H_2O+3CO_2$$

Permanent (noncarbonate) hardness, H_n, is due to the presence of the chlorides, sulphates and nitrates of calcium and magnesium, which remain dissolved on boiling.

Total hardness is the sum of temporary and permanent hardness, and is expressed in mmoles per liter. In its terms, natural waters are classified as follows:

    Soft $H_{tot}<2$ mmol $\cdot$ L^{-1}
    Moderately hard $H_{tot}=2\sim10$ mmol $\cdot$ L^{-1}
    Hard $H_{tot}>10$ mmol $\cdot$ L^{-1}

Chemical oxygen demand (COD) is the quantity of oxygen, in mg $\cdot$ L^{-1}, reqired to oxidize the substances present in a water sample. It is mainly decided by the presence of organic substances and only slightly by the rapid oxidizing compounds of iron, hydrogen sulfide and nitrites. Its value is used as an indirect quantitative parameter to assess the concentration of organic contaminants in water sample. The chemical oxygen demand of artesian waters usually is $1\sim3$ mg $\cdot$ L^{-1}, that of pure lake waters is $5\sim8$ mg $\cdot$ L^{-1}, and that of marsh waters up to 400mg·L^{-1}. The chemical oxygen demand of river waters ranges between broad limits and may be as high as 60mg·L^{-1} or even more.

The pH[①] value of water tells us whether a water sample has an 'acid' or 'alkaline' reaction.

At pH 7 the water is classed as neutral. At a pH value of less than 7 the water is classed as having an acid reaction, while at a pH value of greater than 7 it is classed as having an alkaline or basic reaction. The pH value of natural waters ranges between broad limits: from pH 9～10 in the case alkaline groundwater to pH 1 in the case of acid waters from geothermal sources.

Most commonly, the pH value of natural waters ranges between 6.5 and 8.5. It may be enhanced by an increased concentration of humic acids or when a given water body or water source is polluted by industrial wastes.

The quality of water intended for industrial uses is determined by the requirements of the industrial process involved and the type of the equipment it uses. Chemical factories may use water from rivers, artesian wells, filtered, coagulated, cooled, partially or completely demineralized, potable, etc.

Fresh natural waters need no preliminary treatment when they are to be used in the chemical process industries for the primary treatment of raw materials, to cool products and pieces of equipment, and in various auxiliary operations. In most cases, however, natural waters have to be purified (mainly demineralized) by any one of many processes, depending on the impurities present and the requirement of the manufactering process in question.

Selected from A. M. Kutepov, T. I. Bondareva, M.G. Berengarten, *Basic Chemical Engineering with Practical Application*, 1986, Mir Publishers, Moscow.

Words and Expressions

absorbent [əb'sɔːbənt] *a.* 能吸收的; *n.* 吸收剂
hydrosphere ['haidrəsfiə] *n.* 水界, 水圈
hydology ['haidrələdʒ] *n.* 水文学
subsurface [sʌb'səːfis] *a.* 表面下的; *n.* 地表下的岩石, 地面下的水层
subterranean [ˌsʌbtə'reinnjən] *a.* 地下的; *n.* 地下室
arid ['ærid] *a.* 干旱的, 贫瘠的
geomorphology [dʒiəmɔː'fɔlədʒi] *n.* 地貌学
artesian [ɑː'tiːzjən] *a.* 自流的
water-table *n.* 地下水井
geyser [gaizə] *n.* 间歇(喷)泉 or [giːzə] *n.* 热水锅炉
brackish ['brækiʃ] *a.* 含盐的
saline ['seilain] *a.* 含盐的; *n.* 盐湖
alumosilicate [ə'ljuːməsilikeit] *n.* 铝硅酸盐
humate ['hjuːmeit] *n.* 腐植酸盐

humic ['hju:mik] *n.* 腐植的
leach [li:tʃ] *vt. & vi.* 滤取；*n.* 沥滤器
fulvic acid *n.* 灰黄霉酸
sedimentary ['sedimentəri] *a.* 沉积的
fungus ['fʌŋgəs]，（复）fungi ['fəŋgai] *n.* 真菌
alga [ælgə]，（复）algae [æld3i:] *n.* 水藻，海藻
category ['kætigəri] *n.* 种类
turbidity [tə:'biditi] *n.* 浊度
residue ['rezidju:] *n.* 残余，渣滓
boiler scale 锅炉水垢
marsh [ma:ʃ] *n.* 沼泽，湿地
geothermal [dʒi:ou'θə:məl] *n.* 地热的
demineralize [di:'minərəlaiz] *vt.* 去盐，去离子
potable [pəutəbl] *a.* 可饮的；*n.* 饮料
coagulate [kəu'ægjuleit] *vt. & vi.* 凝结，凝固

Notes

① pH 表示溶液中氢离子浓度对数的负数，$pH = -\log[H^+]$。注意：p 必须是小写，而 H 必须是大写。

Exercises

1. Answer the following questions:
   (1) How many kinds of natural water are there on the earth?
   (2) Why is natural water considered as a solution?
   (3) How do we describe water quality?
   (4) What is the definition of pH value and what does it tell us?
2. According to the passage answer the following questions in full English sentences with at least 30 words.
   (1) Please describe the usage of water in the chemical industries.
   (2) What are the features of natural water and why cannot they be used directly in industries?
3. Translate the following sentences into Chinese:
   (1) Chemical factories today use up between them as much as 1 million cubic meters of water per day.
   (2) The greater proportion of this water is in a continuous movement through the hydrologic cycle under the action of the heat coming from the Sun and from the planet's insides.
   (3) Water from one sea or ocean differs from that from any other in both the overall concentration and make-up of salts.
   (4) Natural water is a complex dynamic system which contains gases, inorganic and

organic substances present in true solution form, in colloidal form, or in suspension.

(5) This is favored by redox reactions, by mixing of water from different sources, by the fact that the dissolved salts may be precipitated due to changes in temperature and/or pressure, the coarse particles may be allowed to settle or be stirred up again, the soil and water may exchange ions, and the microbiological processes may enrich water with microelements.

(6) The suspended solids test tells us what fraction of the total solids present in a water sample is present as suspensions of clay, sand, and soil.

(7) Chemical factories may use water from rivers, artesian wells, filtered, coagulated, cooled, partially or completely demineralized, potable, etc.

(8) In most cases, however, natural waters have to be purified (mainly demineralized) by any one of many processes, depending on the impurities present and the requirement of the manufactering process in question.

Reading Material 19

Chemical Process Industries and Environmental Pollution Abatement

Protection of the environment and judicious use of natural resources in the setting of rapid advances in industry, transport and agriculture are primary concern to any nation.

A prominent place among the measures having as their objective to protect the environment is occupied by the advanced control of all emissions and waste, and this includes their purification and recovery.

Recent years have seen a good deal of effort put into the development of water recirculation schemes, processes that leave little or no waste at all, water treatment, dust removal and gas purification system, and the utilization of solid, liquid and gaseous wastes as secondary raw materials.

The iron and steel, non ferrous, nuclear, petrochemical, electronic and other industries widely use techniques of chemical engineering for the protection of biosphere.

The industrial pollutants found in the biosphere may be classified into two general groups: material pollutants responsible for mechanical, chemical and biological pollution and energy (or physical) pollutants.

Mechanical pollutants include aerosols, solid bodies and particles in water and soil. Chemical pollutants are various gas, liquid and solid chemical compounds which react with the biosphere. Biological pollutants are microorganisms and their wastes; this is an entirely new class of pollutants brought to life by the synthesis of yeast, actinomycetes, bacteria, fungi, and other microorganisms.

Energy pollutants are related to all forms of energy, such as thermal or mechanical (vibration, noise, ultrasound), radiant (visible light, infra-red and ultra-violet rays), electromagnetic, ionizing (alpha, beta and gamma rays, X-rays and neutrons), as left-overs from various processes. Some pollutants, such as radioactive waste, belong to both material and energy groups.

The level of energy (physical) pollution is mainly brought down by shielding sources of noise, electromagnetic fields and ionizing radiations, by noise absorption, and vibration damping.

The sources of biosphere pollution may be classed into concentrated (point-type) and distributed, and also into those operating continuously or intermittently. Pollutants may further be divided into stable (nondegradable) and degradable under the action of chemical and biological processes.

The atmosphere is polluted due to both natural processes and man's activity. Natural pollution comes from dust storms, volcanic activity, forest fires, droplet entrainment from the surface of the seas and oceans, etc. As a result, both solid and gaseous substances find their way into the atmosphere.

Dust lifted off the ground consists of fine particles of rock, soil, and remnants of plants and living organisms.

Volcanic eruption liberate both gaseous substances which contain hydrogen chloride, hydrogen fluoride, ammonia chlorine carbon monoxide and dioxide, sulfur dioxide, hydrogen sulfide, water vapor, and also ash which mainly consists of silica particles.

Droplet entrainment from the surface of the seas and oceans leads to air pollution with the salts of calcium, magnesium, sodium, and potassium present in the seawater in dissolved states. As the droplets vaporized, the salts form tiny crystals which pollute the air.

In addition to particles of inorganic origin, the atmosphere contains varying quantities of minute microorganisms, fungi, bacteria, and spores.

Air pollution from natural sources is taken into account when determining the overall level of atmosphere contamination.

The principal man-made sources of air pollution are emission from large thermal power stations which burn solid, liquid or gaseous fuels, motor vehicles, iron-and-steel works, non-ferrous smelteries, and chemical complexes.

The most typical emissions from iron-and-steel works and non ferrous smelteries are dust, sulfur dioxide, nitrogen oxide, carbon monoxide and hydrocarbons.

The emissions from chemical complexes carry substantially smaller quantities of contaminants, but unfortunately chemical plants are often situated in a close proximity to one another, and their emissions contain a number of extremely toxic compounds. This makes these contaminants especially harmful, and many countries have national standards which set limits of maximum concentration for the substances discharged into the atmosphere.

According to state of matter, all air pollutants in gas emissions are classed into suspended solid particles (aerosols), such as dust and smoke, suspended liquid particles exemplified by spray and mist, and also gaseous and vapor forms.

The major air contaminants in terms of quantity are sulfur dioxide, carbon monoxide, nitrogen oxides, various hydrocarbons and dust. They account for up to 85% of the total pollutants emitted into the atmosphere. For example, the combustion of an organic fuel draws large quantities of atmospheric oxygen and discharges carbon dioxide, water vapor, nitrogen, sulfur and other toxic compounds, and ash.

According to existing records, it took 1.3 thousand million tons of oxygen to burn all kinds of fuel in 1860; and in 1960 the figure rose to 12 thousand million, and it may be expected that in 2000 it will rise to 57 thousand million. At this writing, the annual emission to the atmosphere with products of combustion the world over includes as much as 100 million tones of solid and 150 million tons of sulfur dioxide, 300 tons of carbon monoxide, and 50 million tons of nitrogen oxides.

The toxic emissions to the atmosphere from chemical complexes are organic solvents, amines, aldehydes, chlorine and its derivatives, nitrogen oxides, hydrocyanic acid, fluorine compounds, sulfur dioxide, phosphorus, mercury, hydrogen sulfide, carbon disulfide, organometallic compounds, etc. Sizeable amounts of toxic substances are emitted to the atmosphere in the manufacture of acids, alkalis, fertilizers, cement, soda, ammonia, synthetic fibers, dyes, pesticides, rubber products organic solvents, etc.

A special group of air contaminants includes radioactive wastes discharged in the atmosphere mainly from nuclear and hydrogen weapon tests.

The methods used to purify waste gases depend on the physico-chemical properties, state of matter, degree of dispersion, chemical composition, and concentration of the impurities.

Removal of aerosols. This is done mostly by mechanical and physical methods.

Mechanical methods may be classified into dry and wet processes. Dry processes include sedimentation by gravity, inertial sedimentation and centrifugal sedimentation in a wide range of settling chambers, louvre-type dust catchers and cyclones, and filtration through cloth and fibrous filters.

Wet processes are versatile as they may be used to render a gas free of dust, fumes and mist. Basically they consist in that the gas to be cleaned is scrubbed with a liquid (water) in packed towers, dynamic spray scrubbers, foam dust catchers, Venturi scrubbers, and other types of gas cleaning plant. A very high efficiency in the removal of particles has been shown by film dust and fly-ash catchers, and by spray separation in tray-type and rectifying apparatus with two interfacial zones.

Physical method are electrostatic precipitation and acoustical coagulation.

Electrostatic precipitation is based on the fact that the suspended particles of an aerosol injected into a high-voltage electric field acquire an electrostatic charge, move to one or the other of the grounded collecting electrodes between which the electric field is set up, and settle out there. Electrostatic precipitators are most effective and versatile of all gas cleaning equipment. Among the principal advantages are the capacity to handle large quantities of gas (millions of cubic meters per hour) at a relatively low hydrostatic resistance (60~250 Pa); a high degree of cleaning (90%~99.95% purity); low power requirement (0.06~0.12 kW·hr per 1000m³ of clean gas); and ease of complete automation.

Acoustical coagulation offers a means for speeding up the removal of finely dispersed dust and mist from gases. It consists in that the gas being purified is irradiated with ordinary or ultra sound, and this causes the fine aerosol particles (soot, sulfuric acid mist, fumes and smoke) to coalesce.

Removal of vapors and fumes. This can be done by using liquid absorption, solid adsorption, and catalytic oxidation.

Liquid absorption may be used the selective solubility of impurities (physical absorption) or their chemical reaction with the active components of a liquid absorbent (chemosorption). Liquid absorption is used to remove sulfur dioxide, hydrogen sulfide, other sulfur-bearing compounds, nitrogen oxides, acid fumes (HCl, HF, and H_2SO_4), carbon monoxide and dioxide, various organic compounds (phenol, formaldehyde, volatile solvents, etc.) from gases.

The absorbents used for the purpose are water, ammonia solutions, alkali solutions, suspensions of calcium hydroxide, oxides of manganese and magnesium, ethanol amine, oil, etc. Absorption purification is a cycle operation-when the absorbent is exhausted, it is regenerated. In physical absorption, the absorbent is regenerated by heating and pressure reduction - this causes the absorbed impurities to desorb and increases their concentration. Most chemosorption operations are likewise reversible, so the chemosorbent may be regenerated.

The equipment used for absorption purification is similar to that used for wet aerosol removal.

Solid adsorption is based on the selective adsorption of components from vapor-gas mixtures by suitable particulate materials which have a large specific surface area. Adsorption purification may involve both physical and chemical adsorption (chemosorption). The adsorbents most commonly used are activated carbon, silica gel, alumina gel, natural and man-made zeolites (molecular sieves).

The key requirement that industrial adsorbents are to meet are as follows: high adsorbing capacity, selectivity, thermal endurance, long service life without changes in the structure or surface properties, and ease of regeneration. Adsorption is mainly used to recover organic compounds, above all toxic ones, and also mercury vapor.

Gas cleaning by solid adsorption is effected in batch shelf-type reactors. Special promise is held by fluidized bed adsorbers. Solid sorbents are regenerated by heating (so as to burn out the trapped organic material), and by passing a stream of superheated steam, air, or inert gas (nitrogen) through the sorbent.

Gas purification by catalytic methods is based on the reactions that take place in the presence of solid catalysts. As a result of these catalyzed reaction, the impurities present in the gas being purified are converted to ecologically safe compounds or to compounds readily removable from the gas.

Catalytic purification is used for low-temperature oxidation of toxic organic compounds, carbon monoxide, nitrogen oxides, sulfur dioxide, hydrogen sulfide, and some others. When gases are purified over sorbent catalysts, the process is known as catalytic adsorption. The catalytic methods make it possible to reclaim the heat of reaction, and this in turn provides for power cogeneration in addition to chemical processing.

Thermal methods are used to treat gas emissions carrying alcohols, ethers, esters, ketones, aliphatic and aromatic hydrocarbons, organic acids, and some other compounds when their recovery and recycling is impossible or not warranted. The treatment is effected in thermal combustion units (known as thermal incinerators or afterburners) at a temperature of $923 \sim 1173$ K, the residence time of the gas in the reaction zone being $0.5 \sim 0.7$ s. The throughput in terms of the purified gas stream is 2 to 25 thousand $m^3 \cdot hr^{-1}$, and the degree of purity may be as high as 95%.

When the concentration of combustible organic impurities is close to the lower combustion point, resort is made to flare burning, also known as direct-flame combustion. If the concentration of impurities is below the lower combustion point, the required quantity of heat is supplied by adding a supplemental fuel gas and by burning it in the gas stream being purified. The combustion gases are then passed through a waste heat recovery system to reclaim the waste heat and to reduce fuel requirements.

Selected from A. M. Kutepov, T. I. Bondareva, M.G. Berengarten, *Basic Chemical Engineering with Practical Application*, 1986, Mir Publishers, Moscow.

Words and Expressions

biosphere ['baiəsfiə]　*n.* 生物圈，生命层
pollutant [pə'lu:tənt]　*n.* 污染物
actinomyces [æktinəu'maisi:z]　*n.* 放线菌
entrainment [in'treinmənt]　*n.* 雾沫夹带
remnant ['remnənt]　*n.* 残余，剩余
eruption [i'rʌpʃən]　*n.* 喷发，爆发
spore [spɔ:]　*n.* 孢子，苗子
smaltery ['smeltəri]　*n.* 冶炼厂
proximity [prɔk'simiti]　*n.* 最近，接近，近似
judicious [dʒu(:)'diʃəs]　*a.* 明智的，有见识的
prominent ['prɔminənt]　*a.* 突出的，凸出的，杰出的
yeast [ji:st]　*n.* 酵母
louvre ['lu:və]　*n.* 固定百叶窗，天窗
cyclone ['saikloun]　*n.* 旋风，气旋
scrub [skrʌb]　*vt.* 擦洗，擦净

acoustical [əˈkuːstikəl] a. 听觉的，传音的
coalesce [ˌkouəˈles] vi. 接合，愈合
zeolite [ˈziːəlait] n. 沸石
ecological [ˌekəˈlɔdʒikəl] a. 生态的，生态学的
incinerate [inˈsinəreit] vt. & vi. 把……烧成灰，烧尽

Unit 20　Practical Process Engineering[①]

Modern engineering sciences have their root, according to J. Bronwski, in events in the evolutionary process which occurred about 10,000 years ago. During that period, humans began the gradual change from a nomadic hunter-forager existence to a settled agriculture-based life. The agrarian framework led to the emergence of technologies from which the present-day sciences and engineering disciplines are derived. Rudimentary civil engineering arose as permanent shelters were required and irrigation systems developed. The roots of mechanical engineering lay in the application of the lever in the fashioning of plows and in the invention of the wheel and the pulley to facilitate the movement of burdens.

During the millennia that followed, other engineering technologies along with mathematics, the sciences, the arts, and written means for communication of thought and knowledge gradually developed to meet the increasing needs of evolving civilizations. Included in the process was the development of formal educational institutes which served to define and delineate the various branches of the evolving sciences and engineering fields.

As emerging technologies grew, their application to modern industry became more and more complex. At one time, it was relatively easy for a person to conceive and bring into existence a modest manufacturing operation individually or with assistance of only a few others. However, as cottage industry evolved into the complex plants of modern technology, individuals with more and more specialized knowledge and skills were required in all phases of the planning and operation of the resulting facilities. The trend is reflected in the various curricular that are available in modern universities for engineering disciplines.

While the general emphases of various disciplines differ greatly from one another, there are often overlapping areas of study between the various engineering disciplines so that graduates of several branches can fulfill the needs of certain functions in some specializations. A good example is that of process engineers[②] for the design or operation of chemical and related types of plants, refineries, powerhouses, and similar installations. Large segments of the training received by undergraduates in mechanical and chemical engineering are similar. In addition to the first year's courses in mathematics, physics, chemistry, and basic engineering, which they share with all other engineering disciplines, the mechanical and chemical engineering curricula emphasize fluid flow, heat transfer, and equipment used in the unit operations for associated industrial applications. These areas of studies are basic for a process engineer. Thus, it is common to find a person with either a mechanical or a chemical engineering background functioning as the process engineer on a project. In projects such as boiler-house or power station, where conventional mechanical equipment is involved, a mechanical engineer is more likely to the process engineer. If, however, the process involves chemical-equilibrium evaluations, the application of reaction kinetics, or the application of diffusional operation, a chemical engineer usually serves as the process engineer.

The Role of the Process Engineer

Process engineers have responsibilities in six major areas of a project. In the order in which they occur during the design of a facility, these are:

1. Economic-feasibility studies and estimates of equipment costs.

2. Preparation of a series of documents to define the overall view of the project, present the material and energy balances, and outline the tasks required of the other engineers and piping designers. The latter documents also define the initiating work to be performed by the instrument, electrical, and structural disciplines.

3. Selection of materials of construction for equipment and piping.

4. Process calculations for flows, pressure drops, and heat transfer in piping and for the sizing of equipment.

5. Selection of equipment based on suitability, availability, and cost effectiveness.

6. Purchase of equipment and engineering follow-up.

This book concerns itself with the principal aspects of these major responsibilities of process engineering. It is divided into three sections to coincide with these practical aspects. Chapters 2, 3, and 4 deal with process flow sheets, engineering flow diagrams, and the logistics of flow diagrams, respectively, and together constitute Sec. 1. Chapter 3 also contains a checklist of major items that can be reviewed for inclusion in the preparation of flow diagrams and equipment specifications.

The selection of materials of construction for equipment and piping is reviewed in Chap. 5, which along with various aspects of piping calculation in Chaps. 6, 7, 8, and 9 makes up Sec. 2. Piping calculation have been singled out for special and detailed consideration since the evaluation of pressure loss and other flow parameters is involved in the sizing of almost all process equipment. Even if flow through the unit is not effected in pipes, the theoretical considerations regarding fluid flow reviewed in Chap. 6 can be adapted for analogous situations.

Chapter 7 develops the basic equations necessary for evaluating friction loss in pipes and ducts and their application to incompressible fluids. These equations may be used with compressible and complex fluids when conditions are such that these fluids may be treated as incompressible. Included in this chapter are shortcut methods and a review of various aids for obtaining friction losses with explanations of how they may be extrapolated beyond they stated range. Simplified equations for the quick calculation of flow velocity and Reynold number are given for application to both liquid and gaseous fluids. Simple mnemonic devices are presented to permit the rapid estimation of flow rates and pressure drops.

The piping calculations for compressible fluids are reviewed in Chap. 8. In addition to reviewing the rigorous method for determining pressure drops in adiabatic, isothermal, and polytropic flow, the chapter derives a set of simplified relationships that are analogous to incompressible fluid flow and are suitable for use in most practical applications. Included are means of determining whether or not the approach to sonic velocity and the associated phenomenon of choking is such that use of the rigorous method is required.

Chapter 9 concludes the review of piping calculations by summarizing practical methods for determining flow characteristics of various two-phase-fluid systems. This includes pressure-drop calculation, determination of flow regimes, and minimum-velocity criteria.

Section 3, consisting of Chaps. 10 through 17, reviews the most frequently used major categories of equipment common to most chemical plants, refineries, and power facilities. These include vessels, pumps, blowers and compressors, vacuum equipment, heat exchangers, and mixers and agitators. While the treatment afforded the equipment is comprehensive sufficient description of the items and their applications are given to cover their use in the large majority of the cases in which they are required. Equipment related to unit operations such as distillation, extraction, filtration, centrifugation, crystallization, drying, and similar fields requires special and detailed treatment. While these operations are important and are used extensively in some facilities, their nature is such that their individual use represents only a small portion of the operations in the overall spectrum of processing field. Treatment of these specialized subjects had to be omitted from this general volume, and it is recommended that the reader refer to the specific references book available for the respective topics.

Included in Sec. 3 are brief expositions regarding heat tracing, thermal insulation, and electric power and motors. While responsibility for the subject matter in these two chapters lie primarily with other disciplines, process engineer should be sufficiently conversant with these subjects to make logical and economic choice in the application of respective items.

Once the process engineers have designed equipment, they have a role in completing specification sheets by which the equipment is presented to potential suppliers. Responses to equipment inquiries must be analyzed by process engineers not only for compliance with the process specifications but for determining which of the proposed equipment is the most cost-effective. The basis for making economic analyses and decision is reviewed in a subsequent subsection of this chapter.

After the equipment has been ordered, the process engineers examine the vendor-supplied drawings and literature pertaining to the purchased items to ensure that they meet the specifications in the purchase contract. The process engineers mark necessary corrections on the circulating copies of the drawings and consult with the designers with respect to nozzle orientation and location so that the vendor can eventually issue certified grawings for the project. The certified drawings are used by the process engineers to update the engineering flow diagrams.

The Process Engineer as a Problem Solver

The process engineering tasks just outlined are common to all projects which require a process engineer. However, this by no means implies that process engineering work is routine and can be done by rote. On the contrary, it is rare that any two projects are alike. Even the duplication of a facility to prepare a given product at the same production rate may involve adapting to different utility conditions. Process engineers must be able to formulate and define the problems to be solved, evaluate the alternatives, and make sustainable decisions. They call on their theoretical background and practical knowledge and combine these with imagination and ingenuity to resolve problems and effect decisions to meet the challenge of satisfactorily completing a project on schedule and within its budget. A logical, planned approach is required to resolve both objective and subjective issues.

Process engineers face problems which require either qualitative or quantitative solutions. Questions relating to the selection of processes, process components, or materials are best answered by past experience, a literature search, or consultation with knowledgeable persons. Mathematical models, on the other hand, are used obtain quantitative solutions. Depending on the complexity of the problem and the degree of accuracy demanded for the solution, one can resort to a rule of thumb, a shortcut method, a monograph, a graph, a table, an easy solvable equation, or a set of more complex relationship which requires a programmable calculation or a computer to solve. A judgment as to practicality and cost must be made in choosing the method. In addition, process engineers must be thoroughly familiar with any analytical method used, especially with computer software not written by themselves, to ensure that its constrains or limitations are compatible with the problem being solved

Selected from H. J. Sandler, E. T. Luckiewicz, *Practical Process Engineering*, *A working Approach to Plant Design*, 1988, McGraw-Hill Book Company, New York.

Words and expressions

evolution [ˌi:vəˈlju:ʃən] n. 进展，发展，放出，散出，进化
nomadic [nouˈmædik] a. 游牧的，流浪的
forage [ˈfɔridʒ] n. 草料，饲料
agrarian [əˈgrɛəriən] a. 耕地的，农民的
rudimentary [ˌru:diˈmentəri] a. 基本的，初步的
shelter [ˈʃeltə] n. 掩蔽部，隐蔽处
irrigation [ˌiriˈgeiʃən] n. 灌溉，水利
millennium [miˈleiniəm]，（复）millennia [miˈleniə] n. 一千年，千僖年
delineate [diˈlinieit] vt. 描出……的外形，叙述，描写
curriculum [kəˈrikjuləm] pl. curricula [kəˈrikjulə] n. 学校的全部课程
follow-up 把……探究到底
shortcut [ˈʃɔ:tkʌt] n. 近路，捷径
extrapolate [eksˈtræpəleit] vt. & vi. 推断，外推
mnemonic [ni:ˈmɔnnik] a.（帮助）记忆的
adiabatic [ˌædiəˈbætik] a. 绝热的
isothermal [ˌaisouˈθə:məl] a. 等温的
polytropy [ˈpɔlitrɔpi] n. 多变性

choke [tʃouk] vt. & vi. 堵塞，窒息
regime [rei'ʒi:m] n. 政体，政权，状况，状态
inquiry [in'kwaiəri] n. 询问，调查
vendor [vendɔ:] n. 卖主，小贩
pertain [pə:'tein] vi. 附属
nozzl ['nɔzl] n. 管嘴，喷嘴
orientation [ˌɔ:rien'teiʃən] n. 向东，定位，定向
rote [rout] n. 死记硬背，死搬硬套
budget ['bʌdʒit] n. 预算
ingenuity [ˌindʒi'nju(:)iti] n. 独创性，独出新裁
constraint [kɔn'streint] n. 强迫，强制

Notes

① 本单元材料选自该书中的序言部分。序言一般用来概述全书各章书的内容。阅读本文可了解化工工程师的工作内容。从文笔来讲，序言部分一般较深。在本教科书的最后一个单元学习英语科技书籍的"序言"，有助于了解英语科技书籍的全貌。

② Process Engineer 工艺工程师，指在化工厂或设计院中负责工艺过程设计和生产的工程师，区别于建筑工程师、机械设备工程师和仪表、自动控制工程师等。

Exercises

1. Answer the following questions:
   (1) How much do you know the evolution of the engineering science?
   (2) Do you understand the role of the process engineer now?
   (3) What work should a process engineer do in building a chemical plant?
   (4) How many kinds of valves are there and what are their uses in different conditions?
2. According to the passage answer the following questions in full English sentences with at least 30 words.
   (1) What does a process engineer do with the equipment during the designation of a chemical plant?
   (2) Why must a process engineer have extensive knowledge of various disciplines?
3. Translate the following sentences into Chinese:
   (1) Included in the process was the development of formal educational institutes which served to define and delineate the various branches of the evolving sciences and engineering fields.
   (2) At one time, it was relatively easy for a person to conceive and bring into existence a modest manufacturing operation individually or with assistance of only a few others.
   (3) While the general emphases of various disciplines differ greatly from one another, there are often overlapping areas of study between the various engineering disciplines so that graduates of several branches can fulfill the needs of certain functions in some specializations.

(4) Thus, it is common to find a person with either a mechanical or a chemical engineering background functioning as the process engineer on a project.

(5) In addition to reviewing the rigorous method for determining pressure drops in adiabatic, isothermal, and polytropic flow, the chapter derives a set of simplified relationships that are analogous to incompressible fluid flow and are suitable for use in most practical applications.

(6) While the treatment afforded the equipment is comprehensive sufficient description of the items and their applications are given to cover their use in the large majority of the cases in which they are required.

(7) While responsibility for the subject matter in these two chapters lie primarily with other disciplines, process engineer should be sufficiently conversant with these subjects to make logical and economic choice in the application of respective items.

(8) They call on their theoretical background and practical knowledge and combine these with imagination and ingenuity to resolve problems and effect decisions to meet the challenge of satisfactorily completing a project on schedule and within its budget.

(9) Depending on the complexity of the problem and the degree of accuracy demanded for the solution, one can resort to a rule of thumb, a shortcut method, a monograph, a graph, a table, an easy solvable equation, or a set of more complex relationship which requires a programmable calculation or a computer to solve.

Reading Material 20

Valves

A considerable amount of the work represented on engineering flow diagrams is concerned with piping. The valve is an important aspect which should be kept in mind when preparing the diagrams.

Valves are used to isolate piping or equipment from other portions of the process and to throttle or divert flows; thus, they are an essential part of any piping system. Valves should be designated on engineering flow diagrams by a symbol which not only shows where the valve is required but indicates the type of valve. The process engineer selects the type of valve for each use from among a large variety in accordance with its (1) suitability for the service, (2) availability in required size, pressure and temperature rating, and material of construction, and (3) installed cost.

Fig. 1 lists the more common valves used in various processes together with suggested symbology for representing them on flow diagrams. However, manufacturers' engineering data should be consulted for size, temperature and pressure ranges, and materials of construction for a given valve.

A review of more common valves follows. For specific descriptions and illustrations of

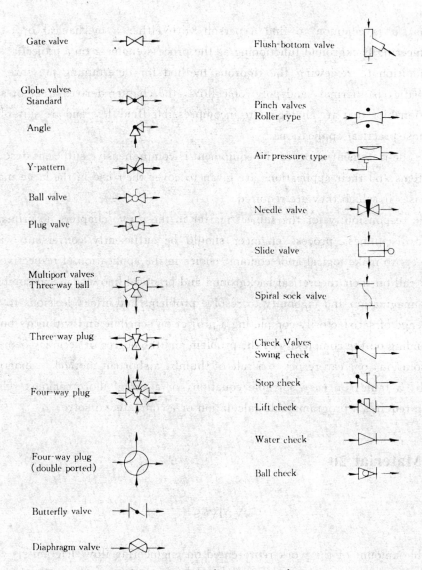

Fig. 1 Types of common valves

the various within each category as well as details of construction, available packing and seal materials, and types of standard connections and flanges, the reader should consult standard references on the subject, special reports in professional journal, or manufacturers' catalogs and engineering data.

Gate valve

1. these valves afford straight-through flow which can be blocked by a disk perpendicular to the line of flow.
2. The disk is lifted through the line of flow by a stem (rising or nonrising).
3. The stem passes through a bonnet fitted with packing to prevent leakage of fluid along the stem.
4. The disk may be a one-piece construction which does not afford tight shutoff, or it may have two pieces, enabling complete closure except for flow with particle matter. A gate

valve with a knife disk can cut through solids to effect a tight closure.
5. Gate valves are used for infrequent on-off service; they are rarely used for throttling except for some slurries or fluids with suspended fibers.
6. They are large in size and weight but are relatively inexpensive and have a low pressure drop when fully open.

Globe valves
1. These valves are available in several designs: standard, angle, and Y-pattern. In all cases, the flow passes through a seat into which a tapered plug id fitted.
2. A stem is attached to the plug and passes through a packed bonnet to a handle or othere operating mechanism.
3. When the stem is all the way in, the plug is in complete contact with the seat and flow stops. As the stem rises, an annular space opens for flow such that the annular area enlarges as the distance of the tapered plug from the seat increases.
4. Globe valves are well suited for throttling flows and for on-off service when they are combined with a regulator.
5. They are comparatively inexpensive but because of the tortuous fluid-flow path exhibit the greatest pressure drop of all common valves but needle valves. The Y-pattern valve has less drop than the angle valve, which has lower drop than the standard globe valve.

Ball valves
1. A ball valve consists of a solid sphere which has a cylindrical port through an axis. The sphere is fitted into a socket in the valve housing so that the axis of the port is in line with the housing's inlet and discharge nozzles.
2. A stem rotates the ball 90°, from fully open to fully closed.
3. Suitable seal rings prevent leakage of fluid around the sphere, and O rings block fluids from escaping at the stem.
4. Ball valves are suited to a wide span of applications, from frequent on-off service to pressure regulation as well flow control. They may be used with slurries and highly viscous liquids in addition to normal clean fluids.
5. They are comparable in price to gate valves and have the advantage of being repairable while the valve body is in a line.
6. They are available in full-port (the diameter of the port is the same as the line size) or reduced-port (70 to 85 percent of line size) types. The pressure drop of a full-port valve is slightly less than that of a gate valve, while the drop for a reduced-port (standard) ball valve is about 3 times as great.

Plug valves
1. These are similar to ball valves except that they use a tapered-plug closure mechanism instead of a sphere.
2. The port is usually oblong and is smaller in cross-sectional area than a circular port in a ball valve of the same nominal size.
3. The precision fit of the tapered plug into its housing and an O ring on a rotating stem

prevents leakage out. Plugs may sometimes be lubricated to prevent galling, bur lubrication must be compatible with the fluid service and operating temperature.

4. Plug valve are suited to on-off and throttling service and are excellent in vacuum conditions.
5. They are somewhat more expensive than ball valves in a comparable material, but the tapered plug can be lined with a polymeric or special material, resulting in an inexpensive valve with the sealing characteristics of a lubricated valve suitable for many corrosive service.
6. The pressure drop across the valve is greater by an order of magnitude than that of a gate valve.

Multiport ball and plug valves

1. Ball valves and plug valves can be constructed to that a fluid enter at one nozzle and leave at one or more of several exit nozzles. The arrangements are known as three-, four-, and five-way valves.
2. A four-way double-ported valve can be used to alternate two streams to and from two sets of equipment.
3. Small directional allows should be entered with multiport valve representations on a flow diagram so that the correct configuration of the valve can be specified.

Butterfly valves

1. A disk (flapper) rotates on a pivotal stem within the valve so that flow is stopped completely when the disk is perpendicular to the flow path and is maximum when it is parallel.
2. Butterfly valves are often used in a wafer form which fits between flanges in a piping section; they are also available with flanged ends.
3. They are well suited for throttling as well as on-off operation. Seats are required for bubbletight shutoff.
4. Butterfly valves are the least expensive valves. They are available in lined material for corrosive service.
5. Their pressure drop is somewhat greater than that of gate valves.

Diaphragm valves

1. Diaphragm valves are usually constructed with a cusp or weir in a housing against which a flexible membrane, or diaphragm, impinges to form a seal. The diaphragm is connected to a stem which passes through the bonnet of the valve.
2. these valves are also constructed in a straight-through weirless design for special slurry applications.
3. They are well suit for throttling and on-off services with slurries.
4. They are available in lined bodies, which are considerably less expensive than high alloy gate valves for corrosive service.
5. They have a high pressure drop.

Flush-bottom valves

1. This type of valve is designed so that there is no fluid in the body or the connecting nozzle when the valve is closed. It is well suited as a draw-off valve for slurries where packing of dead space can occur or for a solution in which unwanted reactions might take place if the solution were unagitated.
2. There are two basic types; the receding-piston, or ram, valve is excellent for slurries, while the lifted-plug type is used with liquids.
3. Small piston or plunger types are used for sampling slurries or liquids when it is important that there be no holdup in the connection to the sampling point. When the valve is closed, the piston is flush with the interior surface of the vessel or pipe.

Pinch or squeeze valves

1. One type of pinch valve consists of a flexible tube between a set of solid rollers which, brought together, squeeze the tube to regulate flow or stop it completely.
2. In another design, the flexible tube is attached internally to both ends of a metallic housing. Regulating the pressure of air admitted to the space between the housing and the tube achieves a throttling of shutoff action.
3. These valves are low-cost, low-pressure-drop units well suited for slurries or gels. Large valves can be used in water systems, as they can effect a shutoff against big solid objects such as rocks logs, or trash.
4. flexible membranes are susceptible to erosion with some slurries and may have to replaced periodically.
5. These valves have limitations of low operation temperature and pressure. Flexible membranes may deteriorate in some solvents or corrosive fluids.
6. These valves cannot be used in actual or incipient vacuum conditions as they tend to close and choke. If they are used on a pump suction, there must be a positive suction head at the valve under all conditions.

Needle valves

1. Needle valves are similar to globe valves except that the plug is an elongate needle which fits into a precisely tapered seat.
2. They are used to obtain precise throttling of low flows of clean fluids.

Slide valves

1. Slide valves are a form of gate valve consisting of a thin rectangular blade that move in and out of a housing.
2. They are used to regulate or block the flow of solids.
3. Elastomeric seals on which the blade can impinge are provided within the housing to prevent gas or vapor leakage when a tight shutoff is required.

Spiral sock valves

1. These valves consist of a twistable fabric or elastomeric sock or tube.
2. They are used to control the flow of powders.

Check valves

1. Several types of check valves are available to prevent reversal of flow in a piping run.
2. Most common for horizontal runs is a swing check which consists of a hinged disk inside a housing. The disk opens when the flow is in the desired direction but is forced closed against a seat if the flow tries to go the other way. If a spring is used at the pivot, the valve may also be installed in a vertical run.
3. A lift check valve has a plug which is lifted when the flow is in the correct path but drops and reseats when the flow is reversed. It usually depends on gravity for closure, but a spring may be included to assist return of the plug (the valve is then known as a piston check valve).
4. A ball check valve is similar to a lift check valve except that a spherical element is forced from its seat under a positive pressure differential and returns to stop the flow. It may be used with some slurries since the spherical surface is self-cleaning.
5. A stop check valve not only prevents flow reversal but can be adjusted to vary the maximum rate of the forward flow.
6. Check valves have high pressure drops owing to a maximum differential imposed by the inertia of the moving and to friction losses resulting from the tortuous paths of the fluid.
7. Most check valves are suited to liquid and high-pressure gas service. A split flapper valve having a thin divided disk pivoting on a hinge, with or without a light spring, is required for low-pressure or vacuum service in which only a nominal pressure drop can be allowed.

Selected from H. J. Sandler, E. T. Luckiewicz, *Practical Process Engineering*, *A working Approach to Plant Design*, 1988, McGraw-Hill Book Company, New York.

Words and expressions

throttle ['θrɔtl] *n.* 节流阀；*vt.* & *vi.* 窒息，闷住
divert [dai'və:t] *vt.* & *vi.* 转移，转向
designate ['dezigneit] *vt.* 指明，指定，选派 or ['dezignit] *a.* 选出而未上任的
flange [flændʒ] *n.* 法兰，凸缘
bonnet ['bɔnit] *n.* 阀门帽
slurry ['slə:ri] *n.* 泥浆
tapered ['teipəd] *a.* 锥形的
annular ['ænjulə] *a.* 环形的
tortuous ['tɔ:tuəs] *a.* 弯曲的，曲折的
socket ['sɔkit] *n.* 座，插座
oblong ['ɔblɔŋ] *n.* & *a.* 长方形，椭圆形
nominal ['nɔminl] *a.* 名义上的，公称的
gall [gɔ:l] *vt.* & *vi.* 擦伤，磨损
compatible [kəm'pætəbl] *a.* 适合的，一致的
flapper ['flæpə] *n.* 片状悬垂物

pivot ['pivət] n. 枢轴
pivotal ['pivətl] a. 枢轴的，中枢的
wafer ['weifə] n. 薄片，圆片
bubbletight [bʌbltait] a. 充满泡沫的
diaphragm ['daiəfræm] n. 隔膜
cusp [kʌsp] n. 尖顶，尖端
weir [wiə] n. 堰，堤
line [lain] vt. 加衬里
impinge [im'pindʒ] vt. & vi. 冲击，撞击
recede [ri:si:d] vi. 收回，撤回
ram [ræm] n. 撞杆，撞锤
erosion [i'rouʃən] n. 腐蚀
susceptible [sə'septəbl] a. 易受影响的，敏感的
incipient [in'sipiənt] a. 开始的，刚出现的
suction ['sʌkʃən] n. 吸，吸收
elongate ['i:lɔŋgeit] vt. & vi. 拉长，伸长
blade [bleid] n. 叶片，桨片，刀片
twistable [twistəbl] a. 可旋转的，可缠绕的
elastomer [i'læstəmə] n. 弹性体
swing [swiŋ] vi. 摇荡，摇摆
hinge [hindʒ] n. 铰链；vt. 装上铰链
inertia [i'nə:ʃjə] n. 惯性
gate valve 闸阀
globe valve 球芯阀
ball valve 球阀
plug valve 旋塞
butterfly valve 蝶阀
diaphragm valve 隔膜阀
flush-bottom valve 平底阀
pinch or squeeze valve 挤压阀
needle valve 针型阀
slide valve 滑板阀
spiral sock valve 螺旋套管阀
check valve 止回阀

PART 5 FRONTIERS OF PHARMACEUTICAL ENGINEERING

Unit 21 Chiral Technology and Single-isomers

Chirality is hardly a new concept in chemistry, yet advances in chiral technology have had a growing impact on pharmaceutical research and development over past few years. Chiral technology now exerts a strong influence on rational drug design. It aids the conception and discovery of new receptor-based or enzyme-inhibiting small molecule drugs, especially where high selectivity of action is sought. Its acceptance is largely because there is now an abundance of technology in place for the manufacture of single-enantiomer chiral drugs.

For those unfamiliar with chiral technology, the term encompasses the range of techniques for producing the single-handed forms (enantiomers) of compounds that have sufficient molecular complexity to be chiral, that is, when molecules cannot be superimposed on their mirror images. Since the specificity of drugs increases as the molecules become more complex, the drive for more specific drugs will lead to a greater proportion being chiral. If a drug is chiral, then in biological terms the enantiomers invariably differ in activity. One may specifically interact with a cell receptor to produce the desired outcome while the other might have no useful application or might have an unwanted effect through some other interaction.

In the clear-cut example where one isomer of a chiral compound is 'good' and the other 'bad', there is obvious benefit from developing the drug as the single isomer to enhance its safety and tolerability. In addition, this can also speed the progress of the drug through regulatory channels, thereby saving R & D costs.

While in the past many drugs developed synthetically have not been chiral, those derived from natural products almost always are (for example, the Penicilins). It is obvious that single-isomer drugs are more specific in mode of action compared with the corresponding racemates. However this, together with the incentives for developing single-isomers for clinical and commercial benefits, does not solely account for the fact that around 80% of drugs entering development are chiral, exclusively now in single-isomer form. Rather this is a consequence of the increased complexity of drug structures today as greater selectivity of action is sought. As an indication of this increased complexity, a drug today will typically need around a dozen steps for its synthesis from basic organic chemicals. About ten years ago, only half this number would, on average, have been required.

Chiral technology has progressed a long way. It is not only confined to its most visible application in pharmaceuticals, but its role extends well into other fields. It has found applications in biochemicals, pesticides, aroma and flavor chemicals, dyes and pigments, liquid crystals, non-linear optical materials, and polymers. In fact, chiral technology represents a huge commercial business opportunity that yet to be fully realized.

A summary of available chiral technology for obtaining single-isomers is listed below. Some of these, such as fermentation and crystallization, have long been available to chemists but their successful application required specialist expertise (for example, microbiology for the former, physical chemistry for the latter). Their use has also been patchy, as experience indicated that they could only address some chiral problems. Together with newer methods, the limitations are being lifted, as the impetus to buy in the special expertise, and the will to integrate different technologies together in a single process, is motivated by the increasing value of the overall expertise in what is now an inescapable need in drug synthesis.

At the point where chirality is first introduced into a synthesis there are three options:

◆ the chirality pool, where the requisite configuration is provided for in the starting materials used and is maintained throughout the remainder of any synthesis;

◆ resolution methods, where the precursor or material is provided as a racemic mixture and has to be separated to give the required isomer. In favorable cases the undesired isomer can be used either by turning it back into raceme which can be resolved again or inverting its configuration so that it too provides the required isomer; or

◆ asymmetric synthesis, where the single-isomer product is derived by introducing the asymmetry directly into a non-chiral material.

Chirality pool methods The simplest access to single isomers is their direct isolation from natural sources and in all cases the inherent chirality of Nature—in plants, animals or microorganisms which are inexpensive and readily available—has been used. An example is the anticancer drug *Taxol*, present in the Pacific Yew tree. *Taxol*'s structure complexity makes total chemical synthesis impractical for drugs supply. However, synthetic chemistry can help by attaching a side chain that is key to *Taxol*'s activity onto a more abundant intermediate from the tree.

Other examples are the penicillins and Merck's[1] cholesterol lowering agent Lovastatin which are derived by microbial fermentation. In both cases synthetic chemistry has also been applied to modify the fermentation products to give better drugs.

Apart from the production of complete drugs, Nature also makes available to the chirality pool useful building blocks like the natural amino acids or sugars. Nowadays, some chemically produced chiral material are becoming commodities and they too can be considered to have entered the chirality pool.

Resolution methods Racemates are easy to make and there are many ways to separate them into enantiomers. The oldest route, classical resolution, uses a chiral acid or base that forms a salt with the racemate. A great many drugs are made in this way. For instance, Syntex[2] has developed a resolution for the (S)-enantiomer anti-inflammatory drug Naproxen using an alkylglucamine resolving agent. A related method covalently binds an auxiliary like menthol or further purification of the separated enantiomers.

Both of these approaches need stoichiometric amounts of another agent but resolution can be done directly by physical methods. Chromatography on chiral stationary phase methods is one, especially useful for providing pre-clinical and early-clinical quantities (as well as, of course, assaying enantiomeric composition). Similar physical separations can be achieved by membrane or extraction systems where on phase contains the racemate and another a chiral selector which will selectively draw out one of the isomers.

Selected from A. Richards & R. Mccagul *Chem. Ind.* (*London*), 1997, (11): 422~425.

Words and Expressions

chirality [kaiə'ræliti] *n.* 手（征）性; chiral; *a.* 手（征）性的
enantiomer [i'næntiəmə] *n.* 对映（异构）体
superimpose [sju:pəim'pəuz] *v.* 加在上面，附加
interact [intə'ækt] *v.* 相互作用，相互影响
racemate [rei'si:meit] *n.* 外消旋体（化合物）
resolution [rezə'lju:ʃən] *n.* 光学拆分（法）
aroma [ə'rəumə] *n.* 芳香（化合物）
flavor ['fleivə] *n.* 香精；香料
pigment ['pigmənt] *n.* 颜料，（植物或动物）天然色素
inescapable [inis'keipəbl] *a.* 无法逃避的
asymmetric [æsi'metrik] *a.* 不对称的; asymmetry; *n.* 不对称
anticancer ['ænti'kænsə] *a.* 抗癌（肿瘤）的
Taxol [tæksəl] *n.* 紫杉醇（抗癌药）
Yew tree [ju:] *n.* 紫杉木；红豆杉（树）
cholesterol [kə'lestərəul] *n.* 胆固醇，胆甾醇
Lovastatin [lɔ:vastatin] *n.* 洛伐他汀（降血脂药）
anti-inflammatory ['æntiin'flæmətəri] *a.* 消（抗）炎的
Naproxen [nə'prɔksən] *n.* 萘普生（非甾体抗炎镇痛药，(S)-构型）
alkylglucamine ['ælkil'glu:kəmi:n] *n.* 烷基葡胺
stoichiometric [stɔiki'ɔmitrik] *a.* 化学计量的

Notes

① Merck 美国著名的制药及精细化学品生产商,其产品几乎涉及精细化学品的各个 领域。
② Syntex 美国著名的制药公司,(S)-萘普生为该公司的专利产品。

Exercises

1. Answer the following questions:
    (1) What role do the chiral drugs play in the pharmaceutical industry?
    (2) Can you give a definition for chirality?
    (3) How have the chiral compounds been produced now?
2. Put the following into Chinese:

The simplest access to single isomers is their direct isolation from natural sources and in all cases the inherent chirality of Nature—in plants, animals or microorganisms which are inexpensive and readily available— has been used. An example is the anticancer drug *Taxol*, present in the Pacific Yew tree. *Taxol*'s structure complexity makes total chemical synthesis impractical for drugs supply. However, synthetic chemistry can help by attaching a side chain that is key to *Taxol*'s activity onto a more abundant intermediate from the tree.

3. Refer to the text above, complete the following notes:

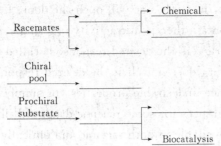

4. Put the following into Chinese:

enantiomer	chiral	optically active	resolution
asymmetric	racemate	biocatalysis	stoichiometric
flavor	pigment	Taxol	anticancer

5. Put the following into English:

固定相	化学计量	制药工业	酶	镜相
消炎的	光学拆分剂	酒石酸	副作用	色素
结晶	天然产物	液晶	胆固醇	色谱

Reading Material 21

When Drug Molecules Look in the Mirror

Almost 150 years have elapsed since Louis Pasteur separated the enantiomers of tartaric acid. Derived from the Greek word "enantio" meaning opposite, enantiomers are nonsuperimposable mirror-image structures. Because the "twins" possess identical physical properties, except for the direction of rotation of polarized light, they are often viewed as a single entity-this is especially true among drug regulating agencies throughout the world. but enantiomers can exhibit distinct chemical behavior when subjected to a chiral environment, that is, surroundings consisting of one twin and not the other.

Differences in the biological activities of the individual enantiomers for dozens of racemic drugs have been reported. While therapeutic activity often resides in one twin, the other can lead to undesirable side effects. The Thalidomide tragedy offers a noteworthy example. In the 1960's, many pregnant women who had taken racemic Thalidomide gave birth to deformed babies. Ensuing investigations showed only the right-handed version of the drug to cause the same birth defects in rat embryos. Had the sedative been administered in the form of L-Thalidomide, the single-enantiomer that rotates polarized light counterclockwise, the disaster may never have occurred.

According to the modern receptor-site theory, drugs attach themselves to specific sites by means of three-dimensional bonding capabilities. The fit of a drug onto a receptor site has been compared to fit of key into a lock. The right drug is the "key" that can fit the receptor "lock" and turn on the desired biological response. Sometimes two slightly different keys will fit inside the same lock, but only one will open the door.

Racemic drugs often contain therapeutic activity in a single enantiomer. The enantiomer that binds to receptor and triggers the desired response is called the agonist. The antagonist binds to the same receptor but does not elicit the desired response. It may display different therapeutic activities, produce undesirable properties, or simply be pharmacologically inert. A look at enantiomeric differences for some racemic drugs will illustrate this point.

Some drugs are made available in both racemic and optically pure form. Methadone and Amphetamine are two examples: Racemic Methadone, used to treat patients in drug withdrawal programs, contains the more active component in the $R(-)$ isomer. However, $R(-)$-Methadone or levadone usually is prescribed in cases involving severe liver damage. While the $S(+)$ isomer of Amphetamine is 3~4 times more potent than its mirror image, both racemic Amphetamine and dexedrine, the $S(+)$ isomer, are prescribed to suppress appetite. Methods for obtaining optically pure drugs not found in nature generally are organized into three categories: Resolution of a racemic mixture, modification of a naturally occurring optically pure substance (chiral pool method), and direct synthesis. While the three approaches for obtaining optically pure drugs vary, they all require a chiral source. Especially direct synthesis of single enantiomers has flourished in the last 30 years from a little studied academic area to an intensely investigated field of commercial importance. Optical activity can be imparted from the reaction of predominantly one of two heterotopic groups or faces. Fermentation, the oldest industrial process for obtaining optically pure compounds, relies on reproduction of microorganisms and takes place in living cells. This method is generally less attractive to industry due to low productivity and large quantities of biomass. However, fermentation is still used widely to produce certain amino acids, antibiotics, and vitamins.

Drug Summary

Name	Desired Enantiomer	Other Enantiomer
Amphetamine	$S(+)$ 3~4 times more potent as stimulant	$R(-)$ produces more adverse cardiovascular effects
L-Dopa	Only $S(-)$ used to treat Parkinson's disease	$R(+)$ contributes to side effects
Ibuprofen	Analgesic activity resides primarily in $S(+)$	
Indacrinone	$R(-)$ has diuretic properties	$S(+)$ induces excretion of uric acid
Ketamine	$S(+)$ 4 times more potent as anesthetic	$R(-)$ produces more side effects

Name	Desired Enantiomer	Other Enantiomer
Methadone	As narcotic, $R(-)$ is 3 times more active than racemate	
L-Methyldopa	$S(-)$ effective in treating hypertension	$R(+)$ produces side effects
Penicillamine	Only $S(-)$ used to treat copper poisoning	$R(+)$ is toxic
Propoxyphene	$2R,3S(+)$ is analgesic	$2S,3R(-)$ is antitussive
Propranolol	Only $S(-)$ effective in treating angina	
Tetramisole	Anthelmintic activity resides primarily in $S(-)$	$R(+)$ produces undesirable side effects
Thyroxine	$S(-)$ prescribed for thyroid deficiency	$R(+)$ decreases serum cholesterol
Timolol	$S(-)$ prescribed for angina and high blood pressure	$R(+)$ prescribed for glaucoma
Verapamil	Both enantiomers increase coronary flow but $R(-)$ produces much less cardiodepressant effect	
Warfarin	$S(-)$ is 2~5 times more potent as anticoagulant $S(-)$ is eliminated 2~5 times more rapidly	

Several amendments to the Act by The Federal Food and Drug Administration (FDA), now require manufacturers to document properties, safety, performance, and toxicity of a new drug, namely, the pharmaceutical companies be compelled to identify optically pure drugs with prefixes of dextro and levo. Eventually the drug industry will be required to generate optically pure products. The advantages are evident: smaller doses, products twice as active, fewer side effects, and superior pharmacological profiles of the active compound.

Selected from "When Drug Molecules Look in the Mirror" *J. Chem Edu*, 1996, 73: 481~484.

Words and Expressions

tartaric acid 酒石酸
polarized light ['pəuləraizd] *n.* 偏振光
Thalidomide [θə'lidə maid] *n.* 沙利度胺（反应停）
sedative ['sedətiv] *n.* 镇静剂（药），止痛药
agonist ['ægənist] *n.* 激动剂，兴奋剂（与拮抗药对立）
antagonist [æn'tægənist] *n.* 拮抗（药）剂，对抗剂，敌手，反对者
Methadone ['meθədəun] *n.* 美沙酮
Amphetamine [æm'fetəmi:n] *n.* 安非他明，甲基苯丙胺
heterotopic [hetərə'tɔpik] *a.* 异位的
cardiovascular [kɑ:diəu'væskjulə] *a.* 心血管的
L-Dopa 左旋多巴

Ibuprofen [aibu'prɔfin] n. 布洛芬
analgesic [ænæl'dʒesik] a. 止痛的；n. 止痛药
diuretic [daijuə'retik] a. 利尿的；n. 利尿剂
uric acid ['juərik'æcid] n. 尿酸
an(a)esthetic [ænis'θetik] a. 麻醉的
narcotic [næ:'kɔtik] n.；a. 催眠药（的）；麻醉剂（的）
L-Methyldopa [meθil'dəupə] n. 左旋甲基多巴
hypertension [haipə:'tenʃən] n. 高血压
antitussive ['ænti'tʌsiv] a. 镇咳的；n. 镇咳药
angina [æn'dʒainə] n. 咽痛；绞痛
anthelmintic [ænθel'mintik] a. 驱肠虫的；n. 驱肠虫药
thyroid ['θaiərɔid] a. 甲状腺的；n. 甲状腺，甲状腺体
thyroxine [θai'rɔksi:n] n. 甲状腺素
glaucoma [glɔ:'kəumə] n. (患)青光眼，绿内障
coronary ['kɔrənəri] a. 冠状的，花冠的
cardiodepressant [kɑ:diəu di'presənt] n. 心抑制药；a. 心抑制的
anticoagulant ['æntikəu'ægjulənt] n. 抗凝（血）剂
dextro ['dekstrəu] a. 右旋的，顺时针的
levo ['li:və,levəu] a. 左旋的

Unit 22 Interferon[①]

Interferon was discovered in 1957 by scientists at the National Institute for Medical Research, U.K. It is a glycoprotein which is induced in response to viral infections and is effective only in species in which it is produced. It was first investigated as an antiviral agent and shown to have a abroad spectrum of activity. Thus, most interferons produce an 80%~100% reduction in the incidence of experimentally-induced common colds and their use is also being further examined in treating chronic hepatitis B, papillomaviruses (warts) and virus infections associated with immunnosuppressed patients following renal transplantation.

Interest in the anticancer activity of interferon first arose due to encouraging results obtained in Sweden whilst treating osteogenic sarcoma and myelomatosis. More recently doctors in Yugoslavia, using human leukocyte interferon preparations injected directly into the tumors, have reported substantial or total remission for cancer of the head and neck. Although the mechanism of anti-tumor activity is not known, they suggest that a direct effect on malignant cells or stimulation of the host's immune system may be responsible.

Despite the intense interest generated by interferons when first discovered, some considerable time elapsed before the compounds were brought into clinical use. The major stumbling block has been problems in their production, coupled with the understandably long time taken in the development of an unusual product. Large doses were required for treatment and only minute amounts, of varying levels of purity, became available from natural sources employing human tissue culture methods. However, from 1980 onwards there have been advances in production techniques, notably the development of recombinant DNA technology which has enabled biosynthetic interferons of high purity to be made available.

Three principal types of interferon (IFN) are known, namely α-IFN produced by leucocytes and other lymphoid (lymphoblastoid) cell, β-IFN produced by fibroblasts and γ- (or immune) IFN. Recently, lymphoblastoid interferon, Wellferon, a complex mixture of α-interferons, and recombinant interferon, Intron A, a pure α-interferon, have become available. These have shown anti-tumor activity in a number of human cancers, e.g. lymphomas, myelomas, myelogenous leukemia and breast cancer. At present, however, they are recommended only for hairy cell leukemia. The mode of anticancer activity is uncertain-interference with the activity of some oncogenes or induction of differentiation of leukemia cells have been suggested. Combination chemotherapy holds promise in some treatment regimes.

Combinations of Intron A with Cisplatinum, Vinblastine, Cyclophosphamide and Melphalan have been evaluated in ovarian, cervical, and pancreatic carcinomas. Toxicity of interferons presents a problem in their potential clinical indications. Side-effects, already observed, are dose related and include influenza-like symptoms, lethargy and depression. Myelosuppression, affection granulocytes, may also occur. Other reported problems are cardiovascular and include hypotension, hypertension and arrhythmias.

In 1986, researchers at Upjohn showed that a new group of 6-phenylpyrimidine derivatives caused the body to produce interferon. The American Association for Cancer Research has demonstrated that the same drugs protect animals against viruses and also improve their defenses against tumor cells. Studies in humans are yet to be done. It has also been suggested that interferon stimulates prostaglandin synthesis and this may help to explain how interferon inhibits cell growth.

A new system of nomenclature for interferon has been devised by an international group of scientists. The group indicate that 'to qualify as an interferon a factor must be a protein which exerts virus non-specific, anti-viral activity at least in homologous cells through cellular metabolic processes involving synthesis of both RNA and protein'. The preferred abbreviation for interferon is IFN. Each interferon is then designated by the animal of origin, e.g. human HuIFN, murine MuIFN, bovine BovIFN. The interferons are next classified into types according to antigen[2] specificities, e.g. α, β and γ, which correspond to previous designations of leucocyte, fibroblast and type II immune, respectively. It was thought that previous type names were misnomers as both leucocytes and fibroblasts can produce each of the two types, α and β, of interferon. If other classes are discovered they will be designated δ, ε, etc. α and β interferons are usually stable in acid media whilst γ interferons are acid-labile. Properly documented differences in molecular size appear to be useful parameters until more stringent criteria such as amino acid sequence and monoclonal antibodies are forthcoming. Molecular weight designations are indicted as HuIFN-α(18K), MuIFN-β(39K).

Selected from H. J. Smith, *Introduction to the Principles of Drug Design*, 2nd ed., Wright, 1988.

Words and Expressions

interferon [intə(:)'fiərɔn] *n.* 干扰素
glycoprotein [glaikəu'prəutin] *n.* 糖蛋白
antiviral ['ænti'vairəl] *a.* 抗病毒的
hepatitis [hepə'taitis] *n.* 肝炎
papilloma [pæpi'ləumə] *a.* 乳头（状）瘤的
wart [wɔ:t] *n.* 疣，瘊子
osteogenic [ɔstiə'dʒenik] *a.* 骨生成的，成骨的
sarcoma [sɑ:'kəumə] *n.* 肉瘤
myelomatosis [maiəu'ləumətəusis] *n.* 骨髓炎
leucocyte(leukocyte) ['lju:kə sait] *n.* 白血球
lymphoid ['limfɔid] *a.* 淋巴（腺）样的，淋巴组织（样）的
lymphoblastoid ['limfəblæst] *a.* 淋巴母细胞的，成淋巴细胞的

fibrobast ['faibrəublɑːst]　n. 成纤维细胞
lymphoma [lim'fəumə]　n.（pl. ~s）淋巴（组织）瘤
myeloma [maiəu'ləumə]　n.（pl. ~s）骨髓瘤
leuk(a)emia [ljuː'kiːmiə]　n. 白血病
Cisplatinum [sis'plætinəm]　n. 顺铂
Vinblastine [vinblɑːstiːn]　n. 长春花碱
Melphalan [melfælən]　n. 苯丙氨酸氮芥
ovarian [əu'vɛəriən]　n.（生理）卵巢
cervical ['səːvikəl]　a. 颈部的
pancreatic [pæŋkri'ætik]　a. 胰腺的
carcinoma [kɑːsi'nəumə]　n.（pl. ~s）癌
lethargy ['leθədʒi]　n. 嗜眠症，不活泼，无生气
granulocyte ['grænjuləusait]　n. 粒细胞，粒性白细胞
hypotension [haipəu'tenʃən]　n. 低血压
arrhythmia [ə'riðmiə]　n. 心率不齐
prostaglandin [prɔstə'glændin]　n. 前列腺素
nomenclature [nəu'menklətʃə]　n. 系统命名法，专门用语
murine ['mjuərain]　a.；n. 鼠科的，鼠科动物
bovine ['bəuvain]　a.；n. 牛科的，牛科动物
antigen ['æntidʒən]　n. 抗原
misnomer ['mis'nəumə]　n. 误称，使用不当的名称

Notes

① interferon：干扰素，是细胞分泌的一类蛋白质，是一种重要的细胞素，简称 IFN，具有较广谱的抗病毒、抗细胞分裂和免疫调节活性；它通过激活细胞其他基团来发挥活性，本身并不能直接抗活病毒。

② antigen：抗原具有免疫原性和反应原性的物质，也称免疫原。免疫原性是指刺激机体的免疫活性细胞产生免疫应答的能力；反应原性是指抗原与抗体或致敏淋巴细胞发生特异性结合而出现可见反应的能力。

Exercises

1. Answer the following questions:
    (1) When and where was the interferon discovered?
    (2) Can you give a definition for interferon?
    (3) How many kinds of interferons are there?
2. Complete the passage of the text above.

　　Interferons have been _____ by an international group of scientists. Above all, to qualify as a(n) a factor must be a protein which exerts virus non-specific, _____ _____ at least in homologous cells through cellular metabolic processes involving synthesis of both _____ and protein. The preferred abbreviation for interferon is IFN. Each interferon is then _____ by the animal of origin, e. g. human HuIFN, murine _____, bovine _____. The interferons are next into types according to _____ specificities, e. g. α, β and γ, which are based on to previous designations of leucocyte, fibroblast and type II immune.

3. Put the following into Chinese:

Interest in the anticancer activity of interferon first arose due to encouraging results obtained in Sweden whilst treating osteogenic sarcoma and myelomatosis. More recently doctors in Yugoslavia, using human leukocyte interferon preparations injected directly into the tumors, have reported substantial or total remission for cancer of the head and neck. Although the mechanism of anti-tumor activity is not known, they suggest that a direct effect on malignant cells or stimulation of the host's immune system may be responsible.

4. Put the following into Chinese:
   murine   hypotension   leuk(a)emia   hepatitis   glycoprotein
   antivirus   infection   recombinant   immune   biosynthetic

5. Put the following into English:
   临床使用   移植   人体组织   主要的   慢性病的
   嗜睡症   病毒   专业术语   低血压   单克隆的

Reading Material 22

Molecular Recognition: Chemical and Biochemical Problems

Molecular recognition (MR) is one of those *in vogue* labels which is being used to describe and advertise a range of enterprises. The subject of the present review is one of the books to be thus identified, and it seems likely to be followed by a range of successors. In reality, this volume provides in print the major part of the proceedings of highly successful international symposium organized by Professor Roberts in Exeter in April, 1989.

The book focuses attention on a range of recent activities in domains of MR which are, for the most part, protein-oriented and in some measure reflect the areas of Professor Roberts' own interests. As editor, he has not attempted to group the subjects and my only justification for doing so here is to try to simplify a summary of the contents of a very wide-ranging series of some 20 research reports.

Four articles from the pharmaceutical industry provide a good insight into modern MR-based methods of analysis and attack upon a variety of problems in drug design. Studies on $α_1$-adrenoceptors, on antiviral agents for rhino- and entero-viruses, on neurokinin receptor antagonists and on renin inhibitors as potential antihypertensives provide a useful introduction, and will be of value for graduate students wishing to know more abut new lines of approach to such problems in the pharmaceutical industry. Some corresponding enterprises in universities are described in articles on penicillin-recognizing enzymes, on β-lactams and on sleeping sickness.

While investigations of this sort generally need to deploy many of the basic methodologies of MR, several articles focus on particular application of s single technique to specific research problems (a large part of which appear to have been published elsewhere). The 'enabling methodology' of peptide synthesis is neatly described in a short essay on peptide immunogens, NMR studies on recognition between small molecules and antibiotics and enzymes give a further view of the activities of Vancomycin an dihydrofolate reductase. The role of computational and graphics methods to provide both structural and dynamic information on ligand binding to receptors is covered in a stimulating account of work on melanin concentrating hormone and phospholipase A_2. The successes and difficulties of protein engineering emerge from a description of studies on tyrosine tRNA synthetase and the continuing relevance for MR of classical mechanistic analysis of enzyme reactions is demonstrated in the context of methylaspartase, a mixed bag of a number of contributions at the organic and physical chemistry end of the spectrum of MR studies cover synthesis to surface phenomena.

If I can single out on highlight, I would choose the article on CAVEAT, which describes a particular method of interrogation of the Cambridge structural database to identify molecules that match three features of tendamistat, a 74-amino acid inhibitor of α-amylase. The description of CAVEAT is stimulating both in its further application to somatostatin and in the tempered skepticism concerning the over-use of designed programs.

In his preface to this book, Professor Roberts says: 'Molecular recognition is a much used expression which means different thing to different scientists.'Very true indeed! There is considerable confusion at the present time over the use (and abuse) of 'MR'. The need for clarification of its use to avoid its undeserved discreditation is urgent. This book is unable to help with this problem. The specific relevance of Roberts' analysis for his own compilation is amply demonstrated by the range of material provided in its 20 articles, whose heterogeneity is immediately apparent from its contents page and is fully confirmed by subsequent reading. Indeed, at times on has to be extremely catholic to identify in certain sections any element of 'molecular recognition'.

Selected from G. M Blackburn *Chem. Ind.* (*London*) 1990, (11): 364~365.

Words and Expressions

recognition [rekəg'niʃən] *n.* 识别，认识
in vogue [in vəug] *a.* 流行的
adrenoceptor [ə driːnəu'septə] *n.* 肾上腺神经受体
rhino- ['rainəu] *n.* (前缀) 鼻的
entero- [entərəu] *n.* (前缀) 肠的
neurokinin [njuərəu'kinin] *n.* 神经激肽
renin ['riːnin] *n.* 肾素，高血压蛋白原酶

β-lactam ['læktæm] n. β-内酰胺
nuclear magnetic resonance spectroscopy(NMR) 核磁共振谱（仪）
dihydrofolate [daihaidrə'fəuleit] n. 双氢叶酸（酯）
reductase [ri'dʌkteis] n. 还原酶
melanin ['melənin] n. 黑色素
tyrosine ['tirəsi:n] n. 酪氨酸
methylaspartase ['meθiləs'pɑ:teis] n. 甲基天门冬氨酸酶
interrogation [interə'geiʃən] n. 讯问，质问
α-amylase ['æmileis] n. α-淀粉（糖化）酶
discreditation [diskredi'teiʃən] n. 怀疑，不名誉
somatostatin [səmətuə'stætin] n. 生长抑素
heterogeneity [hetərəudʒi'ni:iti] n. 异质性，不均匀性

Unit 23 The Marine Drug Potential

In seeking a new revolutionary type of molecular structures and biological activity, we should direct our attention to those areas where they are present in the greatest abundance, namely, marine natural products. In sheer number alone, the comparatively meager number of industrial synthetic chemists throughout the world cannot hope to compete with the infinite number of chemical factories that exist throughout the undersea world.

Marine natural products already show great promise in antitumor and antiviral activity. Research has indicated that a greater number and variety of antitumor and anticancer compounds can be found in marine organisms than in terrestrial species. Many clever chemical constituents are manufactured by the creatures who must compete for space, food, and light in the nutrient rich areas of the ocean.

When one considers the number of biochemical substances within a single specimen of plant or animal-multiplies this by an infinitude of ecological situations which can modify the chemical constituents within an organism and then multiplies in the number of species, the mathematical possibilities of biochemical agents throughout the marine world of natural products staggers the imagination. The seas around us are almost without limit in their potential as a source of new and different pharmaceuticals.

The question that now faces the marine pharmaceutical community is: how can we harness these substances and thereby avail ourselves of these valuable therapeutic and economic resources?

Essentially there are two approaches to the discovery of new "drugs"—namely screening of natural products or chemical synthesis. Increasing knowledge in molecular and cellular biology provides a basis for research aimed at rational drug design. However, screening of natural products for biological activity often leads to new or unanticipated types of action which would probably not be discovered under purely laboratory conditions. "Nature's chemists" also have one major advantage over synthetic chemists, in that from their very beginning they have been manufacturing products that are functional part of a biological system.

The concept of using natural products as a basis for discovery of new therapeutic agents can perhaps best be summed up by quoting the Nobel laureate Ernst Boris Chain[1].

In summary, then, of all past experience in the search for new biodynamic substances, it can be stated that all major advances in this area had at their base a biologic phenomenon discovered by systematic toxicologic, pharmacologic, physiologic and general biologic research, by clinical observations or, in many cases by blind chance. There exists no substitute for this; no so-called rational method based on the advances of the methods of molecular biology or any other physical or chemical method, can replace it in the foreseeable future.

It should be kept clearly in mind that less than one percent of the known species of marine organisms have been studied in even the most cursory manner as to their pharmacological and biochemical properties. As mankind embanks on the great endeavor to procure food and drugs from the sea, a rational systematic approach must be utilized which includes systematics, standardized screening techniques and the use of modern sophisticated analytical tools for isolation, structural elucidation, and chemical determinations. Many different factors come into play and must be orchestrated with care to fine detail if the end product is to be of benefit. Laboratory research frequently yields incomplete results because of inadequate ecological field observations, and documentation.

One of the most frustrating elements in the development of marine pharmaceuticals has been accessibility and availability of raw materials. In most instances marine pharmaceutical field operations require special handling of specimens, including freezing facilities or the use of special preservatives——all of which are costly and inaccessible especially in remote parts of the globe. Well equipped research vessels or facilities are frequently few or non existent in these remote regions.

In order to obtain adequate supplies of properly preserved organisms, a well organized field program is of vital importance. Proper field planning can mean the difference between discovery or defeat. A team of highly skilled marine biologists, divers, photographers, chemists, pharmacologists, pharmacognosists, and taxonomists are essential for a successful procurement program.

Unfortunately no integrated global approach exists to obtain marine biodynamic substances. Procurement programs are currently being handled on a smaller scale by governmental agencies, colleges and universities, research institutes, pharmaceutical companies and other private, commercially funded investigators. For example, a research team in University of California at St. Babara has extracted over 400 chemicals from marine animals and plants since 1977. This is a relatively modest effort considering the National Cancer Institute (NCI) estimate that some 3,000 to 4,000 synthetic compounds must be evaluated before one candidate for clinical trials is obtained. However, 25 of the compounds tested by the team have proved promising, with three reaching the more advanced research stages, and one compound, manoalide[2] (a powerful tumor inhibitor), is expected to be approved by FDA in 1989 for clinical use.

Another factor in the collection of raw materials is the variability of marine organism metabolic chemistry. Biodynamic substances within an organism can fluctuate depending on habitat or food ingested—— a fact which is true in all living systems, including Homo sapiens. The production of many interesting and potentially valuable bioactive compounds is frequently controlled by environmental rather than genetic factors. Therefore, quality documentation is imperative. A precise locality and ecological determination of the collection site is needed for each specimen, along with an accurate taxonomic identification. Thus, the various phases in an organism's life cycle may also play an important role in metabolite products.

Recent improvements in analytical procedures have made the process of isolating, separating, and purifying of bioactive materials from marine sources, and of assigning chemical structures to the compounds somewhat easier. For example, the study of a new antitumor isolated from the marine tunicate, was hastened by advances in high-field nuclear magnetic resonance spectroscopy, high-resolution fast atom bombardment mass spectrometry, and high performance liquid chromatography. As modern science explodes into the 21st century, we can look forward to even greater advances in techniques for isolation and elucidation of natural product chemical constituents.

Research in marine pharmaceuticals begins in the field. And the first step is locating and obtaining the organisms of interest.

Selected from B. W. Halstead, *Chinese Journal of Marine Drugs*, 1990,9(1),6~9.

Words and Expressions

sheer   [ʃiə]   *a.* 纯粹的，真正的
meager   ['mi:gə]   *a.* 贫乏的，欠缺的
terrestrial   [ti'restriəl]   *a.* 地球上的，陆生的；*n.* 陆生动植物
nutrient   ['nju:triənt]   *a.* 营养的，滋养的；*n.* 营养品，养料
infinitude   [in'finitju:d]   *n.* 无穷，无限的范围
rational   ['ræʃənl]   *a.* 理性的，合理的
embank   [im'bæŋk]   *v.* 筑堤，上岸
elucidation   [i'lju:sideiʃən]   *n.* 阐明，解释
orchestrate   ['ɔ:kistreit]   *v.* 使和谐地结合起来
pharmacognosist   [fɑ:mə'kɔgnəsist]   *n.* 生药学家
taxonomist   [tæk'sɔnəmist]   *n.* （尤指动植物）分类学家
procure   [prə'kjuə]   *v.* （努力）取得，实现，达成
Homo sapiens   人类
tunicate   ['tju:nikeit]   *n.* 被囊类动物

Notes

① Ernst Boris Chain，1945 年获得诺贝尔生理与医学奖，曾与 A. Flemming 和 H. Florey 共同合作发现了青霉素，并最终确定青霉素的治疗价值。
② manoalide：其化学物质名称为 4-[3, 6-dihydro-6-hydroxy-5-[4-methyl-6-(2, 6, 6-trimethyl-1-cyclohexen-1-yl)-3-hexenyl]-2H-pyran-2-yl]-5-hydroxy-2（5H）-furanone [75088-80-1]。

Exercises

1. Answer the following questions：

   (1) What role does the sea play in the future?

(2) Do you think that drug potential from sea is economical resources?

(3) Is it necessary that we make complete use of seas in 21st century?

2. Complete the passage of the text above.

Recent improvements in analytical procedures have made the process of _____, _____, and _____ of bioactive materials from marine sources, and of assigning chemical structures to the compounds somewhat easier. For example, the study of a new antitumor _____ from the _____ tunicate, was hastened by advances in high-field _____ _____ _____ spectroscopy, high-resolution fast atom bombardment (FAB) _____ spectrometry, and _____ _____ liquid chromatography. As modern science explodes into the 21st century, we can look forward to even greater advances in _____ for isolation and elucidation of natural product chemical constituents.

3. Put the following into Chinese:

| frustrating | marine organism | clinical trial | fluctuate |
| biodynamic | terrestrial species | unanticipated | orchestrate |

4. Put the following into Chinese:

In summary, then, of all past experience in the search for new biodynamic ubstances, can be stated that all major advances in this area had at their base a biologic phenomenon discovered by systematic toxicologic, pharmacologic, physiologic and general biologic research, by clinical observations or, in many cases by blind chance. There exists no substitute for this; no so-called rational method based on the advances of the methods of molecular biology or any other physical or chemical method, can replace it in the foreseeable future.

5. Put the following into English:

| 治疗用试剂 | 阐明 | 筛选 | 治疗价值 | 合理的 |
| 核磁共振仪 | 高效液相色谱 | 质谱仪 | 高分辨率 |

Reading Material 23

Drugs from the Sea

If asked to name some products of marine origin which are articles of commerce, most people would include sand, salt, fish, shellfish, pearls and precious corals. Some answers would also name algal polysaccharides (alginates, agar, carrageenan), but few would cite a specific organic compound, a drug or fine chemical, such as kainic acid.

If we continued our hypothetical questions into marine-related chemical activities, many would be aware of a substantial research effort during the past decade or two into the secondary metabolites of marine organisms (marine natural products), which has resulted in an impressive chemical literature of molecular structures, many of them new to science and moreover possessing desirable biological properties.

Why has this apparently fruitful basic research not generated a greater awareness of the drugs and other chemicals of marine origin, or perhaps even an actual drug whose name is as familiar as aspirin or penicillin?

Commercial chemicals of marine origin illustrates as follows:

Kainic acid is a rather simple amino acid, a derivative of proline. It was first isolated from a red alga, *Digenea simplex*, in Japan, where the alga had long been used as an anthelmintic drug. Kainic acid proved to be the active principle which was responsible for the drug's ascaridal effect against intestinal parasites. While the crude drug is still used, it was also observed that kainic acid, when injected into the neurons of a rat brain, causes lesions resembling those which occur in Huntington's chorea, a rare but fatal human disorder which exhibits behavioral and motor symptoms. Kainic acid, incidentally, is an example, rare in marine studies, of a modern drug whose genesis is based on folklore.

Okadaic acid[1] has become a tool for the study of molecular mechanisms. It is a long-chain C_{38} fatty acid, a complex polyether, and is structurally related to the antibiotic monensin and the brevetoxins, which are the red tide toxins of the Gulf of Mexico. It was first isolated from two marine sponges, and exhibited unspectacular antitumor properties. Recently okadaic acid was referred to as a new probe for the study of cellular regulation. It is in great demand in the biomedical researches. The supply of this high value specialty chemical is met from microalgal culture and from sponge extraction. A laboratory synthesis of okadaic acid has been achieved, but it is complex and has not been targeted for commercial production.

Antiviral drug Ara-A serves as a template for a synthetic or semi-synthetic drug with the same or improved therapeutic efficiency. This commercial drug may evolve from planned synthetic manipulation, molecular modeling, or from a combination; alternatively it may be the result of a lucky accident—a well-known phenomenon in drug development. At present antiviral drug Ara-A firstly from marine is produced by terrestrial bacterium. This was a quantum leap in drug development as it paved the way for production by well-known fermentation technology.

β-Carotene is a constituent of many plants and animals, terrestrial as well as marine. It plays an important role as provitamin A, as a food and animal feed additive, and has been reported to possess both anti-cancer and anti-ageing properties. The demand has been met by extraction of terrestrial plants and in recent years predominantly by laboratory synthesis. A rich source of β-carotene is the unicellular marine green alga, some strains of which contain β-carotene up to 20 per cent of dry cell weight, in sharp contrast to the classical natural source, carrots. The marine source appears to be competitive vehicle for large scale biotechnology.

The fifth example deals with the development of **a diagnostic tool** rather than a chemical or a drug. The horseshoe crab is an arthropod but not a crustacean like the familiar crabs of the marketplace. Its appearance is characterized by a sharp spike, telson, which extends from its body. Its habitat ranges from the Gulf of Maine to the Gulf of Mexico in the North

Atlantic. Related species are found along the Pacific coasts of Japan and Korea and south to the Philippines. An observation that the blood of horseshoe crabs suffering from an infection would clot led to the discovery that an extract of amoebocyte lysate from polyphemus will clot in the presence of small quantities of bacterial endotoxins. This scientific phenomenon gradually became a widely accepted bioassay for Gram-negative bacterial endotoxins. The demand of crab blood is met by a semiculture, where captured animals are maintained for some time and bled, and eventually returned to the ocean.

In addition Cod liver oil has long been known and used as a food supplement and/or medicine because of its contents of Vitamins A and D. More recently, fish oils have become of increasing interest because of their demonstrated beneficial influence on human cardiovascular health. The polyunsaturated fatty acids, eicosapentaenoic (EPA) and docosahexaenoic(DHA) acids have been subjected to considerable scrutiny.

In view of the fact that 70 per cent of the earth's surface is covered by oceans, which possess a greater diversity of organisms than exist on land, a determined effort combining all necessary elements for success is bound to reach its goal-drugs from the sea.

Selected from P. J. Scheaer *Chem. Ind*, (*London*)1991, (8); 276~278

Words and Expressions

algal ['ælgəl]　*a*. 藻的，藻类的；alga (pl. -gae) *n*.
polysaccharide [pɔli'sækəraid] *n*. 多糖
alginate [æl'dʒineit] *n*. 藻（朊）酸盐
agar ['eigɑ:] *n*. 琼脂，洋菜，石花菜，细菌培养基
carrageenan ['kærəgi:nən] *a*. 角叉菜（藻类）的
kainic acid　海人草酸或红藻氨酸
Digenea simplex　红藻海人草
anthelmintic [ænθel'mintik] *a*. 驱蠕（肠）虫的；*n*. 驱蠕（肠）虫药
ascaridal [æskə'ridəl] *a*. 驱蛔虫的
parasite ['pærəsait] *n*. 寄生物（虫、菌）
lesion ['li:ʒən] *n*. 损伤
monensin [mə'nənsin] *n*. 莫能菌素
brevetoxin [brevi'tɔksin] *n*. 短毒素
β-Carotene ['kærəti:n] *n*. β-胡萝卜素
crustacean [krʌs'teiʃiən] *a*. *n*. 甲壳类的（动物）
arthropod ['ɑ:θrəpɔd] *a*. 节肢动物的；*n*. 节肢动物
telson [telsn] *n*. （动物的）毒刺，（动物的）尾节
amoebocyte [ə'mi:bəsait] *n*. 变形细胞
lysate ['laiseit] *n*. 溶菌液
polypgemus [pɔli'fi:məs] *n*. 大眼水蚤属
endotoxin [endəu'tɔksin] *n*. 内毒素

biota [bai'əutə] n. 生物区系，生物群
eicosapentaenoic acid（EPA） 二十碳五烯酸
docosahexaenoic acid（DHA） 二十二碳六烯酸

Notes

① okadaic acid 化学名称为 9,10-deepithio-9,10-didehydro acanthifolicin，一种蛋白质磷酸酯酶 1 和 2A 的抑制剂。

Unit 24 Catalytic Antibodies[①]: Generation of Novel Biocatalysts

One of the most cogent theories of how enzymes work is that they lower the free energy of the transition state for a reaction relative to the energy of the ground states for the reactants and products. This concept was used to describe the potential capacity antibodies to act as enzymes. It might be possible to 'synthesize a enzyme' by means of antibodies: One way to do this to prepare an antibody to a haptenic group which resembles the transition state of a given reaction. Haptens[②] are macromolecules that carry small chemical haptenic groups which stimulate the production of antibodies.

In 1986, two research groups in California first reported the production of antibodies with enzyme-like activities, known as abzymes which catalyze the hydrolysis of esters and carbonates. While this procedure of eliciting antibodies against transition state analogues was the first successful approach to generating catalytic antibodies, it has some limitations. First, abzymes produced in this way show rate enhancements usually limited to between 10^3 and 10^4. Second, it requires that the transition state for the reaction needs to be understood in some detail. Third, synthesis of a suitably stable transition state analogue must be viable. As a result, scientists have explored other methods in the search for more efficient catalytic antibodies.

Amino acid residues are involved in enzyme catalysis both covalently, for example contributing nucleophilic and general acid-base catalysis at the active site of the enzymes, and electrostatically, either through coulombic interactions or via helix-dipole effects. Charge-charge complementarity also contributes to the exquisite binding specificity exhibited by immunoglobulins. Thus a recent strategy in hapten design uses such electrostatic complementarity to charged haptens to develop catalytic antibodies. This approach has been called the 'bait and switch' strategy. With this method an antibody was produced which catalyzed a β-elimination of ketone. Another component of enzyme catalysis is the ordering of reactants into high energy conformations. Such catalysis particularly involves control of the entropy in the transition state for unimolecular processes and is exemplified by the enzyme chorismate mutase.

Just as enzymes have expanded their catalytic repertoire through the acquisition of co-factors, antibodies have now been modified chemically in order to augment the functionality of the 20 natural amino acids. Two methods have been used for the direct introduction of catalytic groups into the antibody combining site: chemical modification and site specific and mutagenesis.

Chemical modification Antibodies have been modified by the incorporation of natural or synthetic catalysts into their combining sites, the areas in the antibody where the haptens are bound. These have included transition metal complexes, co-factors, and bases or nucleophiles. And nucleophiles have been incorporated into antibody combining sites by the selective chemical modification of existing side chains.

Site-specific mutagenesis Once important binding site residues have been pin-pointed using X-ray crystallography, they can be replaced by other amino acids to allow comparisons of catalytic rates and binding affinities. This method was used to modify the active site of a structurally resolved choline esterase. This enzyme hydrolyses 2,4-dinitrophenyl esters of choline.

In view of the tremendous interest in biocatalysis, it is not surprising that industry has been quick to see the potential of proteins with 'enable' catalytic activity in relation to both the chemical industry and the pharmaceutical field. Since the advent of catalytic antibodies in the mid-1980s, over 70 different chemical reactions have been catalyzed by antibodies. These reactions range from ester or carbonate hydrolysis to carbon-carbon bond forming reactions, and bimolecular amide formation, so their application to general synthetic organic chemistry seems to be very promising.

Catalytic antibodies have a number of advantages for the organic chemist over enzymes. Enzymes have significant limitations in synthesis. First, they only work on compounds similar to the 'natural' substrate and then with rather low affinities. Second, there are many chemical reactions for which there is no known enzyme catalyst. In both situation, abzymes can be of benefit to the synthetic chemist because they are 'programmable'. The range of reactions that can be catalyzed by abzymes appears to be limited only by sufficient knowledge of the transition state for any given reaction and the possibility of synthesis or an appropriately stable transition state analogue. Perhaps the best example of this to date has been the production of a 'Diels-Alderase' catalytic antibody. The Diels-Alder reaction is one of the most useful carbon-carbon bond-forming processes in organic chemistry, for which there are no known enzyme catalyst. Therefore, the acceleration of this reaction by an abzyme has been an important landmark in the field or catalytic antibodies and of considerable potential for chemical synthesis. Another use for catalytic antibodies is in chiral synthesis. Already abzymes have been shown to produce homochiral products from a *meso* substrate and they can also resolve a racemic alcohol mixture using enantiospecific lipase activity.

Although most abzyme catalyzed reactions have been carried out on a small scale, a publication has recently shown that enantioselective reactions can be performed on a gram scale, as in the enantioselective hydrolysis of a 2-benzylcyclopentenyl methyl ether to the corresponding (S)-(-)-2-benzylcyclopentanone. It would appear to be only one step further to put abzymes to work in a bioreactor to move into the kilogram scale of production.

It is clear that, though still young, the use of catalytic antibodies has developed very rapidly to a point where its application in organic chemistry and medicine is imminent. Abzymes have been shown to possess enzyme-like and non-enzyme-like features and they have the capacity to surprise us. From the evidence to date, it can be said of catalytic antibodies that although they may not yet optimize known reactions, they can create new ones. That is just one of the many facets of present interest in the generation of these novel biocatalysts.

Selected from G. H Blaokburn and P. Wen Tworth, *Chem. Ind. (London)*, 1994, (9): 338~342.

Words and Expressions

biocatalyst [baiə'kætəlist] *n*. 生物催化剂
cogent ['kəudʒənt] *a*. 有说服力的，无法反驳的
antibody ['æntibɔdi] *n*. 抗体
hapten ['hæpten] *n*. 半抗原
monoclonal [mɔnəu'kləunəl] *a*. 单一克隆的，单一无性系的
immunoglobulin [i'mju:nəu'glɔbjulin] *n*. 免疫球蛋白
spleen [spli:n] *n*. 脾脏
hybridoma [haibri'dəumə] *n*. 杂交瘤
abzyme [æb'zeim] *n*. 异酶
repertoire ['repətwɑ:] *n*. 全部技能，演奏节目
nucleophile ['nju:kliəfail] *n*. 亲核性，亲核试剂
hydrolysable [haidrəlaizəbl] *a*. 水解性的，进行水解的
disulphide [dai'sʌlfaid] *n*. 二硫化物，连二硫醚化物
electrophilic [ilektrəu'failik] *a*. 亲电性的，亲电（试剂）的
mutagenesis ['mjutədʒenisis] *n*. 突变
choline ['kəuli:n] *n*. 胆碱
affinity [ə'finiti] *n*. 亲合力
disfavour ['dis'feivə] *v*. 不赞成，失宠，不利
bioreactor [baiəuri'æktə] *n*. 生物反应器

Notes

① antibody：抗体，能与抗原（antigen）特异性结合并具有免疫活性的球蛋白，分天然抗体和免疫抗体两类。
② hapten：半抗原，能与对应抗体结合出现抗原-抗体反应，又不能单独激发人或动物体产生抗体的抗原；它只有反应原性，不具免疫原性，也称不完全抗原，包括大多数糖和所有的类脂。

Exercises

1. Answer the following questions:
   (1) How do the catalytic antibodies works in chemical reactions and drug therapy?
   (2) Can you give a definition for the world of science and medicine?
   (3) Do the concept of biocatalysts improve the development of biotechnology?
2. Complete the passage of the text above.

Catalytic antibodies have a number of advantages for the organic chemist over enzymes. Enzymes have significant limitations in synthesis. First, they only _____ on compounds similar to the '_____' substrate and then with rather low affinities. Second, there are many _____ for which there is no known enzyme catalyst. In both situation, abzymes can be of benefit to the chemist because they are 'programmable'. The range of reactions that can be catalyzed by _____ appears to be limited only by sufficient knowledge of the transition state for any given reaction and the possibility of _____ or an appropriately stable transition state analogue. Perhaps the best example of this to date has been the production of a 'Diels-Alderase' _____. The _____ reaction is one of the most useful carbon-carbon bond-forming processes in _____ chemistry, for which there are no known _____ catalyst.

3. Put the following into Chinese:

It is clear that, though still young, the use of catalytic antibodies has developed very rapidly to a point where its application in organic chemistry and medicine is imminent. Abzymes have been shown to possess enzyme-like and non-enzyme-like features and they have the capacity to surprise us. From the evidence to date, it can be said of catalytic antibodies that although they may not yet optimize known reactions, they can create new ones. That is just one of the many facets of present interest in the generation of these novel biocatalysts.

4. Put the following into Chinese:

reactant	immunoglobulin	antibodies	transition state
spleen	nucleophile	repertoire	mutagenesis
sulphide	affinities	choline	hydrolysable

5. Put the following into English:

异酶半抗原	自由能	水解反应	酸碱催化	静电的
突变	底物	酯化酶	消除反应	生物反应器
亲电的				

Reading Material 24

Enzymes in Synthetic Organic Chemistry

Although more than two thousand different enzymes have been described, only a few hundred are commercially available in small quantities and less than two dozen in industrial amounts. Nonetheless, biochemical procedures are slowly becoming accepted as routine in organic synthesis. The main reasons why enzymes have not been used more often in organic chemistry are a lack of motivation and a lack of familiarity on the part of synthetic chemists. On the other hand, chemists are appreciating more and more the potential of enzymes as selective catalysts to construct chiral synthons of complicated compounds, along with the possibility of recycling the biocatalyst if mounted on an immobilized support. The following two examples illustrate that chiral molecules can be obtained directly from achiral precursors.

$$\underset{\text{achiral precursor}}{\overset{\text{COO}^-}{\underset{\text{COO}^-}{\diagup\!\!\!\diagdown}}} + NH_4^+ \xrightarrow{\text{aspartase}} \underset{\text{L-aspartic acid}}{\overset{\text{COO}^-\;\;H}{\underset{^-OOC\;\;\;NH_4}{\diagdown\!\!\!\diagup}}}$$

$$\underset{\substack{\text{MeOOC}\quad\text{COOMe}\\ \text{prochiral center}}}{\overset{X\quad Y}{\diagdown\!\!\!\diagup}} \xrightarrow{\text{esterase}} \underset{\substack{\text{MeOOC}\quad\text{COOMe}\\ \text{chiral molecule}\\ \text{from mono-hydrolysis}}}{\overset{X\quad Y}{\diagdown\!\!\!\diagup}}$$

Of course, one major problem associated with the use enzymes in organic chemistry is that many of the substrates of interest are 'unnatural.' However, enzymes can operate on unnatural substrates by changing the reaction conditions or solvent to change the activity of the enzymes. Enzymes have been divided into six groups and, in each of them, specific enzymes have been used in organic syntheses.

1. *Oxydoreductase* for oxidation and reduction reactions.
2. *Transferase* for transfer of functional groups.
3. *Hydrolase* in hydrolysis reactions of esters, amides, phosphates, etc.
4. *Lyase* for addition to double bonds.
5. *Isomerase* particularly for racemization.
6. *Ligase* for the formation of chemical bonds with ATP cleavage.

Particularly useful for the synthetic chemists is the formation of new carbon-carbon bonds with stereospecific introduction of chiral center. Along these lines, the potential of aldolase-catalyzed aldol reactions as a route to isotopically labeled sugar molecules on a molar scale. For this, dihydroxyacetone is first phosphorylated by a kinase. In the presence of the aldolase (from rabbit muscle), the keto-substrate forms a Schiff base with a lysine residue of the enzyme to give eventually an enamine intermediate that acts as a nucleophile and reacts with an incoming chiral aldehyde. The stereochemistry of the aldol condensation catalyzed by enzyme indicates that two new chiral centers are formed enantiospecifically. This approach has been used for the synthesis of ^{13}C-labeled glucose and fructose.

The use of enzymes as organic tools in the fields of medicinal chemistry, endocrinology, immunology, and biotechnology will become more and more frequent in the coming years. All these disciplines require chemical manipulation of complicated compounds as well as biologically derived or biologically related substances. The utility of high selectivity and the fast rate of enzyme reactions could contribute greatly to the development of rapidly accessible chiral precursors. It is well known that enzymes have the ability to discriminate between enantiomers of racemic substrates. Pig liver esterase (PLE) exhibits a broad tolerance of structural variation in its *meso*-diester substrates. Its enantiotopic specificity has been exploited recently for the preparation of chiral cyclic acid-esters and bicyclic lactones.

In fact, the biochemical methods of enzymatic asymmetric catalysis have the great advantage of being able to generate in high yields bifunctional chiral synthons with optical purities not obtainable otherwise.

Selected from H. Dugas, *Bioorganic Chemistry*, Springer-Verlag, 2nd, 1989.

Words and Expressions

synthon   ['sinθɔn]   *n.* 合成子
immobilize   [i'məubilaiz]   *v.* 使固定，使不动
achiral   [ə'kaiərəl]   *a.* 非手性的
aspartase   [əs'pɑːteis]   *n.* 天门冬氨酸酶
esterase   ['estəreis]   *n.* 酯酶
oxydoreductase   [ɔksidəri'dʌkteis]   *n.* 氧化还原酶
transferase   ['trænsfəreis]   *n.* 转移酶
hydrolase   ['haidrəleis]   *n.* 水解酶
lyase   ['liːəs]   *n.* 裂合酶
isomerase   ['aisəmreis]   *n.* 异构化酶
ligase   ['ligeis]   *n.* 连接酶
aldolase   ['ældɔːleis]   *n.* 醛缩酶
kinase   ['kaineis]   *n.* 激酶
stereochemistry   [stiəriə'kemistri]   *n.* 立体化学
endocrinology   [endəukrai'nɔlədʒi]   *n.* 内分泌学
immunology   [imju'nɔlədʒi]   *n.* 免疫学
discriminate   [dis'krimineit]   *v.* 鉴别，辨出
meso-   [mesəu]   *pref.* 内消旋，中间（物）
lactone   ['læktəun]   *n.* 内酯

Unit 25 Principles of Drug Design

Drug design to day is more of a hope than an achievement. It means the application of previously recognized correlations of biological activity with physicochemical characteristics in the broadest sense, in the hope that the pharmacological success of a not yet synthesized compound can be predicted. Few drugs in use today were discovered entirely in this way. The cholinesterase inhibitor antidote pyridine aldoxime methiodide, the antiulcer drug Cimetidine, and some antimetabolites active against leukemias are examples. One of the principal difficulties in this approach is that the available—and very sophisticated—methods for predicting drug action cannot foretell toxicity and side effects, nor do they help in anticipating the transport characteristics or metabolic fate of the drug *in vivo*. These are, of course, as important in producing a therapeutically successful drug *in vitro* or cellular effect of the pharmacy.

Very often our best efforts are frustrated by basic ignorance of the biology or biochemistry underlying a disease, and we are reduced to what Lewis Thomas, in one of his incisive essays, calls "halfway technology" in reference to the complex and costly management of diseases whose basic causes are not understood. The treatment of rheumatoid arthritis, most malignant tumors, and all mental diseases falls into this category, and contrasts glaringly with the simplicity of dealing with most infectious diseases of bacterial origin and even some viral diseases like poliomyelitis.

Although some practicing medicinal chemists and molecular pharmacologists still regard efforts at rational drug design with some condescension and ill-concealed impatience, a slow but promising development gives renewed hope that progress in this area will not be less rapid than in the application of biology and physical chemistry to human and animal pathology. The explosive development of computer-aided drug design[①] in three dimensions promises to lead to the era of true rational drug design.

Until the early 1960s, drug design was an intuitive endeavor based on long experience, keen observation, serendipity, sheer luck, and a lot of hard work. The probabilities of finding a clinically useful drug were not good; it was estimated that anywhere from 3000 to 5000 compounds were synthesized in order to produce one practical drug. With today's more strict drug safety regulations, the proportions are even worse and the costs skyrocket, retarding the introduction of new drugs to a dangerous extent. The classical method usually applied in drug development was molecular modification—the design of analogues of a proven active "lead" compound. The guiding principle was the paradigm that minor changes in a molecular structure lead to minor, quantitative alterations in its biological effects. Although this may be true in closely related series, it depends on the definition of "minor" changes. The addition of two very small hydrogen atoms to the Δ^8 double bond of ergot alkaloids eliminates their uterotonic activity, but replacement of the N—CH$_3$ substituent by the large phenethyl group in morphine increases the activity less than ten fold. Extension of the side chain of diethazine by only one carbon atom led to the serendipitous discovery of Chlorpromazine and modern psychopharmacology. A retrospective account of classical drug design was provided in 1983.

There are two conclusions to be drawn from these random examples. First, a merely structural change in an organic molecule is meaningless in **structure-activity relationship (SAR)**[2] studies as long as its physicochemical consequences remain unexplored and the molecular basis of its action remains known. Structure, in the organic chemical sense, is only a repository, a carrier of numerous parameters of vital importance of drug activity.

The second conclusion to be drawn from the above examples—and innumerable others—is that the discovery of qualitatively new pharmacological effects is often a discontinuous jump in an otherwise monotonous series of drug analogues and is hard to predict, even with fairly sophisticated methods.

Despite the great success of the classical methods of drug design, their unpredictability and the tremendous amount of wasted effort expended have necessitated the development of more rational methods with a much higher predictive capability, in an effort to elevate drug design from an art to a science. The approach involving the design of analogues of an active lead compound remains unchanged, and the expertise of the medicinal chemist is as much in demand as ever; however, the intuitive process of selecting structural modifications for synthesis becomes circumspect in this approach, and models based on multiple regression analysis and pattern recognition methods, using very powerful computer techniques, are employed as aids. It is obviously much faster and cheaper to calculate the required properties of novel compounds from a large pool of data on their analogues than to synthesize and screen all such new compounds in the classical fashion. Only promising candidates are investigated experimentally. The results gained this way are incorporated into the data base, expanding and strengthening the theoretical search. Eventually, sufficient material accumulates to aid in making a confident decision about whether the "best" analogue has been prepared or whether the series should be abandoned.

Although a beginning has been made, drug design is far from being either automatic or foolproof. The choice of proper lead compound—a necessity in quantitative drug design—is still based on experience, serendipity, and luck, given our basic ignorance of molecular phenomena at the cellular level. Now, however, we can at least have the confidence that the discovery of new drugs and the development of existing ones will be able to keep pace with the progress of biomedical research.

Selected from H. J. Smith, *Medicinal Chemistry*, 2nd ed., Wright, 1988.

Words and Expressions

antidote ['æntidəut]　*n.* 解毒剂

aldoxime [æl'dɔksi:m] n. 醛肟化合物
methiodide ['meθaiədaid] n. 甲基碘化物
antiulcer ['æntiʌlsə] a. 抗胃溃疡的
Cimetidine [sai'metidi:n] n. 西咪替丁（抗胃溃疡药）
rheumatoid ['ru:mətɔid] a. 风湿性的，害风湿病的，类风湿病的
arthritis [ɑ:'θraitis] n. 关节炎
poliomyelitis [pɔliəumaii'laitis] n. 脊髓灰质炎，小儿麻痹症
condescension [kɔndi'siʃən] n. 屈尊，恩赐的态度
pathology [pə'θɔlədʒi] n. 病理学，病状
serendipity [serən'dipiti] n. 意外发现，偶然发现
paradigm ['pærədaim] n. 范例，示例
ergot ['ə:gət] n. 麦角碱，麦角菌（病）
uterotonic [ju:tərəu'tɔnik] n. 子宫收缩的；a. 子宫收缩药
Morphine ['mɔ:fi:n] n. 吗啡
Chlorpromazine [klɔ:'prəuməzin] n. 氯丙嗪（治精神病药）
psychopharmacology [saikəu fɑ:mə'kɔlədʒi] n. 精神药理学
foolproof [fu:lpru:f] a. 极简单明了的，有安全装置的

Notes

① **CADD**：Computer-Aided Drug Design，计算机辅助药物设计，即利用计算机进行药物分子活性结构的分析，从而设计出新的药物分子结构，使合成出的新药物具有较优疗效及较少的副作用或定向地合成具有特定疗效的药物。

② **SAR**：structure-activity relationship，构效关系，即药物结构与生物活性间的关系。药物的构效关系研究，就是根据某一类型药物结构上的变化，导致生物活性的变化，设法寻找某些构效关系的规律性，以指导药物的研究和合成。

Exercises

1. Answer the following questions:
   (1) Do you think CADD methods are rational?
   (2) Can you give a definition for CADD?
   (3) How many drugs have successfully been produced by CADD today?

2. Complete the passage of the text above.

   There are two conclusions to be _____ from these random examples. First, a merely _____ change in an organic molecule is meaningless in _____ relationship studies as long as its consequences remain unexplored and the molecular _____ of its action remains known. Structure, in the organic chemical sense, is only a repository, a carrier of numerous parameters of vital importance of _____ _____.

   The second _____ to be drawn from the above _____ and innumerable others is that the discovery of _____ new pharmacological effects is often a discontinuous jump in an otherwise monotonous series of drug _____ and is hard to predict, even with fairly sophisticated methods.

3. Put the following into Chinese:

The classical method usually applied in drug development was molecular modification—the design of analogues of a proven active "lead" compound. The guiding principle was the paradigm that minor changes in a molecular structure lead to minor, quantitative alterations in its biological effects. Although this may be true in closely related series, it depends on the definition of "minor" changes. The addition of two very small hydrogen atoms to the Δ^8 double bond of ergot alkaloids eliminates their uterotonic activity, but replacement of the N—CH_3 substituent by the large phenethyl group in morphine increases the activity less than ten fold. Extension of the side chain of diethazine by only one carbon atom led to the serendipitous discovery of chlorpromazine and modern psychopharmacology.

4. Put the following into Chinese:
   antidote   antiulcer   serendipity   foolproof   poliomyelitis
   intuitive   malignant   morphine   antimetabolite   pathology

5. Put the following into English:
   生物效应   单调的   构效关系   定性的   生物碱
   结构识别   参数   先导化合物 细胞的   生物医学

Reading Material 25

On Computer-Aided Drug Design

The development of new drugs has been responsible for decreasing human morbidity and mortality more than any other scientific endeavor in our lifetime. These products have dramatically improved the quality of life across all age ranges and socioeconomic groups. Moreover, modern drugs are a highly cost-effective form or treatment. They can prevent illness or, when illness occurs, speed recovery, reduce hospital stays, and decrease the need for surgery.

Drugs can be discovered in a number of ways. Sometimes they are found by accident. Most frequently, they are developed as part of an organized effort to discover new ways to treat specific diseases. With the general acceptance of the molecular basis of disease has come the realizations that the disease process can be understood at the chemical level, and consequently the disease can be interrupted chemically. This has led to the mechanistic approach for the development of drugs to treat diseases.

The mechanistic approach to drugs discovery begins with knowledge of the disease process itself. It also requires that one know about the chemical structures of the interacting molecules. Since substrates, ligands, or drugs that mimic them (effectors) and their enzymes or receptors (targets) interact via a lock-and-key type mechanism, knowledge of their three-dimensional structures is of critical importance. Once these are known, scientists can begin to design new chemical entities to influence the targets which are involved in the disease process.

Because of the vast amount of information involved in determining the three-dimensional structures of the effector and its target, and in the use of this information for the design of new medicinal agents, computers have been a major requirement for this process. Consequently this approach to new drug design has frequently been called "computer-aided drug design" (CADD). Such a designation, however, loses sight of the fact that the computer functions as a tool in the drug design process. CADD is critically dependent on the physical techniques of crystallization and spectroscopy to provide the practical parameters for its calculations, and on the wisdom of the medicinal scientists to interpret and utilize its output data.

This book has been written to provide an overview of the process of mechanistic, computer-aided drug design. To accomplish this, the book has been divided into two sections: "Methods" and "Applications." It is intended to be of use to students who plan to enter the field of drug design and to individuals who are currently involved with drug research but may not be fully familiar with the approaches used in CADD. Since this is a very rapidly moving field, some of the theoretical sections present concepts that are at the forefront of this technology; consequently this book should also be of use to scientists who are intimately involved with CADD.

The process of mechanistic design of new drugs is only in its infancy. This is because the knowledge base about both disease processes and the structures and interactions of molecules is still developing. This in no way prevents the use of this technology in discovering new pharmaceuticals. Rather it challenges the creativity of the scientist to supplement current knowledge with ingenuity. The Applications section of the book has been added as a complement to the Methods section in order to demonstrate how scientists are currently coping with the available knowledge base and at the same time successfully developing new drugs.

Selected from T. J. Perun, C. L. Propst, *Computer-Aided Drug Design: Methods and Applications*, Marcel Dekker Inc., N.Y., 1989.

Words and Expressions

morbidity [məˈbiditi] n. 发病率，致病率
mortality [mɔːˈtæliti] n. 死亡率，死亡数
socioeconomic [ˌsəusiəu iːˈkənɔmik] a. 社会经济学的
substrate [ˈsʌbsteit] n. 基质，底物
ligand [ˈligənd] n. 配体，配合物
effector [iˈfektə] n. 效应器
mimic [ˈmimik] a.; n. 模仿的，拟似的，模仿物，拟形
entity [ˈentiti] n. 实体，本质
infancy [ˈinfənsi] n. 初期，幼时，婴儿期
ingenuity [ˌindʒiˈnjuːiti] n. 机灵，机智，巧妙

APPENDIXES

Appendix 1

The General Principles for Nomenclature of Chinese Approved Drug Names *

I. General Guidance

1. The term "drug" refers generally to all kinds of drugs including chemical drugs, antibiotics, biochemicals, biological preparations, radiopharmaceuticals and chemical identities isolated from natural drugs with the exception of Chinese traditional drugs.

2. The drug names established in accordance with the general principles are Chinese Approved Drug Names (CADN). The Chinese Pharmacopoeia Commission is authorizes to be in charge of the devising and establishment of CADN and reporting to the Ministry of Public Health for registration.

3. Drug names should be scientific, distinctive and short in words. Definite stems should be translated wherever possible to express the homologous series systematically.

4. Drug names that are likely to convey to a patient an anatomical, physiological, pathological or therapeutic prophecy or hint should be avoided. Figures or number used as drug names are not accepted.

5. The English drug names of International Nonproprietary Names (INN) published by World Health Organization are adopted as far as possible. For drug names not yet established in INN, appropriate English names may be used.

6. If the alteration of a drug name in conventional use for a long time deems necessary, the used name may be admitted for a transition period. The interval of the transition should follow the related regulations of the Ministry of Public Health.

7. The category as a note after a drug name is based on the principal pharmacological action, action mechanism or brach of science, or translated directly from categories designated in INN. It is admitted for reference only.

8. Trade name (including foreign and Chinese name) of a drug should not be used as generic name for the drug. The generic name (including INN) and the specific stems of English and Chinese translation are not to be used as trade name or to form a trade name for trade

---

* 选自中华人民共和国卫生部药典委员会编. 中国药品通用名称. 北京:化学工业出版社,1997 第 XV～XIX 页.

mark registration.

II. Nomenclature of drug substances

9. The translation of English approved drug names to Chinese is based on phonetics, definition or a combination of both, with phonetic translation as the first preference. The Chinese names must be in best correspondence with the English names.

10. For inorganic chemical drugs use their chemical names, if they are commonly used and simple; Popular names may be used in case chemical names are not commonly used, such as: hydrochloric acid and borax. Acid salt in acidic state is expressed with "氢", such as:"碳酸氢钠" instead of "重碳酸钠"; for basic salt, the use of "次" is avoided, such as, "碱式硝酸铋" is used instead of "次硝酸铋".

11. For organic chemical drugs, the chemical name is used for those of short name such as, benzoic acid; the conventional popular name may be used as far as the conditions of the use of the drugs are met, such as Saccharin Sodium and Glycerin.

   For long names, the nomenclature follows the following principles.

(1) Drug names assigned phonetically. English names of a few syllables may be translated completely, for example, Codeine is translated from the conplete pronunciation of the name. For names of many syllables are abridged, for example, Amitriptyline is translated from the first 2 and last 2 syllables in phonetics to make four Chinese words for the drug name. Drug names translated on the basis of phonetics should be easy to pronounce and read, the words adopted be common, refined and not miss leading. The accent of English names should be realized in the translation.

(2) Drug names assigned by structural, categorial consideration or in combination of phontics (including nomenclature for chemicals and abridged chemical groups or radicals). Whenever the translation of drug names is in difficult or names of multiple or excessive syllables, the direction should be adopted, such as chlorpromazine, cefadroxil, etc. The Chinese translation is 氯丙嗪, here 氯 stands for Chloro of English, 丙嗪 for the rest from the combination of structure and stem of action, Cefadroxil is translated into 头孢羟氨苄 similarly.

12. For drug names of salts or esters from an acid, the name of the acid precedes the base (or base group) and are in inverted order with the English names, as with Streptomycin Sulfate 硫酸链霉素, Hydrocortisone Acetate 醋酸氢化可的松.

   For salts from organic acid, the Chinese words denoting acid is generally omitted as in Poldine Metisulfate 甲硫泊尔定 and Sorbitan Laurate 月桂山梨醇.

   Drugs of esters with suffix of "ate" may be translated into "ester", such as Fedrilate 非屈酯. For drug of ester obtained from the condensation group, "ester" is in the last of words order in Chinese, for example, Cefcanel Daloxate 头孢卡奈达酯.

13. For drug names of quaternary ammonium salts, the chlorine, bromine in Chinese names generally precede the ammonium, as in: Benzalkonium Bromide 苯扎溴铵 with the exception of some conventional names.

Chinese drug names from quaternary ammoniun salts of organic acid start with the name of the acid generally with the omission the Chinese word "acid", as in Amezinium Metilsulfate 甲硫阿镁铵 instead of 甲硫酸阿镁铵.

14. The English names of biochemical drugs are generally based on INN; for drug names not yet listed in INN refer to NC-INB or ICBN published names. For translation into Chinese it is nedessary to consider the pharmaceutic characteristics or generally used name in addition to the biochemical names published by the Committee for Biochemical Names of the Chinese Biochemical Association, for example, Urokinase is translated into 尿 (uro) 激酶 (kinase); Trypsin into 胰蛋白酶; Adenosine Triphosphate into 三磷腺苷.

    For growth hormones, both source and pharmaceutic property are considered in the translation into Chinese through the combination of phonetic and category, for example: 生长释素 for Soma torelin, 牛亮氨生长素 for Somavubove, 猪诺生长素 for Somenopor.

15. For monoclonal antibody and interleukin, the combination of phonetic and category of abridged English name is used in translation into Chinese, for example: Dorlimomab Aritox, Biciromab; Teceleukin are translated into 4~5 Chinese words respectively as 阿托度单抗, 比西单抗, 替西白介素. (Underlined is translation from category).

16. For radiopharmaceuticals, immediately after the Chinese name of the nuclide, the symbol of the nuclide with mass number is labeled in square brackers, for example 碘 [^{125}I] 化钠.

17. For extracts from natural drugs of known chemical identity, if the drug name is derived from the botanieal genus or species, it is accepted in the nomenclature for the Chinese name with reference to the genus or species, for example: 青蒿素 for Artemisinin; 青霉胺 for Penicillamine. Otherwise translation phonetically is preferable, for example: 吗啡 for Morphine, 阿米卡星 for Amikacin.

    If the chemical structure is unknown or not yet establshed, the translation is based on the abridgment of the source and function, for example: 杆菌肽 for Bacitracin.

    The word root for glucoside is now translated into "苷" to replace "甙" which has been used in the past in agreement with the nomenclature for chemicals in China.

III. Nomenclature of Pharmaceutical Preparations

18. For the nomenclature of pharmaceutical preparations, name of the active ingredient precedes the dosage form, for example: 吲哚美辛胶囊 for Indometacin capsules.

19. It is advisable to describe the use or property precedes the drug name of pharmaceutical preparation, for example: 吸收性明胶海绵 for Absorbable Gelatin Sponge.

20. For the drug name of pharmaceutical preparation of single active ingredient should be in agreement with that of the pharmaceutical substance, for example 布美他尼片 for Bumetanide Tablets.

21. The drug names for compound pharmaceutical preparations are referred to the following conditions.

(1) Named by the active ingredient preceded with "Compound", for example：复方碘化钾溶液 for compound Iodine Solution.

(2) Named after some drugs or their abbreviations, or adopted the phonetic and category of the English name in abridgment. For example：葡萄糖氯化钠注射液 for Glucose and Sodium Chloride Injection，氨酚待因片 for Paracetamol and Codeine Tablets，安钠咖注射液 for Caffeine and Sodium Benzoate Injection.

If the name of the active ingredient can not be abridged satisfactorily, the words "复方" (compound) are use to precede the abridged name.

(3) For compound pharmaceutical preparations of many active remedies that are difficult in abridgment, the member of the pharmaceutical substances may be used for the nomenclature of the preparation, for example: Injections of 15 Amino Acids is named as Compound Amino Acids (15). If the side chain amino acid should be expressed, the drug name Compound Amino Acids Injection (15HBC) may be used.

For amino acids of similar composition but different in proportions, a series number may be added for its identity, as in Compound Amino Acids Injection (15-1).

For compound preparation of multivitamins or vitamins and trace elements, the same principle may be applied as 多维维生素片 (15) for Multivitamin Tablets (15)，多维元素片 (31) for Multivitamins and Elements Tablets (31).

Appendix 2

INN 采用的词干及其中文译名*

一、抗微生物药

1. 抗生素

-bactam	-巴坦	β-内酰胺酶抑制药类，如溴巴坦
cef-	头孢-	头孢菌素类
-cidin	-西定	不属于其他类的天然抗生素
-cillin	-西林	青霉素类
-cycline	-环素	四环素类
-gillin	-洁林	曲霉菌属抗生素
-kacin	-卡星	卡那霉素类
-micin	-米星	小单孢菌属抗生素
-monam	-莫南	单巴坦类抗生素
-mycin	-霉素	链霉菌属抗生素
-oxef	-氧头孢	头孢霉素衍生物类
-parcin	-帕星	糖肽类
-penem	-培南	亚胺培南类
rifa-	利福-	利福霉素类
-rubicin	-(柔)比星	柔红霉素类抗肿瘤抗生素
-tricin	-曲星	多烯类

2. 抗真菌药

-conazole	-康唑	咪康唑类
-fungin	-芬净	抗真菌类抗生素
-pirox	-吡罗	吡啶酮衍生物类

3. 合成抗菌药

-dapsone	-(氨)苯砜	氨苯砜类抗麻风药
nifur-	硝呋-	硝基呋喃类
-oxacin	-沙星	萘啶酸类
-prim	-普林	甲氧苄啶类

* 选自中华人民共和国卫生部药典委员会编. 中国药品通用名称. 北京:化学工业出版社,1997 第 XX～XXX 页。

sulfa-(-sulfa-)	磺胺-(-磺胺-)	磺胺类	-metacin	-美辛	吲哚美辛类
4. 抗病毒药			-nixin	-尼辛	苯氨烟酸类
-mantadine	-曼(他)定（或金刚）	金刚烷衍生物类	-oxicam	-昔康	苯并噻嗪类
			-profen	-洛芬	布洛芬类
-motine	-莫汀	喹啉衍生物类	-quazone	-喹宗	喹唑啉衍生物类
-uridine	-尿苷	尿嘧啶类	**4. 抗精神失常药**		
-vir	-韦	阿昔洛韦类	-giline	-吉兰	B型单胺氧化酶抑制药
二、抗寄生虫药			-mox	-莫辛	单胺氧化酶抑制药,肼衍生物类
-antel	-尔太	驱肠蠕虫药			
-bendazole	-苯达唑	噻苯达唑类	-oxepin(e)	-塞平	西多塞平类抗抑郁药
-ectin	-克丁	阿巴美丁类	-oxetine	-西汀	氟西汀类
-fos	-磷(或-福司)	磷衍生物类	-perone	-哌隆	氟哌丁苯类
			-pramine	-帕明	米帕明类
-nidazole	-硝唑	甲硝唑类	-pride	-必利	舒必利类
-oxanide	-沙奈	水杨苯胺衍生物类	-tepine	-替平	甲替平类
三、神经系统药			-tixene (-thixene)	-噻吨	噻吨衍生物类
1. 麻醉药			-triptyline	-替林	三环类抗抑郁药
-caine	-卡因	局部麻醉药	**5. 镇静催眠药**		
-curium	-库铵	神经肌肉阻断剂,箭毒样物质	-azam	-(巴)占	氯巴占类安定药
			-azepam	-西泮	地西泮类
-flurane	-氟烷	含氟吸入麻醉药	-bamate	-氨酯	氨甲酸酯类
nal	纳	去甲吗啡类麻醉拮抗药/促效药	-barb	-巴比	
			-barbital	-巴比妥	巴比妥类
2. 镇痛药			-spirone	-螺酮	替螺酮类抗焦虑药
adol(-adol或-adol-)	多		-zafone	-扎封	阿氯扎封类安定药
			-zolam	-唑仑	苯并二氮䓬类
-adom	-朵	替氟朵衍生物类	**6. 抗癫痫药**		
-azocine	-佐辛	苯并吗吩烷类	-toin	-妥英	乙内酰脲衍生物类
-eridine	-利定	哌替啶类	-zepine	-西平	三环类抗惊厥药
-fenine	-非宁	格拉非宁类	**7. 食欲抑制剂**		
-fentanil	-芬太尼	芬太尼类	-orex	-雷司	苯乙胺衍生物类
-orph-	-啡-		**8. 益智药**		
-orphan	-啡烷	吗啡烷类	-racetam	-(拉)西坦	吡拉西坦类
3. 消炎镇痛药			**9. 抗震颤麻痹药**		
-ac	-酸	异丁芬酸类	-dopa	-多巴	多巴胺受体激动药
-arit	-(扎)利	氯丁扎利类抗关节炎药	**10. 苯并二氮䓬类拮抗药**		
			-azenil	-西尼	氟马西尼类
-bufen	-布芬	丁酸衍生物类	-carnil	-卡奈	咔啉衍生物类
-butazone	-泰宗	保泰松类	**四、心血管系统药**		
-buzone	-布宗	保泰松衍生物类	**1. 抗心律失常药**		
-fazone	-法宗	哒嗪衍生物类	-afenone	-非农	普洛帕酮类
-fenamate	-芬那酯	芬那酯衍生物类	-bradine	-雷定	减缓心律药
-fenamic acid	-芬那酸	邻氨基苯甲酸衍生物类	-cainide	-卡尼	利多卡因衍生物
			-darone	-达隆	胺碘酮类

2. 抗高血压药

词干	中文	类别
-anserin	-色林	5-羟色胺拮抗药
-azosin	-唑嗪	哌唑嗪类
-dralazine	-屈嗪	肼酞嗪类
guan-	胍-	胍乙啶类
-kalim	-卡林	钾通道激活药
-nidine	-尼定	咪唑啉衍生物类
-pril	-普利	卡托普利类
-prilat	-普利拉	
-serpine	-舍平	利血平类

3. 血管舒张药（包括部分抗心绞痛药）

词干	中文	类别
dil	地尔	
-dipine	-地平	硝苯地平类
-pamil	-帕米	维拉帕米类
-tiazem	-硫䓬	地尔硫䓬类钙通道阻滞药

4. β受体阻滞药

词干	中文	类别
-dilol	-地洛	普齐地落类
-olol	-洛尔	普奈洛尔类

5. 降血脂药

词干	中文	类别
-fibrate	-贝特	氯贝丁酯（氯贝特）类
-nicate	-烟脂	烟酸酯类
-vastatin	-伐他汀	洛伐他汀类

6. 血管收缩药

词干	中文	类别
-azoline	-唑啉	抗组胺药、局部血管收缩药安他唑啉类
-pressin	-加压素	加压素类

7. 强心剂

词干	中文	类别
-dan	-旦	依马唑旦类
-rinone	-力农	氨力农类

五、影响血液及造血系统药

词干	中文	类别
-arol	-香豆素	双香豆素类
-grel (-grel-)	-格雷	抗血小板聚集药
-pafant	-帕泛	血小板活化因子拮抗药
-parin	-肝素	肝素衍生物凝血药
-plase	-普酶	纤维蛋白溶酶原激活药
-poetin	-泊丁	红细胞生成素型血液因子

六、消化系统药

词干	中文	类别
-aldrate	-铝	铝盐制酸药
-cic	-西克	具羧基的保肝药
-prazole	-拉唑	苯并咪唑衍生物抗消化性溃疡药
-tidine	-替丁	H_2受体阻滞药

七、呼吸系统药

词干	中文	类别
-ast	-司特	抗过敏药
-cromil	-罗米	色氨酸类抗过敏药
-drine	-君	苯乙胺衍生物拟交感神经药
exine	-克新	溴己新类祛痰药
-frine	-福林	苯乙基衍生物拟交感神经药
-fylline	-茶碱	茶碱衍生物类
-steine	-司坦	粘液溶解药
-terol	-特罗	苯乙胺类支气管扩张药
-xanox	-咕诺	咕诺酸类抗过敏药

八、利尿药

词干	中文	类别
-crinat	-利那	依他尼酸衍生物类
-etanide	-他尼	吡咯他尼类
-pamide	-帕胺	氨碘酰苯甲酸衍生物类
-renone	-利酮	螺内酯类醛甾酮拮抗药
-semide	-塞米	呋塞米（呋喃苯胺酸）类
-tizide (-thiazide)	-噻嗪	氯噻嗪类

九、抗肿瘤药

词干	中文	类别
-arabine	-拉滨	阿糖呋喃衍生物类
-citabine	-(西)他滨	安西他滨类
mito-(-mito)	-米托	核毒素类
-mustine	-莫司汀	氯乙胺类
-platin	-铂	顺铂类
-sulfan	-舒凡	甲磺酸盐烷化剂类
-tepa	-替派	塞替派类
-trexate	-曲沙	叶酸拮抗药
vin-	长春-	长春碱类

十、激素类药

词干	中文	类别
-actide	-克肽	具促皮质素作用的合成多肽类
andr	雄	雄激素类
bol	勃	同化激素类
cort	可	皮质甾类，可的松衍生物
estr	雌	雌激素类
gest	孕	孕激素类
-ifene	-米(或昔)芬	氯米芬或他莫昔芬类抗雌激素药
-met(h)asone	-米松	泼尼松龙类，雷那诺龙类麻醉药
-olone	-龙	雄诺龙类性激素及甘草酸衍生物等
-onide	-奈德	含缩醛基的局部用皮质激素类

pred	泼	皮质激素类	十五、酶类药及其抑制药		
predni	泼尼		-ase	酶	酶类药
-relin	-瑞林	垂体激素释放刺激药	stat	司他	酶抑制药
-relix	-瑞里(克)	垂体激素释放抑制药	十六、诊断用药		
som-	-生长素	生长激素类	io-	碘	含碘造影剂
-sterone	-睾酮	雄激素类药	-fenin	-苯宁	甲基亚氨乙酸衍生物利苯宁类
-tocin	-缩宫素	缩宫素类	gado-	钆-	钆衍生物类
十一、降血糖药			十七、其他		
-formin	-福明	双胍类	-crine	-吖啶	吖啶衍生物类
gli-(-gli-)	格列-	磺酰脲类	-dronic acid	-膦酸	钙代谢调节药,药用辅料
十二、抗变态反应药					
-astine	-斯汀	抗组胺药	erg(erg-,-erg-)	麦角	麦角生物碱衍生物类
-pendyl	-喷地	丙硫喷地类抗组胺药	-golide	-高莱	多巴胺受体激动药及麦角林衍生物类
十三、前列腺素类药					
prost	前列		-mer	-姆	多聚物类
十四、免疫系统药			nab	大麻	大麻酚衍生物类
-dismase	-地酶	超氧歧化酶类	-oxan(e)	-克生	苯并二噁烷衍生物,肾上腺素能受体拮抗药
imex	美克	免疫兴奋药			
-imod	-莫特	免疫调节药	-piprazole	-哌唑	苯哌嗪衍生物促精神药(psychotropics)
-imus	-莫司	免疫抑制药			
-leukin	-白介素	白细胞介素类免疫调节药	retin	维A	维生素A衍生物类
-monab(-mab)	-单抗	单克隆抗体类免疫调节药	sal	柳或水杨	水杨酸衍生物类
-ribine	-立宾	吡唑呋林型、呋喃核糖衍生物类免疫调节药	-stigmine	-斯的明	抗胆碱酯酶药
			trop	托(品)	阿托品衍生物副交感神经阻滞药或抗胆碱能药
-stim	-司亭	免疫调节药(集落生成刺激因子)	-verine	-维林	平滑肌解痉药

Appendix 3

英汉对照新药名选编*

药 名		药理分类	药 名		药理分类
英文名	中文名		英文名	中文名	
A			Aceclofenac	醋氯芬酸	消炎镇痛药
			Acetorphan	醋托泛	止泻药
Abacavir	阿巴卡韦	抗HIV药	Aciclovir	阿昔洛韦	抗病毒药
Abciximab	阿昔单抗	抗血栓药	Acitretin	阿维A	抗癌,治牛皮癣药
Abecarnil	阿贝卡尼	抗焦虑药	Aclacinomy-cin A	阿克拉霉素A	抗癌药
Acadesine	阿卡地新	血管疾病药			
Acarbose	阿卡波糖	降血糖药	Acrivastine	阿伐司丁	抗组胺药

---

* 主要参考尹勇、李威,药学进展,1995、1996各期连载的新药名选编,并对1996年后的重要新药名作了补充,供读者阅读参考。

续表

药名 英文名	药名 中文名	药理分类	药名 英文名	药名 中文名	药理分类
Actarit	阿克他利	免疫调节剂	Arginosuccina-telyase	精氨酸琥珀酸酯裂解酶	β-葡糖酶刺激剂
Adenosine	腺苷	抗心律失常药	Artemether	蒿甲醚	抗疟药
Alacepril	阿拉普利	抗高血压药	Artemisinin	青蒿素	抗疟药
Albendazol	阿苯达唑	驱肠虫药	Artesunate	青蒿琥酯	抗疟药
Alendronate sodium	阿伦膦酸钠	抗骨质疏松药	Asparaginase	门冬酰胺酶	抗癌药
Alfacalcidol	阿法骨化醇	血钙调节剂	Aspoxicillin	阿扑西林	抗生素
Alfuzosin	阿夫唑嗪	降血压,抗前列腺增生药	Astemizole	阿司咪唑	抗组胺药
			Atenolol	阿替洛尔	心血管药
Alglucerase	阿糖脑苷酶	脑苷酶类药	Atevirdine	阿替韦啶	抗病毒药
Allopurinol	别嘌醇	抗痛风药	Atrimustine	阿莫司汀	抗癌药
Almitrine	阿米三嗪	中枢神经系统药	Atrinositol	阿曲肌醇	神经肽激抗药
Alprazolam	阿普唑仑	抗焦虑药	Atorvastatin	阿伐他汀	降血脂药
Alprostadil	前列地尔	前列腺素类药	Atovaquone	阿托夸酮	杀原虫药
Altretamine	六甲蜜胺	抗癌药	Aureobasidin A	金担子素 A	抗真菌的抗生素
Ambamustine	氨莫司丁	抗癌药	Avandia	阿丸迪亚	治疗Ⅱ型糖尿病药
Ambroxol	氨溴素	祛痰药	Azaquinone	阿扎夸酮	合成的抗生素,抗药性肺病用药
Amfebutamone	安非他酮	抗抑郁药			
Amifloxacin	氨氟沙星	抗菌药	Azasetron	阿扎司琼	5-羟色胺受体阻滞药
Amifostine	氨磷丁	抗辐射药			
Amikacin	阿米卡星	抗生素	Azelaic acid	壬二酸	抗痤疮药
Amiloride	阿米洛利	利尿药	Azealastine	氮草司汀	抗组胺药
Aminogluteth-imide	氨鲁米特	抗癌药	Azinomycin	阿嗪霉素 B	抗生素
			Azithromycin	阿奇霉素	大环内酯抗生素
Amisupride	氨磺必利	抗精神病药	Aztreonam	氨曲南	抗生素
Amlexanox	氨米咕诺	抗过敏药	**B**		
Amlodipine	氨氯地平	抗高血压药			
Amocarzine	阿莫卡嗪	抗丝虫病药	Bambuterol	班布特罗	支气管扩张药
Amonafide	氨萘非特	抗癌药	Bariprazole	巴利拉唑	抗溃疡药
Amorolfine	阿莫罗芬	抗真菌药	Barnidipine	巴尼地平	钙拮抗剂
Amosulalol	氨磺洛尔	β受体阻滞药	Batimastat	巴马司他	抗癌药
Amperozide	安哌齐特	抗精神病药	Baclomethasone	倍氯米松	肾上腺皮质激素
Amphotericin B	两性霉素 B	抗生素	Befloxatone	贝氟沙通	抗抑郁药
Ampiroxicam	安吡昔康	消炎镇痛药	Belfosdil	贝磷地尔	抗高血压药
Amrinone	氨力农	强心药	Benazepril	贝那普利	降压药
Amsacrine	安吖啶	抗肿瘤药	Benidipine	贝尼地平	血管扩张药
Anagrelide	阿那格雷	抗凝血药,抗血栓	Benzydamine	苄达明	消炎镇痛药
Anastrozole	阿那舒唑	抗肿瘤药	Bepridil	苄普地尔	血管扩张药
Ancrod	安克洛酶	抗凝药	Beractant	贝雷克坦	肺表面活性剂
Angiotensin Ⅱ	血管紧张素Ⅱ	升压药	Beraprost	贝前列素	前列腺素
Aniracetam	茴拉西坦	益智药	Bermoprofen	柏莫洛芬	消炎镇痛药
Antarelix	安雷利克斯	释放激素	Bertosamil	柏托沙米	抗局部缺血药
Apraclonidine	阿可乐定	眼科手术用药	Besigomsin	贝西冈新	保肝药
Aprotinin	抑肽酶	促凝血药	Betafectin	倍他非丁	免疫调节剂
Arbaprostil	阿巴前列素	前列腺素类药	Betamipron	倍他普隆	抗菌素
Arbutamine	阿布他明	心脏兴奋药	Betanidine	倍他尼定	降压药
Argatroban	阿加曲班	抗血栓药	Betaxolol	倍他洛尔	β-受体阻断剂
Arginase	精氨酸酶	抗癌药			

续表

药名 英文名	药名 中文名	药理分类	药名 英文名	药名 中文名	药理分类
Bevantolol	贝凡洛尔	β-受体阻断剂	Cefpirome	头孢匹罗	头孢菌素
Biciromab	比西单抗	诊断用药	Cefpodoxime proxetil	头胞泊肟丙酯	头孢菌素
Bidisomide	比地索胺	抗心律失常药	Cefprozil	头孢丙烯	头孢菌素
Bifemelane	二苯美仑	益智药	Cefquinome	头孢喹肟	头孢菌素
Bilirubin oxidase	胆红素氧化酶	胆红素氧化酶刺激剂	Cefsulodin	头孢磺啶	头孢菌素
Bimakalin	比卡林	钾通道激活剂	Ceftazidime	头孢他啶	头孢菌素
Binifibrate	比尼贝特	降血脂药	Cefteram pivoxil	头孢特伦新戊酯	头孢菌素
Bioxalomycin	草酸氢酰霉素	DNA 合成抑制药	Ceftibuten	头孢布烯	头孢菌素
Bisoprolol	比索洛尔	β-受体阻滞药	Ceftizoxime	头孢唑肟	头孢菌素
Bopindolol	波吲洛尔	β-受体阻滞药	Ceftriaxone	头孢曲松	头孢菌素
Botulinum toxin-2	肉毒素-2	肌松弛药	Cefuroxime	头孢呋辛	头孢菌素
			Celadin	西拉丁	细菌粘连抑制剂
Bovactant	勃法克坦	肺表面活性剂	Celiprolol	塞利洛尔	β-受体阻滞药
Brimonidine	溴莫尼定	α₂-受体激动药	Centchroman	苯并二氢吡喃	避孕药,抗癌药
Brodimoprim	溴莫普林	抗菌药	Centoxin	桑托新	败血症
Bromerguride	溴麦角脲	多巴胺拮抗药	Centpropazine	桑普罗帕嗪	抗抑郁药
Bromfenac	溴芬酸	消炎镇痛药	Ceranapril	西那普利	降压药
Bropirimine	溴匹立明	抗肿瘤药	Cercainide	西卡尼特	抗心律不齐药
Broxaterol	溴沙特罗	β₂ 受体激动剂(止喘药)	Cericlamine	西立氯腰	抗抑郁药
			Cerivastatin	塞伐他汀	降胆固醇药
Bryostatin-1	薯司他丁-1	抗癌药	Ceronapril	西罗普利	抗高血压药
Bucindolol	布新洛尔	β-受体阻滞剂	Cetamolol	塞他洛尔	β-受体阻滞药
Bucricaine	丁吖卡因	局麻药	Cetefloxacin	西替沙星	抗菌药
Budesonide	布地奈德	抗哮喘药	Cetirizine	西替立嗪	抗组胺药
Bunazosin	布那唑嗪	抗高血压药	Cetrorelix	西曲瑞克	抗肿瘤药
Bupivacaine	布比卡因	局麻药	Chandonium iodide	碘利多乐	神经肌阻断剂
Buprenorphine	丁丙诺啡	麻醉镇痛剂			
Buspirone	丁螺环酮	抗焦虑药	Chlorhexidine	洗必泰	消毒防腐剂
Butenafine	布替奈芬	抗真菌药	Chlorsulfaquinoxalone	氯磺喹噁酮	抗癌药
Butibufen	布替布芬	消炎药			
Butoconazole	布托康唑	抗真菌药	Cibenzoline	西苯唑啉	抗心律失常药
Butorphanol	布托啡诺	镇痛药,镇咳药	Cicaprost	西卡前列素	前列腺素类药
			Ciclesonide	环索奈德	止喘药
C			Cicletanine	西氯他宁	利尿药
Captopril	卡托普利	抗高血压药	Ciclosporin A (Cyclosporin A)	环孢素 A	免疫抑制剂
Carvedilol	卡维地洛	血管扩张药	Cilansetron	西兰司琼	5-羟色胺受体拮抗药
Cefotaxime	头孢噻肟	头孢菌素			
Capecitabine	卡倍他滨	抗癌药	Cilazapril	西拉普利	降压药
Cefaclor	头孢克洛	头孢菌素	Cilnidipine	西尼地平	钙通道阻滞药
Cefotetan	头孢替坦	头孢菌素	Cilostazol	西洛他唑	抗凝药
Cefotiam	头孢替安	头孢菌素	Cimitidine	西咪替丁	组胺 H₂ 受体阻滞药
Cefotiam hexetil	头孢替安己酯	头孢菌素			
Cefozopran	头孢唑兰	头孢菌素	Cinolazepam	西诺西泮	催眠药
Cefpimizole	头孢唑咪	头孢菌素	Cinoxacin	西诺沙星	抗感染药

药名 英文名	药名 中文名	药理分类	药名 英文名	药名 中文名	药理分类
Cioteronel	塞奥罗奈	抗雄激素药	Dirithromycin	地红霉素	抗生素
Ciprofibrate	环丙贝特	降血脂药	Disopyramide	丙吡胺	抗心律不齐药
Ciprofloxacin	环丙沙星	抗菌药	Ditiocarb sodium	二硫卡钠	免疫调节药
Cisapride	西沙必利	镇吐药	Dobutamine	多巴酚丁胺	抗休克药
Cistinexine	西替克新	祛痰药	Docorpamine	多卡巴胺	强心剂
Citalopram	西酞普兰	抗抑郁药	Dofetilide	多菲利特	抗心律失常药
Citicoline	胞磷胆碱	精神兴奋剂	Domperidone	多潘立酮	止吐药
Clarithromycin	克拉霉素	抗生素	Dopexamine	多培沙明	升压药
Clemastine	氯马斯丁	抗组胺药	Dorzolamide	多佐胺	治青光眼药
Clindamycin	林可霉素	抗生素	Doxacurium chloride	多库氯胺	神经肌肉阻断剂
Clobetasol	氯倍他索	抗炎药	Doxazosin	多沙唑嗪	抗高血压药
Clomipramine	氯米帕明	抗抑郁药	Doxifluridine	去氧氟尿苷	抗癌药
Clonazepam	氯硝西泮	抗惊厥药	Doxofylline	多索茶碱	支气管扩张
Clopidogrel	氯吡格雷	抗凝药	Droloxifene	屈洛昔酚	抗乳腺癌药
Cloricromen	氯克罗孟	抗凝药	Dronabinol	屈大麻酚	镇吐药
Closiramine	氯西拉敏	抗组胺药	Droxicam	屈昔康	消炎镇痛药
Cloxazosin	氯噁唑嗪	α-阻滞剂	Droxidopa	屈昔多巴	抗震颤麻痹药
Clozapine	氯氮平	抗精神病药			
Colfosceril palmitate	棕榈胆磷	肺表面活性剂			
Crilanomer	克立诺姆	外科用药			
Croconazole	氯康唑	抗真菌	**E**		
Cromolyn sodium	色甘酸钠	抗过敏药	Ebastine	依巴司汀	抗组胺药
Cyclobenzaprine	环苯扎林	抗抑郁药	Ecabet	依卡倍特	抗溃疡药
Cyproterone	环丙孕酮	雄激素拮抗剂	Efadroxil	头孢羟氨卡	头孢菌素
Cytarabine	阿糖胞苷	抗癌药,抗病毒药	Eflornithine	依氟乌氨酸	抗原虫药
D			Dfonidipine	依福地平	钙通道阻滞药
			Elcitonin	依西妥宁	胃溃疡治疗剂
Dalteparin sodium	达肝素钠	抗凝药	Emedastine	依美斯丁	抗组胺药
Dapiprazole	达哌唑	抗溃疡病药	Enalapril	依那普利	抗高血压药
Delapril	地拉普利	抗高血压药	Enflurane	恩氟烷	吸入麻醉剂
Denopamine	地诺帕明	强心药	Enoxacin	依诺沙星	抗菌药
Deprodone propionate	丙酸地泼罗酮	肾上腺皮质激素药	Enoxaparin	依诺肝素	抗凝药
			DEnoximone	依诺苷酮	强心药
Desflurane	地氟烷	麻醉药	Epalrestat	依帕司他	醛糖还原酶抑制剂
Desmopressin	去氨加压素	抗利尿药	Eperisone	乙哌立松	解痉药
Dexrazoxane	右雷佐生	放疗/化疗保护药	Epinastine	依匹斯汀	抗组胺药
Dextromethorphan	右美沙芬	镇痛,镇咳药	Epirubicin	表阿霉素	抗生素
			Erythropoietin	促红细胞生成素	抗贫血
Dideoxyinosine	双脱氧肌苷	抗病毒药			
Dihydroartemisinin	双氢青蒿素	抗疟药	Esmolol	艾司洛尔	心血管药
			Etodolac	依托度酸	抗炎药
Diltiazem	地尔硫草	冠脉扩张药	Etoposide	足叶乙甙	抗癌药
Dinoprostone	地诺前列酮	子宫收缩药	Exifone	依昔苯酮	抗凝药

续表

药名英文名	药名中文名	药理分类
F		
Fadrozole	法屈唑	抗恶性肿瘤药
Famciclovir	泛昔洛韦	抗带状疱疹药
Famotidine	法莫替丁	抗酸药及治疗消化性溃疡病药
Fasudil	法舒地尔	钙拮抗剂
Felbamate	非尔氨酯	抗惊厥药
Felodipine	非洛地平	钙拮抗剂
Filgrastim	非格拉司替姆	治白细胞减少症
Finasteride	非那雄胺	抗前列腺增生药
Fenoterol	非诺特罗	支气管扩张药
Flecainide	氟卡尼	抗心律失常药
Fleroxacin	氟罗沙星	抗菌药
Flomoxef	氟氧头孢	头孢菌素
Flosequinan	氟司喹南	抗高血压药
Flucloxacillin	氟氯西林	抗生素
Fluconazole	氟康唑	抗真菌药
Fludarabine	氟达拉宾	抗白血病药
Flumazenil	氟马西尼	抗焦虑药
Flunarizine	氟桂利嗪	抗心绞痛
Fluosol-DA	氟索	血浆代用品
Fluoxetine	氟西汀	抗抑郁药
Flupirtine	氟吡汀（氨酯）	镇痛药
Flurbiprofen	氟比洛芬	消炎镇痛药
Flurithromycin	氟红霉素	抗生素
Flutamide	氟他胺	抗雄激素类
Fluticasone	氟替卡松	抗过敏药
Flutrimazole	氟曲马唑	抗真菌药
Flutropium bromide	氟托溴胺	抗胆碱药
Fluvastatin	氟伐他汀	降血脂药
Fluvoxamine	氟伏沙明	抗抑郁药
Formestane	福美坦	抗乳癌药
Formoterol	福莫特罗	抗支气管扩张药
Foscarnet sodium	膦甲酸钠	抗病毒药
Fosinopril	福辛普利	抗高血压药
Fosphenytoin	磷苯妥英	抗癫痫药
Fotemustine	福莫司汀	抗癌药
Fraxiparin	弗希肝素	抗血栓药
G		
Gabapentin	加巴喷丁	抗焦虑药
Gadoteridol	钆特醇	诊断剂
Ganciclovir	更昔洛韦	抗病毒药
Gemcitabine	吉西他滨	抗癌药
Gemfibrozil	吉非罗齐	降血脂药
Gestodene	孕二烯酮	避孕药
Gliclazide	格列齐特	降血糖药
Glipizide	格列吡嗪	降血糖药
Glucagon	高血糖素	胰岛素拮抗药
Glyburide (glibenclamide)	格列本脲	降血糖药
Glycosaminoglycans	葡胺聚糖	抗血栓药
Gonadorelin	戈那瑞林	促性激素释放药
Goserelin	戈舍瑞林	促性激素释放药
Granisetron	格拉司琼	镇吐药
Guamecycline	胍甲环素	抗生素
Guanabenz	胍那苄	降压药
Guanfacine	胍法辛	抗高血压药
Gusperimus	胍立莫司	免疫调节剂
H		
Halofantrine	卤泛群	抗疟药
Halometasone	卤米松	肾上腺皮质激素类药
Histrelin	组氨瑞林	治子宫内膜异位药
I		
Ibopamine	异波帕胺	利尿药
Idarubicin	伊达比星	抗生素
Idebenone	艾地苯醌	脑代谢改善药
Iloprost	伊洛前列素	前列腺素类药
Imidapril	咪达普利	抗高血压药
Imipenem	亚胺培南	抗生素
Indalpine	吲达品	抗抑郁药
Indecainide	英地卡尼	抗心律失常药
Indeloxazine	茚洛秦	抗心律失常药
Indium (In) quino-line complex	喹啉铟络合物	血栓形成诊断剂
Indobufen	吲哚布芬	消炎镇痛药
Indometacin	吲哚美辛	消炎镇痛药
Iodixonal	碘克沙醇	X-线造影剂
Iotrolan	碘曲仑	诊断剂

药名		药理分类	药名		药理分类
英文名	中文名		英文名	中文名	
Ipratropium bromide	异丙托溴铵	支气管扩张药	Lovastatin	洛伐他汀	降血脂药
			Lufrinol	鲁夫利醇	治肝硬化药
Ipriflavone	伊普黄酮	治骨质疏松	**M**		
Iproplatin	异丙铂	抗肿瘤药	Manidipine	马尼地平	血管扩张药
Isepamicin	异帕米星	抗生素	Masoprocol	马索罗酚	抗肿瘤药
Isotretinoin	异维A酸	角质溶解药	Mefloquine	甲氟喹	抗疟药
Isradipine	伊拉地平	血管扩张药	Meropenem	美罗培南	抗生素
Itraconazole	伊曲康唑	抗真菌药	Mesalazine	美沙拉秦	消炎药
			Metformin	二甲双胍	降血糖药
K			Metoclopramide	甲氧氯普胺	镇吐药
Ketoconazole	酮康唑	抗真菌药	Metolazone	美托拉宗	利尿,抗高血压药
Ketoprofen	酮洛芬	消炎镇痛药	Metoprolol	美托洛尔	心血管病治疗药
Ketorolac	酮咯酸	消炎镇痛药	Miconazole	咪康唑	抗真菌药
			Mifepristone	米非司酮	避孕药
L			Metrifonate	美曲膦酯	抗老年痴呆症药
Lacidipine	拉西地平	血管扩张药	Milrinone	米力农	强心药
Lactitol	拉克替醇	保肝药	Miltefosine	米替福新	抗癌药
Lamivudine	拉米夫定	抗病毒药	Minocycline	米诺环素	抗生素
Lamotrigine	拉莫三嗪	抗惊厥药	Minoxidil	米诺地尔	降压药
Lansoprazol	兰索拉唑	抗溃疡药	Miocamycin	乙酰麦迪霉素	抗生素
Laratadine	氯雷他定	抗组胺药	Mirtazapine	米氮平	抗抑郁药
Leflunomide	来氟米特	消炎镇痛药	Misoprostol	米索前列醇	前列腺素类药
Lenograstim	来格司亭	免疫调节药	Mitomycin C analogues	丝裂霉素C类似物	抗肿瘤药
Lentinan	香菇多糖	抗癌药			
Leustatin	亮司他汀	抗癌药	Mitoxantrone	米托蒽醌	抗肿瘤药
Levobunolol	左布诺洛尔	β-受体阻滞药	Mivacurium chloride	米库氯铵	神经肌肉阻断剂
Levocabastine	左卡巴斯丁	抗过敏药			
Levodropropizine	左羟丙哌嗪	镇咳药	Mivazerol	咪伐折醇	α_2肾上腺素能激动剂
Levofloxacin	左氧氟沙星	抗菌药			
Limaprost	利马前列素	治脉管炎药	Mizolastine	咪唑司汀	抗组胺药
Lisinopril	赖诺普利	降压药	Mizoribine	咪唑立宾	免疫抑制剂
Lobaplatin	洛巴铂	抗癌药	Moclobemide	吗氯贝胺	抗抑郁药
Lodoxamide tromethamine	洛度沙胺	眼科抗过敏药	Modafinil	莫达非尼	精神兴奋剂
			Moexipril	莫昔普利	抗高血压药
Logiparin	诺吉肝素	抗凝血药	Mofezolac	莫苯唑酸	消炎镇痛药
Lomefloxacin	洛美沙星	抗菌药	Molgramostim	莫拉司亭	免疫调节药
Lonidamine	氯尼达明	生育调节药	Mometasone	莫米松	抗炎药
Loperamide	咯哌丁胺	止泻药	Montelukast	孟鲁司特	治疗哮喘药
Loprinone	洛普利酮	心脏兴奋剂	Moracinize	莫雷西嗪	抗心律失常药
Loracarbef	氯碳头孢	头孢菌素	Mosapride	莫沙必利	镇吐药
Loratadine	氯雷他定	抗组胺药	Moveltipril	莫维普利	抗高血压
Losartan	洛沙坦	抗高血压药	Moxalactam	莫沙头孢	头孢菌素
Losigamone	洛加酮	抗癫痫药	Moxifloxacin	莫喜沙星	抗菌药

续表

药名		药理分类	药名		药理分类
英文名	中文名		英文名	中文名	
Mycophenolate mofetil	麦考酚酯	免疫抑制剂	Oxaliplatin	奥沙利铂	抗癌药
			Oxaprozin	奥沙普秦	消炎药
			Oxatomide	奥沙米特	平喘药
N			Oxazepam	奥沙西泮	安定药
			Oxcarbazepine	奥卡西平	抗惊厥药
Nabazonil	大麻折尼	抗惊厥药	Oxendolone	奥生多龙	同化激素类药
Nabilone	大麻隆	抗焦虑药	Oxiconazole	奥昔康唑	抗真菌药
Nabitan	大麻坦	镇痛药	Oxiracetam	奥拉西坦	益智药
Naboctate	大麻克酯	治青光眼药,镇痛药	Ozagrel	奥扎格雷	抗凝药
Nabumetone	萘丁美酮	消炎镇痛药	**P**		
Nadifloxacin	那氟沙星	抗菌药	Paclitaxel	紫杉醇	抗癌药
Nafamostat	奈莫司他	蛋白酶抑制剂	Panipenem	帕尼培南	抗生素
Nafarelin	那法瑞林	治子宫内膜异位	Pantoprazole	泮托拉唑	抗溃疡药
Nafazodone	那法唑酮	抗抑郁药	Paroxetine	帕罗西汀	抗抑郁药
Naftifine	奈替芬	抗真菌药	Pefloxacin	培氟沙星	抗菌药
Nalmefene	纳美芬	吗啡拮抗药	Pemirolast	吡嘧司特	抗过敏药
Naloxone	纳洛酮	解毒药	Penciclovir	喷昔洛韦	抗病毒药
Nanofloxacin	纳诺沙星	抗菌药	Pentagastrin	五肽胃泌素	诊断用药
Nazasetron	那扎西隆	镇咳药	Pentamidine	喷他脒	抗感染药
Nebupent	戊烷脒	治卡氏囊虫肺炎药	Pentazocine	喷他佐辛	镇痛药
Nedocromil	奈多罗米	抗过敏药	Pentostatin	喷司他丁	酶抑制药
Nefazodone	奈法唑酮	抗抑郁症药	Perfosfamide	培磷酰胺	抗肿瘤药
Nemonapride	奈莫必利	多巴胺受体激动药	Pergolide mesilate	甲磺酸培高利特	多巴胺激动剂
Neticonazole	奈康唑	抗真菌药			
Neuquinoron	新喹隆	抗菌药	Perindopril	培哚普利	降压药
Nicardipine	尼卡地平	血管扩张药	Pidotimod	匹多莫德	免疫调节剂
Nicorandil	尼可地尔	冠脉扩张药	Pilsicainide	吡西卡尼	抗心律失常药
Nifedipine	硝苯地平	抗心绞痛药	Pimobendan	匹莫苯	强心药
Nivaldipine	尼伐地平	血管扩张药	Pinacidil	吡那地尔	降压药
Nimesulide	尼美舒利	消炎药	Pipecuronium bromide	哌库溴铵	肌松药
Nimodipine	尼莫地平	脑血管扩张剂			
Nipradilol	尼普洛尔	血管扩张药,β受体阻滞剂	Piracetam	吡拉西坦	益智药
			Pirarubicin	吡柔比星	抗生素
Nisoldipine	尼索地平	血管扩张药	piretanide	吡咯他尼	利尿药
Nitrendipine	尼群地平	降压剂	piroxicam	吡罗昔康	非甾抗炎药
Nizofenone	尼唑苯酮	抗惊厥药	Podopgyllotoxin	鬼臼毒素	抗病毒药
O			Porcine lung surfactant	泊辛肺表面活性剂	治呼吸窘迫剂
Octreotide	奥曲肽	胃肠道止血药			
Ofloxacin	氧氟沙星	抗菌药	Porfimer sodium	卟吩姆钠	光致敏药
Olanzapine	奥氮平	多巴胺受体阻滞药			
Omeprazole	奥美拉唑	抗溃疡药	Pramiracetam	普拉西坦	益智药
Ondansetron	奥丹司琼	5-羟色胺拮抗药	Pravastatin	普伐他汀	降血脂药
Ormaplatin	奥马铂	抗癌药	Prazosin	哌唑嗪	抗高血压药

药名		药理分类	药名		药理分类
英文名	中文名		英文名	中文名	
Propentofylline	丙戊茶碱	大脑调节剂	Saralasin	沙拉新	降压药,诊断辅助药
Propionic acid	丙酸	抗真菌药			
Propiram	丙吡兰	镇痛药	Sargramostim	沙格司亭	免疫调节药
Propiverine	丙哌维林	泌尿系统用药	Sarpogrelate	沙格雷酯	抗血小板凝聚药
Propofol	丙泊汾	全身麻醉药	Seroxat	赛乐特	抗抑郁症药
Propranolol	普萘洛尔	降压,抗心律不齐,心绞痛药	Serrapeptase	舍雷肽酶	抗炎剂
			Sertaconazole	舍他康唑	抗真菌药
Pro-urokinase	尿激酶前体	纤维蛋白溶解剂	Sertraline	舍曲林	抗抑郁药
Pulmozyme	脱氧核糖核酸酶	治囊性纤维变性药	Sevoflurane	七氟烷	吸入麻醉剂
			Sibutramine	西布曲明	减肥药
Pumactant	肺脉坦	肺表面活性剂	Sildenafil citrate	枸橼酸西地那非	磷酸二酯酶V抑制剂
Pyrroindomicin	吡咯吲哚霉素	抗生素			
			Simvastatin	昔伐他丁	降血脂药
Q			Sincalide	辛卡利酯	利胆药
Quazepam	夸西泮	安定药	Sinteplase	辛普拉斯	抗血栓形成药
Quinapril	喹那普利	抗高血压药	Sisomicin	西索米星	抗生素
			Sorivudine	索立夫定	抗病毒药
R			Sotalol	索他洛尔	降压,抗心绞痛,心律不齐药
Raloxifene	雷咯昔芬	抗骨质疏松药			
Ramipril	雷米普利	抗高血压药	Sparfloxacin	司氟沙星	抗菌药
Remacemide	瑞马酰胺	抗癫痫药	Spirapril	螺普利	抗高血压药
Remoxipride	瑞莫必利	抗精神病药	Stavudine	司他夫定	抗HIV病毒药
Repaglinide	瑞格利奈	糖尿病治疗药	Stiripenetol	司替戊醇	抗癫痫药
Resperidone	利司哌酮	安定药	Streptozocin	链佐辛	抗肿瘤药
Reviparin	瑞肝素	抗凝药	Sulconazole	硫康唑	抗真菌药
Ribavirin	利巴韦林	抗病毒药	Sulfadoxine	硫胺多辛	抗菌药
Rifabenthiazon	利福苯噻唑	抗生素	Sulprostone	硫前列酮	前列腺素类药
Rifabutin	利福布丁	抗生素	Sultamicillin	舒他西林	抗生素
Rifapentin	利福喷丁	抗菌药	Sumatriptan	舒马普坦	治偏头痛
Rilmazafone	利马扎封	催眠药			
Riluzole	利鲁唑	肌萎缩侧索硬化治疗药	**T**		
			Tacacitol	他卡化醇	抗银屑病药
Rivastigmine	雷伐斯的明	抗早老年性痴呆药	Tacrine	他克林	益智药
Rokitamycin	罗他霉素	抗生素	Tacrolimus	他克莫司	免疫抑制剂
Rolipram	咯利普兰	抗精神失常药	Tamoxifen	他莫昔芬	雌激素拮抗剂,抗癌药
Romurtide	罗莫肽	免疫调节剂			
Roxithromycin	罗红霉素	抗生素	Tamsulosin	他洛新	α-受体阻滞剂
Rufloxacin	卢氟沙星	抗菌药	Tazobactam	他唑巴坦	抗感染药
			Teceleukin	替西白介素	免疫调节剂
S			Teicoplanin	替考拉宁	抗生素
Salbutamol	沙丁胺醇	平喘药	Telmesteine	替美斯坦	祛痰药
Salmeterol	沙美特罗	支气管扩张药	Temocarpril	替莫普利	抗高血压药
Sapropterin	沙丙喋呤	抗苯丙氨酸血症药	Tenidap	替尼达普	非甾抗炎药
			Teniposide	替尼泊苷	抗癌药

药名 英文名	中文名	药理分类	药名 英文名	中文名	药理分类
Tenoxicam	替诺昔康	消炎镇痛药	Tranexamic acid	氨甲环酸	止血药
Teprenone	替普瑞酮	抗溃疡药	Tretinoin	维A酸	皮肤科用药
Terazosin	特拉唑嗪	降血压药	Triamcinolone acetonide	曲安奈德	抗炎药
Terbinafine	特比萘芬	抗真菌药			
Terbutaline	特布他林	平喘药			
Terfenadine	特非他定	抗组胺药	Triazolam	三唑仑	安定药
Teriparatide	特立帕肽	诊断药	Trimetrexate	三甲曲沙	抗肿瘤药
Thioridazine	硫利达嗪	抗精神病药	Trimoxazole	曲莫沙唑	抗感染药
Thymosin alpha-1	胸腺素 α-1	免疫调节剂	Troglitazone	曲格列酮	降血糖药
			Tropisentron	托吡西隆	镇吐药
Tiagabine	噻加宾	抗癫痫药	**U**		
Tiamenidine	噻美尼定	降血压药			
Tianeptine	噻奈普汀	抗抑郁药	Urofollitropin	尿促卵泡素	促性激素类药
Tiapride	硫必利	抗精神病药	**V**		
Tibolone	替勃龙	雄激素,同化激素类药			
			Valaciclovir	伐昔洛韦	抗疱疹药
Ticlopidine	噻氯匹定	血小板抑制药	Venlafaxine	文拉法辛	抗抑郁药
Tilisolol	替利洛尔	β-受体阻滞剂	Verapamil	维拉帕米	降血压药
Tinazoline	替那唑啉	血管收缩药	Vesnarinone	维司力农	抗心力衰竭药
Tioconazole	噻康唑	抗真菌药	Vigabatrin	氨己烯酸	抗癫痫药
Tiopronin	硫普罗宁	保肝药	Vincristine	长春新碱	抗癌药
Tirapazamine	替拉扎明	抗癌药	Vinorelbine	长春瑞滨	抗癌药
Tirilazad	替拉扎特	治神经病药	Virend	维恩德	抗病毒药
Tirofiban	替罗非班	抗心绞痛药	Vorozole	伏氯唑	抗肿瘤药
Tizanidine	替扎尼定	解痉药	**Z**		
Tocoretinate	托考维甲酸酯	创伤药			
Tolnaftate	托萘酯	抗真菌药	Zafirlukast	扎鲁司特	治疗哮喘药
Toloxatone	托洛沙酮	抗抑郁药	Zalcitabine	扎西他宾	抗病毒药
Tolrestat	托瑞司他	治糖尿病药	Zaltoprofen	扎托洛芬	消炎镇痛药
Topiramate	托吡酯	抗癫痫药	Zamoterol	扎莫特罗	心兴奋剂
Torasemide	托拉塞米	利尿药	Zidovudine	齐多夫定	抗病毒药
Toremifene	托瑞米芬	抗癌药	Zinostatin	净司他丁	抗癌药
Tosufloxacin	托氟沙星	抗菌药	Zolpidem	唑吡坦	催眠药
Tramadol	曲马多	镇痛药	Zonisamide	唑尼沙胺	抗癫痫药
Trandolaprilat	群多普利拉	抗高血压药	Zopiclone	佐匹克隆	催眠药

总 词 汇 表

A

a heart tonic 强心药
abate [ə'beit] vt. 减少,减轻
abbreviate [ə'bri:vieit] vt. 将……缩短,省略;简写
abrade [ə'breid] vt. 磨,擦,擦伤
abrasion [ə'breiʃən] n. 擦伤(掉、去),磨损,
abrasive [ə'breisiv] n. 磨料,研磨剂;a. 磨料的
abscissa [æb'sisə] n. 横(坐)标,横线
absorbent [əb'sɔ:bənt] a. 能吸收的;n. 吸收剂
abuse [ə'bju:z] vt. 滥用
abzyme [æb'zeim] n. 异酶
accrue [ə'kru:] n. 自然增加,产生
accumulation [ə'kju:mjuleiʃən] n. 积累,积聚物
acetate ['æsiteit] n. 乙酸盐(酯)
acetic acid ['əsi:tik 'æsid] n. 乙酸,醋酸
acetone ['æsitoun] n. 丙酮
acetoxy group 乙酰氧基
acetylcholine [ˌæsitil'kəuli:n] n. 乙酰胆碱
achiral [ə'kaiərəl] a. 非手性的
Achyranthes aspera 倒扣草,土牛膝
acidification [əˌsidifi'keiʃən] n. 使发酸,酸化
acidify [ə'sidifai] v. (使)酸化
acoustical [ə'ku:stikəl] a. 听觉的,传音的
acquisition [ˌækwi'ziʃən] n. 获得,获得物
actinomyces [ˌætinəu'maisi:z] n. 放线菌
acumen [ə'kju:men] n. 敏锐,聪明
acute [ə'kju:t] a. 急性的,敏锐的
acyl- ['æsil] n. 酰基
acylamino- [ˌæsi'læminəun] n. 酰氨基
adaptogenic [əˌdæptə'dʒenik] a. 适应原的
adenine ['ædəni:n] n. 腺嘌呤
adenosine [ə'denəsi:n] n. 腺苷,腺嘌呤核苷
adenosinetriphosphate 三磷酸腺苷
adenylic acid 腺苷酸,腺嘌呤核苷酸
adhesive [əd'hi:siv] n. 胶粘剂,粘合剂
adiabatic [ˌædiə'bætik] a. 绝热的,不传热的
administration [ədˌminis'treiʃən] n. (药的)服法,给药
admix [əd'miks] v. (使)混合,掺和
adrenal [ə'dri:nl] n.;a. 肾上腺(的)
adrenaline [ə'drenəlin] n. 肾上腺素
adrenergic [ˌædrə'nə:dʒik] a. 肾上腺素的
adrenoceptor [əˌdri:nəu'septə] n. 肾上腺素能受体,肾上腺素神经受体
adrenocortical hormone 肾上腺皮质激素
adsorption [æd'sɔ:pʃən] n. 吸附(作用)
adulteration [ədˌʌltə'reiʃən] n. 掺杂
adverse ['ædvə:s] a. 逆的,相反的,反向的
aerobe ['ɛərəub] n. 需氧菌,需氧生物,
aerobic [ɛə'rəubik] a. 需氧的,有氧的
afferent ['æfərənt] a. 传入的
affinity [ə'finiti] n. 亲合力,吸引力,密切关系
agar ['eigɑ:] n. 琼脂,洋菜,石花菜,细菌培养基
agglomeration [əg'ləməreiʃən] n. 团聚(作用)
aggregate ['ægrigit] n. 聚集,总量;a. 聚集的
aggregation [ægri'geiʃən] n. 聚集(作用)
aglucone n. 配质,配基(葡糖苷的)非糖部
agonist ['ægənist] n. 激动剂,兴奋剂
agrarian [ə'grɛəriən] a. 耕地的,农民的
akin [ə'kin] a. 类似的
alanine ['æləni(:)n] n. 丙氨酸
alditol acetate 乙酸醛醇酯
aldolase ['ældɔ:leis] n. 醛缩酶
aldoxime [æl'dɔksi:m] n. 乙醛肟
alga [ælgə], (pl) algae [ældʒi:] n. 水藻,海藻
algal ['ælgəl] a. 藻的,藻类的
alginate ['ældʒineit] n. 藻(胶)酸盐
alkaline ['ælkəlain] a. 碱的,碱性的
alkaloid ['ælkəlɔid] n. 生物碱
alkaloidal [ˌælkə'lɔidl] a. 生物碱的
alkylglucamine ['ælkil'glu:kəmi:n] n. 烷基葡胺
allergenic [ælə'dʒenik] a. 过敏原的
allergic [ə'lə:dʒik] a. 过敏的,患过敏症的
alleviate [ə'li:vieit] vt. 减轻,缓和
alternately [ɔ:l'tə:nitli] ad. 交替地,预备地
alumosilicate [ə'lju:məsilikeit] n. 铝硅酸盐

amebic dysentery 阿米巴痢疾
amenable [əˈmiːnəbəl] a. 有责任的，有义务的
amide [ˈæmaid] n. 酰胺
amine [ˈæmiːn] n. 胺
amino acid n. 氨基酸
aminocephalosporanic acid n. 氨基头孢烷酸
aminoglycoside [ˌæminəuˈglaikəusaid] n. 氨基糖苷类
aminopenicillanic acid 氨基青霉烷酸
ammoniacal [ˌæmouˈnaiəkəl] a. 氨的，氨性的
amoeba [əˈmiːbə] [pl] amoebae [əˈmiːbiː] 或 amoebas n. 变形虫，阿米巴
amoebocyte [əˈmiːbəsait] n. 变形细胞
Amoxycillin n. 阿莫西林
Amphetamine [æmˈfetəmiːn] n. 安非他明
amphibian [æmˈfibiən] n. 两栖类动物
Ampicillin n. 氨苄西林
ampul [ˈæmpuːl] n. 安瓿 针剂瓶，细颈瓶
α-amylase [ˈæmileis] n. α-淀粉（糖化）酶
anaerobic [əˌneiəˈrɔbik] a. 厌氧微生物的
anaesthesia [ˌænisˈθiːzjə] n. 麻醉（法），感觉缺乏
anaesthetic [ˌænisˈθetik] a. 麻醉的，麻木；n. 麻醉剂
analgesia [ˌænælˈdʒiːziə] n. 无痛觉，镇痛
analgesic [ˌænæˈdʒiːsik] n. 止痛药，镇痛剂
analogous [əˈnæləgəs] a. 类似的
anchor [ˈæŋkər] n. 锚；v. 抛锚，锚定
angina [ænˈdʒainə] n. 咽痛，绞痛
angiosperm [ˈændʒiəspəːm] n. 被子植物
anhydrase [ænˈhaidreis] n. 脱水酶
annular [ˈænjulə] a. 环形的
annulus [ˈænjuləs] n. 环（带，形，状）物
antacid [æntˈæsid] n. 抗酸剂，解酸药；a. 抗酸的，解酸的
antagonism [ænˈtægənizm] n. 对抗（性，作用）
antagonist [ænˈtægənist] n. 反对者，（医）对抗剂
antagonize [æŋˈtægnaiz] v. 对抗
anthelmintic [ˌænθelˈmintik] a.；n. 驱蠕（肠）虫（的）
anthracene [ˈænθrəsiːn] n. 蒽
anthrax [ˈænθræks] n. 炭疽热
anti-anxiety [æntiæŋˈzaiəti] n. 抗焦虑药；a. 抗焦虑的
antibacterial [ˌæntibækˈtiəriəl] n. 抗菌药；a. 抗菌的
antibiotic [ˌæntibaiˈɔtik] n.；a. 抗生素，抗菌素
antibody [ˈænti bɔdi] n. 抗体
anticancer [ˈæntiˈkænsə] a. 抗癌的
anticancer [ˈæntiˈkænsə] a. 抗癌（肿瘤）的
anticoagulant [ˈæntikəuˈægjulənt] n. 抗凝（血）剂
anticold [ˈæntikould] n. 抗感冒，抗伤风
anti-convualsant [ˈæntikənˈvʌlsənt] adj. 抗痉挛的
antidote [ˈæntidəut] n. 解毒剂
Aantifebrin [ˈæntiˈfebrin] n. 乙酰苯胺
antifoaming [ˈæntifəmiŋ] a. 防沫的，消沫的
antifungal [ˈæntiˈfʌŋgəl] a. 杀真菌的，抗真菌的
antigen [ˈæntidʒən] n. 抗原
antigenic [ˈæntiˈdʒenik] a. 抗原的
antigenicity [ˈæntidʒəˈnisiti] n. 抗原性
anti-infective 抗传染的，防传染的
anti-inflammatory [ˈæntiinˈflæmətəri] a. 消炎的，抗炎的
antileukaemic [ˌæntiljuːˈkiːmik] a. 抗白血病的
antimalaria [ˌæntiməˈlɛəriə] n. 抗疟疾，抗疟疾药
antimicrobial [ˌæntimaiˈkrəubiə] a.；n. 抗菌药
antioxidant [ˌæntiˈɔksidənts] n. 抗氧剂
antiparallel [ˌæntiˈpærəlel] a. 反平行的
antiseptic [ˌæntiˈseptik] n.；a. 防腐剂，防腐的
anti-stress 抗紧张的
antithrombin [ˌæntiˈθrɔmbin] n. 抗凝血酶
antitoxin [ˌæntiˈtɔksin] n. 抗毒素
anti-tubercular 抗结核的
antitumour [ˌæntiˈtjuːmə] n. 抗肿瘤
antitussive [ˌæntiˈtʌsiv] a.；n. 镇咳的，镇咳药
antiulcer [ˌæntiˈʌlsə] a. 抗胃溃疡的
antiviral [ˌæntiˈvaiərəl] a. 抗病毒的
aorta [eiˈɔːtə] n. 主动脉
arabinose [əˈræbənəus] n. 阿戊糖，阿（拉伯）糖
arbitrary [ˈɑːbitrəri] a. 任意的，独裁的，专断的
arid [ˈærid] a. 干旱的，贫瘠的
aroma [əˈrəumə] n. 芳香
arrhythmia [əˈriðmiə] n. 心律不齐
arrhythmogenic [əriðməˈdʒenik] a. 致心律不

齐的
arrow poison 箭毒
arsenal ['ɑ:sinl] n. 军火库，兵工厂
arsenic [ɑ:'senik] n. 砷
artemisia [ˌɑ:ti'miziə] n. 艾属植物，艾
Artemisia annua L. 黄花蒿属植物，青蒿属植物
Artemisinin 青蒿素
arteriosclerosis [ɑ:ˌtiəriəuˌskliə'rəusis] n. 动脉硬化（症），闭塞性动脉硬化
artesian [ɑ:'ti:zjən] a. 自流的
arthritic [ɑ:'θritik] a. 关节炎的
arthritis [ɑ:'θraitis] n. 关节炎
arthropod ['ɑ:θrəpɔd] a.；n. 节肢动物
ascaridal [æskə'ridəl] a. 驱蛔虫的
ascertain [æ'sətein] vt. 查明，弄清
aseptic [æ'septik] a. 无菌的，防腐的；n. 防腐剂
asparagine [ə'spærədʒi:n] n. 天门冬酰胺 asn＝asparagine 天冬酰胺的缩写
Asparagus cochinchinensis 天冬草，天门冬
aspartase [əs'pɑ:teis] n. 天门冬氨酸酶
Aspirin ['æspirin] n. 阿司匹林
Assyrian [ə'siriən] a.；n. 亚述的，亚述人（语）
asthma ['æsmə] n. 哮喘
asthmatic [æs'mætik] a. 气喘的，患气喘病的
asymmetric [ˌæsi'metrik] a. 不对称的
asymmetry [æ'simitri] n. 不对称
atomize ['ætəmaiz] vt. 使雾化，喷雾，散布
atrial ['ɑ:triəl] a. 房的，有关心房的
atrioventricular [ˌeitriəuven'trikjulə] a. 房室的，心房与心室的
Atropine ['ætrəpin] n. 阿托品
attrition [ə'triʃən] n. 摩（擦、损、耗），互（研）磨
augment [ɔ:g'ment] v. 增大（加，长），扩大（张）
auriculoside [ɔ:ˌrikjulə'said] a. 房侧的
autoclave ['ɔ:təkleiv] vt. 用高压锅蒸（消毒）；n. 高压锅（釜），高压灭菌器
autolyze [ˌɔ:tə'laiz] v. 自溶，自体溶解
autopsies ['ɔ:təpsais] n. (pl.) 尸体解剖（检验）
availability [əˌveilə'biliti] n. 有效性，效力
Ayurveda 印度草医学

azo ['æzəu] n. 偶氮
AZT 即 zidovudine [zai'dəuvjudi:n] 叠氮胸苷，齐多夫定
Aztreonam ['æztriəˌnæm] n. 氨曲南

B

bacillary dysentery 杆菌状痢疾
bacillus [bə'siləs] n. 杆状细菌，任何细菌
bacitracin [ˌbæsi'treisin] n. 杆菌肽
bacterial strain 细菌系，细菌株
bactericidal [bækˌtiəri'saidl] a. 杀菌的，杀菌性的
bacterium's ribosome 细菌的核糖体
Bacteroides fragilis 脆弱拟杆菌
Baeyer-Villiger oxidation 拜耳-维列氧化反应
baffle ['bæfl] n. 隔板，导流片，折流板
barbiturate [bɑ:'bitjurit] n. 巴比妥酸盐
barbituric acid n. 巴比妥酸
barium acetate 乙酸钡
barley ['bɑ:li] n. 大麦
batch [bætʃ] a. 间歇的，分批的；n. 一批，批料
batch-to-batch 一批批
beaker ['bi:kə] n. 烧杯
beef lung [bi:f lʌŋ] 牛肺
belladonna [beləˈdɔnə] n. 颠茄，莨菪，颠茄制剂
benzene ['benzi:n] n. 苯
bicyclic [ˌbai'saiklik] a. 双环的
bile acid 胆汁酸
binder ['baidə] n. 粘合剂
bioassay [ˌbaiəuə'sei] n. 生物鉴定，生物测定
bioavailability [baiəuˌəvailəbiliti] n. 生物利用度
biocatalyst [ˌbaiəu'kætəlist] n. 生物催化剂，酶
biochemical ['baiəu'kemikəl] a. 生物化学的
bioengineered [baiəu'endʒi'niərid] a. 生物工程的
biology [bai'ɔlədʒ] n. 生物学，生物（总称）
bioreactor [ˌbaiəuri'æktə] n. 生物反应器
biosphere ['baiəsfiə] n. 生物圈，生命层
biosynthesis [ˌbaiəu'sinθisis] n. 生物合成
biosynthetic [ˌbaiəu'sinθetik] a. 生物合成的
biota [bai'əutə] n. 生物区（系），生物群
biotechnologic ['baiəutek'nɔlədʒik] a. 生物技术的
biotechnology [ˌbaiəutek'nɔlədʒi] n. 生物工艺学
bisglycoside 双糖苷

bisulfite [bai'sʌlfait] n. 重亚硫酸盐，酸性亚硫酸盐
Black Death 黑死病（鼠疫）
bluff [blʌf] a. 陡峭的；n. 悬崖，天然陡坡
blur [blə:] v. 弄脏（污），（使）变模糊；n. 污点
boiler scale n. 锅炉水垢
bonnet ['bɔnit] n. 阀门帽
borosilicate [bɔrəsilikeit] n. 硼硅酸盐
botanical [bɔ'tənikəl] a. 植物学的
botanically [bə'tænikəli] ad. 植物（学）地
Botrytis cinerea 灰葡萄孢（霉）
bouncing ['baunsiŋ] a. 强壮的，大的，活跃的
bovine ['bəuvain] a. & n. 牛科；牛科动物
bovine pancreas 牛胰腺
brackish ['brækiʃ] a. 含盐的
bradykinin [,brædi'kainin] n. 缓激肽（血管舒张药）
breakage ['breikidʒ] n. 破损
brevetoxin [brevi'tɔksin] n. 短毒素
brine [brain] n. 盐（卤）水，海水；v. 用海水泡
briquette [bri'ket] n. 煤饼（球，砖），坯块，试块
bronchial asthma 支气管哮喘
bronchitis [brɔŋ'kaitis] n. 支气管炎
broth [brɔθ] n. 肉汤，液体培养基
bubble cap 泡罩
bubbletight [bʌbltait] a. 充满泡沫的
bubonic [bju:'bɔnik] a. 腹股沟腺炎的
buffer [bʌfə] vt. 缓冲；n. 缓冲剂
bulldoze ['buldouz] v. 威吓
Bunsen burner 本生灯（一种煤气灯）
buoy [bɔi] vt. 漂浮，浮起，装浮标，振作；n. 浮标
buoyant ['bɔiənt] a. 有浮力的，轻快的
Bupleurum radix 柴胡属植物的根
butterfly valve 蝶形阀
t-butylglycylamido t-丁基甘氨酰胺基

C

cactus ['kæktəs] n. 仙人掌
caffeine ['kæfi:n] n. 咖啡因，咖啡碱
calcitonin [,kælsə'tɔnin] n. 降血钙素
calcium carbonate 碳酸钙
cancellation [kænsə'leiʃən] n. 删除，取消
Canscora diffusa 多枝叶穿心草属
capillary [kə'piləri] a. 毛细（管）的；n. 毛细血管
capitalize on (upon) 利用
capsule ['kæpsju:l] n. 胶囊
carbohydrate [,ka:bou'haidreit] n. 碳化合物，糖类
carboxyl group 羧基
carboxylation [ka:bɔksi'leiʃən] n. 羧化（作用）
carboxylic acid 羧酸
carcinogen [ka:'sinədʒən] n. 生癌物质；诱癌因素
carcinogenic [ka:sinəu'dʒenik] a. 致癌的
carcinoma [,ka:si'noumə] ([pl] carcinomas 或 carcinomata [,ka:si'noumətə] n. 癌
cardiac ['ka:diæk] n. 强心剂，心脏病患者；a. 心脏的
cardiodepressant [ka:diəu di'presənt] n. 心抑制药；a. 心脏抑制的
cardiotonic [ka:diəu'tɔnik] n. 强心剂；a. 强心的
cardiovascular [ka:diəu'væskjulə] a. 心血管的
carnation [ka:'neiʃən] n. 麝香石竹（康乃馨）
β-carotene ['kærəti:n] n. β-胡萝卜素
carrageenan ['kærəgi:nən] a. 角叉菜（藻类）的
casing ['keisiŋ] n. 包装，保护性的外套
casual ['kæʒjuəl] a. 偶然的，临时的，随便的，非正式
catalyze ['kætəlaiz] v. 催化，促进
catechin ['kætikin] n. 儿茶酸
catecholamine [,kæti'kəuləmi:n] n. 儿茶酚胺
category ['kætigəri] n. 种类
Catharanthus roseus 长春花
cavity ['kæviti] n. 洞，腔
Ceftazidime ['sefteizidi:m] n. 头孢他啶
cellular ['seljulə] a. 细胞的
cellulose [se'ljulous] n. 纤维素
centrifugation [sentrifju'geiʃən] n. 离心分离
Cephaelis ipecacuanha Rich. 头九节波状吐根属
cephalosporium [,sefələu'spɔ:riəm] n. ; pl. cephalosporia [,sefələu'spɔ:riə] 假头状孢子头
Cephalosporium acremoniu 假头状孢子头枝顶孢属
cereal ['siəriəl] a. 谷类（的），谷子（的）；n. 谷物
cerebral ['seribrəl] a. 脑的，大脑的
cervical ['sə:vikəl] a. 颈的（如宫颈的）
chalcone ['kæl,kəun] n. 查耳酮，芳丙烯酰芳烃
check valve 止回阀

chelating　['kiːleitiŋ]　a. 螯合的
chemotherapy　[ˌkeməu'θerəpi]　n. 化学治疗法
chirality　[kaiə'ræliti]　n. 手（征）性
Chloramphenicol　[ˌklɔræm'fenikəl]　n. 氯霉素
chloroform　['klɔːrəfɔrm]　n. 氯仿
chlorophyll　['klɔːrəfil]　n. 叶绿素
Chloroquine　[ˌklɔːrə'kwiːn]　n. 氯喹
Chlorpromazine　[klɔː'prəuməzin]　n. 氯丙嗪
Chlortetracycline　[ˌklɔːtetrə'saiklain]　n. 金霉素
cholesterol　[kə'lestərəul]　n. 胆固醇；胆甾醇
choline　['kəuliːn]　n. 胆碱
Chondrodendron　[ˌkɔndrə'dendrɔn]　n. 南美防己属
chopper　['tʃɔpə]　n. 粉碎机
choriocarcinoma　[ˌkəuriəuˌkɑːsi'nəumə]　n. 绒膜癌
chromatogram　['krəumətəgræm]　n. 色谱（分离），层析谱
chromatographic　[ˌkrəumə'tɔgrəfik]　a. 色谱（分析）的
chromatography　[ˌkrəumə'tɔgrəfi]　n. 色谱法
chromatoplate　['krəumətəˌpleit]　n.（薄层）色谱板
chromogenic　[ˌkrəumə'dʒenik]　a. 发色的，发色体的
chrondroitin　n. 软骨素
chronic　['krɔnik]　a. 慢性的，长期的
chronological　[ˌkrɔnə'lɔdʒikəl]　a. 按年代顺序排列的
chute　[ʃuːt]　n.（斜，滑，流）槽，沟，斜道（管）
Cimetidine　[sai'metidiːn]　n. 西咪替丁
Ciprofloxacin　['siprəu'flɔksəsin]　n. 环丙沙星
circumvente　[səːkəm'vent]　vt. 包围
Cisplatinum　[sis'plætinəm]　n. 顺铂
citrate　['sitreit]　n. 柠檬酸盐（酯）
citric　['sitrik]　a. 柠檬酸的
cladinose　n. 二脱氧甲基己糖，克拉定糖
clandestine　[klæn'destin]　a. 秘密的
Clavulanic acid　克拉维酸
claxon　[klæksn]　n. 电气警笛，电器喇叭
clinical　['klinikəl]　a. 临床的，病房用的
clinician　[kli'niʃən]　n. 临诊医师，门诊医师
clone　[kləun]　n.；v. 克隆，无性繁殖，无性系
clot　[klɔt]　n.（血液等的）凝块；v.（使）凝结

clump　[klʌmp]　vi. 结块，结团；n.（土，铀）块，群，丛
coagulate　[kou'ægjuleit]　v. 凝结；a. 凝结的
coagulation　[kouˌægju'leiʃən]　n. 凝结，凝结物
coalesce　[ˌkouə'les]　vi. 接合，愈合
Cocaine　[kəu'kein]　n. 可卡因
Codeine　['koudiːn]　n. 可待因
codification　[ˌkɔdifi'keiʃən]　n. 整理，编纂
codon　['koudən]　n. 密码子，基码
coefficient　[kəui'fiʃənt]　n. 系数
cogent　['kəudʒənt]　a. 有说服力的，无法反驳的
colony　['kɔləni]　n.（生物）群体
colorant　['kʌlərənt]　n. 颜料，着色剂
coloration　[ˌkʌlə'reiʃən]　n. 染色，着色
colorimetric　[kʌləri'metrik]　a. 比色的
Column chromatography　柱色谱法，柱层析法
comatose　['kəumətəus]　a. 昏迷的，麻木
commensurate　[kə'menʃərit]　a. 同量的，同等的
compaction　[kəm'pækʃən]　n. 压紧
compassionate　[kəm'pæʃənət]　a. 富于同情心的
compendium　[kəm'pendiəm]　pl. compendiums 或 compendia　[kəm'pendiə]　n. 概要，概略，纲要
Compositae　n. 菊科
compressibility　[kəmpresi'biliti]　n. 可压缩性
compressive　[kəm'presiv]　a. 压缩的；n. 有压力的
concomitant　[kən'kɔmitənt]　a.；n. 伴生（随）的
condensation　[ˌkɔnden'seiʃən]　n. 缩合，浓缩
condescension　[ˌkɔndi'siʃən]　n. 屈尊，恩赐的态度
conformation　[ˌkɔnfɔː'meiʃən]　n. 构象
conformational　[ˌkɔnfɔː'meiʃənəl]　a. 构象的
conformational isomerism　构象异构现象
conifer　['kounifə]　n. 松类植物，针叶树
conjunctivitis　[kənˌdʒʌŋkti'vaitis]　n. 结膜炎
conspicuous　[kən'spikjuəs]　a. 明显的，显著的
constipation　[ˌkɔnsti'peiʃən]　n. 便秘
constituent　[kən'stitjuənt]　n. 成分，要素；a. 组成的
constraint　[kən'streint]　n. 强迫，强制
contamination　[kənˌtæmi'neiʃən]　n. 玷污，污染，污染物
contiguous　[kən'tigjuəs]　a. 邻近的，接近的，毗边的

contractile [kən'træktail] a. 会缩的，有收缩性的
contractility [kənˌtræktə'biliti] n. 收缩性，伸缩力
contraindication [ˌkɔntrəˌindi'keiʃən] n. 禁忌症
controversial [ˌkɔntrə'və:ʃəl] a. 争论的，争议的
convection [kən'vekʃən] n.（热，电）对流
conveyor = conveyer [kən'veiə] n. 输送机（设备）
corn steep liquor 玉米浸液
Cornus florida 佛罗里达的山茱萸
coronary ['kɔrənəri] a. 冠状的
corrugate ['kɔrugeit] v. 成波（纹）状，起皱
Costus speciosus 闭鞘姜
cough-suppressing 镇咳的
countercurrent ['kauntəˌkʌrənt] n. 逆流
countermeasure ['kauntəmeʒər] n. 对策，反措施
counterpart ['kauntəpɑ:t] n. 配对物，副本
cradle ['kreidl] n. 摇篮
cream ['kri:m] n. 霜剂
crest [krest] n. （峰）顶，脊，振幅，齿顶
Cross-hatch ['krɔ:shætʃ] vt. 给……近交叉阴影线
crossover ['krɔsouvə] n. 交叉，天桥，转线路
crustacean [krʌs'teiʃən] a.; n. 甲壳类的（动物）
crystallography ['kristə'lɔgrəfi] n. 结晶学，结晶论
culmination [ˌkʌlmi'neiʃən] n. 巅峰，最高点，累积
culture medium （细菌的）培养基
curare [kju'rɑ:ri] n. 箭毒，马钱子（也叫番木鳖）
curriculum [kə'rikjuləm]（pl）curricula [kə'rikjulə] n. 学校的全部课程
cursory ['kə:səri] a. 草率的，仓促的，疏忽的
cusp [kʌsp] n. 尖顶，尖端
cyanamid n. 氨基氰，腈胺
cyanosis [ˌsaiə'nəusis] n. 青紫
cyclic ['saiklik] a. 环状的，循环的
cyclone ['saikloun] n. 旋风，气旋
cytidine ['saitədin] n. 胞嘧啶核苷
cytidylic acid 胞（嘧啶核）苷酸
cytosine ['saitəsi:n] n. 胞嘧啶

D

dammarane ['dæmərein] n. 达玛烷
ddI 即 dideoxyinosine 双脱氧肌苷
de novo [di'nouvou] n. 重新，更始
debris ['debri] n. 碎片
decarboxylation [di:'kɑ:bɔksileʃən] n. 脱羧
decolorization [di:ˌkʌlərai'zeiʃən] n. 脱色，漂白
decolorize [di:'kʌləraiz] vt. 使脱色，将……漂白
decomposition [di:kɔmpə'ziʃən] n. 分解（作用）
decongestant [ˌdi:kən'dʒestənt] n. 减轻充血药
degradation [ˌdegrə'deiʃən] n. 降解，递降分解
degrade [di'greid] v. 使降解，（使）退化
deleterious [deli'tiəriəs] a. 有害（毒）的
delineate [di'linieit] vt. 描出……的外形，叙述，描写
6-demethyl-6-deoxytetracycline 6-去甲基-6-脱氧四环素
demineralize [di:minərəlaiz] vt. 去盐，去离子
denature [di:'neitʃə] vt. 变性，使……变性
deoxyadenylic acid 脱氧腺苷酸
deoxycytidylic acid 脱氧胞苷酸
deoxyguanylic acid 脱氧鸟苷酸
deoxyribonuclease [di:'ɔksiˌraibou'nju:klieis] n. 脱氧核糖核酸酶
deoxyribonucleic acid 脱氧核糖核酸（即 DNA）
deoxyribonucleoside triphosphates 三磷酸脱氧核糖核苷酸
deoxyribose [di:'ɔksiˌraibous] n. 脱氧核糖
2-deoxyribose 2-脱氧核醣
deoxythymidylic acid 脱氧胸腺嘧啶核苷酸
depict [di'pikt] vt. 描述，描写
depletion [di'pli:ʃən] n. 用尽，损耗，缺乏，亏损
depot ['depəu] n. 储存，基地
depressant [di'present] n.; a. 镇静剂 抑制剂
deprivation [depri'veiʃən] n. 脱除，剥夺，免职
derivative [di'rivətiv] n. 衍生物；a. 衍生的
derivatization n. = derivation 衍生（作用），导出
dermal ['də:məl] a. 皮肤的，真皮的
dermatan sulfate 硫酸皮肤素
desiccant ['desikənt] n. 干燥剂
desiccation [desi'keiʃən] n. 干燥
desoctapeptide [di:ˌzɔktə'peptaid] n. 脱八肽
detergent [di'tə:dʒənt] n. 清洁剂

deterioration [ditiəriə'reiʃən] n. 变坏，降低（品质）
detrimental [detri'mentl] a.；n. 有害（损）的
dextro ['dekstrəu] a. 右旋的；顺时针的
Dextromethorphan [ˌdekstrə'meθəfen] n. 右美沙芬
dextrorotatory [ˌdekstrəu'rəuteitəri] a. 右旋的
D-galactose D-半乳糖
diabetes [daiə'bi:ti:z] n. 糖尿病，多尿症
diabetic [daiə'betik] n. 糖尿病患者；a. 糖尿病的
dianthus caryophyllus 康乃馨，洋石竹
diaphoretic [ˌdaiəfə'retik] a. 发汗的；n. 发汗药
diaphragm ['daiəfræm] n. 隔膜
diaphragm valve 隔膜阀
diastereoisomer [ˌdaiəˌsteriəu'aisəumə] n. 非对映异构体
diazotize [dai'æzətaiz] v. 使重氮化
dictate [dik'teit] n. 指令，指示
die [dai] n. 冲磨，死亡
dielectric [daii'lektrik] a. 不导电的，绝缘的
diffraction [di'frækʃən] n. 衍射
diffusivity [difju'siviti] n. 扩散性（率）
Diflunisal [dai'flu:nisæl] n. 二氟苯水杨酸，二氟尼柳
2,4-difluoroaniline n. 2,4-二氟苯胺
digalloyl group 鞣酰基
Digenea simplex n. 红藻海人草
digest [dai'dʒest] vt. 蒸煮（某物），煮解（某物）
digestion [di'dʒestʃən] n. 消化力，消化作用，蒸煮
digitalis [didʒi'teilis] n. 洋地黄
Digitalis lanata 毛花洋地黄
Digitalis purpurea 紫花毛地黄
digitoxigenin n. 毛地黄毒苷配基，β-[丁烯酸内酯]-14-羟甾醇
digoxigenin n. 毛地黄毒苷，地谷新配基
3,4-dihydro-2-phenyl-2H-1-benzopyran 3,4-二氢-2-苯基-2H-1-苯并吡喃
dihydrofolate [dai haidrə'fəuleit] n. 二氢叶酸（酯）
7,4'-dihydroxy-8-methylflavan 7,4'-二羟基-8-甲基黄烷
7,4'-dihydroxyflavan 7,4'-二羟基黄烷
diluent ['diljuənt] a. 稀释的；n. 稀释剂

dilute [dai'lju:t] a.；v. 淡的，稀释的
dimer ['daimə] n. 二聚物
dimeric [dai'merik] a. 二聚的，形成二聚物的
dimerise ['daimərais] vt. 使聚合成二聚物
p-dimethylaminobenzaldehyde p-二甲基胺基苯甲醛
N,N-dimethylglycylamido N,N-二甲基甘氨酰胺基
1,3-diphenylpropane 1,3-二苯基丙烷
disaccharide [dai'sækəraid] n. 二糖
disassemble [disə'sembl] vt. 拆卸，分解
discreditation [diskredi'teiʃən] n. 怀疑，不名誉
discrete [dis'kri:t] a. 不连续（接）的，分离（散）
discriminate [dis'krimineit] v. 识别，区分
disfavour [dis'feivə] v. 不赞成，失宠，不利
disintegrant [dis'intigrənt] n. 崩解剂
disintegration [dis'intigreiʃən] n. 崩解
dislodge [dis'lɔdʒ] vt. 移（挪，调）动，移去
dispense [dis'pens] vt. 分配，配药
dissimilar [di'similə] a. 不一样的，不同的
dissociate [di'səuʃieit] vt. 使分离，使离解
distillation [disti'leiʃən] n. 蒸馏
distillation flask 蒸馏瓶
distilled water 蒸馏水
distribution [ˌdistri'bju:ʃən] n. 分布状态，分配，
distribution function 分布函数
disulfide [dai'sʌlfaid] n. 二硫化物
diuretic [daijuə'retik] a.；n. 利尿的，利尿药
divert [dai'və:t] vt.；vi. 转移，转向
dividend ['dividend] n. 股份红利，股息
docosahexaenoic acid（DHA） 二十二碳六烯酸
dome [dəum] n. 圆（拱，穹）顶，圆顶帽，穹面
L-Dopa (levo-dopamine) [levəu'dəupəmi:n] n. 左旋多巴
dopamine ['dəupəˌmi:n] n. 多巴胺
dorsal ['dɔ:səl] a. 背面的，背部的
dosage ['dəusidʒ] n. 下药，配药，剂量，用量，
dossier ['dɔsiei, dəu'siei] n. 病历表册，病历夹
downcomer n. 泄水管，下气道
drape [dreip] vt. 披盖；n. 布单，被单
droplet ['drɔplit] n. 小滴
duplex ['dju:pleks] a. 双的，二重的
dyscrasia [dis'kreizjə] n. 体液不调，恶液质

E

ebullating-bed 沸腾床
ecological [ˌekəˈlɔdʒikəl] a. 生态的，生态学的
effector [iˈfektə] n. 效应物，效应器（神经）
efficacious [ˌefiˈkeiʃəs] a. 有效验的，灵验的
effluent [ˈefluənt] a.，流出（的）；n. 流出物，废水，废液
efflux [ˈeflʌks] n. 流出物，流出
eicosapentaenoic acid (EPA) 二十碳五烯酸
ejection [iˈdʒekʃən] n. 排斥，喷出
elastomer [iˈlæstəmə] n. 弹性体
electrophilic [ˌilektrəuˈfailik] a. 亲电子的
electrophoresis [iˈlektrəufəˈri:sis] n. 电泳
elicit [iˈlisit] vt. 引（抽，诱，得）出，使发出
elixir [iˈliksə] n. 酏剂
elongate [ˈi:lɔŋgeit] vt. & vi. 拉长，伸长
eluant [ˈeljuənt] n. 洗提（脱）液，展开剂
elucidation [iˈlju:sideiʃən] n. 阐明，解释
elution [iˈlju:ʃən] n. 洗脱
embank [imˈbæŋk] v. 筑堤，上岸
embody [imˈbɔdi] vt. 体现，包含
emboss [imˈbɔs] vt. 使浮凸于（表面）上，使凸起，作浮雕
emetic [iˈmetik] n. 催吐剂；a. 催吐的
emetine [ˈemətiːn] n. 吐根碱，吐根素，依米丁
emission [iˈmiʃən] n. 发射，散发
empiric [emˈpirik] a. 经验性的
emulsin [iˈmʌlsin] n. 苦杏仁酶
emulsion [iˈmʌlʃən] n. 乳浊液，乳剂
enantiomer [enˈæntiəumə] n. 对映体，对映异构物
enantiomorphic [enˈæntiəˈmɔːfik] a. 对映异构的
encode [inˈkəud] n. 编码
endocrinology [ˌendəukraiˈnɔlədʒi] n. 内分泌学
endocyclic [ˌendouˈsaiklik] a. 桥环的
endogenous [enˈdɔdʒənəs] a. 内生的，内源的
endoperoxide [ˌendoupəˈrɔksaid] n. 内过氧化物
endothermic [ˌendəˈθəːmik] a. 吸热的，内热的
endotoxin [ˌendəuˈtɔksin] n. 内毒素
entail [inˈteil] vt. 使必需，使承担，遗传给
entero- [ˈentərəu] n. （前缀）肠
enterococcal [ˌentərəuˈkɔkəl] a. 肠球菌的
enterococcus [ˌentərəuˈkɔkəs] n. pl. enterococci [ˌentərəuˈkɔksai] 肠球菌
entity [ˈentiti] n. 实体，本质，病种
entrainment [inˈtreimənt] n. 雾沫夹带，挟带
entrusted [inˈtrʌst] vt. 委托，托管，信托
enzymatic [ˌenzaiˈmætik] a. 酶的，酶促的
enzymatically [ˌenzaiˈmætikəli] ad. 酶地，促酶地
enzyme [ˈenzaim] n. 酶
Ephedra [iˈfedrə] n. 麻黄属
ephedrine [eˈfedrin] n. 麻黄碱，麻黄素
epinephrine [ˌepiˈnefrin] n. 肾上腺素
episode [ˈepisoud] n. （一系列事件中的）一个事件
epoxide [ˈepɔksaid] n. 环氧化物
ergot [ˈəːgət] n. 麦角
erosion [iˈrouʃən] n. 腐蚀
erythromycin [iˌriθrouˈmaisin] n. 红霉素
escalation [ˌeskəˈleiʃən] n. 逐步上升，逐步升级
Escherichia coli 大肠杆菌，埃（舍利）希氏杆菌，大肠埃希氏杆菌（缩写为 E. coli）
ester [ˈestə] 酯
esterase [ˈestəreis] n. 酯酶（水解酯的酶）
esterify [esˈterifai] v. （使）酯化
ethambutol [ɪˈθæmbjutɔl] n. 乙胺丁醇
ethanol [ˈeθənɔl] n. 乙醇，酒精
ether [ˈiːθə] n. 醚
ethics [ˈeθiks] n. 道德规范
ethyl acetate 乙酸乙酯
ethylenediamine [eθili:ˈdaiəmi:n] n. 乙二胺
evolutionary [ˌiːvəˈlju:ʃənəri] a. 进化的，发展的
exaggerate [igzˈædʒəreit] v. 夸大，夸张
excipient [ikˈsipiənt] n. 赋形剂
excretion [eksˈkriʃən] n. 排泄，分泌
exemplify [igzempˈlifai] vt. 例证，示范
exogenous [ekˈsɔdʒinəs] a. 外生的，外源的
exothermic [eksəuˈθɔːmik] a. 放热的，发热的
expectorant [eksˈpektərənt] a., n. 祛痰的，祛痰剂
expiration [ekspaiəˈreiʃən] n. 呼气，终止，截止
exponential [ekspəuˈnenʃəl] a. 指数的；n. 指数
extemporaneous [ekstempəˈreinjəs] a. 即席的，临时的
extra-chromosomal 染色体外的
extract [iksˈtrækt] vt. 榨出，萃取，提取
　　　　[ˈekstrækt] n. 萃取物，提取物

extraction [iks'trækʃən] n. 提取，萃取，抽出物
extraneous [eks'treniəs] a. 外部裂化，新异反射
extrapolate [eks'træpəleit] vt.；vi. 推断，外推
extrapolation [ˌekstrəpəu'leiʃən] n. 外推法，推断
extrusion [eks'tru:ʒən] n. 挤（压，喷，推）出

F

fauna ['fɔ:nə] n. 动物群，动物区系
feedstuff ['fi:dstʌf] n. 饲料
fermentation [ˌfə:men'teiʃən] n. 发酵
festoon [fes'tu:n] n. 花彩，垂花饰；vt. 结彩
fibrillation [ˌfaibri'leiʃən] n. 原纤维形成作用
fibrobast ['faibrəublɑ:st] n. 成纤维细胞
fibrous ['faibrəs] a. 纤维的，含纤维的
file [fail] vt. 提出申请
filter paper n. 滤纸
filtrate ['filtrit] n. 滤（出）液，['filtreit]；v. 过滤
flange [flændʒ] n. 法兰，凸缘
flapper ['flæpə] n. 片状悬垂物
flavan ['fleivən] n. 黄烷
flavan-3,4-diols 黄烷-3,4-二醇
flavanone ['fleivənoun] n. 黄烷酮
flavonoid pigment 黄酮类颜料
flavonol ['fleivənɔl] n. 黄酮醇
flavor ['fleivə] n. 香精，香料
flocculation [ˌflɔkju'leiʃən] n. 絮凝（作用）
flowability [ˌfləuebiliti] n. 可流动性
fluctuation [ˌflʌktju'eiʃən] n. 波动
fluoroquinolones n. 氟喹诺酮
flurry ['flʌri] n. 阵风，飓风
flush-bottom valve 平底阀
foaming [fɔmiŋ] n. 发泡，起泡
foetal ['fi:tl] a. 似胎儿的，胎儿的（=fetal）
follow-up 把……探究到底
foolproof [fu:lpru:f] a. 极简单明了的，有安全装置的
forage ['fɔridʒ] n. 草料，饲料
formic acid 甲酸，蚁酸
formidable ['fɔ:midəbəl] a. 可怕的，难对付的
formula ['fɔ:mjulə] n. 公式方案，处方，配方
foul up 搞糟，弄乱，做坏
foxglove ['fɔksglʌv] n. 毛地黄
fractionate ['frekʃəneit] vt. 使分馏

fractionation [ˌfrækʃə'neiʃən] n. 分馏
fracture ['fræktʃə] v. & n. 破裂，断口（面），折断
fragment ['frægment] n. 碎片，断片，片段
friability [ˌfraiə'biliti] n. 脆性，易碎性
friable [fraiəblə] a. 易碎的，脆的
froth [frɔθ] n. 泡，泡沫，废物；vt. 使生泡沫
fucose ['fju:kous] n. 岩藻糖
fulvic acid n. 褐菌酸
fungal [fʌŋgəl] a. =fungous 真菌的
fungitoxic [ˌfʌndʒi'tɔksik] a. 真菌毒性的
fungus ['fʌŋgəs]，pl. fungi ['fəŋgai] n. 真菌
furostanol ['fjuərəstənəl] n. 呋甾醇
fusion [fju:ʒən] n. 熔化，熔解

G

galactosamine [gəˌlæk'təusəˌmi:n] n. 半乳糖胺，氨基半乳糖
gall [gɔ:l] n. 胆汁，五倍子，没食子；vt.，vi. 擦伤，磨损
gallic acid 五倍子酸，没食子酸
galvanic [gæl'vænik] a.（电池）电流的，电镀的
gamut ['gæmət] n. 全部，全（整个）范围，音阶
gastrointestinal (GI) [ˌgæstrəuin'testinəl] n. 肠胃道的
gate valve 闸阀
gauze [gɔ:z] n.（线、纱、滤、金属丝）网，纱布
gelatine ['dʒelə'tin] n. 骨胶，明胶（亦作：gelatin）
Gelonium multiflorum (缩写为 G. multiflorum) 多花白树属
gene [dʒi:n] n.（遗传）因子，（遗传）基因
generic [dʒi'nerik] a. 一般的，非特殊的
genetic [dʒi'netik] a. 遗传的，起源的
genin ['dʒenin] n. 配质，配基
genome ['dʒi:noum] n. 基因组，染色体组
genomic ['dʒi:nəumik] a. 染色体组的，基因组的
genus ['dʒi:nəs] pl. genera ['dʒenərə] n. 类，种类
geomorphological [dʒiəmɔ:'fɔlədʒikəl] a. 地貌学的
geothermal [dʒi:ou'θə:məl] n. 地热的
germicidal [dʒə:mi'saidəl] a. 杀菌的
germinate ['dʒə:mineit] v. 发芽，发育，使生长
geyser [gaizə] n. 间歇（喷）泉，[gi:zə]

n. 热水锅炉
gland [glænd] n. 腺体，腺
glaucoma [glɔ:'kəumə] n. (患)青光眼，绿内障
gln=glutamine 谷氨酰胺
globe valve 球阀
globular ['glɔbjulə(r)] a. 球状的
glucosamine [ˌglu:kous'æmi:n] n. 葡糖胺，氨基葡糖
glucose ['glu:kous] n. 葡萄糖，右旋糖
glucosyloxy flavan 葡糖氧基黄烷
glucuronic acid 葡糖醛酸
glutamate ['glu:tə'meit] n. 谷氨酸盐（酯或根）
glyceraldehyde [glisə'rældəhaid] n. 甘油醛
glycine ['glaisi:n, glai'si:n] n. 甘氨酸，gly. 甘氨酸的缩写
glycoalkaloid [ˌglaikou'ælkəlɔid] n. 配糖（生物）碱
glycogen ['glaikoudʒen] n. 糖原，动物淀粉
glycone ['glaikoun] n. (=glycerin suppository) 甘油栓
glycopeptide [ˌglaikəu'peptaid] n. 糖肽
glycoprotein [ˌglaikou'prouti:n] n. 糖蛋白
glycosidase [glai'kəusideis] n. 糖苷酶
glycoside ['glaikəˌsaid] n. 苷，配糖物
glycosylate ['glaikəsileit] vt. 糖基化
glycylcyclines n. 甘氨酰环素
Gnetales 买麻藤目
gradient ['greidiənt] n. 坡度，斜率，梯度变化曲线
granulation ['grænju:leiʃən] n. 成粒，制粒
granule ['grænju:l] n. 颗粒，细粒，微粒
granulocyte ['grænjuləusait] n. 粒细胞
gravimetric [grævi'metrik] a. 重量分析的，重量的
grepafloxacin 格帕沙星
groove [gru:v] n. 凹槽，最佳状态，惯例
gross [grous] n. 总额；a. 总的，毛重的
strophanthin g-羊角拗质
guanine ['gwɑ:ni:n] n. 鸟嘌呤（即 2-amino-6-oxypurine 2-氨基-6-氧代嘌呤）
guanylic acid 鸟苷酸
guaosine ['gwɑ:nəsin] n. 鸟（嘌呤核）苷
guideline ['gaidəlain] n. 方针
guinea-pig ['ginipig] n. 豚鼠，天竺鼠
gymnosperm [dʒimnəspə:m] n. 裸子植物

Gymnospermae 裸子植物纲
gyrase ['dʒaiəreis] n. 促旋酶

H

hagfish ['hægfiʃ] n. 八目鳗类鱼
hallucination [həlu:si'neiʃən] n. 幻觉，幻想
handling ['hændliŋ] a. 触摸的，处理的
hapten ['hæpten] n. 半抗原
hardness [hɑ:dnis] n. 硬度
heat sink 换热器，散热片，散热装置，冷却套
henbane ['henbein] n. 天仙子
heparin ['hepərin] n. 肝素
hepatical ['hepətikəl] a. 肝的
hepatitis [hepə'taitis] n. 肝炎
herbalism ['hə:bəlizəm] n. 草药医术学
herpes ['hə:pi:z] n. 疱疹
heterocyclic [hetərə'saiklik] a. 杂环的
heterogeneity [ˌhetərəudʒi'ni:iti] n. 异质性；不均匀性
heterogeneous ['hetərəu'dʒi:niəs] a. 不均匀的，多相的.
heterotopic [hetərə'tɔpik] a. 异位的
heuristics [hjuə'ristiks] n. 直观推断，试探法
hexamer ['hekseimə] n. 六聚物，六壳粒（病毒）
hexane ['heksein] n. 己烷
Hexobarbital ['heksəu'bɑ:bitæl] n. 海索比妥，环己巴比妥
hexosamine [hek'sɔsəmi:n] n. 氨基己糖，己糖胺
hiatus [hai'eitəs] n. 脱落，裂缝
high performance liquid chromatography 高压液相色谱（简写 HPLC）
highlight ['hailait] v. 强调
high-speed mixer/granulator 高速混合制粒机
hinge [hindʒ] n. 铰链；vt. 装上铰链
Hirsch funnel 赫尔什漏斗
histidine ['histidi:n] n. 组氨酸
Homo sapiens n. 人类
homogeneous [ˌhɔmə'dʒi:njəs] a. 均一的，均相的
hopper ['hɔpə] n. 漏斗，布（给）料器，斗仓
hordenine 大麦芽碱，对二甲氨乙基苯酚
hormone ['hɔ:moun] n. 激素，荷尔蒙
humate ['hju:meit] n. 腐植酸盐
humic ['hju:mik] n. 腐植的

hurdle ['hə:dl] vt. 用篱笆围住，跳过（栏栅），克服
hybridoma [,haibri'dəumə] n. 杂交瘤
hydraulic bowl a. 水压的，液压的
hydrofoil ['haidrəfɔil] n. 水叶，着水板，水翼
hydrology [hai'drɔlədʒ] n. 水文学
hydrolase ['haidrəleis] n. 水解酶
hydrolysable [haidrəlaizəbl] a. 水解性的
hydrolysate [hai'drɔliseit] n. 水解产物，水解液
hydrolysis [hai'drɔlisis] n. 水解（作用）
hydrolyzable ['haidrəlaizəbl] a. 可水解的
hydrolyze ['haidrəlaiz] vi. 水解
hydrosphere ['haidrəsfiə] n. 水界，水圈
hydrostatic ['haidrə'stætik] a. 流体静力（学）的
hydroxyflavan 羟基黄烷
hydroxyl [hai'drɔksil] n. 羟基
hydroxyl group 羟基
hygienic [hai'dʒi:nik] a. 卫生学的，卫生的
hygroscopic [haigrə'skɔpik] a. 吸湿的，温度计的
hyoscine ['haiəsin] n. 莨菪碱，天仙子碱
hypertension [haipə:'tenʃən] n. 高血压
hyperthermia ['haipə(:)'θə:miə] n. 体温过高，高热
hypnosis [hip'nousis] n. 催眠，催眠状态
hypnotic [hip'nɔtik] a.; n. 催眠的，催眠药
hypochlorite [,haipə'klɔ:rait] n. 次氯酸盐
hypotension [,haipəu'tenʃən] n. 低血压
hypothetical [,haipəu'θetikəl] n. 假设的，有前提的

I

Ibuprofen [ai'bjuprəufən] n. 布洛芬
iduronic acid 艾杜糖醛酸
imidazole [,imi'dæzoul] n. 咪唑，1,3-二氮杂茂
immerse [i'mə:s] vt. 沉浸
immiscible [i'misibəl] a. 不能混合的，不融和的
immobilize [i'məubilaiz] v. 使固定，使不动
immune [i'mju:n] a. 免疫的；n. 免疫者
immunodeficiency [,imju:noudi'fiʃənsi] n. 免疫缺陷
immunoglobulin [i'mju:nəu'glɔbjulin] n. 免疫球蛋白
immunological [,imju:'nɔlədʒikəl] a. 免疫学的
immunology [imju:'nɔlədʒi] n. 免疫学

immunopotentiate [i'mju:noupə'tenʃieit] v. 免疫加强
impair [im'pɛə] n. 损害，使弱
impeller [im'pelə] n. 叶轮，涡轮，推进器
impetus ['impitəs] n.（原，推）动力，动（冲）量
impinge [im'pindʒ] v. 碰撞，冲（撞，打）击
implantation [im'plɑ:nteiʃən] n. 植入法
implicit [im'plisit] a. 含蓄的，固有的
impurity [im'pjuəriti] n. 杂质
in vitro [in'vaitrəu] 在体外，在玻璃试管内，在玻璃容器内
in vivo [in'vi:vəu] a.（活）体内的
in vogue [in vəug] a. 流行的
inactivate [in'æktiveit] v. 使钝化，使不活泼
incidence ['insidəns] n. 影响范围，落下的方式
incinerate [in'sinəreit] vt.; vi. 把……烧成灰，焚化
incipient [in'sipiənt] a. 开始的，刚出现的
incorporate [in'kɔ:pəreit] v.（使）合并（并加）
increment ['inkrimənt] n. 增加（大，长，收，益）
incrustation [inkrʌ'steiʃən] n. 结硬壳，积垢
incubate ['inkjubeit] v. 使发展，孵化
indentation [inden'teiʃən] n. 刻（压）痕，缺口
indigenous [indi'dʒinəs] a. 本土的，固有的
inertia [i'nə:ʃiə] n. 惯性
inescapable [inis'keipəbl] a. 无法逃避的
infancy ['infənsi] n. 初期，幼时，婴儿期
infection [in'fekʃən] n. 传染，感染，影响
infectious [in'fekʃəs] a. 有传染性的，易传染的
inferential [infə'renʃəl] a. 推论的，推理的
infinitude [in'finitju:d] n. 无穷，无限的范围
inflammation [,inflə'meiʃən] n. 怒火，燃烧，发炎
inflammatory [in'flæmətəri] a. 发炎的
ingenuity [,indʒi'nju(:)iti] n. 独创性，独出新裁
ingestion [in'dʒestʃən] n. 咽下，吸收，摄取
ingredient [in'gri:djənt] n. 成分，配料，成份
inhaler [in'heilə] n. 吸入器
inherent [in'hiərənt] a. 固有的，内在的
inhibitor [in'hibitə] n. 抑制剂
inhibitory [in'hibi,təri] a. 抑制的
injection [in'dʒekʃən] n. 注射，注射剂
innate [i'neit] a. 先天的，天生的
inoculate [i'nɔkjuleit] vt. 接种，嫁接

inoculum [i'nɔkjuləm] *pl.* inocula [i'nɔkjulə] *n.* 接种体，接种物，培养液
inotropic [ˌinəu'trɔpik] *a.* 影响（肌）收缩力的，变力的（心神经纤维）
in-process control 过程中控制
Insulin ['insjulin] *n.* 胰岛素
integrity ['inteːgriti] *n.* 完整性
interdependent [ˌintədi'pendənt] *a.* 互相依赖的
interferon [ˌintə'fiərɔn] *n.* 干扰素
intermediate [ˌintə'miːdiət] *n.* 中间体
interplay ['intəplei] *n.*；*v.* 相互影响
interrogation [interə'geiʃən] *n.* 讯问，质问
interstice [in'təːstis] *n.* 空隙，间隔，裂缝
interval ['intəvəl] *n.* （时间的）间隔
intervention [ˌintə'venʃən] *n.* 干涉
intestinal [in'testinl] *a.* 肠的，肠内的
intestinal mucosa 肠粘液
intimately ['intimitli] *ad.* 亲密地，熟悉地
intracellular [ˌintrə'seljulə] *a.* 细胞内的
intractable [in'træktəbl] *a.* 难处理的，难治的
intratracheal [ˌintrə'treikiəl] *a.* 气管内的
intravenous [intrə'viːnəs] *a.* 静脉内的
intravenous injection 静脉注射
intravenously [ˌintrə'vinəsli] *ad.* 静脉内
intriguing *a.* 引起兴趣（或好奇心）的
intubation [ˌintju'beiʃən] *n.* 插管，插管法
invasive [in'veisiv] *a.* 侵略的，侵害的，侵袭的
investigational [investi'geiʃənəl] *a.* 研究的
Ipecacuanha [ˌipikækju'ænə] *n.* 吐根，吐根制剂
irrigate ['irigeit] *vt.* 冲洗
irrigation [ˌiri'geiʃən] *n.* 冲洗，冲洗法，冲洗液
ischemia [is'kiːmiə] *n.* 局部缺血，局部贫血
isobaric [aisəu'bærik] *a.* 等压（线），恒压的
isoleucine [ˌaisou'ljuːsiːn] *n.* 异白氨酸，异亮氨酸
isomerase [ai'sɔməreis] *n.* 异构化酶
isomeric [ˌaisəu'merik] *a.* 同分异构的
isoniazid [ˌaisəu'naiəzid] *n.* 异烟肼
isopenicillin [ˌaisəˌpe'nisilin] *n.* 异青霉素
isosterism [ˌaisəu'sterizm] *n.* 等排性，电子等排同物理性
isotherm ['aisəuθəːm] *n.* 等温线
isothermal [aisou'θəːməl] *a.* 等温的

J

judicious [dʒuː'diʃəs] *a.* 明智的，有见识的

junction ['dʒʌŋkʃən] *n.* 连接，接合，汇合处
jurubine 圆椎茄碱
juxtaposition [ˌdʒʌkstəpə'ziʃən] *n.* 并列，毗邻

K

kainic acid 海人草酸或红藻氨酸
kammogenin ['kæməˌdʒənən] *n.* 莰模配质，莰模皂苷元
ketolides *n.* 吲哚内酯类
ketone ['kiːtoun] *n.* 酮
Ketoprofen ['kiːtəu'prəufen] *n.* 酮洛芬
kiln [kiln] *n.* （砖，瓦）窑，（火）炉
kinase ['kaineis] *n.* 激酶，致活酶
kinetic [kai'netik] *a.* 动力学的，运动的

L

β-lactams β-内酰胺类抗生素
lactate [læk'teit] *n.* 乳酸盐（酯）；*v.* 分泌乳汁
lactobacillus [ˌlæktəubə'siləs] *n.* 乳酸杆菌属
lactone ['læktəun] *n.* 内酯
lactose ['læktous] *n.* 乳糖
lag [læg] *vt. vi. n.* 滞后
laminar ['læminɑː] *a.* 层（式，状，流）的
lance [lɑːs] *v.* 切开，刺破；*n.* 长枪，喷枪
larynx ['læriŋks] *n.* 喉
latency ['leitənsi] *n.* 潜在（因素），隐藏
latex ['leiteks] *n.* 乳液，胶乳，橡浆
leach [liːtʃ] *vt. & vi.* 滤取；*n.* 沥滤器
leakage ['liːkidʒ] *n.* 漏，泄漏，漏出物
lesion ['liːʒən] *n.* 损害，身体上的伤害
lethal ['liːθəl] *a.* 致命的，致死的
lethargy ['leθədʒi] *n.* 嗜眠症，不活泼，无生气
leucocyte (leukocyte) ['ljuːkə sait] *n.* 白血球
leuk(a)emia [ljuːˈkiːmiə] *n.* 白血病
levo- ['liːvə, levəu] [构词成分] 左，向左，左旋
levorotatory [ˌliːvəu'rəutətəri] *a.* 左旋的
lifespan ['laif'spæn] *n.* 寿命，平均生命期
ligand ['laigənd, 'ligənd] *n.* 配体，配合物
ligase [li'geis] *n.* 连接酶
light petrol 轻气油
ligroin ['ligrouin] *n.* 轻石油，石油醚
line [lain] *vt.* 加衬里
linearize ['liniəraiz] *v.* 使……线形化
lining ['lainiŋ] *n.* 衬里（套，垫，层，板）

liquorice ['likəris] n. =licorice 甘草,甘草属植物
louvre ['lu:və] n. 固定百叶窗,天窗
Lovastatin n. 洛伐他汀
lubricant ['lju:brikənt] n. 润滑剂
lyase ['li:əs] n. 裂合酶
lymph [limf] n. 淋巴,淋巴液
lymphoblastomid [ˌlimfə'blæstəumid] n. 成淋巴细胞瘤疹
lymphocytic ['limfə'sitik] a. 淋巴球的,淋巴细胞的
lymphoid ['limfɔid] a. 淋巴(腺)样的,淋巴组织的
lymphoma [lim'foumə] n. 淋巴瘤
lymphosarcoma [ˌlimfəusɑ:'kəumə] n. 淋巴肉瘤
lyophilization [laiˌɔfilaizei∫ən] n. (低压)冻干(结),升华干燥,冷冻脱水
lysate ['laiseit] n. 溶菌液,(细胞)溶解产物
lysis ['laisis] pl. lyses ['laisi:z] n. (病的)渐退,消散,细胞溶解

M

Ma Huang 麻黄
macrolide ['mækrəlaid] n. 大环内酯
macromolecule [ˌmækrəu'mɔlikju:l] n. 大分子
Madagascar [mædə'gæskə] n. 马达加斯加岛
magma ['mægmə] n. 岩浆,稠液,(稀)糊
mal- (词头)不(正确),非,不良
malaria [mə'lεəriə] n. 疟疾
malignant [mə'lignənt] a. 有害的,恶性的(指肿瘤)
maltodextrin [ˌmɔ:ltəu'dekstrin] n. 麦芽糖糊精
mandrake ['mændreik] n. 曼德拉草(根)
manipulation [məˌnipju'lei∫ən] n. 触诊,操作法,处理
mannose ['mænous] n. 甘露糖
marginal ['mɑ:dʒinəl] a. 边缘的,边际的
marsh [mɑ:∫] n. 沼泽,湿地
mass [mæs] vt. 聚集;n. 团
maxim ['mæksim] n. 格言,准则,谚语
meager ['mi:gə] a. 贫乏的,欠缺的
mechanism ['mekənizəm] 机理,历程,机构
mediate [mi:dieit] v. 调停,调解,中介
megohm ['megəum] n. 兆欧(姆)
melancholia [ˌmelən'kəuliə] n. 精神忧郁症

melanin ['melənin] n. 黑色素
melon ['melən] n. (各种的)瓜
melphalan ['melfələn] n. 苯丙氨酸氮芥
membrane ['membrein] n. 膜,隔膜,细胞膜
memorabilia [ˌmemərə'biliə] [复] n. 大事记
mental disorder 精神错乱
Meperidine [mə'peridi(:)n] n. 哌替啶(镇痛药)
meso- [mesəu] (前缀)内消旋,中间(物)
metabolic [ˌmetə'bɔlik] a. 新陈代谢的
metabolism [me'tæbəlizəm] n. 新陈代谢
metabolite [me'tæbəlait] n. 代谢物
metachromatic [ˌmetə'krəumətik] a. 因光易色的
Methadone ['meθədəun] n. 美沙酮(镇痛药)
methanol ['meθənɔl] n. 甲醇
methanolic sulphuric acid 硫酸甲醇液
methanolysis [ˌmeθə'nɔlisis] n. 甲醇分解作用
methemoglobinuria [ˌmetˌhi:məuˌgləubi'njuəriə] n. 正铁血红蛋白尿
Methicillin [ˌmeθi'silin] n. 美替西林,二甲氧基苯青霉素
methiodide [meθ'aiədaid] n. 甲基碘化物
methodology [ˌmeθə'dɔlədʒi] n. 方法论,方法学
methoxyflavan 甲氧基黄烷
methyl group 甲基
methylaspartase ['meθil əs'pɑ:teis] n. 甲基天门冬氨酸酶
methylate ['meθileit] vt. 使甲基化,向……导入甲基
methylation [ˌmeθi'lei∫ən] n. 甲基化
L-Methyldopa n. 左旋甲基多巴
metronidazole [ˌmetrə'naidəzəul] n. 甲硝唑
microbial [mai'krəubiəl] a. 微生物(或细菌)的
microbiologic ['maikrəubaiə'lɔdʒik] a. 微生物学的
micrococcal nuclease 微球菌核酸酶
microorganism ['maikrou'ɔ:gənizəm] n. 微生物
microporous [maikrəu'pɔ:rəs] a. 微孔性的,多孔的
mill [mil] vt. 碾磨
millennium [mi'leiniəm] pl. millennia [mi'leniə] n. 一千年
mimic ['mimik] a.;n. 模仿的;拟态的;模仿物
minocycline [ˌminəu'saikli:n] n. 二甲胺四环素

misbrand [mis'brænd] vt. 贴错标签
miscellaneous [misi'leiniəs] a. 多方面的；其他的
miscible [misibl] a. 易溶合的
misnomer ['mis'nəumə] n. 误称；使用不当的名称
mistletoe ['misltou] n. 槲寄生
mnemonic [ni:'mɔnik] a.（帮助）记忆的
mobile phase 流动相
modification [ˌmɔdifi'keiʃən] n. 修改，改变，更改
molasses [mə'læsiz] n.（废）糖浆，糖蜜
moldy ['məuldi] (=mouldy) a. 发（生）霉的，霉烂的
momentum [mou'mentəm] n. 动量，要素
Momordica charantia 苦瓜
monensin [mə'nənsin] n. 莫能菌素
monitor ['mɔnitə] vt. 监控；n. 监视器，（病人）监护仪
monoclonal [mɔnəu'kləunəl] a. 单细胞系的，单克隆的
monocyclic [ˌmɔnə'saiklik] a. 单环的
monomer ['mɔnəmə] n. 单体
monosaccharide [ˌmɔnə'sækəraid] n. 单糖
monotonous [mə'nɔtənəs] a. 单调的
morbidity [mɔ:'biditi] n. 发病率，致病率
morphine ['mɔ:fi:n] n. 吗啡
morphine methyl ether 吗啡甲基醚
mortality [mɔ:'tæliti] n. 死亡率，死亡数
mould [məuld] n. 霉菌
mRNA =messenger RNA 信使核糖核酸
mucoitin [mju'kɔuitin] n. 粘多糖，粘液素
mucosa ['mju:kəusə] n. pl. mucosae ['mju:kəusi:], -s 粘膜（粘液膜）
mucous ['mju:kəs] a. 粘液的，分泌粘液的
mulberry ['mʌlbəri] n. 桑树，桑葚，深紫红色
multidrug 多药物
multiparticulate [mʌltipə'tikjulit] n. 多颗粒
multisulfonamide n. 多磺酰胺
munition [mju:'niʃən] n.（常用复数）军需（用）品，军火
murine ['mjuərain] a.；n. 鼠科的，鼠科动物
mustard ['mʌstəd] n. 芥（禾），芥子气
mustard-gas n. 芥子气
mutagenesis ['mjutədʒenisis] n. 突变
mutant ['mju:tənt] a. 变异的；n. 突变异种
mutation [mju:'teiʃən] n. 变化，（生物物种）突变
Mycobacterium tuberculosis 结核杆菌（缩写为 M. tuberculosis）
mycobiological ['maikouˌbaiə'lɔdʒikəl] a. 真菌生物学的
myeloma [maiə'ləumə] n.（pl. ~s）骨髓瘤
myelomatosis [ˌmaiələumə'təusis] n. 骨髓瘤（病），多发性骨髓瘤

N

nanometer ['nænouˌmi:tə] n. 纳米，毫微米（即 nm）
Naproxen [nə'prɔksən] n. 萘普生（非甾体抗炎镇痛药，(S)-构型）
Narcissus pseudonarcissus L. 假水仙属植物
narcotic [nɑ:'kɔtik] n. 麻醉药，起麻醉作用的东西
nasal ['neizəl] a. 鼻的，鼻音的；n. 鼻音
nasal septum 鼻隔膜
nascent ['næsnt] a. 初生的
nausea ['nɔ:sjə] n. 恶心，反胃，晕船
needle valve 针型阀
neuralgic [njuə'rældʒik] a. 神经痛
neuroblastoma [ˌnjuərəblæs'təumə] n. 成神经细胞瘤
neurokinin [njuərəu'kinin] n. 神经激肽
neuromuscular [ˌnjuərou'mʌskjulə] a. 神经肌肉的
neuron ['njuərɔn] n. 神经元，神经细胞
neutral ['nju:trəl] a. 中性的
neutralize [nju:trə'laiz] vt. 中和
nitrate ['naitreit] n. 硝酸盐（酯）
p-nitroaniline 对硝基苯胺
nitrofurantoin [ˌnaitrəufjuə'ræntɔin] n. 呋喃坦啶
Nitroglycerin ['naitrəu'glisərin] n. 硝酸甘油，三硝酸甘油酯
Nocardia [nəu'kɑ:diə] n. 诺卡氏菌属，土壤细菌属
Nocardicin 诺卡杀菌素，诺卡地菌素
node [nəud] n. 节结
nomadic [nou'mædik] a. 游牧的，流浪的，无定的
nomenclature [nəu'menklətʃə] n. 命名法
nominal ['nɔminl] a. 标（公）称，标定的，规定的

non-hydrolyzable 不可水解的
nonreproducible ['nɔnˌri:prə'dju:səbl] a. 不能繁殖的，不能再生产的，不能再生长的
nonsteroidal ['nɔnste'rɔidl] a. 非甾族化合物，非类固醇的
nonthermal a. 无热量的
nonwoody plants 非木本植物
noradrenaline [ˌnɔ:rə'drenəlin] n. = norepinephrine 去甲肾上腺素
norepinephrine [ˌnɔrepi'nefrin] n. 去甲肾上腺素
norspirostanol 18-降螺甾烷醇
noscapine ['nɔskəpi:n] n. 那可汀
nozzle ['nɔzl] n. (喷管)嘴，喷油嘴
nuclear magnetic resonance spectroscopy (NMR) 核磁共振谱（仪）
nucleation [ˌnju:kli'eiʃən] n. 成核（现象，作用），核化
nucleic acid n. 核酸
nucleophile ['nju:kliəfail] n. 亲核性，亲核试剂
nucleoside ['nju:kliəsaid] n. 核苷
nucleotide ['nju:kliətaid] n. 核苷酸
nucleotidylation 核苷酸化作用
nutrient ['nju:triənt] a.；n. 营养的，滋养的；营养品

O

oblong ['ɔblɔŋ] n.；a. 长方形，椭圆形
obviate ['ɔbvieit] vt. 排除，避免，事先预防
octadecylsilylated a. 十八烷基硅烷基化的
ointment ['ɔintmənt] n. 软膏，药膏，油膏
oligonucleotide [ˌɔligəu'nju:kliətaid] 低（聚）核苷酸，寡核苷酸
oligosaccharide [ˌɔligou'sækəraid] n. 低聚糖
onset ['ɔnset] n. 发作
ophthalmic [ɔf'θælmik] a. 眼的；n. 眼药
opium ['oupjəm] n. 鸦片
optical isomerism 旋光异构现象
optimize ['ɔptimaiz] vt. 使尽可能完善；n. 最佳化
optimum ['ɔptiməm] a. 最好的，最佳的；n. 最适条件
orchestrate ['ɔ:kistreit] v. 使和谐地结合起来
ordinate ['ɔ:dinit] n. 纵坐标，竖标距；a. 有规则的

orientation [ˌɔ:rien'teiʃən] n. 向东，定位，定向
orifice ['ɔrifis] n. (小)孔，小洞，喷嘴，孔板
oscillation [ˌɔsi'leiʃən] n. 震动，摇动
osmosis [ɔz'məusis] n. 渗透，渗透作用
osteogenic [ˌɔstiə'dʒenik] a. 骨生成的，成骨的
outcome ['autkʌm] n. 结果，成果
ovarian [ou'vɛəriən] a. 卵巢的，子房的
overlap ['əuvə'læp] v. 重叠
overly ['əuvəli] ad. 过度地，极度地
overweight a. 过重的
oxazolidinone [ˌɔksə'zəulidəun] n. 噁唑烷酮
oxidase ['ɔksideis] n. 氧化酶
oxidation [ˌɔksi'deiʃən] n. 氧化（作用）
oxydoreductase [ˌɔksidə ri'dʌkteis] n. 氧化还原酶
oxygenation [ˌɔksidʒi'neiʃən] n. 氧化，以氧气处理
ozone ['ouzoun] n. 臭氧

P

paddle [pædl] vt. 搅打；n. 桨，搅拌器
painkiller ['pein'kilə] n. 止痛药
paintbrush ['peintbrʌʃ] n. 画笔，漆刷
Panax ginseng 高丽参
pancreas ['pæŋkriəs] n. 胰腺
pancreatic [ˌpæŋkri'ætik] a. 胰腺的
pancreatin ['pæŋkriətin] n. 胰酶制剂
Papaver somniferum 罂粟
papilloma [ˌpæpi'ləumə] n. 乳头（状）瘤
papyrifera (Broussonetia papyrifera 的缩写) 构树
paradigm ['pærədaim] n. 范例，示例
paralyse ['pærəlaiz] vt. 使麻痹，使瘫痪，使无力
paralysis [pə'rælisis] n. 瘫痪，麻痹
parameter [pə'ræmitə] n. 参数
paramount ['pærəmaunt] a. 最高的，首要的
parasite ['pærəsait] n. 寄生物（虫，菌）
parasitemia [ˌpærəsai'ti:miə] n. 寄生虫血症
parenteral [pæ'rentərəl] a. 非肠道的
parillin n. 杷日灵，副菝葜皂苷
paroxysm ['pærəksizəm] n. (病)发作，突发；暴发
partially [pɑ:ʃəli] ad. 部分地，不完全地
partition coefficient 分配函数
pasty [peisti] a. 糊状的
pathogen ['pæθədʒin] n. 病原体，病原菌

pathogenic [pæθə'dʒenik] a. 致病的，病源的
pathology [pə'θɔlədʒi] n. 病理学，病状
pathway ['pɑ:θwei] n. 路径
peanut meal 花生粉
pellet ['pelit] n. 药丸，小球
pelletize v. 造球，制粒，做成丸
penetration [,peni'treiʃən] n. 渗透，穿透力
Penicillin ['penicilin] n. 青霉素
Penicillium chrysogenum 黄青霉，产黄青霉
penicillium notatum 青霉菌，特异青霉，点青霉
pentapeptide [,pentə'peptaid] n. 五肽
peptide ['peptaid] n. 多肽
percentage [pə'sentidʒ] n. 百分数比例，利润，佣金
perforate ['pə:fəreit] v. 穿（钻，打，冲）孔，打眼
perforation [pə:fə'reiʃən] n. 穿孔
peripheral [pə'rifərəl] a. 外周的，周围的
periwinkle ['periwiŋkəl] n. 长春花属植物，玉黍螺
permanganate [pə'mæŋgənit] n. 高锰酸盐
permeability [,pə:mjə'biliti] n. 渗透，渗透性
permeable ['pə:miəbl] a. 可渗（穿）透的
permeation [pə:mi'eiʃən] n. 渗透，充满
permethylation 全甲基化
permissable [pə:'misəbl] a. 可允许的，许可的
peroral [pə'rɔ:rəl] a. 经口的
peroxide [pə'rɔksaid] n. 过氧化物
perspiration ['pə:spə'reiʃən] n. 排汗，汗
pertain [pə:'tein] vi. 附属 (to)
pervious ['pə:vjəs] a. 透光（水）的，有孔的，能通过的，能接受的，
petroleum ether 石油醚
phage [feidʒ] n. 噬菌体
pharmaceutical [,fɑ:mə'sju:tikəl] n. 药品；a. 药物的
pharmacist ['fɑ:məsist] n. 药剂师，配药师
pharmacognosist [fɑ:mə'kɔgnəsist] n. 生药学家
pharmacokinetics ['fɑ:məkəukai'netiks] n. 药物动力学
pharmacological [fɑ:məkə'lɔdʒikəl] a. 药理学的
pharmacologically [,fɑ:məkə'lɔdʒikəli] ad. 药理学地
pharmacopoeia [,fɑ:məkə'pi:ə] n. 药典
phe=phenylalanine 苯基丙氨酸的缩写

Phenacetin [fi:'næsitin] n. 非那西汀
phenethylamine 苯乙胺
phenol ['fi:nɔl] n. 酚，石炭酸
phenolic [fi'nɔlik] a. 酚的
phenothiazine [,fi:nəu'θaiəzi:n] n. 吩噻嗪
phenoxyacetic acid 苯氧基乙酸
phenylacetic acid 苯基乙酸
phenylalanine [,fenil'æləni:n] n. 苯基丙氨酸
Phenylbutazone [,fi:nil'bju:təzəun] n. 保泰松，苯基丁氮酮，（止痛退热药）
2-phenylchroman 2-苯基色满
phosphate ['fɔsfeit] n. 磷酸盐（酯）
phosphoric acid 磷酸
phosphorylation [fɔ,sfəri'leiʃən] n. 磷酸化（作用）
photolysis [fəu'tɔlisis] n. 光分解
phototoxicity [,foutoutɔk'sisiti] n. 光毒性
physicochemical [,fizikəu'kemikəl] a. 物理化学的
physiologically [,fiziə'lɔdʒikəli] ad. 生理学地
phytoalexin [,faitəuə'leksin] n. 植物抗毒素，植保菌素
phytochemistry [,faitou'kemistri] n. 植物化学
pigment ['pigmənt] n. 颜料，天然色素
pilot ['pailət] a. 试验性
pilot-plant n. 中试工厂，小规模试验性工厂（设备）
pinch or squeeze valve 挤压阀
pivot ['pivət] n. 枢轴
pivotal ['pivətl] a. 枢轴的，关键的
placebo [plə'si:bəu] n. 安慰剂
plague [pleig] n. 瘟疫，鼠疫；vt. 使得灾祸，折磨
planetary mixer n. 行星齿轮混合器，行星式的混合器
plasma ['plæzmə] n. 血浆，浆，淋巴液，等离子体
plasmid ['plæzmid] n. 质体，质粒
Plasmodium falciparum 恶性疟原虫，镰状疟原虫
platelet ['pleitlit] n. 血小板；小板，小盘
ploy [plɔi] n. 策略，趣味，工作
plug valve 旋塞阀
pneumatic [nju:'mætik] a. 气体的，空气的，气体（力）学的
pneumococcal [,nju:mə'kɔkəl] a. 肺炎双球菌的
polar solvent 极性溶剂
polarity [pou'læriti] n. 极性

polarize ['pəuləraiz] vt. 使偏振，使极化
polarized light n. 偏振光
polarographic [pəulærə'græfik] a. 极谱（法）的
poliomyelitis [pɔliəumaii'laitis] n. 脊髓灰质炎，小儿麻痹症
poliovirus ['pəuliəu,vaiərəs] n. 脊髓灰质炎，病毒
pollutant [pə'lu:tənt] n. 污染物质
polyacrylamide [,pɔliə'klilimaid] n. 聚丙烯酰胺
polyamide [pɔlimaide] n. 聚酰胺
polymerase ['pɔlimæreis] n. 聚合酶
polymeric [,pɔli'merik] a. 聚合的，聚合体的
polymerization [,pɔlimærai'zeiʃən] n. 聚合（作用）
polypeptide [,pɔli'peptaid] n. 多肽
polypgemus [pɔli'fi:məs] n. 大眼水蚤属
polysaccharide [pɔli'sækəraid] n. 多糖，多聚糖
polytropy ['pɔlitrɔpi] n. 多变性
poppy ['pɔpi] n. 罂粟，鸦片，麻醉品
porcine ['pɔ:sain] a. 猪的
postulate ['pɔstjuleit] v. 要求，假定，假设
potable ['pəutəbl] a. 可以喝的；n. 饮料
potency ['pəutənsi] n. 效力，能力，潜力，力量
potent ['pəutənt] a. 有力的，有效的
potentiate [pə'tenʃieit] vt. 加强，更有效
potentiation [pəu,tenʃi'eiʃən] n. 增效作用，增强作用
potpourri [pəu'puəri] n. 混合香料，杂烩，混合物
preamble [pri:'æmbl] n. 序言，绪论
pre-antibiotic era 指使用抗生素之前的时期
precipitant [pre'cipitənt] n. 沉淀剂（物）
precipitate [pri'sipiteit] vt. 使沉淀；vi. 沉淀，[pri'sipitit] n. 沉淀物
precipitation [pri,sipi'teiʃən] n. 沉淀（作用）
precipitous [pri'sipitəs] a. 险峻的，陡峭的，突然的
preclinical [pri'klinikəl] a. 临床前的，临症前期的
precursor [pri'kə:sə] n. 前体
prednisolone [prəd'nisəlɔun] n. 强的松龙，泼尼松龙
predominant [pri'dɔminənt] a. 占优势的，主要的
preparation [prepə'reiʃən] n. 准备，制备，制剂
preparative [pri'pærətiv] a. 制备的，预备的；n. 制备，预备，准备
prepurification [pri:,pjurifikeiʃən] n. 预纯化

prescribe [pris'kraib] v. 规定，命令，开（药方）
prescription [pris'kripʃən] n. 处方，药方，规定
preservation [prizə:'veiʃən] n. 保存，储藏
preservative [pri'zə:vətiv] a. 防腐的，保存的；n. 防腐剂
pressor ['presə] n. 升高血压的物质；a. 有使血压增高的，收缩血管的
prevalence ['prevələns] n. 流行，盛行
prevalent ['prevələnt] a. 普通的，一般的，流行的
priority [prai'ɔriti] n. 优先权
probenecid [prə'benisid] n. 丙磺舒，羧苯磺胺
problematic [prɔblə'mætik] a. 成问题的，有疑问的
procoagulant [,prəukəu'ægjulənt] a. 促凝血的，n. 前凝血剂
procure [prə'kjuə] v. （努力）取得，实现，达成
procurement [prə'kjuəmənt] n. 获得
proinsulin [,prəu'insjulin] n. 胰岛素原
proliferation [,prəlifə'reiʃən] n. 增殖
proliferative [prou'lifəreitiv] a. 增殖的，增生的
prominent ['prɔminənt] a. 突出的，凸出的，杰出的
propensity [prə'pensiti] n. 倾向
prophylactic [,prɔfi'læktik] n. 预防药，避孕药；a. 预防疾病的
proprietary [prə'praiətəri] a. 专利的，有专利权的；n. 所有（权），所有人，专利药
prosapogenin 前皂配基
prostaglandin [,prɔstə'glændin] n. 前列腺素
prostate adenocarcinoma 前列腺癌
protein ['prouti:n] n. 蛋白质，朊；a. （含）蛋白质的
proteinaceous [,proutii'neiʃəs] a. 蛋白质的
proteoglycan [,prəutiə'glaikæn] n. （含）蛋白多糖
proteolytic [,proutiə'litik] a. 分解蛋白质的
proven [pru:ven] a. 证实的
provision [prə'viʒən] n. 预备，措施，设备，条款
provoke [prə'vouk] vt. 驱使，惹起，激怒，挑拨
proximity [prɔk'simiti] n. 最近，接近，近似
pseudo ['psju:dəu] a. 假的，伪的
psychopharmacology [saikəu fɑ:mə'kɔlədʒi] n. 精神药理学
purge [pə:dʒ] v. 清（吹，扫，消）除，（使）净

化，催泻；n. 净化，泻药
purine ['pjuəri:n] n. 嘌呤
putrefaction [ˌpju:tri'fækʃən] n. 腐烂；腐败；腐败物
pyrazinamide [ˌpirə'zinəmaid] n. 吡嗪酰胺
pyridone n. 吡啶酮，羟基吡啶
pyrimidine [pai'rimidi:n] n. 嘧啶
pyrogen ['paiərədʒən] n. 致热质，热原
pyrophosphate [ˌpaiərou'fɔsfeit] n. 焦磷酸盐（酯），焦磷酸

Q

quiescent [kwai'esnt] a. 静（止）的，不动的
Quinacrine ['kwinəkrin] n. 阿的平（抗疟疾药）
quinine [kwi'ni:n] n. 奎宁
quinolone n. 喹诺酮，2-羟基喹啉
quinovose ['kwinəvəus] n. 奎诺糖，鸡纳糖，6-脱氧葡糖

R

racemate [rei'si:meit] n. 外消旋体（化合物）
racemic [rə'simik] a. 外消旋的
racemization [ræsimai'zeiʃən] n. 外消旋（作用）
radial ['reidiəl] a. 径向的，（沿）半径的，放射的
radical ['rædikəl] a. 基本的，基团的；n. 基，基团
ram [ræm] n. 撞杆，撞锤
rash [ræʃ] n. 皮疹
rearrangement [ˌri:ə'reindʒmənt] n. 重排
recalcify 再钙化
recede [ri:'si:d] vi. 收回，撤回
reclaim [ri'kleim] vt. 回收，再生，恢复，收回
recognition [ˌrekəg'niʃən] n. 识别，认识
recombinant [ri'kɔmbinənt] n. 重组细胞，重组体
recrystallization [ri'kristəlai'zeiʃən] n. 重结晶
reduce [ri'dju:s] vt. 减少
reductase [ri'dʌkteis] n. 还原酶
reduction [ri'dʌkʃən] n. 还原作用
refine [ri'fain] -v. 精炼，精制，使文雅高尚
reflux ['ri:flʌks] n. 回流
refractory [ri'fræktəri] a. 耐熔（火）的，难治的，顽固性的
refurbish [ri:'fə:biʃ] vt. 再刷新，再磨光
regime [rei'ʒi:m] n. 制度，状态，生活方式
regimen ['redʒimən] n. 疗法
regiment ['redʒimənt] n. 一大群，大量
regiospecific reaction 区域专一性反应
regulatory ['regjulətəri] n. 调整的，调节的
reimburse [ˌri:im'bə:s] vt. 偿还，偿付
reiterate [ri:'itəreit] vt. 重做，重申
relaxation [ˌri:læk'seiʃən] n. 松弛，缓和，减轻
relegated ['religeitid] a. 驱逐的，使降级，归于……的
reliability [riˌlaiə'biliti] n. 可靠度
remedy ['remidi] n. 治疗法，药物；vt. 治疗
remnant ['remnənt] n. 残余，遗留物
renal ['ri:nl] a. 肾的，肾脏的
renaturation ['ri:ˌneitʃə'reiʃən] n. 复原，复活
renin ['ri:nin] n. 肾素，高血压蛋白原酶
repertoire ['repətwɑ:] n. 全部技能，演奏节目
repetitively [ri'petitivli] ad. 重复地
replenishment [ri'pliʃmənt] n. 补给（充），充实
replica ['replikə] n. 复制品
replication [ˌrepli'keiʃən] n. 复制（品），复制过程
repro ['ri:prəu] n. 复制品
requisite ['rekwizit] a. 必备的，需要的；n. 必需品
residence time 滞留时间
residue ['rezidju:] n. 残余，渣滓
resolution [ˌrezə'lju:ʃən] n. 光学拆分（法）
respiration [ˌrespə'reiʃən] n. 呼吸，呼吸作用
respiratory ['respireitəri] a. 呼吸（作用）的
response [ris'pɔns] n. 响应，反应
resurgent [ri'sə:dʒənt] a. 复活的，苏醒的
rhabdomyosarcoma [ˌræbdəuˌmaiəusɑ:'kəumə] n. 横纹肌肉瘤
L-rhamnose L-鼠李糖
rheumatoid ['ru:mətɔid] a. 类风湿性的，风湿病样的
rhino- ['rainəu] n. （前缀）鼻
ribose sugar ['raibəus] 核糖
ribosomal [ˌraibə'səuməl] a. 核糖体的，核（糖核）蛋白体的
rifampin ['rifəmpin] n. 利福平
rigor ['raigɔ:] n. 僵硬，强直
rinse [rins] v. 冲洗，漂洗；n. 漂清，冲洗
ritual ['ritjuəl] n. 仪式，典礼；a. 仪式的，典礼的
roche 岩石，废弃的粗沙岩

rodent ['rəudənt] n. 啮齿动物
rote [rout] n. 死记硬背，死搬硬套
routinely [ruːˈtiːnli] ad. 常规地，惯例地
rudimentary [ˌruːdiˈmentəri] a. 基本的，初步的
runt [rʌnt] n. 侏儒（指矮小动植物）
ruscogenin 鲁士可宁
ruscoside n. 鲁士可宁甙

S

salicylate [sæˈlisileit] n. 水杨酸盐或酯
salicylic acid 水杨酸
salient [ˈseiliənt] a. 凸（突）的，显著的 n. 突出部分
saline [ˈseilain] a. 含盐的；n. 盐湖
saliva [səˈlaivə] n. 唾液，涎
sapogenin [ˌseipəˈdʒenin] n. 皂草配基，皂角甙配基
saponify [səˈpɔnifai] vt & vi (使)皂化
saponin [ˈsæpənin] n. 皂草苷，皂角苷
sarcoma [sɑːˈkəumə] n. 肉瘤，恶性毒瘤
Sardinian [sɑːˈdinjən] n. 撒丁岛人，撒丁岛语
sarsaparilloside 葡萄糖洋菝葜皂苷
sawdust [ˈsɔːdʌst] n. 锯屑
scale [skeil] n. 锅垢
scopolamine [skəuˈpɔləmin] n. 莨菪胺
score [skɔː] v. 擦伤，刻，划线，打记号，计算
screening [ˈskriːniŋ] n. 筛网，过筛
scrub [skrʌb] vt. 擦洗，擦净
scrupulously [ˈskruːpjuləsli] ad. 审慎地，严格地
scrutiny [ˈskruːtini] n. 详细审查
sedation [siˈdeiʃən] n. 镇静作用
sedative [ˈsedətiv] a. 镇静的；n. 镇静药
sediment [ˈsedimənt] n. 沉淀
sedimentary [ˈsedimentəri] a. 沉积的
seed vessel 果皮
segragation [segriˈgeiʃən] n. 分开，隔离，离析
semiconservative [ˈsemikənˈsəːvətiv] a. 半保留的，半保存的
semi-micro a. 半微（量）
semi-synthetic a. 半合成的
sensitivity [sensiˈtiviti] n. 敏感性，灵敏度
separatory funnel 分液漏斗
sequence [ˈsiːkwəns] n. 序列，次序，顺序
serendipity [serənˈdipiti] n. 偶然发现，意外发现

serotonin [ˈserəˌtɔnin] n. 5-羟色胺（一种神经递质）
serum [ˈsiərəm] n. 血清，血浆，浆液
sesquiterpene [ˌseskwiˈtəːpiːn] n. 倍半萜烯
sex hormone 性激素
sheer [ʃiə] a. 纯粹的，真正的
shipment [ˈʃipmənt] n. 装货，装运，载物量
shock [ʃɔk] n. 冲击打击，休克，中风
short circuit 短路，短接
shortcut [ˈʃɔːtkʌt] n. 近路，捷径
Si gel 硅胶
side-chain 侧链
sieve [siv] n. 筛，筛子，滤网
silica gel n. 硅胶
simplex [ˈsimpleks] a. 单一的，单纯的
simulate [ˈsimjuleit] vt. 模拟
size and shape 大小形状
sizing [ˈsaiziŋ] n. 填料，上浆
skeletal [ˈskelitl] a. 骨骼的，骸骨的
slide valve 滑动阀
slot [slɔt] n. 缝，隙，槽，条板
slurry [ˈsləːri] n. 稀（泥，沙）浆，悬浮体（液）
smealtery [ˈsmeltəri] n. 冶炼厂
soapy lather 肥皂泡
sober [ˈsəubə] a. 清醒的，适度的；vt. 使清醒
socioeconomic [ˌsəusiəuˌiːkəˈnɔmik] a. 社会经济学的
socket [ˈsɔkit] n. 座，插座
sodium carbonate 碳酸钠
sodium hyposulfite 次亚硫酸钠
Solanaceae [ˌsəuləˈneisiiː] n. 茄科
solanaceous alkaloids 茄科生物碱
solanine [ˈsəuləniːn] n. 茄碱
solid-state [ˈsɔlidˈsteit] a. 固态的
solubility [ˌsɔljuˈbiliti] n. 溶（解）度，溶（解）
solubilize [ˈsɔljubilaiz] v. 增溶，溶解
solubilizing [ˈsɔljubilaiziŋ] a. 增溶的
solution [səˈljuːʃn] n. 解答，溶液，溶解
somatostatin (SRIF) [səumətəuˈstætin] n. 生长抑素
somatotropin [ˌsəumətəuˈtrəupin] n. 生长激素
sorbitol [ˈsɔːbitɔl] n. 山梨醇
sorbose [ˈsɔːbəus] n. 山梨糖

sorcerer ['sɔ:sərər] n. 男巫，魔术师
soybean ['sɔi'bi:n] n. 大豆，黄豆
sparger ['spɑ:dʒə] n. 分布器，喷雾器
spasm ['spæzəm] n. 痉挛，一阵发作
spatial ['speiʃəl] a. 空间的
specification [spesifi'keiʃən] n. 说明书，规格
spectroscopy [spek'trɔskəpi] n. 光谱学，波谱学，
spectrum ['spektrəm] (pl. spectra) n. 谱图
spillage ['spilidʒ] n. 溢出，洒落
spinal ['spainl] a. 针的，脊骨的，脊柱的
spinal cord 脊髓
spirostane 螺甾烷
spirostanol n. 螺甾烷醇
splash [splæʃ] vt. 溅污
splashings n. 喷溅物
spleen [spli:n] n. 脾
sponsor ['spɔnsə] n. 发起人，主办人
spore [spɔ:] n. 孢子；vi. 长孢子
sporulate ['spɔrjuleit] vi. 形成孢子
spout [spaut] v. 喷（出，射）；n. 喷管，喷流
sprain [sprein] n. & vt. 扭，扭伤
spray [sprei] n. 喷雾；v. 喷
squeeze [skwi:z] n. 压榨，挤；v. 压榨，挤，挤榨
staphylococcal [,stæfilou'kɔkəl] a. 葡萄球菌的
staphylococcus [,stæfilou'kɔkəs] pl. staphylococci [,stæfilou'kɔksai] n. 葡萄球菌
Staphylococcus aureus 金黄色酿脓葡萄球菌（缩写为 S. aureus）
starch [stɑ:tʃ] n. 淀粉，浆（糊）
stationary phase 固定相
statistically [stə'tistikli] adv. 统计学地
stave off 避免，避开，延缓
stereochemistry [stiəriə'kemistri] n. 立体化学
stereospecific reaction 立体专一性反应
sterile ['sterail] a. 不能生育的，无细菌的
sterilization [sterilai'zeiʃən] n. 消毒，杀菌，绝育
steroid ['steroid] n. 甾族化合物，类固醇
sterol ['sterɔl] n. 甾醇，固醇
stilbesterol [stil'bestrɔl] n. 己烯雌酚
still [stil] n. 蒸馏器；v. 蒸馏
stipulation [stipju'leiʃən] n. 规定，约定，合同
stoichiometric [stɔiki'ɔmitrik] a. 化学计量的
stoichiometry [stɔiki'ɔmitri] n. 化学计算，化学计量（法，学），理想配比法

stopper ['stɔpə] v. 塞住；n. 塞子
stopwatch ['stɔpwɔtʃ] n. 秒表，跑表
storage ['stɔridʒ] n. 储藏，存储
stratification [strætifi'keiʃən] n. 分层
Streptococcus pneumoniae 肺炎链球菌，肺炎双球菌（缩写为 S. pneumoniae）
streptococcus [,streptou'kɔkəs] pl. streptococci [,streptou'kɔkai] n. 链球菌
streptogramin n. 链阳性菌素
streptokinase ['streptəu'kaineis] n. 链激酶
Streptomyces [,streptəu'maisi:z] n. 链霉菌属
Streptomycin [,streptə'maisin] n. 链霉素
strip [strip] vt. 汽提，解吸
striped [straipt] a. 有斑纹的
k-strophantoside n. k-羊角拗糖甙，绿毒羊角拗甙
Strychnos ['striknɔs] n. 马钱子属，毒鼠碱
subacute [sʌbə'kju:t] a. 亚急性的
subdivide ['sʌbdi'vaid] vt. 把……再分，分装
sublimation ['sʌblimeiʃən] n. 升华（作用）
submission [səb'miʃən] n. 屈从，降服
subside [səb'said] vi. 下沉，沉淀，衰减
substantiate [səb'stænʃieit] vt. 证实
substitute ['sʌbstitju:t] n. 取代，替代物；v. 取代，替代
substrate ['sʌbsteit] n. 基质，底物
subsurface ['sʌb'sə:fis] a. 表面下的；n. 地表下的岩石，地面下的水层
subterranean [,sʌbtə'reinnjən] a. 地下的；n. 地下室
subunit [sʌb'ju:nit] n. 亚单位，副族，亚基
succumb [sə'kʌm] vi. 屈从，屈服
sucrose ['sju:krəus] n. 蔗糖，（砂糖）
suction ['sʌkʃən] n. 吸，吸力
suction funnel 吸滤漏斗
suitability [sju:tə'biliti] n. 适合性，适应性
sulfhydryl [sʌlf'haidril] n. 硫氢（基），巯（基）
sulfonate ['sʌlfəneit] = sulphonate n. 磺酸盐（酯）；vt. 使磺化
sulphonamide [,sʌlfou'næmid, sʌl'fɔnəmaid] n. 磺胺，磺胺药物
sulphur ['sʌlfə] n. 硫，硫磺
superimpose [sju:pəim'pəuz] vt. 加在上面，叠加
supernatant [sju:pə'neitənt] a. 浮在上层（表面）的，漂浮的；n. 上层清液

superstition [ˌsjuːpəˈstiʃən] n. 迷信
supplant [səˈplɑːnt] vt. 代替，取代
surveillance [səːˈveiləns] n. 监视，看守
susceptible [səˈseptəbl] a. 敏感的，易感染的
suspension [səsˈpenʃən] n. 悬浮液
sustain [səsˈtein] vt. 维持
swallow [ˈswɔləu] n. 吞咽，咽喉，食道 vt.；vi 吞下
sweetener [ˈswiːtenə] n. 甜味剂
symposium [ˈsimpəuziəm] n. 专题讨论会，学术报告会
synapse [siˈnæps] n. 突触
syndrome [ˈsinˌdrɔm] n. 并发症状，综合症
synergy [ˈsinədʒi] n. 药的协同作用
synergistic [ˌsinəˈdʒistik] a. 增效剂的，配合剂的
synthesis [ˈsinθisis] n. 合成（法）
synthesize [ˈsinθisaiz] vt. 合成，综合
synthetic [sinˈθetik] a. 合成的，人造的，综合的
synthon [ˈsinθɔn] n. 合成子
syphilis [ˈsifilis] n. 梅毒
syringe [ˈsirindʒ] n. 注射器；vt. 注射
syrup [ˈsirəp] n. （糖，糊，膏）浆，糖汁

T

tablet [ˈtæblit] n. 药片，片剂
Taka-diastase [ˈtɑːkə ˈdaiəsteis] n. 高峰淀粉酶
tannin [ˈtænin] n. 丹宁，丹宁酸，鞣酸
tapered [ˈteipəd] a. 锥形的
tarragon [ˈtærəgən] n. 龙蒿，龙蒿叶
tartaric acid 酒石酸
taste masking 味觉模糊
tautomerism [tɔːˈtɔmərizm] n. 互变（异构）现象，互变异构
Taxol [ˈtæksɔl] n. 紫杉醇（一种抗癌药名）
taxonomist [tækˈsɔnəmist] n. （尤指动植物）分类学家
Taxus breviofolia 短叶红豆杉
telson [ˈtelsn] n. （蝎类的）毒刺，（昆虫的）尾节
template [ˈtempleit] n. 模板
teratology [ˌterəˈtɔlədʒi] n. 畸形学，怪异研究
terminology [ˌtəːmiˈnɔlədʒi] n. 专门名词，术语
terrestrial [tiˈrestriəl] a. 地球上的，陆生的，陆生动植物
tertian [ˈtəːʃən] a. 间日的，隔日（发作）

Tetracycline [ˌtetrəˈsaiklain] n. 四环素
Thalidomide [θəˈlidəmaid] n. 沙利度胺，反应停
thaw [θɔː] n. 解冻
the central nervous system (CNS) 中枢神经系统
the Pacific yew tree 太平洋紫杉，太平洋红豆杉
the peripheral nervous system (PNS) 外周神经系统
the protozoan Entamoeba histolytica 溶组织内阿米巴原虫，痢疾阿米巴原虫，痢疾变形虫原虫
therapeutical [ˌθerəˈpjuːtikəl] a. 治疗（学）的
therapeutically [ˌθerəˈpjuːtikəli] ad. 治疗（学）地
therapy [ˈθerəpi] n. 治疗，疗法
Thienamycin [ˌθaiˌenəˈmaisin] n. 硫霉素
thin layer chromatoplate 薄层色谱板
thiol [ˈθaiɔl] n. 硫醇，巯基
thornapple [ˈθɔːnˌæpl] n. 曼陀罗
threonine [ˈθriːəni(ː)n] n. 苏氨酸，羟丁氨酸
thrombin [ˈθrɔmbin] n. 凝血酶
thrombocytopenia [ˌθrɔmbəusaitəuˈpiːniə] n. 血小板减少（症）
throttle [ˈθrɔtl] n. 节流阀；vt. & vi. 窒息，闷住
throughput [ˈθruːˈput] n. 生产量（率，能力），容许量
thwart [θwɔːt] vt. 阻碍，反对，横过；a. 横放的
thymidine [ˈθaimidiːn] n. 胸（腺嘧啶脱氧核）苷
thymidylic acid 胸（腺嘧啶脱氧核）苷酸
thymine [ˈθaimiːn] n. 胸腺嘧啶（也即 2,6-dioxy-6-methyl-pyrimidine 2, 6-二氧-6-甲基嘧啶）
thyroid [ˈθaiərɔid] a. 甲状腺的；n. 甲状腺
thyroxine [θaiˈrɔksiːn] n. 甲状腺素
tissue [ˈtisjuː] n. 组织，薄纸
toll [tɔl] n. 费，代价
toluene [ˈtɔljuiːn] n. 甲苯
tonicity [təˈnisiti] n. 强壮，强健
topical [ˈtɔpikəl] a. （医）局部的
topoisomerase [ˌtəupəuaiˈsɔmərei s] n. 拓扑异构酶
topology [təˈpɔlədʒi] n. 拓扑，布局，局部解剖学
tortuous [ˈtɔːtjuəs] a. 弯曲的，曲折的
tow [təu] v.；n. （丝，纤维）束，麻屑，短纤维
toxin [ˈtɔksin] n. 毒素
tracheal [trəˈkiːəl] a. 气管的，导管的，呼吸管的
tract [trækt] n. 系统，道束（医）

tranquillizer ['træŋkwilaizə] n. 安定药
transferase ['trænsfə reis] n. 转移酶
transfusion [træns'fju:ʒən] n. 注入，输血，输液
transpose [træns'pouz] vt. 使互换位置，变换，vi. 进行变换
trauma ['traumə] n. 外伤，创伤
tray [trei] n. 分馏塔盘，塔板
Tribulus terrestris 刺蒺藜
tribute ['tribju:t] n. 颂词，礼物，贡品
Trichosanthes kirlowii 栝楼，瓜蒌
triethylamine [traieθi'læmin] n. 三乙胺
trimethoprim [ˌtrai'meθəprim] n. 甲氧苄啶
triterpenoid [ˌtrai'tə:pə'nɔid] n. 三萜(烯)化合物
trophoblastic [ˌtrɔfəu'blæstik] a. 滋养层的
tropine ['trəupi:n] n. 托品，莨菪碱
trovafloxacin 特伐沙星
trypsin ['tripsin] n. 胰蛋白酶
tuber ['tju:bə] n. 块茎，结节，突起
tubercle ['tju:bəkl] n. 结核(结)节，结节
tubercle bacillus 结核菌
tuberculosis [tju(:)bə:kju'lousis] n. 结核(病)，肺结核
d-tubocurarine [tju:bəukju'rɑ:rin] n. 管箭毒碱
tubular ['tju:bjulə] a. 管(状，形)的，管式的
tumour ['tju:mə] n. 瘤，肿瘤，肿块
tunicate ['tju:nikeit] n. 被囊类动物
turbidity [tə:'biditi] n. 浊度
turbo- (词头) 涡轮，透平
twistable ['twistəbl] a. 可旋转的，可缠绕的
tyrosine ['taiərəsi:n] n. 酪氨酸[缩写，tyr.]

U

ubiquitous [ju'bikwətəs] a. 无所不在的，到处都有的
ulcer ['ʌlsər] n. 溃疡，腐烂物
underweight ['ʌndə'weit] n.; a. 不足的重量，标准以下的重量
uniformity [ju:ni'fɔ:miti] n. 一样，一式，一致(性)
unprecedented [ʌn'presidentid] a. 空前的
unremitting [ˌʌnri'mitiŋ] a. 不间断的，持续的
unsaturated [ʌn'sætjuretid] a. 不饱和的
unsubstitute [ʌn'sʌbstitju:t] v. 无取代
uracil ['juərəsil] n. 尿嘧啶

uric acid n. 尿酸
uridine n. 尿嘧啶(核)苷
uridylic acid 尿苷酸
urinary ['juərinəri] a. (泌)尿的
uronic acid 糖醛酸
uterotonic [ˌju:tərəu'tɔnik] n. 子宫收缩药；a. 子宫收缩的
uterus ['ju:tərəs] n. 子宫

V

vaccine ['væksi:n] n. 疫苗 a. 疫苗的，牛痘的
vagina [və'dʒainə] n. 叶鞘，阴道，鞘
validation [ˌvæli'deiʃən] n. 确认，证实
valine ['væli:n] n. 缬氨酸[缩写：val]
valve [vælv] n. 阀(门)，活门，气门，闸门
Vancomycin [ˌvæŋkə'maisin] n. 万古霉素
vascular ['væskjulə] a. 脉管的，血管的，有脉管的
vasodilation [ˌveizəudai'leiʃən] n. 血管舒张
vegetative ['vedʒitətiv] a. 生长的，植物性的
vehicle ['vi:ikl] n. 赋形剂，运载工具
vendor ['vendɔ:] n. 卖主，小贩
venom ['venəm] n. (蛇的)毒液，恶意，怨恨
Venturi [ven'tu:ri] n. 文氏管，文杜里管(喷嘴)，缩喉管
verification [verifi'keiʃən] n. 检验，鉴定，核实
versus ['və:səs] prep. 对，与……相对
vertebrate ['və:tibreit] n. 脊椎动物；a. 脊椎动物的，有椎骨的，有脊椎的
vesicant ['vesikənt] a. 起疱的，腐烂性的；n. 起疱剂
viability [ˌvaiə'biliti] vt. 生存力
viable ['vaiəbl] a. 能生存的，有生存力的，可行的
vial ['vaiəl] n. 小瓶，小玻璃瓶 vt. 放……于小瓶中
vicinity [vi'siniti] n. 附近，邻近，近处，接近
Vinblastine [vin'blɑ:sti:n] n. 长春花碱
Vinca ['viŋkə] n. 长春花
Vincristine ['vinkristi:n] n. 长春新碱
Vincristine sulphate 硫酸长春新碱
Vinleurosine n. 环氧长春碱
Vinresidine n. (=leurosidine)异长春碱，洛诺西丁
violation [vaiə'leiʃən] n. 违反，妨碍
viral ['vaiərəl] a. 病毒的

virulent ['virjulənt] a. 有病毒的，毒害的
viscosity [vis'kɔsiti] n. 粘性，粘滞性
vitamin ['vitəmin] n. 维生素，维他命
void [vɔid] a. 空的，作废的；n. 空隙，真空；vt. 排泄，放空，使无效
volatile ['vɔlətail] a. 易挥发的，易变的

W

wafer ['weifə] n. 薄片，圆片，糯米纸囊剂
wart [wɔ:t] n. 疣，肉赘
water-table n. 地下水位
weight variation 重量差异
weir [wiə] n. 堰，溢流堰，低坝；v. 用坝挡住
whooping cough 百日咳
World Health Organization 世界卫生组织（缩写为WHO）
wormwood ['wə:mwud] n. 蒿属植物（尤指洋艾），苦艾
wrap [ræp] vt. 包装

X

xanthone ['zænθəun] n. 咕吨酮，(夹)氧杂蒽酮
xylem ['zailem] n. 木质部
xylene ['zaili:n] n. 二甲苯
xylose ['zailous] n. 木糖，戊醛糖

Y

yeast [ji:st] n. 酵母
Yersinia pestis 耶尔森氏菌属鼠疫，耶尔森氏菌属瘟疫
Yew tree 紫杉木；红豆杉（树）

Z

zeolite ['zi:əlait] n. 沸石
zinc [ziŋk] n. 锌

内 容 提 要

《制药工程专业英语》是根据《大学英语教学大纲(修订本)》(高等学校本科用)的专业阅读部分的要求编写的。供理工科制药工程专业(包括化学制药专业和药物制剂专业)或相关专业的三、四年级学生使用,也可供同等英语程度的科技人员学习。

本书包括课文及阅读材料共 25 个单元(50 篇),均选自原版英文教科书、专著、大型参考书及专业期刊(大部分是国外 80 年代末及 90 年代以来的出版物)。其中第一部分 1~5 单元介绍药物化学;第二部分 6~10 单元介绍生物制药;第三部分 11~15 单元介绍工业药剂;第四部分 16~20 单元介绍制药工程,第五部分 21~25 单元介绍制药工程前沿的研究领域。每个单元由一篇课文和一篇阅读材料构成。附录有:The General Principles for Nomenclature of Chinese Approved Drug Names,INN 采用的词干及其中文译名,英汉对照新药名选编和总词汇表。每篇课文均配有阅读理解练习和词汇练习。为便于学生自学,本书每单元均配有单词和词组表,并作了必要的注释。